The Measurement of Sensation

OXFORD PSYCHOLOGY SERIES

1. *The neuropsychology of anxiety: an enquiry into the functions of septohippocampal system*
   Jeffrey A. Gray
2. *Elements of episodic memory*
   Endel Tulving
3. *Conditioning and associative learning*
   Nicholas J. Mackintosh
4. *Visual masking: an integrative approach*
   Bruno G. Breitmeyer
5. *The musical mind: the cognitive psychology of music*
   John Sloboda
6. *Elements of psychophysical theory*
   Jean-Claude Falmagne
7. *Animal intelligence*
   Edited by Lawrence Weiskrantz
8. *Response times: their role in inferring elementary mental organization*
   R. Duncan Luce
9. *Mental representations: a dual coding approach*
   Allan Paivio
10. *Memory, imprinting, and the brain*
    Gabriel Horn
11. *Working memory*
    Alan Baddeley
12. *Blindsight: a case study and implications*
    Lawrence Weiskrantz
13. *Profile analysis*
    D. M. Green
14. *Spatial vision*
    R. L. DeValois and K. K. DeValois
15. *The neural and behavioural organization of goal-directed movements*
    Marc Jeannerod
16. *Visual pattern analysers*
    Norma V. Graham
17. *Cognitive foundations of musical pitch analysis*
    C. L. Krumhansl

18. *Perceptual and associative learning*
    G. Hall
19. *Implicit learning and tacit knowledge*
    A. S. Reber
20. *Neuropsychology of communicative behaviour*
    D. Kimura
21. *The frontal lobes and voluntary action*
    R. E. Passingham
22. *Classification and cognition*
    W. Festes
23. *Vowel perception and production*
    B. D. Rosner and J. B. Pickering
24. *Visual stress*
    A. Wilkins
25. *Electrophysiology of mind*
    Edited by M. D. Rugg and M. G. H. Coles
26. *Attention and memory: an integrated framework*
    N. Cowan
27. *The visual brain in action*
    A. D. Milner and M. A. Goodale
28. *Perceptual consequences of cochlear damage*
    B. J. C. Moore
29. *Binocular vision and stereopsis*
    Ian P. Howard and Brian J. Rogers
30. *The measurement of sensation*
    Donald Laming

The Measurement of Sensation

DONALD LAMING
Department of Experimental Psychology,
University of Cambridge

OXFORD PSYCHOLOGY SERIES
NO. 30

OXFORD NEW YORK TOKYO
OXFORD UNIVERSITY PRESS
1997

Oxford University Press, Great Clarendon Street, Oxford OX2 6DP
Oxford New York
Athens Auckland Bangkok Bogata Bombay
Buenos Aires Calcutta Cape Town Dar es Salaam
Delhi Florence Hong Kong Istanbul Karachi
Kuala Lumpur Madras Madrid Melbourne
Mexico City Nairobi Paris Singapore
Taipei Tokyo Toronto Warsaw

and associated companies in
Berlin Ibadan

Oxford is a trade mark of Oxford University Press

Published in the United States
by Oxford University Press, Inc., New York

A catalogue record for this book is available from the British Library

Library of Congress Cataloging in Publication Data
Laming, D. R. J. (Donald Richard John)
The measurement of sensation / Donald Laming.
(Oxford psychology series; no. 30)
Includes bibliographical references and index.
1. Senses and sensation–Testing. 2. Psychology, Experimental.
I. Title. II. Series.
QP435.L34 1997 612.8'028'7–dc21 97-3966

ISBN 0 19 852342 4

Typeset by Hewer Text Composition Services, Edinburgh

Printed in Great Britain by
Biddles Ltd,
Guildford & King's Lynn

Preface

In 1957 S.S. Stevens published his famous paper 'On the psychophysical law' and ignited a controversy which has continued ever since. That controversy has shifted its ground somewhat over the years; it has, as it were, spawned sub-controversies. But three recent compendia in *Behavioral and Brain Sciences* (Krueger 1989; Lockhead 1992; Murray 1993) show that it still continues. This book traces the development of that controversy.

I have organized the book around a succession of theoretical ideas that have been proposed to explain why it is that people's judgments of sensory quantities sometimes diverge sharply from physical reality. There is, to my mind, a particular intellectual appeal to this succession. Each idea appears to accommodate a wide range of experimental findings and to answer the particular problems which confounded its predecessor; but then itself founders on some new and hitherto unforeseen result. I give some examples.

1. S.S. Stevens supported his initial statement 'that the sensation Ψ is proportional to the stimulus S raised to a power n' (Stevens 1957b, p. 162) with a large number of experiments on the magnitude estimation of different sensory attributes. To these he subsequently added the estimation of inverse attributes (paleness, softness of sounds, smoothness of textures), the production of a stimulus to match a given number, and cross-modality matching. All these results conformed neatly to the generalization just cited, and they were consistent with the suggestion—which S.S. Stevens espoused whole-heartedly—that internal sensations could be measured on a ratio scale like length and weight. Now, ratio-scale quantities (to be precise, *extensive* ratio-scale quantities) can be added and subtracted as well as multiplied and divided. But, when that experiment was carried out (Beck and Shaw 1967), the estimation of differences in loudness seemed to require a *different* scale to the estimation of single loudnesses. That finding meant that loudness could not be an extensive ratio-scale quantity after all.

2. A possible reason for this apparent divergence was at hand. Attneave (1962) had already suggested that numbers had their own subjective values like other stimulus attributes. The differencing of loudnesses, it was suggested, takes place at some intermediate stage and the result is expressed as a number which bears a power law relationship to the difference thus estimated. (This would make the numerical estimates measurable on a particular *non-extensive* ratio scale.) In the hands of Dwight Curtis, Stanley Rule and others this formula accommodated many summation and differencing experiments, restoring the notion of internal power law transforms (now two of them) between the stimulus variable and the numerical response. But then Marks (1978a, b, 1979a, b) compared the summation of *successively* presented loudnesses with the total loudness of *simultaneous* stimuli, using tones in different critical bands or in different ears. The question, whether two simultaneous or two successive sensations were to be combined, proved critical.

3. One idea that initially promised to address all these problems was the matching of just-noticeable differences, matching equal numbers of jnds on different sensory continua. If both continua obey Weber's Law (most of the sensory attributes used in these experiments do), a power law transform results. But the matching of differences in sensation need no

longer generate the same scale as single stimuli, ultimately because a matching between two single stimuli is now meaningless. Only jnds can be matched. Single stimuli are, instead, assumed to be judged relative to some implicit reference stimulus which is not ordinarily controlled. The total loudnesses of simultaneous and successive stimuli now differ because different reference stimuli are implicit in the judgment of two successively presented components. But this idea too founders. It predicates a precise relationship between the power law exponent and the Weber fraction, which does not obtain in nature.

At each stage the accumulated experimental results—and there have been very many experiments—seem to admit a simple and precise synthesis, sufficiently simple to attract a large number of psychologists to the problems that remain and sufficiently precise to admit some elegant mathematical argument. Here, surely, is a problem which should rapidly yield to mathematical analysis! But it has not proved so.

Each of the theoretical positions I have sketched (and there are others besides) incorporates a number of prior assumptions, some of them acknowledged, others unwitting. The experimental finding which shows that this or that theory will not, after all, suffice does so by focusing on the consequences of one or another of the unwitting assumptions which is thereby exposed to view. On careful examination, of course, that unwitting assumption proves to be false. The controversy then has, in a sense, to backtrack to where that false assumption was taken on board and follow a different route from that point on. The question now is: how far do psychologists have to go back in time to arrive at a consistent understanding of internal sensation?

I think the answer is to 22 October 1850. For it was on that morning, Fechner tells us, that whilst lying abed he conceived the idea of making 'the relative increase of bodily energy the measure of the increase of the corresponding mental energy' (Boring 1950, p. 280). What is wrong with that intuition is not so much the acknowledged logarithmic transform, against which S.S. Stevens fulminated so vehemently, but the *implicit* assumption that sensation admitted measurement on any kind of continuum at all—that mental events could be formulated within a system like classical physics. That is an idea which every psychophysicist since has unwittingly accepted. But physics abandoned the classical nineteenth century framework long ago; it is now time for psychophysics to do likewise.

Many readers will immediately ask: if there is no underlying continuum, how did Stevens repeatedly obtain such lawful results from his experiments? Imagine subjects giving a larger number than previously if the present stimulus seems greater than the previous one, and a smaller number if it seems smaller. An average calculated over a sufficient number of subjects, who have experienced the stimuli in different random orders, will appear to show an orderly relationship to the stimulus magnitude. Individual estimates, of course, will be very variable—and that is just what happens.

The progression of theoretical ideas, experimental studies, analyses, and controversies stemming from Stevens' 1957 article occupies the latter two-thirds of this book, from Chapter 5 onwards. Chapter 1 details the nineteenth century antecedents of that controversy and Chapter 2 examines the debate, which began long before Stevens entered the arena, about whether sensation is, in fact, measurable in any ordinary sense of that term.

Thereafter come two chapters on Fechner's Law which stand somewhat apart from the rest of the argument. This is not to be wondered at, because Fechner's Law looks at a quite distinct kind of experiment—concerning the measurement of discriminable differences—

from Stevens' 'direct' methods. But those two chapters have a more than merely historical relevance. When, ultimately, magnitude estimation and kindred methods are found not to lead to any scale of sensation distinct from the natural physical measure of the stimulus, it is tempting to return to Fechner's Law and interpret the logarithmic transform in a purely operational sense as the metric of a theory of sensory discrimination. What recent research has shown, however—research in which I have myself been deeply involved—is that a yet more comprehensive and wider ranging account of sensory discrimination is possible, in which the metric is the natural physical measure of the stimulus. Whatever experimental justification there might once have seemed to be for introducing some distinctive measure of internal sensation evaporates under critical examination.

That, then, is the character and structure of this book. It endeavours to bring together an increasing diversity of ideas and multiplication of experiments, a diversity and a multiplication which has otherwise tended to fragment the field of subjective sensation into separate subdivisions. Individual psychologists involved in one or another subcontroversy, especially those actively supporting their arguments with fresh experiments, tend to concentrate their attention on just their subdivision of the field. So one purpose of this book to provide all those participants with an overview of a wider whole.

Such an exercise involves judgments about the relative importance of different arguments to the whole and the amount of space and detail to devote to this or that line of experimental work, and I expect most readers to disagree somewhere or other. Psychologists actively involved in arguing some particular point of view inevitably do so from a distinctive standpoint. That can be seen especially clearly in the different contributions from Stanley Rule and Dwight Curtis on the one hand, and Michael Birnbaum on the other, arguing whether there are two distinct judgments to be made of the relationship between two stimuli or only one. There is one important respect in which readers will also find it here.

I have chosen to debate solely the question how the strength of internal sensation might be related to physical stimulus magnitude. That takes the argument principally to the 'direct' ratio-scale methods introduced by Stevens (1957b) and to developments of those methods by his colleagues and successors. But some psychophysicists (e.g. Krueger 1989), perhaps many, see absolute identification and category judgment experiments as addressing substantially the same question. Both classes of experiment support some kind of subjective scaling of the stimuli. They also exhibit a number of phenomena in common.

But, in practice, the data from these two classes of experiment are analysed in different ways. Magnitude estimates are usually just averaged, and the immediate question of interest concerns the relation of those averages to the physical stimulus magnitudes. But averaging of responses is not meaningful with absolute identification, and a much more complicated analysis is required of the pattern of misidentifications. That more complicated analysis lies beyond the scope of this present book, and absolute identification data are called upon only when the implications they afford about the nature of the underlying judgment process are needed to support the interpretation of experiments about sensation. The treatment of both magnitude estimation and absolute identification in terms of an ordinal scheme of judgment in Chapters 10 and 11 reflects my own perspective on the matter. I think that kind of bias is inevitable.

A primary organization of this book in terms of theoretical ideas means that I do not attempt a comprehensive review of the experimental evidence. There are many too many experiments for that to be feasible; though many of the experiments have already been surveyed elsewhere (e.g. Stevens 1975; Poulton 1989) from particular points of view. But where some conclusion critical to the theoretical development is at issue, I have endeavoured to summarize all of the experimental evidence known to me on the grounds that, on the most important empirical issues, the reader should have the opportunity to assess that evidence for himself or herself. So, for example, my collection of corresponding pairs of Weber fractions and power law exponents is presented in Fig. 8.2 (so that the reader can form his or her own impression what kind of relationship exists in nature); the numerical data and their sources are set out in Tables 8.2 and 8.3 (so that the reader can answer questions about subsets of attributes); and notes on the original experiments have been put in an appendix (so that the reader can apply his or her own criteria which experiments are reasonably included in this comparison and which ones should be struck out). Other readings of the accumulated data are possible, and the experimental evidence most critical to this or that theoretical position is exhibited in this degree of detail in order to facilitate the examination of those other readings.

I now have some intellectual debts to acknowledge. The arguments and the reanalyses of data in this book are the results of thinking about the problem of sensation, on and off, over a long period of time. The greatest influence on the evolution of that thinking has undoubtedly been Christopher Poulton. Looking at what I wrote 20 years ago (Laming 1973, Chapter 3), I see that at that time I accepted Stevens' idea of ratio-scale measurement. It was Christopher Poulton who weaned me away from that acceptance. Much more recently, I owe the idea that people perceive objects and abstract their judgment of the attribute from the total perception of the object to the review article by Greg Lockhead (1992). But the contribution which has, perhaps, given me the greatest cause for head-scratching has been the complex of seemingly simple results in two papers by Robert Teghtsoonian (1971, 1973). Finally, I thank Duncan Luce, Sandy MacRae, and Malcolm Sharpe for some very incisive criticism at a late stage in the preparation of this manuscript.

3 July 1996 D. L.

Contents

1 The origins of a controversy

There is a fundamental distinction to be made between a physical stimulus and that same stimulus as it is experienced by an observer. I use two separate sets of words to obviate confusion between the two.

1. The amount of light reflected by this page is its *luminance* and can be measured with an exposure meter such as photographers use.
2. The *brightness* of the page is that reflected light as experienced by the reader. Brightness may be deceptively related to luminance; that is why photographers use exposure meters.

Suppose, by way of another example, you are listening to television late at night. Although the volume control has not been touched, the sound nevertheless appears gradually to get louder. If you listen past midnight, your next-door neighbour may protest about a level of sound that passed unnoticed earlier in the evening. The auditory power produced by the television set's loudspeaker is one thing, its apparent loudness as experienced by you (and your next-door neighbour) quite another.

Again, there is a trick question: which is heavier, a pound of feathers or a pound of lead? Without thinking, you say 'lead'—and are then told that they both weigh the same! But taking 'heaviness' to mean the *feel of weight* as one or the other is picked up, the pound of lead is indeed heavier. In my classroom demonstration a pillow weighing 720 g is matched to one of a set of lead weights. The matches chosen so far range from 30 to 225 g. The heaviest weight in the set (320 g) has never yet been selected.

These three examples are ways in which people become aware that their sensory impressions are sometimes at variance with the world around them. If such discrepancies were rare, then questions about sensations as entities distinct from physical attributes of stimuli would probably never have arisen. Certainly, if our perception was always veridical, such questions could never be resolved; and there would be no book to be written on *The measurement of sensation.* But, as things are, a careful distinction needs to be maintained between the physical attributes of a stimulus and the subjective experience of those attributes, and I accordingly use two distinct sets of words.

In the arguments that follow, luminance, sound pressure, frequency, weight, etc. will always refer to the physical attributes of a stimulus as those attributes are measured by a photometer, a sound level meter, a frequency meter, a scale pan, and so on, while brightness, loudness, pitch, and heaviness will denote the corresponding subjective experiences. Whether the terms reserved for subjective experiences refer to sensations internal to the observer, or whether they refer to the observer's estimates of physical stimulus attributes, and whether those two notions are empirically distinct, are questions which I postpone for the present. But it would be well to bear in mind that even though the experimenter may specifically ask his subjects, on the one hand, to judge the physical stimulus or, on the other, to report on their internal sensations, what the subjects actually do might be another matter.

Physical science tells us how to make objective measurements of luminance and of other attributes of the world in which we live; but how should sensation be measured? That question has played a seminal role in the development of experimental psychology. Of the various elements that came together in the middle of the nineteenth century to form the new science of experimental psychology, the most influential and enduring was Fechner's *Elemente der Psychophysik* (1860); and Fechner was driven to that work by an idea of how sensation might be measured. On the basis of this measure Fechner proposed to develop a 'physics of the mind' and thereby open the way for the scientific study of mental events. A moment's reflection shows that sensation cannot be measured in the same objective way as luminance, sound pressure, frequency, and weight; that was the forthright conclusion of a committee set up in 1932 by the British Association for the Advancement of Science to report on the possibility of 'Quantitative estimates of sensory events' (Ferguson *et al.* 1940). Some prior assumption is needed before any kind of measurement of sensation is possible, and the entire subject has been dominated by controversies between the advocates of different prior assumptions. In the first place, this critique is concerned with a careful examination of those different assumptions.

In this first chapter I trace the origins of a controversy which still continues today, unresolved (see, e.g., Krueger 1989 and the commentaries which follow his article). Those origins provide a simple introduction to the most important of the ideas with which we shall be concerned.

1.1 FECHNER'S LAW

In his *Zend-Avesta* (1851) Fechner relates how, while lying abed on the morning of 22 October 1850, he conceived an idea which led him to a nine-year programme of psychophysical experimentation and, ultimately, to the *Elemente der Psychophysik* in 1860. That idea was to make 'the relative increase of bodily energy the measure of the increase of the corresponding mental intensity' (Boring 1950, p. 280). In 1834, and again in 1846, Weber had published the empirical generalization which bears his name: if X and $X + \Delta X$ are the magnitudes of two stimuli which can just be distinguished, then

$$\Delta X/X = \Theta, \tag{1.1}$$

where Θ is a constant which depends on the stimulus attribute. If, now, a 'just-noticeable difference' ΔX be taken, as Fechner took it, to be a unit of 'mental intensity'—to correspond to an increment in sensation of constant size—then the relation between this measure of sensation and the physical stimulus magnitude must be of the form

$$S = \ln X, \tag{1.2}$$

since, if $(X + \Delta X)/X$ is constant, so too is $\{\ln(X + \Delta X) - \ln X\}$. Today eqn 1.2 is known as Fechner's Law and 1.1 as Weber's Law.

Fechner's interest in the question of measuring sensation was ultimately philosophical.

He was much preoccupied with the relation between mind and matter and, with respect to that question, was antipathetic to the materialist tide of his time. If it were possible to measure mental events, then they could thereby be shown to have the reality that Fechner sought for them. Consequent on the centenary of his death (1887) there has been renewed interest in Fechner's conception of psychophysics as a science and in his ideas in general, with translations published of further extracts from his works (Murray 1993; Heidelberger 1987, 1988, 1993, 1994; Scheerer 1987, 1989, 1992; also Adler 1966). Fechner's personal contribution to psychophysics is not a matter that will concern us here. It is sufficient that eqns 1.1 and 1.2 offer the possibility of an indirect measurement of sensation in terms of the resolving power of the sensory system. That is an important idea to be evaluated. The objections that have been raised to Fechner's derivation of eqn 1.2 from 1.1 (e.g. Luce and Edwards 1958; Luce 1993; but see also Krantz 1971; Laming 1997) will also not concern us. In case this seems a cavalier attitude, I comment that if we should come across an alternative idea, as we shall, unequivocally superior to Fechner's, the objections of Luce and Edwards will be neither here nor there.

1.2 ANTECEDENTS OF STEVENS' POWER LAW

In default of any alternative, Fechner's Law was generally accepted for about a hundred years as the way to measure sensation. While there were psychologists who doubted its validity, there was no body of experimental work of sufficient substance to support an alternative formula, until Stevens (1957b; see also Stevens and Galanter 1957). Stevens argued vigorously that sensations *could* be measured directly (by simply asking a subject how loud a sound seemed to be), and that direct measurements made in this manner did not conform to Fechner's Law but to a power law (eqn 1.5 below) instead. The *idea* of a power relation between physical stimulus magnitude and sensation had, however, been suggested in the nineteenth century (as Stevens 1957b, 1961b, readily acknowledged); it had been proposed by Plateau (1872b) and Brentano (1874), among others.

Plateau (1872b) reported this experiment: at his request eight oil-painters mixed a grey mid-way between a given white and a given black, working by natural daylight. Although Plateau did not report this experiment until 1872, he tells us (p. 377) that it had been carried out about 20 years before the publication of Fechner's *Elemente* (i.e. about 1840), which makes it the very earliest experimental study of the problem of sensation. It was reported in 1872 in the course of an introduction to a much more substantial dissertation by Delboeuf (1873, of which more below). The significant result was that the eight greys turned out to be nearly all the same ('*presque identiques*'). Since the intensity of natural daylight can vary greatly from one painter's studio to another's, Plateau argued that the selection of a grey mid-way between the given white and black must have been independent of the absolute level of illumination and therefore a function of the *relative* intensities only of the light reflected from the black, the grey, and the white. If, now, the intensities of the *sensations* evoked by the three stimuli also preserve common ratios as the incident light is varied, the relation of the sensation to the luminance of the stimulus must be a power function.

Plateau's argument was defective. He took the mid-grey mixed by his artists to be such that the *difference* between the sensations evoked by the white and the grey was equal to the *difference* between the sensations of the grey and the black. Since his experiment showed no more than that the match depended on the relative luminances only of the white, the grey, and the black, it was compatible with both a power law relation (as Plateau proposed) and also a logarithmic law.[1] When Plateau (1872a) saw Delboeuf's much more comprehensive set of results (below) he realized his mistake.

Stevens (e.g. 1975, pp. 6–7) was fond of quoting Plateau's work as anticipating his own,[2] but failed to appreciate the profound difference of view expressed in this inspired intuition:

> When we experience, either simultaneously or successively, two physical sensations of the same sort, but of different intensities, we can easily judge which of the two is the stronger and we can, moreover, decide whether the difference between them is great or small. But there, it seems, the comparison must end, at least if we admit only direct judgments, and we appear to be incapable of estimating the numerical ratio between the intensities of two sensations in this way. (Plateau, 1872b, p. 377; Laming and Laming, 1996, p. 136)

Ordinarily, according to Plateau, numerical judgment of sensations is impossible. But the particular task that Plateau set his painters is an exception, because a professional artist is able to match the contrast of the grey against the white to that of the black against the grey. Whether that technique of matching contrasts gives the same intermediate grey that one might obtain by other methods (e.g. magnitude estimation or category judgment) remains to be discovered.

At about the same time Delboeuf (1873) substantially repeated Plateau's experiment in the laboratory, collecting adjustments of the white to match a much wider range of greys and blacks. Delboeuf's idea was to add a small constant to the stimulus magnitude in Fechner's Law to give

$$S = \ln\{(X + X_0)/X_0\}, \tag{1.3}$$

where the X_0 might be the residual level of activity in the retina (Helmholtz's *Eigenlicht*; von Helmholtz, 1909–11, vol. II, p. 12) or, in other modalities, a part of the weight of the arm lifting a weight (Fechner 1860; pp. 155–6 in Adler's, 1966, translation) or an irreducible

[1] Let L_w, L_g, and L_b be the luminances of the white, the grey, and the black, and let $S(L_w)$, $S(L_g)$, and $S(L_b)$ be their respective brightnesses. Plateau interpreted the values of L_g selected by his eight artists to be such that

$$S(L_w) - S(L_g) = S(L_g) - S(L_b).$$

The fact that substantially the same match was made under different levels of illumination means that, for any positive k,

$$S(kL_w) - S(kL_g) = S(kL_g) - S(kL_b).$$

If

$$S(L) = aL^{\beta},$$

then multiplying each luminance by k increases each subjective difference by the same factor k^{β}, while if

$$S(L) = \ln a + \beta \ln L,$$

multiplication by k leaves both subjective differences unchanged.

[2] Stevens (1961b, p. 80, 1975, p. 7) is incorrect when he attributes to Plateau the idea that his artists were matching subjective *ratios.*

error of adjustment which Fechner (p. 186 in Adler, 1966) called Volkmann's constant. Murray (1993, pp. 119–20) describes Delboeuf's experiment in detail, reproduces some of his numerical data, and, important for the present argument, examines in a footnote (Murray 1993, footnote 3) how well those data conform both to Fechner's original formula (eqn 1.2) and to a power law (eqn 1.5 below). Murray finds very little difference between these three formulae in the accuracy with which they are able to represent Delboeuf's data, and that underlines two important lessons:

1. The fact that one formula works very well does not mean that other formulae will not perform similarly; it may simply be that the experiment is uninformative with respect to the empirical differences between the different formulae.
2. Careful design of the experiment is needed (or careful selection amongst already published experiments) if there is to be any empirical discrimination between the different ideas that have been proposed for the relation of internal sensation to physical stimulus magnitude.

The other significant anticipation of the power law came in an article by Brentano (1874), and his argument was much closer to Stevens' subsequent point of view. Starting from Weber's Law (eqn 1.1), Brentano noted that the increment in the stimulus which produces a just noticeable increase in the strength of the sensation is proportional to the magnitude of the stimulus to which it is added. But he rejected, as by no means self-evident, Fechner's assertion that all just-noticeable increases in sensation are *equal*; all one can say is that they are *equally noticeable*. What 'equally noticeable' means when applied to differences in sensation remains to be determined. Arguing by analogy with the physical domain, but without recourse to any experimental observations, Brentano asserted that Weber's Law applied equally to the subjective domain. If this argument is valid, then equal ratios of physical stimulus magnitudes map onto equal ratios at the subjective level of description (though the subjective ratios need not be the same as the physical ones; see Brentano, 1874; pp. 66–8 in Rancurello *et al.*'s, 1973, translation), and that mapping is compatible only with a power law. This was first shown to be so by Fechner (1877); I shall give a proof later (Chapter 7, p. 87) in its proper place. Brentano anticipated not only Stevens' Power Law, but also the suggestion by Ekman (1956, 1959) that Weber's Law should apply at the subjective level of description as well. Ekman's idea is examined in Chapter 8 where it is shown to lead to a certain relationship between Weber fractions (at the physical level of description) and power law exponents. But even more important in all these preliminaries is the fact that the transition from Weber's Law to either Fechner's Law or to a power law is a matter of *assumption*, not of empirical observation.

1.3 THE SONE SCALE

In default of any alternative, Fechner's Law was generally accepted as the way to measure sensation for nearly a hundred years. It failed, however, in the face of a practical problem in acoustical engineering.

Acoustic intensity (sound pressure level) is conventionally measured in decibels on a logarithmic scale because the range of intensities met in nature is so large. Table 1.1 lists a number of common environmental sounds whose energy levels range from 1 to 10^{14}. An increase of 10 dB corresponds to a 10-fold increase in acoustic power, 20 dB to a 100-fold increase, and so on. The conventional point of reference (0 dB) is 20 $\mu N/m^2$, which is a lowish estimate of the absolute threshold at 1000 Hz for a very keen ear and therefore the lowest level likely to be of interest in human audition. A simple application of Fechner's Law says that 100 dB (the sound of an underground train arriving at a station) should sound twice as loud as 50 dB (the level of background conversation in, say, a library); but most people would say that the underground train sounds much more than twice as loud. Herein lies a problem for acoustic engineers in communicating with their technically unsophisticated clients: how can they express the effect of their work in terms of what the client will hear?

Table 1.1 Decibel levels of some common environmental sounds

Sound	Sound level in dB
Softest audible sound	0
Normal breathing	10
Open country at night	20
Soft whisper	30
Very quiet living room	40
Quiet conversation (e.g. library)	50
Average speaking voice at 5 ft	60
Television, typical sound level	70
Motor car at 65 mph, from 25 ft	80
Motor cycle 25 ft away	90
Underground train entering station	100
Chainsaw (unprotected operator)	110
Loud rock group	120
Machine gun fire at close range	130
Jet engine at take-off, from 100 ft	140

From 'Psychophysics' by D. Laming, p. 259, in A. M. Colman (ed.) *Companion encyclopedia of psychology*, vol. 1. © 1994, Routledge. Reprinted by permission.

The practical problem of devising a scale which would enable the engineer to interpret esoteric acoustic measurements to a lay client was first tackled experimentally in 1930. In those early experiments observers, often the engineers themselves, were asked to judge the ratio of the loudnesses of two successive tones (Richardson and Ross 1930; Ham and Parkinson 1932) or to adjust a tone to sound half or twice as loud as a given standard (Geiger and Firestone 1933). These and further experiments (summarized by Churcher 1935) culminated in the *sone* scale (Stevens 1936). On the sone scale a sound pressure level of 40 dB generates a loudness of 1 sone; a level of 50 dB generates 2 sones; 60 dB, 4 sones, and so on, each increase of 10 dB doubling the sone value of the loudness. So

$$\text{loudness in sones} = (10^{-2}A)^{0.6}, \qquad (1.4)$$

where A is the amplitude of a tone in units of 20 $\mu N/m^2$.

Twenty years later Stevens' sone scale formed the basis of an international standard for the measurement of loudness (ISO Recommendation R.232; see Stevens 1956a, 1957a). Without going into details, the loudness of a complex sound is calculated by first measuring the sound pressure level within each of a series of octave or third-octave frequency bands. Those sound pressure levels are individually converted into loudness levels according to eqn 1.4 (slightly modified according to the frequency band; see Stevens 1957a, p. 15, fig. 4 and p. 19, fig. 7) and the numbers of sones aggregated over the different bands. If desired, that total loudness level can then be converted back into an equivalent sound pressure level using eqn 1.4 again, but in the inverse direction.

1.4 STEVENS' POWER LAW

About 1953 Stevens turned his attention to the problem of measuring not just loudness, but the sensations evoked by a multitude of other stimulus attributes as well, i.e. sensation in general. This occupied him almost full-time for the remainder of his life. The international standard for the measurement of loudness was one outcome of his renewed attention, but other products of Stevens' work are of much greater importance for this critique. He developed a group of new experimental methods for measuring sensation—the 'direct' or ratio-scaling methods of which magnitude estimation is the best known. In magnitude estimation the subject is presented with a sequence of stimuli and asked to assign a number to each in proportion to its (subjective) magnitude—in proportion to the loudness, say, of each of a sequence of tones. These methods I describe in detail in Chapter 5.

Based on the data he obtained, especially from magnitude estimation, Stevens proposed this generalization to relate the intensity of sensation to the physical magnitude of the stimulus:

$$S = aX^{\beta}, \tag{1.5}$$

where a is a constant which depends on the scale unit of sensation and β is an exponent which characterizes the attribute being judged. Equation 1.5 was supported by a large body of experimental work (Stevens and Galanter 1957, and many later studies; see Stevens 1975) and provided the alternative which was needed to call Fechner's Law (eqn 1.2) into question.

I remark, however, that Stevens uses the notion of 'subjective sensation' in a somewhat different way to Fechner. Both writers conceive of sensation as an intermediary between sensory input and perception. For Stevens, the numbers uttered by subjects in his magnitude estimation experiments are direct observations of that intermediary. But for Fechner, sensation cannot be measured directly—it can only be inferred from the precision of discrimination between similar stimuli. Herein lies a critical difference: Fechner's concept can alternatively be viewed as an operational construct in a theory of sensory discrimination. We shall see in Chapter 3 that Fechner's logarithmic law gives an accurate account of discriminations between two separate stimuli—between, say, two separate flashes of light in darkness—and the accuracy of that account, and therefore the operational status of his logarithmic law, is entirely independent of any results that Stevens might obtain from magnitude estimation and similar experiments.

1.5 FOUR BASIC IDEAS

I have now introduced four ideas which will run throughout this book. These ideas all bear on the relation between the physical magnitude of a stimulus and the internal sensation it evokes, a relation which is conventionally known as the 'Psychophysical Law'. For convenience, I summarize here:

1. Fechner's Law (eqn 1.2), which posits a logarithmic relation between sensation and the physical stimulus magnitude. This generalization is based on data from discrimination experiments and takes the resolving power of sensory discrimination as its unit of measurement.
2. Stevens' Power Law (eqn 1.5), which posits a power law relation where Fechner's Law posits a logarithmic one. This generalization is based on data from ratio-scaling procedures in which subjects are asked to estimate the magnitude of each stimulus directly, as it appears to them.
3. Brentano proposed, in addition to the power law, that a relation analogous to Weber's Law applied at the subjective level of description. This relation, known today as Ekman's Law (Ekman 1956, 1959; Stevens 1966a), has recently been a focus of interest because it offers a possible answer to the question of how judgments of sensation, on the one hand, and sensory discrimination, on the other, might be related.
4. In contradistinction to these authors, Plateau was sceptical that any numerical estimate of sensation was possible. The view he expressed in the passage cited is *exactly* the hypothesis I used (Laming 1984, but in ignorance of Plateau's writing) to develop quantitative accounts of several otherwise baffling results concerning the variability of sensory judgments.

The arguments which follow are concerned, in the first instance, to discriminate between these four ideas as basic principles on which to rest the analysis of experiments which seek to measure internal sensations. It will turn out that each idea is partly empirical, partly extra-empirical. When, for example, Fechner asserts that just-noticeable differences at different parts of the scale of stimulus magnitude are subjectively equal, that implies, in the first place, that the discrimination of, say, luminance at one part of the scale is isomorphic to discrimination at any other part of the scale, differing only by a multiplicative factor. That can be tested by experiment. In the second place, Fechner's assertion also implies that the differences in sensation corresponding to different just-noticeable differences are all equal. That cannot be tested by experiment; it is, instead, a definition of a measure of sensation.

I propose to compare these four ideas strictly according to their empirical implications because, if those empirical implications are not mirrored in the state of nature, there is no measurement of sensation to be had. But there is, as a preliminary, an alternative approach to examine, based on an extrapolation from the principles of dimensional analysis in the physical sciences. This approach appears, at first blush, to obviate much hard work; but that appearance turns out to be deceptive. Examining this alternative approach will help to put mathematical argument *per se* in its proper place.

1.6 DIMENSIONAL ANALYSIS

Luce (1959) sought to argue that the relation between physical stimulus magnitude and internal sensation could, logically speaking, take one of only a small number of mathematical forms. The basis of his argument is best explained by an example.

The length of a line can be measured in inches and also in centimetres. It is the same length however it is measured and should evoke the same internal sensation. This means that the form of the relation between physical stimulus magnitude and sensation ought, logically, to be independent of the units in which the physical magnitude is measured. In like manner, it ought to be independent also of the units in which sensation is measured. The particular constraint which that consideration imposes on the mathematical form of the relation between the two depends on the type of scale on which each variable is measured, and that notion of scale type itself requires some explanation.

Stevens (1951) distinguished four kinds of measurement scale: nominal, ordinal, interval, and ratio. To illustrate, in April of each year some 35 000 runners line up at Greenwich at the start of the London marathon. They are identified by their names, which constitute a nominal scale: those names distinguish the different competitors, but do not, of themselves, tell us anything about how any individual will fare in the race. At the end of the race the competitors finish in some specific order—an ordinal scale. The order of finishing tells us only that; it says nothing about how long each competitor took or how fast he ran. To reduce congestion on the course different sections of the competitors are started at different times. So finishing times are values on an interval scale; they need to be corrected for the actual time of starting. Finally, corrected time enables us to say how much faster one competitor ran than another. It constitutes a ratio scale like length and weight. Subsequently Stevens (1959b) introduced the log interval scale, distinguished by the property that the logarithm of the scale variable is measured on an interval scale. It is a matter of taste whether one regards this as a fifth type of scale or simply as an alternative way of formulating an interval scale.

Depending on whether the physical scale of measurement was of ratio, interval, or log interval type, and depending on the scale type used to measure sensation (nine combinations are possible), Luce was able to identify the mathematical form which the relation between the two had to take if the constraint of independence from the units of measurement was to be satisfied. He proved nine theorems. One of those theorems is particularly striking: if both physical stimulus magnitude and sensation are measured on ratio scales, the relation has to be a power law like eqn 1.5. Its proof is essentially the argument I give later in Chapter 7 (p. 87).

Luce's (1959) argument generalized the technique of dimensional analysis in physics (Bridgeman 1922; Krantz *et al.* 1971, Chapter 10) to the less constrained procedures of psychophysical scaling. In a relation between physical ratio-scale quantities defined in terms of the fundamental dimensions of angle, charge, length, mass, temperature, and time, the combinations of dimensions of the different quantities in the equation have to balance—anything else would be to equate chalk with cheese—and that requirement often dictates the mathematical form of the relation. It is reasonable, very reasonable, to expect the *form* of the relation obtaining in nature to be independent of the units which the scientist has chosen for the measurement of the different (ratio-scale) quantities. A change from inches to centimetres for the measurement of length should lead to no more than a corresponding change in the unit of measurement for some other quantity. In the psychophysical application in which scales of measurement other than the ratio scale have to be envisaged, this expectation transposes into the requirement that an admissible transformation of the physical scale should lead only to an admissible transformation of the subjective scale, the mathematical form of the relationship between the two remaining unchanged.

At first sight the argument looks compelling and very restrictive. But, as Luce (1959, pp. 90–1) acknowledged, if the relation between the physical stimulus magnitude and sensation contains a dimensional constant, then a change from inches to centimetres as the unit of measurement would be absorbed in a change in the value of that constant. The stimulus variable representing length is then effectively *dimensionless* and Luce's argument has no implication for the mathematical form of the relation. The constraint which Luce identified on the possible forms of the Psychophysical Law applies only if there are no dimensional constants involved (Luce 1964).

In a critique of the original argument, Rozeboom (1962a,b) pointed out that the quantities entering into almost any law can be de-dimensionalized, so that Luce's principle of theory construction arguably has no applicability to psychophysics. Luce (1962) concurred. In magnitude estimation, for example, a pure (dimensionless) number is assigned to a physical stimulus with the dimension of length, or energy, or luminance and it is difficult to see how the condition that there be no dimensional constant can be satisfied.

Recently Luce (1990) and Narens and Mausfeld (1992) have sought to establish more abstract and general principles which might constrain the possible mathematical forms of the relation between the physical and the subjective. Narens and Mausfeld proposed an Equivalence Principle which is illustrated by the following example. The level of a pure tone may be measured either by its amplitude (A) or by its energy ($\propto \frac{1}{2}A^2$). But it is the same tone however it is measured, and should evoke the same internal sensation. In fact, the exponent of the power law for a pure tone has long been taken to be 0.3 with respect to energy, but 0.6 with respect to amplitude; this satisfies the requirement of equivalence.

Luce (1990) turned his attention specifically to cross-modal matching because this finesses the problem of what scale type is appropriate for the measurement of internal sensation. Sensation is not something that can be measured directly, and its scale is a matter of assumption. Cross-modality matching, on the other hand, is a matching between two physical dimensions for which the scales of measurement are known—one can choose two stimulus continua that both admit ratio scales—and no assumption about the scale type of sensation need be made. Luce applied essentially the same principle as before (1959) to the matching relation between two stimulus dimensions and showed, by the same argument, that the matching relation had to be a power law. However, the problem of dimensional constants has not gone away. In Fig. 5.6 (p. 67), to take one example, force of handgrip, measured in pounds weight, is matched to stimuli on nine other continua, measured in a variety of different units (but not pounds weight). The dimensions do not balance, and dimensional constants have to be included in the matching relation which thereby admits expression as a relation between two dimensionless quantities. Luce's principle of theory construction still exerts no leverage.

As a matter of philosophical principle, mathematical argument can never tell us, by itself, what the state of nature is. The state of nature can only be discovered from empirical observation. What mathematics can do is to spell particular arguments out in explicit step-by-step detail and thereby expose their validity to rigorous examination. An argument is accepted, as a whole, if each step is individually judged to be valid. Verbal arguments can deceive; the steps in a mathematical argument are more easily seen to be true or false, as the case may be. So, given the premises set out in Luce (1959, 1964 or 1990), the Psychophysical Law has to be a power law. But what the successive arguments by Luce and by Narens and Mausfeld have achieved is not to tell us what form the Psychophysical Law must take in nature, but merely to refine the premises which are needed, mathematically speaking, to ensure that the form that it does take is a power law.

One might, alternatively, look on Luce's mathematical result (1990, Theorem 1) as a putative relation awaiting experimental test. If a power law matching relationship is found to hold generally in nature, Luce's mathematics provides a sophisticated underpinning applicable to a wide variety of similar experiments—experiments, moreover, in which the stimuli need not necessarily be metric. But it is already known that the mathematics oversimplifies experimental reality in one critical respect. Subjects typically select different matches for the same stimulus value presented on different trials of an experiment. That is to say, the matching relation is not 1 : 1. A 1 : 1 relation exists between the stimulus values and the (geometric) mean matches (as in Fig. 5.6, p. 67), but some particular design of experiment is required, allowing averages to be calculated over some number of randomly ordered trials, to permit that mean to be estimated. That circumstance introduces the possibility, which I consider carefully in Chapter 11, that Stevens' Power Law results from the design of the experiment, rather than from some transform internal to the subject. In such a case a power law result would in no way validate Luce's mathematical theory.

No argument is stronger than its weakest, most unreliable, link. Luce (1990) assumes, explicitly, that in cross-modality matching a single value of one physical attribute is matched to a unique value of the other. Krantz (1972) called this a *mapping theory* because each stimulus continuum is mapped thereby onto the other. Krantz was drawing a distinction with *relation theories*, which suppose that what the subject judges is the relation between a pair of stimuli, the notion of judging a single stimulus being meaningless. Luce (1990, p. 67) reviews a particular argument by Shepard (1981) and rejects the relational idea ultimately in these terms:

> Shepard (1981, p. 36) made an additional argument to the following effect: Absolute judgments are highly variable, whereas discriminations between stimulus ratios are much less so, and subjects should therefore favor ratio judgments when they have the opportunity because that will lead to higher quality performance. Discriminations between two stimuli certainly provide evidence for a less variable internal representation of signals than is found with the absolute identification. . . . However, in regard to the intensity of signals, . . . the relevant studies are of variability in magnitude estimates, ratio estimates, and cross-modal matches. These show a variability comparable with and often greater than that found in absolute judgments (Green & Luce, 1974; Green, Luce, & Duncan, 1977; and Luce, Green, & Weber, 1976). Matching judgments of signal intensity behave more like absolute judgments and less like ratio discriminations, so I do not believe that Shepard's (1978, 1981) argument has force for signal intensity.

That argument assumes that absolute identification experiments (Luce *et al.* 1976) invoke a true absolute mode of judgment. That assumption is implicit, without collateral support, notwithstanding that detailed analysis of such experiments (Laming 1984) suggests the contrary, that absolute identification judgments are, psychologically speaking, judgments of relations between stimuli. A more sophisticated argument is needed if Shepard's suggestion is to be rebutted.

In fact, Shepard's idea turns out to be correct. Much later, in Chapter 10, I look at certain findings from magnitude estimation experiments, specifically at the correlation between successive log magnitude estimates. Ironically, one of the sources of such data is the study by Green *et al.* (1977) cited above; it shows that subjects in magnitude estimation and production tasks are indeed judging the relation of one stimulus to its predecessor. That implication is inescapable and cannot be controverted by any mathematical argument. While the argument from dimensional analysis might be justifiable as an exercise in axiomatization, it contributes nothing to psychophysics.

Before turning to a systematic examination of experimental data, there is one further idea to call in question—the idea that sensation is indeed measurable on a ratio, or at least an interval, scale. That idea is so fundamental that it has a chapter to itself.

2 Can sensation be measured?

Most readers will be taking it for granted that internal sensations are graded in strength and should therefore be measurable in the conventional sense of that term, on a ratio or at least on an interval scale, if only a reliable way could be found of carrying out the measurements. That would seem to be implicit in the very title of this book. Most of those who have contributed to this field have taken a similar view. However, that idea is *assumption*, not fact. This is so important and fundamental a matter that I spend an entire chapter sketching an alternative point of view.

The idea that internal sensations are measurable is so 'obvious' that many people do not even see it as an assumption. To see why this is so, I try, as a preliminary, to get inside the mind of such a person, to state explicitly the ideas which they hold implicitly, unaware. It is difficult to characterize a point of view that one does not oneself hold; but the commentaries on the articles by Krueger (1989) and by Lockhead (1992) reveal so great a variety of contemporary viewpoints that it is likely that my sketch will strike a chord with someone or other somewhere. Thereafter I characterize two, quite distinct, dissenting points of view. It should not be supposed, however, that I concur entirely with either of those dissenting views. In the remainder of this chapter I set out a fourth stall which underlies the empirical arguments to come.

2.1 'OF COURSE SENSATION IS MEASURABLE'

The three illustrative examples at the beginning of Chapter 1, among others, show that physical stimulus magnitude is one thing and what an observer says about it may be quite another. There has to be some distinct intermediary. Since physical stimulus magnitudes are, most of them, measurable on ratio scales, and since people's judgements increase continuously with the stimulus magnitude, that intermediary—sensation—has itself to be continuous. It must therefore be measurable, at least on an interval scale, if only a reliable way could be found to measure it.

I see this as approximately Stevens' implicit point of view; but he would probably have added that since asking subjects the direct question 'How loud does this tone sound?' gave systematic answers, those answers must be the required measure of sensation. Sensation is seen as a distinct intermediary, the metric according to which the mind works whilst processing the input, closely related to the neurophysiological substrate. The perception of objects, in context, is in no way denied; but the proper business of psychophysics is with the intermediary, sensation. The dimensions of sensation are defined by reference to the physical attributes of stimuli, because the physical theory which describes the properties of those stimuli must ultimately extend to the receptors and sensory neurons which respond to them.

Although the context in which an object is presented and its associated stimulus parameters (e.g. the physical size of a weight) modify its perception, such phenomena are seen as no more than 'puzzles to be solved rather than as counterexamples' (Krueger 1989, p. 300). Sensation is preliminary to contextual interaction and is veridically measured when the stimulus field is so devised as to eliminate such interference or, at the least, to minimize it by the averaging of data. This predicates a simple stimulus situation in which only the physical attribute of interest is manipulated. Whether that simple stimulus situation actually delivers a measure of sensation of the generality desired is an empirical question that we shall look at in due course. Stevens was sufficiently aware of the deficiencies of this approach to include a final chapter in his *Psychophysics* (1975) entitled 'Hazards and Remedies'.

2.2 'INTERNAL SENSATIONS CANNOT BE MEASURED'

There have always been a few psychologists calling the sensationist bluff on the grounds that sensations cannot be observed directly, only reported on. von Kries (1882) was one of the earliest. He asserted that it is meaningless to say that two sensations or two differences between sensations are equal. Quantitative sensations, according to von Kries, are no more comparable than are qualitative. Sensations are not the sort of thing that can be measured, certainly not in the sense in which length and weight and time are measurable. 'In my opinion, the whole attempt to measure dimensions of intensity of inner experience is nothing more than a rash and unjustified carrying-over of the measurement of dimensions of intensity from physics' (von Kries 1882, p. 274).[1] There is no argument; but, then, there is no argument which will prove a null hypothesis. The controversy which ensued between von Kries and Fechner is recounted by Murray (1993, pp. 126–7) and elaborated by Heidelberger (1993) and van Brakel (1993) in their commentaries on Murray's article.

The same objection (the *quantity objection*) has been pressed by James (1890) in a much-quoted remark:

> To introspection, our feeling of pink is surely not a portion of our feeling of scarlet; nor does the light of an electric arc seem to contain that of a tallow-candle in itself. (James 1890, vol. 1, p. 546)

It was also pressed by the physicist members of the committee appointed by the British Association for the Advancement of Science (Ferguson *et al.* 1940), and more recently by Savage (1970), Zuriff (1972), Tumarkin (1981), and Boynton (1989) among others. To appreciate the force of this objection, it will help to examine more closely what the notion of measurement involves.

'Measurement' means assigning numbers to the entities on a continuum so that empirical relations between the entities are represented by arithmetical relations between the numbers. If I have a scale pan, two weights A and B which balance are *a fortiori* equal; so they are assigned the same number. If A and B in one scale pan balance C in the other, C is assigned twice the number assigned to both A and B. A scale of weight can be constructed on that basis, which is known as *extensive measurement.* A similar basis suffices to construct a scale of length. Two sticks side by side, coincident at both ends, are equal in length. Now place those two sticks end to end; a third stick which coincides with the beginning of the first and

[1] Translated by Janet Laming.

with the end of the second, when placed side by side with the two, is of twice the length. And so on. In principle, time can be defined in the same way by reference to an hour glass or an egg timer; but it happens to be more convenient to measure time with a pendulum or other oscillatory device. But how are two internal sensations to be placed side by side so that their equality can be demonstrated? And how, thereafter, can they be concatenated, end to end?

This is actually too strict a characterization of measurement. Many measurements are indirect, measurements of some other quantity which physical theory tells us is precisely related to the quantity of interest. Time is conventionally measured by counting the swings of a pendulum or some other periodic device such as a quartz oscillator, successive swings of a pendulum each taking the same amount of time. Another example, closer to the present field of application, concerns the sensitivity of the hand to vibration. In most experiments the stimuli are supplied through a probe vibrating with a prescribed amplitude normal to the skin. The probe is often a rod (known as a *contactor*) oscillating along its length (e.g. Verrillo, 1962). How can the amplitude of those oscillations, which may be tiny, of the order of microns, be measured? It is not possible to set the contactor at one extreme position or the other and use methods for the measurement of small, but stationary, displacements because the motion of the contactor is controlled by a current-driven vibrator which responds to input current with acceleration, not with displacement. The usual solution is an accelerometer mounted on the contactor. But an accelerometer gives a piezo-electric output proportional to acceleration, not to displacement; and physical theory is then required to recover the amplitude of oscillation of the contactor from its acceleration. The point of this example is that if there were an analogous theory of the experimental procedures which have been promoted to measure sensation, then the basis of measurement of internal sensations might be similarly assured.

Matching one luminance to another (e.g. Heinemann 1955) is arguably a comparison of two sensations 'side by side'. And actual concatenation of sensations, placing them 'end to end', may not be necessary. When one volume of water at 10 °C is mixed with an equal volume at 20 °C, the resultant mix has a temperature of 15 °C, not 30 °C; but that does not prevent the measurement of temperature. So, it would be premature to decry, at this stage, all possibility of measuring sensation.

2.3 'PEOPLE JUDGE OBJECTS, NOT ATTRIBUTES'

In short, everyone makes the 'stimulus error' (Boring 1921). This point of view has recently been argued vigorously by Lockhead (1992) on the ground that the kinds of judgments which are conventionally used as the basis for measuring sensation are much subject to the contexts in which they are made. Lockhead specifically cites the effects of simultaneous contrast on perceived brightness (see later, pp. 83–5), the complexities of visual illusions such as Ames' rooms (Ittelson 1952, pp. 39–52; cf. below, p. 16), and the effect of preceding stimuli on category judgments, especially in a previously unpublished experiment on the judgment of the loudness of tones varying in frequency as well as sound pressure level.

There is, in addition, a yet more powerful argument which he overlooked. If a disc in some slanted orientation be matched by an ellipse placed normal to the line of sight, subjects are generally able to match the real shape of the stimulus, but are systematically biased towards that real shape when asked to match the disc's perspective shape, that is, to match the elliptical pattern cast by the slanted disc on the retina. Analogous results are obtained from the matching of a disc at one distance by a comparison disc at another—matches of perspective size are biased towards real size—and from the matching of whiteness and colour (Thouless 1931a,b; Hering 1925). It needs to be emphasized that intermediaries, shapes and sizes corresponding geometrically to the perspective, are physically present in the pattern of stimulation on the subject's retina—are *simultaneously* present on the subject's retina—and feed through into proportionate afterimages:

> . . . two circular discs of different sizes adjusted to phenomenal equality give unequal after-sensations, whereas when adjusted to stimulus equality they give equal after-sensations, although the objects appear unequal at the time of fixation. This last experiment is a particularly striking one, since the subject is astonished at the contrast between the relative phenomenal sizes during fixation and in the after-sensation. (Thouless 1931b, p. 9)

Nevertheless, it is impossible to make direct use of those intermediaries (except when they are juxtaposed in the stimulus field; e.g. Gibson 1950, pp. 176–7, fig. 70). It is as though the subject has to calculate backwards from the perceived object, what the perspective shape and size of the retinal image ought to be, and those calculations are systematically biased. Phenomenal regression is therefore a 'stimulus error' and it seems to be unavoidable.

If all the perceptual cues to distance and orientation be eliminated by, for example, viewing the stimulus through a reduction tube against a black velvet background and under diffuse illumination, the phenomenal shape can then be matched without bias (Thouless 1931b). But subjects then have no idea of the distance or the orientation of what they are looking at. Reintroduce those cues, and the bias towards the real object reappears. The bias is less in trained artists than in control subjects (Thouless 1932), but it is not entirely absent, suggesting that attention to the sensation *per se*, as Titchener demanded (Titchener 1905, pp. xxvi–xxvii), is actually impossible. Artists are taught to view their model through partially closed eyes—this throws the model out of focus and partially destroys the cues to its distance and orientation—or to transfer angular extents, such as the height of a tree, to the sketchpad by holding a pencil at arm's length and marking the angular extent with a thumbnail. That is the only way in which the artist can get the size of the tree 'right'.

Another, especially compelling, example is cited by Warren (1989, p. 297):

> . . . it is impossible for us to perceive the gross spectral changes produced by head shadowing and pinna reflections when a sound source moves. These changes in peripheral stimulation (which can exceed 20 dB for particular spectral bands) are perceived in an automatic and obligatory fashion as changes in position of the source rather than as changes in the quality of the sound or the relative intensity of spectral components. As pointed out by Helmholtz, 'we are exceedingly well trained in finding out by our sensations the objective nature of the objects around us, but . . . are completely unskilled in observing these sensations *per se*; . . . the practice of associating them with things outside of us actually prevents us from being distinctly conscious of the pure sensations (Warren and Warren 1968).

The dependence of observation on context does not, of itself, preclude valid measurement; it merely means that context has to be controlled. But we can know about internal sensations only through the medium of judgments made by experimental subjects. The examples just cited suggest that identification of the stimulus as an object is primary and the judgment of sensation derived therefrom. This raises the critical question whether 'sensation' can be defined in a way that is independent of the object from which it is abstracted. Lockhead's conclusion is that the relation between the physical attributes of the stimuli being judged and the judgments made by human subjects is so complex that the enterprise undertaken by Stevens, his colleagues, and his students is fundamentally misconceived. Perception is what psychophysicists should study, not sensation.

If I agreed entirely with that point of view, there would be no *The Measurement of Sensation* for me to write. In the remainder of this chapter I set out yet another point of view which underlies the empirical enquiries to come.

2.4 PERCEPTION WITHOUT 'SENSATION'

Stimulation of the sense organs generates a pattern of activity within the sensorium that is experienced by the observer as a percept 'out there'. The percept is a construction, a model of a part of the world outside. As an example, Fig. 2.1 shows Kanizsa's (1955) triangle; an opaque white triangle can be 'seen' obscuring the central part of the figure.

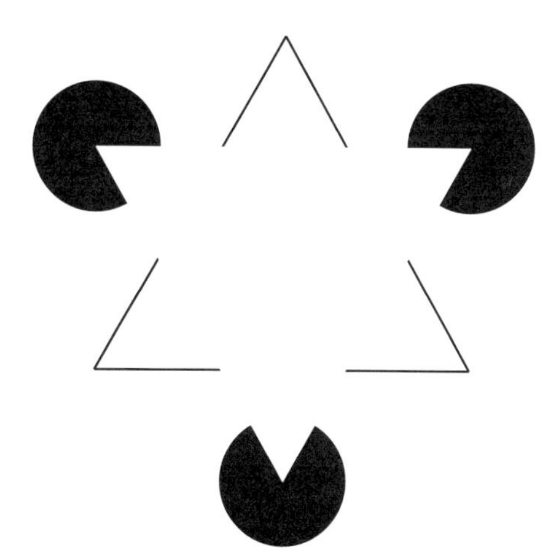

Fig. 2.1 Kanizsa's triangle. The figure appears to consist of a black outline triangle and three filled circles partially obscured by an opaque white triangle. The white triangle is not explicit in the stimulus field; it disappears if the filled circles are covered. When they are uncovered, it reappears. (From 'Margini quasi-percettivi in campi con stimolozione omogenea', by G. Kanizsa, *Rivista di Psicologia*, vol. 49, p. 16. © 1955, Giunti Gruppo Editoriale, Firenze. Reproduced by permission.)

Indeed, not only did all my subjects say that they clearly saw a white triangle superimposed on another triangle and partly covering it, but many of them also insisted that they had the impression that there really was a second triangle cut from another whiter sheet of paper and pasted on the first. They could not see any difference between the edges of this whiter triangle and the real boundaries that one sees when a figure is truly distinct from its background. (Kanizsa 1955, pp. 16–18; [Translated by Janet Laming.])

The whiter triangle is not actually there to be seen—'seen' now used in its literal sense. It is constructed by the perceiver.

Kanisza's triangle illustrates this idea: the visual field and patterns of stimulation in other sensory modalities provide the observer with data about the outside world. On the basis of that data a model of the world is constructed. That is the percept. The process of construction is internal, but the model is projected into the world outside where things are seen and heard. If the percept is referred to a location inside the body—if we feel pain or palpitations or if we itch—then it is legitimate to talk about an internal sensation. But if the brightness, loudness, or heaviness is referred to a percept 'out there', there are no grounds for supposing that there is, *in addition* and by analogy with sensations of pain or itch, an internal sensation which might provide the basis for a separate judgment. To suppose so is an *illusion of grammar.* Indeed, Thouless' (1931a,b) experiments on the constancies indicate that no such separate judgment can be made.

S.S. Stevens might well have replied that in his laboratory subjects routinely assign numbers, systematically, to the loudness of pure tones, to the loudness as they hear it. What is that, if not measurement? *But what is it that is being measured?* How do we know that it is an internal sensation? The tones to be judged are presented one at a time, by themselves, in quiet. The stimulus situation preferred by psychophysicists is analogous to viewing Thouless' slanted disc through a reduction tube. Just as the elimination of all cues to the disc's orientation prevents the subject from matching anything other than its perspective shape—the information needed to make any other kind of match is entirely lacking—so, the stimulus presented for magnitude estimation is likewise stripped of context, so far as that can be achieved. But the subject is, none the less, estimating the intensity of a tone heard 'out there'.

A more sophisticated philosophical analysis, one with which I believe Stevens would have agreed, says that certainly the subject is estimating the intensity of a tone heard 'out there'; but when that tone is entirely devoid of context, and only then, the subject's judgments reflect, in an unbiased way, his internal sensation. That is why psychophysicists use such absurdly simple stimulus configurations. If the tone had, instead, been one note of a melody, the percept would have been quite different and so also would the judgment of loudness, irretrievably compromised by context. But presenting that tone in isolation from any other stimulus reveals the internal metric of the sensory system according to which it is processed.

The idea that the judgment of stimuli in complete isolation reveals the internal metric of the sensory system is pure assumption. In practice, complete isolation is unachievable. There is always, at the least, the instructions from experimenter to subject whose influence on the responses is demonstrable (see later, pp. 183–5) and, in due course, we shall discover other implicit contexts in magnitude estimation experiments (see Chapter 10). So, while the effect of context is demonstrable, what about the hypothetical contribution from internal sensation? In our present state of knowledge there is no way of distinguishing the reports by Stevens' subjects from judgments of the physical attributes of stimuli, of highly impoverished stimuli, the judgments being expressed on a response scale devised by the experimenter. The possibility has to be considered that the results Stevens achieved in his laboratory reflect no more than a pragmatic randomization between different sorts of contextual influences.

2.5 THEORETICAL FORMULATIONS

Of course, to formulate an understanding of perceptual processes, some regime is needed intermediate between the stimulus and the judgment. But that intermediate regime is a theoretical construct, not a matter for direct observation and measurement. It is far from clear that the most appropriate regime is a simple reformulation of the physical attributes of the stimuli at a subjective, psychophysical level of description—as brightness, loudness, pitch, heaviness etc.—or that the best experimental basis for that reformulation is magnitude estimation and other 'direct' procedures. In fact, so long as our perception is veridical or, at the least, we remain unaware of systematic discrepancies, we cannot tell how our perception works and our choice of intermediate regime matters little. But, exceptionally (e.g. Fig. 2.1), we perceive elements which are known not to be physically present in the stimulus—illusions—and we obtain some insight into the process.

Given our presently limited understanding of perception, I consider it better to formulate that intermediary regime in terms of information, in terms of what the stimulus tells the subject about the outside world, rather than proceed directly to a subjective physics. A frame of reference which treats the stimulus as a source of data makes direct contact with a wealth of experiments on sensory discrimination, and the kind of theory which results will be the subject of Chapter 3. Meanwhile, I cite another example to show how this approach can illuminate specifically perceptual phenomena.

If Fig. 2.2 be viewed from a distance of about 50 cm, faint grey diagonal lines may be seen passing through the white spaces. The discovery of these lines is attributed by Lindsay and Norman (1977, p. 40) to one Robert Springer, although this is one of several similar figures studied by Prandtl (1927). At a greater distance, about 1.5 m, bright horizontal and vertical lines, brighter than the surrounding white, may be seen in the horizontal and vertical white spaces. The ranges of distances within which these illusory lines may be seen correspond roughly to the ranges over which certain sinusoidal components of the figure, different components for the two sets of lines, are at or below threshold. That suggests an explanation in terms of the partial loss of information in the course of sensory analysis (Laming 1992).

If, in passage through our sensory apparatus, certain information provided by the physical stimulus is blocked, not transmitted, then we are insensitive to the corresponding features of the stimulus field. A simple example is metameric lights. Although such lights have different physical spectra, no information about their spectral differences passes beyond the receptors. Information about colour is transmitted through three channels only, red, green, and blue. Two lights which, though of different spectral compositions, happen each to excite the red, the green, and the blue channels to the same three extents, cannot be distinguished.

Springer's figure (Fig. 2.2) can be decomposed into sinusoidal components which are passed selectively through different wavenumber-sensitive channels in the visual system (see e.g. Laming, 1991c). At the other end of those parallel transmission lines the separate wavenumber-selective messages are reassembled and the overall pattern of black squares reconstructed. But, at a certain distance of view, two adjacent harmonics which both have peaks running through the centres of the diagonal white spaces are jointly at or below threshold and therefore of a critical contrast (relative to their wavenumber) at which they become subject to subthreshold compression (see Laming 1986, Chapter 8). That subthreshold compression is an actual loss of information and a consequent effective loss of contrast, but only a partial loss, so that when the pattern is reconstructed at the end of the visual transmission line, there is a noticeable defect relative to the pattern of black squares on a white ground. That defect shows as the diagonal grey lines.

Fig. 2.2 Springer's lines. Faint grey diagonal lines running through each white space may be seen on close inspection. From a greater distance bright white horizontal and vertical lines, brighter than the white surround, become apparent, again running through each white space. (From 'Précis of *Sensory analysis*' by D. Laming, *Behavioral and Brain Sciences*, vol. 11, p. 286. © 1988, Cambridge University Press. Reproduced by permission.)

At a greater distance, the harmonic components producing those diagonal grey lines are sufficiently far below threshold that the defect thereby created becomes itself imperceptible. (As distance increases, so also do the wavenumbers of individual sinusoidal components. Since the components of interest have wavenumbers sufficiently great that further increase of wavenumber is accompanied by an increase in threshold, one can usefully think of increase of distance as producing a decrease of contrast, even though this is technically incorrect.) At that greater distance certain other harmonic components, now oriented horizontally and vertically, enter the critical region of contrast where subthreshold compression takes hold, and illusory vertical and horizontal lines can be seen. The illusory lines are now bright, brighter than the white surround, because these harmonics both have troughs running through the centres of the horizontal and vertical white spaces. Partial suppression of those troughs is perceived as a bright line.

What this particular example illustrates is a relation between what is perceived when Springer's figure is viewed from various distances and quantitative details of the visibility of sinusoidal gratings, specifically their modulation thresholds (van Nes 1968) and the shapes of their detectability functions (Laming 1986). The tracing of that relation depends on an intermediate regime which sees the physical stimulus as a source of data on which the perceptual judgment is based. Whether that kind of formulation proves to be generally appropriate depends on how many other similar relationships need to be taken account of, and some further examples are presented in Chapter 6. Meanwhile, there is a another reason why it is helpful to look on perception as the interpretation of data.

2.6 PRIOR EXPECTATIONS

Hollingworth (1909) reported this experiment on the reproduction of guided movements. A narrow slit of the required length was cut in a strip of cardboard which was then pasted onto a similar strip to form a furrow. This furrow could be readily traced with a pencil held by a blindfolded subject. Two seconds later the subject attempted to produce a movement of the same amplitude on a sheet of plain paper (i.e. with no furrow to guide him) and two seconds later a second reproduction. Different prescribed amplitudes were presented in random order, each followed by two reproductions, until a total of 50 reproductions of each standard amplitude had been recorded. Figure 2.3 shows the mean amplitudes of the reproductions of each prescribed amplitude of movement.

In different sessions different series of standard amplitudes were presented for reproduction: Series A ranged from 10 to 70 mm, Series B from 30 to 150 mm, and Series C from 70 to 250 mm. Within each series, the shorter movements were overproduced while long movements were underproduced, and log mean reproduction was approximately a linear function of log standard amplitude. Mean reproductions are biased towards a fixed point internal to the stimulus series; but different series are biased towards *different* fixed points, showing that the bias depends on the particular amplitudes the subjects had recently traced. But if a standard amplitude is presented repeatedly, by itself, in a separate session (filled points in Fig. 2.3), the bias is negligible.

What this experiment shows is that the length of the reproduction is a compromise between the actual length of the guided movement on that particular trial and the length which the subject has come to expect on the basis of previous trials, recently experienced. As another example, I have already mentioned the size–weight illusion, in which a physically larger object feels lighter relative to its physical weight. Harper and Stevens (1948) constructed their *veg* scale of heaviness by having subjects choose from an array of comparison weights the one which felt half as heavy as a given standard. The weights were all of the same physical size and half-heaviness corresponded to about 62 per cent of the weight of the standard. When Warren and Warren (1956) repeated the experiment, they compared sets of comparison weights equal in size to the standard (replicating Harper and Stevens 1948; half-heaviness equivalent to 65 per cent of the standard), comparison weights half the physical size of the standard (half-heaviness now equivalent to 52 per cent of the standard), and comparison weights one-quarter the physical size of the standard (half-heaviness 41 per cent). Plainly, physical size enters systematically into the (subjective) estimation of physical weight. How to formulate the combination of such disparate factors poses a problem for the theorist.

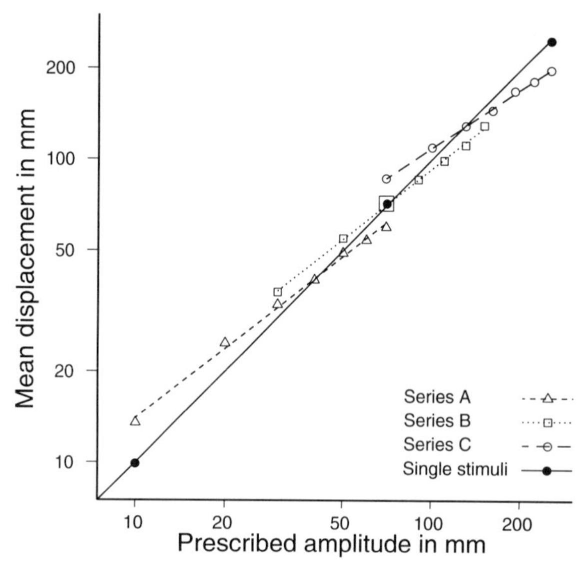

Fig. 2.3 Mean reproductions of standard amplitudes of movement from Hollingworth (1909). Series A, B, and C are from different sessions in which different ranges of amplitudes were presented for reproduction. The filled points display the results of three further sessions in which one amplitude only was presented repeatedly.

A visual stimulus, a flash of light say (borrowing an example from Lockhead 1992), is seen against a pre-existing background luminance (which might be complete darkness). It is an empirical question whether the significant stimulus parameter is the absolute luminance of the flash, or its excess over the background; and Lockhead argues on several different grounds that the significant input to the visual process consists of temporal changes in luminance. If that be so, then the scaling of luminance *per se* needs to be replaced by the scaling of temporal changes in luminance. But Hollingworth's data in Fig. 2.3 and much similar data elsewhere (e.g. Ward and Lockhead 1971; Laming 1968, Chapter 8) pose a more difficult conceptual problem. It is easy to envisage a differential input to the visual system which confers a specific sensitivity to temporal changes (Laming 1986, Chapter 5), but what kind of machinery is going to interact with individual preceding stimuli, individual stimuli presented several trials previously?

Invocation of a graded internal sensation rather commits one to a mechanical view of the matter and it is then difficult to incorporate the effects of past experimental trials in any simple manner. I prefer to think of those past trials as contributing data which ranks *pari passu* with the similar data contributed by the guided trial. The amplitude of reproduction in Hollingworth's experiment is then chosen in the light of all available data and the movement the subject actually makes is his best estimate of what is required. I conjecture that previous trials enter into the process of reproduction because the recall of past experience enables the subject to be more precise. That precision comes from the increased volume of data. It comes at the expense of a bias; but, since the subject received no feedback, that bias is not something of which he can be aware.

2.7 FUNCTIONAL MEASUREMENT

Suppose, now, that an accurate, quantitative description be formulated for a substantial body of experimental data, ostensibly judgments of the intensity of sensation, as succinct a description as may be. Sensation cannot be measured except through the judgments of experimental subjects. One might say it does not exist apart from those judgments. Suppose that in that succinct, accurate description some simple relation between the physical stimulus magnitude and the judgments recorded—Fechner's Law or Stevens' Power Law or some other formula yet to be discovered—some simple relation comes to assume a fundamental role analogous, say, to the inverse square law of gravitational attraction. Then, that simple relation, whatever it may be, provides a rational basis for the measurement of sensation; and the precise meaning of 'sensation' is determined by the operations by which that measurement is effected.

This outline could be construed as the approach which Anderson has promoted under the title 'Functional Measurement'. Anderson's ideas have been developed mostly in the field of person perception, studying the way in which different descriptors combine in the assessment of the whole person (see Anderson 1974). But the functional approach has also been applied to the size–weight illusion (Anderson 1970, 1972) to deliver a subjective scale of weight.

In a typical experiment (Anderson 1970) there are several weights, each combined in a complete factorial design with the same set of different physical sizes, and subjects rate each size–weight combination on a 1 to 20 scale or by dividing a line on a slip of paper. Mean ratings typically generate approximately parallel lines as functions of size, a separate line for each weight. Conformity to an averaging model is tested through the interaction term in an analysis of variance. Some experiments give significant results, but the deviations from the parallel are not great. Anderson's interpretation of such data is that the intercepts of the lines for different weights constitute an interval scale of subjective heaviness; the analogous intercepts for different sizes constitute an interval scale for expected heaviness as a function of size; and the compatibility of data with model means that the 20-point rating scale is the 'correct' response measure to use (rather than the magnitude estimates espoused by S.S. Stevens). As a validation of this approach, Anderson (1972) showed that ratings of the average of two weights (functional measurement requires two independent variables in an orthogonal experimental design to permit the calculation of an interaction term and cannot therefore be applied to the judgment of single weights) generate a scale that is linear with the scale of heaviness obtained from size–weight data.

Functional measurement sounds simple, clean, and atheoretical. But it is only fair to point out that the ranges of weight explored are not large: 150–250 g in Anderson (1970) and 200–600 g in Anderson (1972). Neither are the ranges of size large: 40–72 mm cubes and cylinders 6 cm in diameter and 3.3–15.3 cm in height, respectively. Moreover, responses are ushered into the centre of the rating scale by the use of anchor stimuli; and Anderson's (1972, p. 390) comment on one of his significant interaction terms suggests that he has found the anchors to be very necessary. It is therefore legitimate to interpolate Anderson's functional scale of heaviness within the narrow ranges of weight and size explored, but not to extrapolate it outside. The reason is that within those narrow ranges of the independent variables there is little non-linearity for the interaction term to pick up, and interpolated values will be accurate; but, tested over much wider geometric ranges of stimulus magnitudes (as Stevens does), Anderson's averaging model might well collapse.

I nevertheless wish to retain a functional approach. It will become apparent that the measurement of sensation is bedevilled by prior assumptions, often assumptions of no empirical content, which nevertheless constrain subsequent argument. Those prior assumptions have to be identified as such and called into question. However, instead of modelling the results of custom-designed two-factor experiments, I propose to direct attention to those traditional experiments which already exist aplenty, not only measurements of thresholds, but magnitude estimation and production and cross-modality matching as well. A functional approach, to my mind, subsists in accounting for as many of the experimental phenomena as accurately and as economically as may be. The treatment of sensory discrimination in Chapter 3 will illustrate what I mean. If, in that accurate and economical account, some simple relation emerges between some intermediate variable and the physical stimulus magnitude, then, whatever that relation might be, the intermediate variable is a potential measure of sensation. But if, on the other hand, that approach requires the abandonment of some long-treasured idea, so be it. Even if that approach means discarding the initial question of interest, the very idea of measuring sensation, again, so be it. For the assertion that sensation is indeed measurable is the one of those prior assumptions that most needs to be questioned.

The first task of this critique is to look and see whether Fechner's Law (Chapters 3 and 4), on the one hand, or Stevens' Law (Chapters 5–7), on the other, fulfils such a fundamental role with respect to the judgment of sensation. But at this point a subtle difficulty emerges which is most simply illustrated by rewriting Fechner's Law (eqn 1.2) in this more general form:

$$S = \ln a + \beta \ln X, \qquad (2.1)$$

which puts the zero ($\ln a$) and the unit (β) of the scale at our disposal. If, now, both sides of eqn 2.1 be exponentiated,

$$e^S = aX^\beta, \qquad (2.2)$$

and Stevens' measure of sensation appears (on comparing eqn 2.2 with eqn 1.5) to be nothing more than the exponential of Fechner's measure. Is the long-continued controversy between Stevens' and Fechner's scientific disciples merely a quarrel about how the psychological theory (the same theory) should be formulated mathematically? That is a question I investigate in Chapter 8.

Although the protagonists in the controversy have not seen the issue in this light, it should be noted that Fechner's Law depends *essentially* on the fiat that all just-noticeable differences are subjectively equal; and that the power law originally proposed by Brentano (1874) depends on the equally arbitrary assertion that the subjective domain is structured like the physical, so that just-noticeable differences in sensation satisfy a relation analogous to Weber's Law. Neither of these assertions, which are antecedents of the measurement of sensation, not consequences, has any empirical foundation. Indeed, neither of them has any empirical content! So the possibility must again be considered that the controversy between Stevens' and Fechner's scientific disciples is artificial, incapable of empirical resolution.

It will turn out, as an empirical matter, that no stimulus can be judged in isolation, absolutely, but only in relation to some other stimulus. The experiments by Stevens and his colleagues depend on suitably randomizing the effects of that implicit reference stimulus. But an adequate treatment of the measurement of sensation must take this relative nature of sensory judgment explicitly into account. Judgments of sensory magnitudes are known to be much subject to bias (Poulton 1968, 1979, 1989). A theory of the measurement procedure would tell us how to avoid those biases or, at least, how to correct for them. Exploration of the implications of the relative nature of sensory judgement, of relational theories of sensation, occupies Chapters 8–10.

At the end of the day, it may be that a theory of the experiments which have been promoted as measuring sensation will fail to deliver any scale of measurement distinct from the physical. If the reproduction of a guided movement can be modelled without invoking an internal sensation, so also might magnitude production and estimation. We therefore have to beware of the *sensation error*. The *stimulus error*, recall, subsists in attending to the objective stimulus and judging that, rather than the sensation it produces. By the *sensation error* I mean taking judgments of the physical stimulus to be judgments of some internal sensation, when there is actually no distinct process which might serve as a basis for such a judgment.

Now, if our enquiry reduces purely to a consideration of physical measures, the application of dimensional analysis by Luce (1959, 1964, 1990), especially in application to cross-modality matching, might be expected to exert some leverage. But while averaged matches (and estimates) can be measured on a ratio or an interval scale, individual judgments might be no better than ordinal. That idea is explored in Chapters 11 and 12. Since people can usually say whether one stimulus is stronger or weaker than another, a nominal scale can be excluded. But a theory of sensory judgment must concern itself with the individual judgments, and it is logically possible that the psychological component, the component that elsewhere provides the experimental basis for measuring sensation, is no better than ordinal. In that case Luce's (1959) theorems prescribe no particular form of relationship.

2.8 THE SCOPE OF ENSUING ARGUMENTS

Experiments in which subjects have been asked to make judgments about single stimuli, presented one at a time, raise two broad classes of question:

1. Assuming that each stimulus evokes an internal sensation of some strength on which the judgment is based, how is that strength of sensation related to the physical stimulus magnitude? It is easy to see that this question provides a motivation for such experiments in the first place; Stevens' (1956b) method of magnitude estimation is the example above all others.
2. An alternative motivation arises sometimes from a purely practical problem. For example, what is the most effective way of indicating altitude to the pilot of an aircraft? The pilot's ability to resolve small differences in pointer position against a set of scale marks is limited, and, rather than having the pointer continuously adjustable, it might be more effective to limit it to a small number of distinct positions. That practical question was addressed by Hake and Garner (1951) in an experiment which required the subjects to read the position of a pointer against two scale marks when that position was drawn at random from differently sized sets of possible values. Their experiment concerned the accuracy of absolute identification, and the second broad class of question asks how that accuracy is related to a variety of experimental parameters and, by implication, what is the nature of the process underlying such judgments.

I emphasize that in the arguments which follow I address the first of these questions only. But some psychophysicists, perhaps many, see magnitude estimation experiments and 'ratio scaling' methods on the one hand and absolute identification and category judgment on the other as addressing substantially the *same* questions. Both kinds of experiment support some kind of subjective scaling of the stimuli. Garner and Hake (1951) showed how identification data could be used to scale the stimuli in terms of their discriminability. Their method was an adaptation of Thurstone's (1927) Law of Comparative Judgment and similar to Guilford's (1931, 1954) treatment of pair-comparison data. The two kinds of experiment also exhibit a number of phenomena in common—they both display sequential effects and an increase of response variability with the (log) range of stimulus values. So my restriction of argument to the first question alone requires some justification.

In practice, the two broad questions I have distinguished above typically dictate experiments of different design and, even more to the point, different analyses of the data. The analysis of data from magnitude estimation and other 'ratio scaling' methods usually consists of the calculation of (geometric) mean judgments. Those calculations are relatively simple. The immediate question of interest concerns the relation of the geometric means to stimulus magnitudes. But if, addressing the second question, an absolute identification design is used, mean judgments are hardly meaningful since the numbers attached to different response categories are properly no more than an ordered set of labels. Instead, an analysis is required of the pattern of misidentifications. The appropriate analytical technique is Torgerson's (1958) Law of Categorical Judgment—Braida and Durlach (1972) present some fine examples of its application—but the calculations are now quite different in kind and much more complex. The reason for restricting subsequent argument to the first question alone is simply this difference in analytical technique. An adequate treatment of absolute identification and category judgment would require a prior investment in the technicalities of Torgerson's model and that, in turn, requires a separate book.

I do not dispute the phenomenal similarity between magnitude estimation and absolute identification experiments. Indeed, it will become apparent during the ensuing argument that I consider the empirical value of magnitude estimation to reside in the *precision* of the numerical judgments, not in their means, and that Torgerson's analytical techniques are appropriate for magnitude estimation data too. But the complexity of two quite different analytical philosophies within one book would be too much. In this book, therefore, I address only the question whether there is empirical evidence sufficient to establish some scale of internal sensation distinct from the physical measure of the stimulus. Absolute identification experiments frequently include feedback to the subjects so that an objectively correct response is operationally defined. That precludes absolute identification data bearing directly on the question of internal sensation, and such evidence is called upon (in Chapter 10) only when its implications about the nature of the underlying judgment process are needed to support the argument about sensation.

In this book, then, I investigate theories which might support this or that procedure as a measure of internal sensation. My ultimate conclusion will be that there is no internal sensation to be measured—no sensation distinct from subjective estimates of *physical* stimulus magnitudes, that is, estimates of stimulus magnitudes as they are perceived, not as they are physically presented, but estimates of physical magnitudes, not of some internal intermediary. This conclusion could well have been left until the end, when the many ways of looking at sensation that psychologists have developed will all have been tried and found to fail. But it is characteristic of the arguments to come that each begins with an intuition which initially promises much, promises to meet all those problems on which previous ideas have foundered, but then itself comes to grief on some new experimental finding. I state my conclusion now in the belief that it will illuminate those coming arguments.

There are several related ideas to explore, each of which is capable of organizing a large volume of experimental results, different, though overlapping, volumes falling into place with different ideas. I shall ultimately argue that all those ideas fail because they incorporate the assumption that sensation can be measured on at least an interval scale. Scalability of internal sensation is an assumption underlying all the controversies surveyed in this book. Take away that assumption, and the controversies evaporate. The arena is then cleared for study of the second broad class of questions distinguished above, concerning the process underlying judgments of single stimuli. But if, notwithstanding that it is false, the assumption of the scalability of sensation be retained, there is no empirical basis on which existing controversies might be resolved.

3 Fechner's Law—the normal model

Fechner's Law

$$S = \ln X, \tag{3.1}$$

can be split into two independent assertions:

1. the phenomena of sensory discrimination are uniform with respect to the logarithm of stimulus magnitude; and
2. that logarithmic metric measures the sensation experienced by the subject.

In this chapter I begin an examination of Assertion 1, which is actually a restatement of a strong form of Weber's Law. If, as will appear in the next chapter, the phenomena of sensory discrimination can be described equally accurately in terms of some formula other than the logarithmic, and if, as will also appear in the next chapter, that other formula accommodates a significantly wider range of phenomena, then there is no need to discuss Assertion 2, which is extra-empirical.

In Fechner's day the phenomenon from which his law was derived was the difference threshold, as determined by the methods of constant stimuli, of limits, and of average error. But since then the variety of experimental paradigms for the study of sensory discrimination, and the detailed procedures within those paradigms, has increased greatly, so that it is now possible to bring results from signal detection experiments, from studies of psychometric functions, as well as conventional determinations of thresholds, to bear on the empirical validity of Assertion 1. More to the point, these changes in experimental practice have brought with them a change in our collective understanding of a 'threshold', so that a fair examination of Fechner's Law must begin with an attempt to understand the notion of a threshold as he conceived it.

3.1 THE NOTION OF A 'THRESHOLD'

If, as in the last chapter, perception is viewed as the construction of a model of the world—a model which is projected 'out there', rather than representing a sensation 'inside'—then, for a stimulus to be perceived, there must be a certain minimum amount of information about the stimulus received from the sense organs, sufficient to specify what the stimulus is. If some lesser amount only is available, no perceptual model of acceptable reliability can be constructed and the stimulus is not perceived; but once the necessary minimum of information is exceeded, the stimulus is seen for what it is. If the flood waters do not come over the threshold of the door, the house remains dry; but once the level of that threshold is exceeded, the whole house is inundated to the full depth of the flood and the threshold might as well not be there. It would, however, be foolish for the householder to say that, because no water has yet entered the house, there is no danger of flooding; and the psychophysical equivalent, the assertion that a stimulus which fails to exceed threshold has no effect, has also proved to be mistaken.

The controversy, whether there is a psychophysical threshold—by which I mean the idea that stimuli below threshold are imperceptible, unavailable as a basis for judgment—or whether the notion of a threshold is no more than a statistical abstraction (e.g. Swets 1961), seems still to be unresolved. The facts of the matter are that subjects can adjust a stimulus, a flash of light, say, or a brief tone in noise, to be 'just detectable' or to be 'just noticeably greater than' a standard stimulus and can do so with some consistency. Figure 3.1 exhibits one example. For that to be so, a 'threshold' has to be more than a mere statistical abstraction. At the same time, the same subjects can make better-than-chance discriminations between stimuli that are below 'threshold', so the idea that a 'threshold' marks the limit of sensibility is contraindicated. I propose the following resolution.

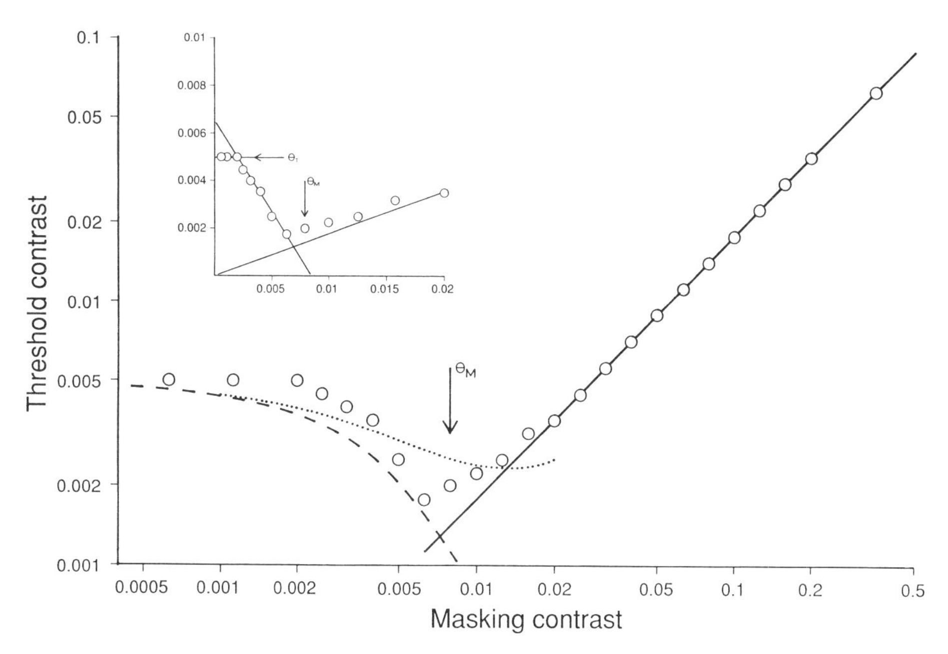

Fig. 3.1 Thresholds for the detection of increments added to the contrast of a 10 cycles/deg sinusoidal grating determined by the method of adjustment. The masking contrast was continuously present and the test contrast was added every alternate second. The inset diagram presents part of the data with respect to linear coordinates and shows that near absolute threshold the subject used three different threshold criteria over different ranges of the masking contrast. (Data from Campbell and Kulikowski, 1966. Figure from *Sensory analysis*, by D. Laming, p. 146. © 1986, Academic Press. Reproduced by permission.)

If there is sufficient information about a stimulus to permit its reconstruction in a model of the world, then it is perceived. That limiting amount of information defines a pragmatic 'threshold' of perceptibility. A variable stimulus can be adjusted about that critical level until it is 'just noticeable'. Weaker stimuli, providing less than that critical level of information, are not ordinarily noticed. But that does not mean that the lesser level of information such weaker stimuli provide is forfeit. On the contrary, meaningful discriminations are possible with respect to all levels of a standard stimulus, including levels below detection threshold, levels too low to be perceived. Laming (1986, Chapter 8) presents many examples. Moreover, this influence below threshold is by no means restricted to the simple stimuli used by psychophysicists; Marcel (1983) has demonstrated that words briefly presented and masked to prevent awareness can nevertheless affect a variety of subsequent discriminations.

Demonstrating meaningful discrimination with respect to stimuli below threshold generally requires the use of a two-alternative forced-choice (2AFC) or a signal-detection experimental paradigm, with immediate knowledge of results, in which the subject is impelled to be as accurate as possible. In that way subjects can be driven to find some way of discriminating between stimuli which, though they are known to be there, cannot ordinarily be perceived. Such experiments can measure the information actually afforded by subthreshold stimuli, and the manner in which that information varies with stimulus magnitude, still 'subthreshold', is a topic of particular interest within sensory discrimination. But it bears no close relation to the nineteenth-century notion of a threshold.

Alternatively, the subject can be allowed to adjust the stimulus until it is 'just noticeable'. In the experiment reported in Fig. 3.1 (Campbell and Kulikowski 1966), the subject viewed a sinusoidal grating of 10 cycles/deg filling a circular field, 2° in diameter, set in a uniform surround equal to the space average luminance (40 cd/m^2) of the grating. The contrast of the grating switched once per second between the levels C and $C + \Delta C$, and the subject's task was to adjust the ΔC to be just noticeable. The main diagram in Fig. 3.1 is plotted on logarithmic coordinates, but part of the data is replotted on linear coordinates to display clearly the rectilinear nature of the subject's contrast settings for very low contrasts C. Those settings may be summarized as follows:

1. If $C \leqslant 0.002$, $\Delta C = \theta_T$, where $\theta_T = 0.005$ is the absolute threshold for the alternating test grating ΔC by itself, alternating at 0.5 Hz.
2. If $0.002 \leqslant C \leqslant 0.006$, $C + b\Delta C \sim \theta_M$, where $\theta_M = 0.008$ is the absolute threshold for the static masking grating C.
3. If $0.02 \leqslant C$, $\Delta C/C = 0.175$.

As statistical abstractions from 2AFC data, these rectilinear characteristics look bizarre. But, interpreted as the stimulus levels needed to construct a coherent percept of the stimulus, they make sense. For $C \leqslant 0.002$, the subject is adjusting the ΔC until he can just see the grating alternating, one way or the other, once every second. For $0.002 \leqslant C \leqslant 0.006$, the subject is adjusting the total contrast until he can just see the static grating of contrast $C + \Delta C$ every other second. The setting of ΔC above $C = 0.02$ is again atypical (usually the threshold for discrimination of contrast between two separate gratings increases approximately as the 0.7 power of contrast; Laming 1986, p. 16, Fig. 1.11; Legge 1979, 1981), but is possibly another setting for the perceptibility of a change in contrast, one way or the other, occurring once every second. The message is that while subjects can adjust stimuli to threshold perceptibility quite consistently, those settings may not always parallel the results from direct measurement of the information afforded by the stimuli as assessed by modern 2AFC methods.

There is also another problem which becomes comprehensible when a 'threshold' is seen as the limit of perceptibility. In the traditional method of limits (or serial exploration), a comparison stimulus which is clearly greater than the standard is progressively reduced in small steps until it appears equal and, to balance, a comparison stimulus clearly less than the standard is progressively increased. What is observed is that subjects tend to perseverate their judgments so that a descending series of comparison stimuli will usually generate a lower estimate of the threshold than will an ascending series. Laming (1986, p. 20, Fig. 2.2) displays an example from the judgment of differences in length of line by Kiesow (1925/26). Now, in a descending series the subject has a clear idea of what the difference between the stimuli looks like and therefore requires a lesser quantity of information from the comparison stimulus in order to reconstruct that difference perceptually. A descending series benefits from prior knowledge what to look for, analogous to a prior expectation; this will be particularly relevant when determining an absolute threshold. But in an ascending series, beginning below threshold, the subject may be somewhat uncertain what the stimulus to be detected actually looks like and may require a stronger stimulus in consequence. Markowitz and Swets (1967) have suggested a very similar process in signal-detection experiments with only a small proportion of signal trials.

To sum up, stimuli presented for discrimination or detection provide the subject with information, the information depending on their magnitudes. The amount of information may be determined as accurately as desired and, it seems, with very little bias in a modern 2AFC discrimination or signal detection paradigm (Green and Swets 1966, p. 105). One may also have the subject adjust a variable stimulus until it is just detectable, and that criterion I take to correspond to an amount of information sufficient to enable the stimulus to be reconstructed perceptually. But the information utilized in a perceptual reconstruction is information about some particular feature of the stimulus and may not be all the information there is. That is, the method of 'just-noticeable differences' may be of variable efficiency. Moreover, the amount of information required may be partly met from prior knowledge or expectation; and the particular features on which the perceptual reconstruction is based may be different at different levels of physical stimulus magnitude, so that the method of adjustment may give results curiously variable in comparison with modern 2AFC methods. So, the 'threshold' as traditionally conceived and the statistical abstraction from modern experimental procedures are two distinct notions. What needs to be labelled as false, however, is the assertion that when a stimulus fails to exceed threshold, it is as though it had never been presented. That idea is contraindicated by the experiments of Swets *et al.* (1961), and since that time numerous studies of negative masking have succeeded in measuring discrimination thresholds between pairs of stimuli of which one is below the detection threshold (see Laming 1986, Chapter 8 for a review, and Laming 1988a,b).

3.2 THE NORMAL MODEL

The phenomena of sensory discrimination to which Fechner's Law relates arise from signal detection, psychometric function, and threshold experiments which might use stimuli from any part of a sensory continuum. To facilitate a concise discussion of the matter, a model of an entire sensory continuum is desirable. Envisage that the presentation of each level of luminance, or of noise, or length of line, or weight is represented by a random sample from a normal distribution with fixed variance σ^2 and mean proportional to the logarithm of the stimulus magnitude,

$$\mu(L) = \ln L. \tag{3.2}$$

The use of the variable L in eqn 3.2 simply reflects that the argument which follows is illustrated with data from the discrimination of luminance levels (L). But, to the extent that other sensory modalities have been explored, the argument applies equally to all sensory continua, and eqn 3.2 and similar equations to follow should be read with that generality.

The function $\mu(L)$ is, of course, the measure of sensation proposed in Fechner's Law (eqn 1.2); but the normal model is to be used here merely for the calculation of experimental predictions and for the analysis of data. When two particular luminances are selected for presentation in a simple two-choice discrimination, a model for that experiment may be constructed by inserting the corresponding normal distributions in a conventional signal-detection model as in Fig. 3.2. A variation in the level of one of the luminances, when using, for example, the method of constant stimuli, is represented by replacement of one of the distributions (equivalent, in the present model, to varying the separation between them). The variance σ^2 determines the precision of discrimination and will depend *inter alia* on the continuum. This scheme for the representation of an entire continuum of stimuli originated with Thurstone (1927). To the extent that it gives an accurate account of the data, the function in eqn 3.2 is operationally defined.

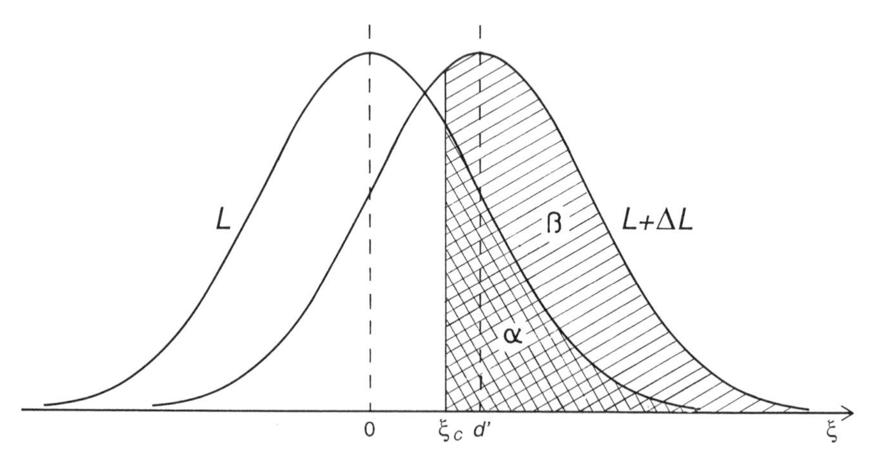

Fig. 3.2 The normal signal-detection model of Tanner and Swets (1954). Presentations of luminance L and of luminance $L + \Delta L$ are respectively represented by random samples drawn from the corresponding distributions, which are taken to be normal, here scaled to unit variance, and separated by a difference in mean d'. The parameter d' measures the discriminability of the difference ΔL. The choice of criterion ξ_C reflects the subject's motivational bias and determines the two operating probabilities α and β. The probability α is the probability of incorrectly identifying the flash as the brighter one when the luminance is actually L; β is the probability of correctly reporting the brighter flash when it is presented. (Figure adapted from *Sensory analysis* by D. Laming, p. 27. © 1986, Academic Press. Reproduced by permission.)

This model (eqn 3.2) expresses a simple relation between Fechner's Law and the data from discrimination experiments. My initial concern in this chapter is to discover how well it works. I shall examine evidence concerning the validity of Weber's Law, and then look in more detail at the properties of *difference discriminations*, that is, discriminations between two separate stimuli presented in silence. Those properties will support the statement of a strong form of Weber's Law which applies not merely to thresholds, but to discriminability functions and to signal-detection characteristics as well. There is, however, some incisive criticism to be made of the normal model; that criticism is left until the next chapter.

I shall illustrate my argument with experimental data drawn from experiments on the discrimination of luminance. But it should not be supposed that the argument applies only to that particular attribute. To the extent that relevant experiments have been carried out, similar findings have been reported from all of the other sensory modalities. The most important of those findings are reproduced in Laming (1986, 1987, 1988a,b, 1989a).

3.3 WEBER'S LAW

In their comment on Krueger's (1989) review of the psychophysical law Brysbaert and d'Ydewalle (1989, p. 271) write '. . . it is surprising that Weber's law still needs to be refuted in a 1989 review article'. I take this opportunity to set the experimental findings straight.

The empirical relation between threshold and stimulus magnitude depends on the configuration of the two stimulus levels to be compared. For a difference discrimination between two stimuli presented against a silent background, typical behaviour is as illustrated by the filled data points in Fig. 3.3 from Leshowitz *et al.* (1968). On each trial of this experiment Leshowitz *et al.* presented two successive flashes of light to the dark-adapted eye of their subject. The flashes were 1° in diameter, 32 ms (filled circles) or 320 ms (squares) in duration, and of luminances L and $L + \Delta L$. The filled symbols estimate those values of ΔL which would have been discriminated with 75 per cent accuracy in this 2AFC experiment and they cluster with acceptable accuracy around the continuous straight line, which has gradient 1 and therefore represents Weber's Law (eqn 1.1) with respect to the logarithmic coordinates. Conformity to that straight line continues downwards to about the absolute thresholds which are indicated by the arrows labelled, respectively, θ_{32} and θ_{320}. The Weber fraction (Θ in eqn 1.1) is given by the location of the straight line in Fig. 3.3 with respect to the logarithmic axes; for the subject in this experiment, $\Theta = 0.28$.

This pattern of threshold characteristic has been demonstrated for the discrimination of intensity in all five primary sensory modalities (hearing: Harris 1950; Hanna *et al.* 1986; smell: Stone 1963; Stone and Bosley 1965; Stone *et al.* 1962; taste: Schutz and Pilgrim 1957; temperature (cold): Johnson *et al.* 1973; touch: Hamer *et al.* 1983; Craig 1974; vision: Cornsweet and Pinsker 1965; and Fig. 3.3 here). In addition, Weber's Law has been shown to describe sensitivity in many derived attributes by, among others, Campbell *et al.* (1970), Gatti and Dodge (1929), Gaydos (1958), Indow and Stevens (1966), Mountcastle *et al.* (1969), Oberlin (1936), Panek and Stevens (1966), Treisman (1963), and Volkmann (1863).

Two exceptions are known. The difference threshold for the amplitude of a pure tone (but not Gaussian noise) conforms to a power law with an exponent of about 5/6. This is probably because higher levels of tone produce a broader spread of excitation along the length of the basilar membrane and thereby stimulate an increasing number of primary fibres. In this way, the particular value 5/6 can be related to mechanical properties of the cochlea (Laming 1986, Chapter 10). Gaussian noise shows accurate conformity to Weber's Law, however, because the particular limit to discrimination which that law describes is actually implicit in the statistical structure of the physical stimulus. Discrimination of the contrast of a sinusoidal grating conforms to a power law with an exponent of about 0.7 (Laming 1986, pp. 16 and 210). It is likely that this exception will ultimately admit a similar explanation with respect to the multiplicity of visual channels. Numerousness may prove yet another exception with an exponent of about 0.75, but the evidence is still slight (Burgess and Barlow 1983; Krueger 1984).

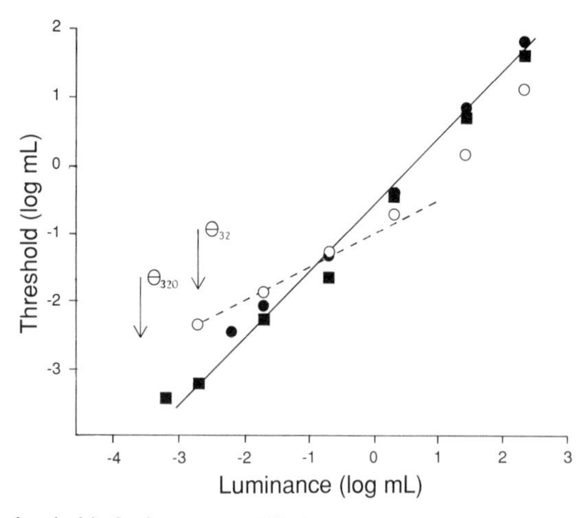

Fig. 3.3 Difference thresholds for luminance (filled symbols) and increment thresholds (open circles) in the temporal 2AFC experiment by Leshowitz *et al.* (1968). The continuous line has gradient 1 (Weber's Law) and the broken line ½. The arrows at −2.7 and −3.6 log mL mark the values on the abscissa of the absolute thresholds for a 32 ms (circles) and a 320 ms flash (squares), respectively. (From *Sensory analysis* by D. Laming, p. 10. © 1986, Academic Press. Reproduced by permission.)

The reason why the validity of Weber's Law is so frequently questioned (e.g. Krueger 1989) does not relate, however, to either of these known exceptions, but to confounding with thresholds for the detection of an increment to a continuous background. It is commonly said, quite correctly, that the Weber fraction (calculated from increment thresholds) is fairly constant for the middle ranges of stimulus values, but increases at both extremes (Holway and Pratt 1936; Boring 1942, p. 45). The increase in the Weber fraction observed at high stimulus levels is probably due to saturation of the receptors. This has been dramatically demonstrated by Alpern *et al.* (1970) in circumstances (20 ms flash of white light superimposed on a 100 ms background) in which the failure of discrimination cannot be attributed to light adaptation. But the rise in the Weber fraction at low stimulus levels depends specifically on calculating the fraction for detection of an increment.

Increment detection, that is, detection of a single stimulus of size ΔL added to a pre-existing background of level L, displays a systematically different threshold relation which is most clearly exhibited by contrast thresholds for sinusoidal gratings (van Nes and Bouman 1967; Hess and Nordby 1986). Up to a certain illuminance (which depends on the wavenumber of the grating) the contrast threshold increases only as the square root of the illuminance; thereafter it conforms to Weber's Law (see Laming 1991a). Bearing in mind that an increment of square (rather than sinusoidal) profile can be expressed as a Fourier sum and therefore behaves as an amalgam of grating components, it is to be expected that visual increments will display a similar threshold characteristic, though transiting less sharply from square root to Weber law segments. The open circles in Fig. 3.3 are increment thresholds for the same stimulus configuration and the same subject as before, but with the luminance L presented continuously. The experimental procedure was unchanged. At high luminances (in excess of 10 mL) the increment thresholds conform to Weber's Law (continuous line of gradient 1 in Fig. 3.3), but at low luminances (below 1 mL) the data tend to a square root asymptote, shown by the broken line of gradient ½.

This pattern is clearly evident only in the case of luminance. There are weak indications from Harris (1950, 1963) that a similar relation holds for hearing, and from McBurney and Pfaffmann (1963, data reanalysed by Laming 1987) for the taste of sodium chloride. Other sensory modalities remain to be explored.

The astonishing remark from Brysbaert and d'Ydewalle (1989) above, however, results from their own experiment (Brysbaert and d'Ydewalle 1990) on the discrimination of luminance. For two luminous discs of 8.2° diameter against a background of 11.5 cd/m^2 they obtained difference thresholds which increased steadily with luminance, a little ragged maybe, but not an adequate basis for questioning Weber's Law. Their stimuli for comparison were actually two Masson discs,[1] and the process of adjusting the black and white sectors between each trial in a staircase procedure must have been very tedious. Their questioning of Weber's Law derives from repeating the experiment against a background of 160 cd/m^2, all threshold measurements being made at luminances (12.4–155.6 cd/m^2) *less than* the surround. At luminances in excess of 121.9 cd/m^2 (75.2 cd/m^2 for a second subject) in this repetition of their experiment the threshold *decreased* in absolute terms as the luminance at which it was measured was further increased, whereas Weber's Law says the threshold should continue to increase. But, when the standard luminance is sufficiently close to that of the surround, comparison with that surround provides an additional cue to improve the accuracy of discrimination. It is not to be wondered at if subjects take advantage of that comparison. Suppose (underlining this point with another example in which the informativeness of an additional cue is taken to an extreme) the study concerned discrimination of length of line, the lines being placed end to end. Envisage a graduated ruler to be placed alongside each line to be compared . . .

Underlying Brysbaert and D'Ydewalle's remark is some particular, but unspoken, assumption about the intermediate process supporting the discrimination of luminance

[1] If a black and white sectored disc be rotated faster than the eye can follow the flicker, it appears a uniform grey. According to the Talbot–Plateau Law the intensity of the grey is equal to the time average of the black and the white. By placing sectors of different widths at different distances from the centre, carefully calculated gradations of grey can be created. The invention of the technique is credited to Masson (1845), and the best historical account of it is in von Helmholtz (1909–11, vol II, pp. 206–15 in English translation). The Masson disc is very much a nineteenth century technique, though it is still used when some particularly elaborate profile of luminance is required (e.g. Cornsweet 1970, pp. 272–5; Lockhead 1992, p. 548). Its use (as here) to measure difference thresholds is tedious beyond belief.

which imparts a certain, but evidently inappropriate, interpretation to Weber's Law. In modelling their data they endeavoured to fit a power law relation, a product of powers of both the absolute luminance of the stimuli and of the difference of luminance with respect to the background, simultaneously to both sets of thresholds. That is indicative of their different conception.

Weber's Law holds for a discrimination between two separate stimuli sufficiently in excess of the background against which they are presented; it specifies, rather accurately, the amount of discriminative information which such a configuration affords about the different magnitudes of those stimuli. But when the surround luminance is greater than that of the two stimuli, an additional cue becomes available and the behaviour of the threshold is more complex (Whittle 1986). That is not a good reason to decry Weber's Law.

There is, finally, one further kind of objection to Weber's Law which needs to be addressed. Link (1992) analysed certain data from Fechner (see Adler 1966, p. 155, the one-handed series) for the discrimination of two lifted weights, a standard and a comparison weight either 4 or 8 per cent greater. Even though the proportionate difference in weight is fixed, discrimination is demonstrably better with respect to heavier weights. A relation like

$$\Delta W/(W + W_0) = \Theta, \tag{3.3}$$

where W_0 is a small constant, is needed to fit the data. The Weber fraction $\Delta W/W$ again increases at small stimulus magnitudes in an experiment where the configuration of the stimuli cannot be cited as the cause.

Fechner (see Adler 1966, pp. 155–6) was aware of this problem and suggested that the weight of his arm and of his shirt sleeves should also enter into the equation (see also p. 4 here). My own estimate of that additional weight, based on Fechner's (Adler 1966, p. 154) two-handed series, is 237 g (Laming 1986, p. 7), whereas the corresponding estimate from Oberlin's (1936, Experiment 1) thresholds for lifted weights is only 66 g. Why the difference? I argue in the next chapter that only changes in the stimulus input are available as a basis for discrimination. Those changes include the additional feel of heaviness as a weight is hefted, but not the constant weight of the arm which is ever present; that constant weight should be of no effect. Certainly, repeating the experiment with a heavy (500 g) cuff on the wrist (Gregory and Ross 1967) does not increase the difference threshold as eqn 3.3 would require. A different explanation is needed.

Differential sensitivity might vary from day to day and, to protect against such variation, experimenters usually make an equal number of measurements at each stimulus magnitude of interest within each experimental session. Fechner (see Adler 1966, p. 153) describes such a design in detail. The subject will thereby build up some idea what weight to expect, and reference to the results from Hollingworth (1909) in Fig. 2.3 shows that estimation of the stimuli will be biased, being drawn towards a centre of gravity. Figure 3.4 shows the variable errors[2] of movement amplitude from Hollingworth's experiment plotted against the means, this

[2] If x is the length of reproduction of some prescribed amplitude A on some particular trial of Hollingworth's (1909) experiment in Fig. 2.3, and if X is the mean reproduction of amplitude A, then $(X - A)$ is the *constant error* and $(x - X)$ is known as the *variable error*. The variable error therefore measures the precision of repeated reproductions about their mean. The data in Fig. 3.4 are averages of the *absolute* variable error $|x - X|$ (rather than, as one would calculate today, root mean squares). If the distribution of variable error is normal, the absolute error is equal to 0.80 times the standard deviation.

time with a linear abscissa. The different standard amplitudes were presented in random order within each session, so that the bias on each judgment from the last few trials varies from one presentation of a given standard to another. That variation in prior expectation feeds through into a greater variability of adjustment in Series A, B, and C (the sessions with several different standards intermixed) compared with the three sessions (filled points) in which one standard only was presented by itself. The data from the mixed sessions conform roughly to

$$\Delta X = \Theta X + X_0, \tag{3.4}$$

where X_0 represents the additional variability from the variable prior expectation. (A similar equation fitted to the filled data points gives an additional error of 1 mm which is arguably the limiting accuracy to which the subjects could draw a line blindfold.)

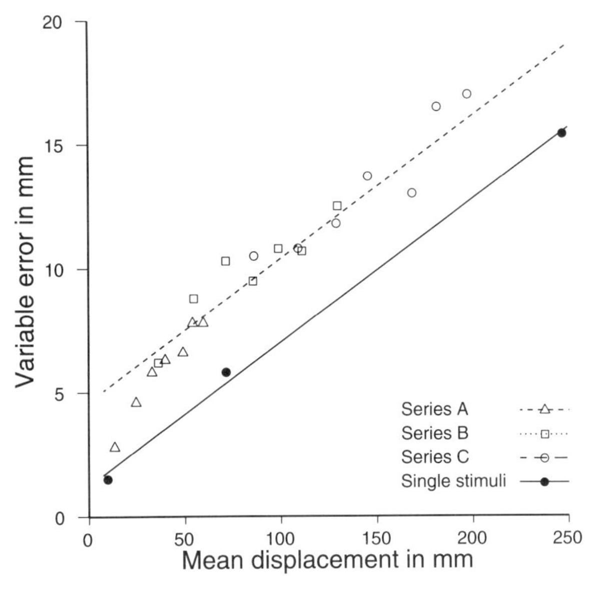

Fig. 3.4 The variable errors of reproduction from Hollingworth (1909, cf. Fig. 2.3). As before, Series A, B, and C are from different sessions in which different ranges of amplitudes were presented for reproduction. The filled points display the results of three further sessions in which one amplitude only was presented repeatedly.

So Link's objection may signify no more than the involvement of prior expectations which vary from one trial to another depending on the identities of the stimuli recently presented. The scale of those prior expectations will be proportional to the weights actually lifted; and in this connection it is relevant that Fechner (1860), working with standard weights from 300 to 3000 g, measured thresholds which require an additive constant equivalent to 237 g, while Oberlin's (1936) thresholds for weights from 50 to 550 g require an additive constant of only 66 g. Until the interaction of the accuracy of discrimination with the detailed order of presentation of different stimulus magnitudes is understood, it would be premature to dismiss Weber's Law on the basis of eqn 3.3.

3.4 DIFFERENCE DISCRIMINATIONS

The normal model (eqn 3.2) describes not merely the difference threshold (i.e. Weber's Law), but the entire discriminability function and the signal-detection operating characteristic as well. It generates directly the normal, equal variance, signal-detection model of Tanner and Swets (1954) shown in Fig. 3.2. The criterion (ξ_C in Fig. 3.2) determines two probabilities, α (false positive) and β (correct detection). But the location of the criterion is a free parameter and as ξ_C ranges through its possible values, α and β co-vary, tracing out a curvilinear relation in the unit square. Figure 3.5(a) displays two examples, corresponding to two different values of d', the separation between the means of the distributions of Fig. 3.2 in units of standard deviation. The data from a signal-detection experiment consist of pairs of proportions of false positives and correct detections, and the test of the model turns on whether the set of data points can be reasonably accommodated by some one of the admissible operating characteristics (Fig. 3.5(a) again).

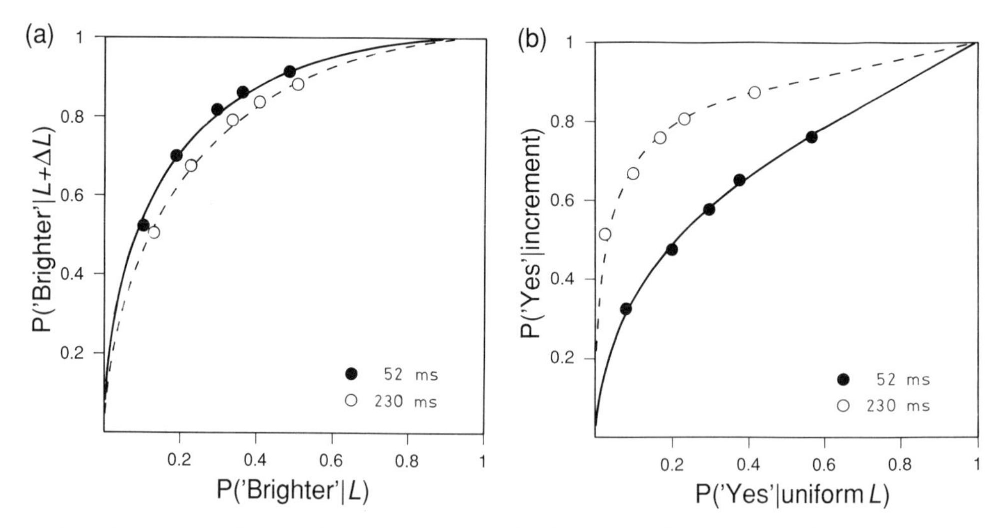

Fig. 3.5 Signal-detection data from two experiments by Nachmias and Steinman (1965, Experiments II and III) for a discrimination between two luminances L and $L + \Delta L$. (a) Difference discrimination: the two luminances were presented briefly in darkness for either 52 or 230 ms. The subject expressed her posterior confidence that the brighter flash had been presented on an ordered six-point scale. (b) Increment detection: the increment was a fine bright line added to the same uniform field. Each stimulus (uniform field or field with superimposed line) was exposed for either 52 or 230 ms. Except for the different signal to be detected, this experiment was the same as (a), as also was the subject. The Asymmetric operating characteristics are calculated from a non-central χ^2 model. (From *Sensory analysis* by D. Laming, pp. 26 and 94. © 1986, Academic Press. Reproduced by permission.)

Figure 3.5 presents the data from two experiments by Nachmias and Steinman (1965). On each trial of the first experiment (Fig. 3.5(a); the second experiment in Fig. 3.5(b) will be examined in the next chapter, in explicit comparison with the first) the subject observed a flash of light filling a circular field 1° in diameter. The luminance of the flash was either L or $L + \Delta L$ where ΔL represented an increase of 26 per cent. After each stimulus the subject reported whether she thought the 'brighter' or the 'dimmer' flash had been presented; more precisely, she reported her posterior confidence on a six-point scale. That enabled five pairs of proportions, of false positives and correct detections, to be calculated from the one block of trials (see Green and Swets 1966, pp. 99–107). The experiment was conducted with two different durations of flash, 52 and 230 ms, and in each case the data points conform nicely to an operating characteristic calculated from the normal model with d' equal to 1.39 and 1.18, respectively.

This result is typical. A signal detection experiment performed with two separate stimuli presented in silence invariably generates a symmetric operating characteristic conforming to the normal, equal variance model proposed by Tanner and Swets (1954). Examples from other sensory modalities may be found in Viemeister (1970), Mountcastle *et al.* (1969), Linker *et al.* (1964), and Semb (1968).

The next question concerns the manner in which the proportion of correct identifications increases with the difference in luminance ΔL. If the criterion in Fig. 3.2 is located centrally between the two distributions, the absolute proportion of correct responses is a maximum, assuming equal frequencies of the stimuli L and $L + \Delta L$. But that proportion depends on the separation between the means of the distributions, d' in Fig. 3.2, where

$$\begin{aligned} d' &= \sigma^{-1}[\mu(L + \Delta L) - \mu(L)] \\ &= \sigma^{-1}\ln(1 + \Delta L / L) \\ &\approx \sigma^{-1}\Delta L / L. \end{aligned} \tag{3.5}$$

On the basis of the normal signal-detection model (Fig. 3.2) the proportion of correct identifications in a 2AFC task ought to increase as the normal integral transform of $d'/\sqrt{2}$; that is,

$$\text{P. correct} = \Phi(\Delta L / \sqrt{2}\sigma L), \tag{3.6}$$

where $\Phi(\ )$ denotes the normal probability integral.

The data in the left-hand panel of Fig. 3.6 speak to this point. These data from the same experiment by Leshowitz *et al.* (1968) are, in fact, some of the discriminability data from which the difference thresholds in Fig. 3.3 were estimated by interpolation. The filled symbols on the left-hand side of Fig. 3.6 represent the proportions of correct responses obtained in this 2AFC task as a function of $\log(\Delta L/L)$. The origin of the abscissa has been translated so that $\log(\Delta L/L) = 0$ corresponds artificially to 75 per cent correct responses; and differently shaped symbols represent proportions recorded with respect to different standard luminances L. The continuous curve is the upper half of a normal probability integral with respect to ΔL, plotted here with respect to a logarithmic abscissa. The filled data points deviate slightly from this curve because the approximation in eqn 3.5 overstates the value of the natural logarithm at large values of $\Delta L/L$.

The experimental findings in Fig. 3.6 are again quite general. Examples from other sensory modalities may be found in Mountcastle *et al.* (1969), Brown (1910), Hanna *et al.* (1986), McBurney *et al.* (1967), and Stone and Bosley (1965).

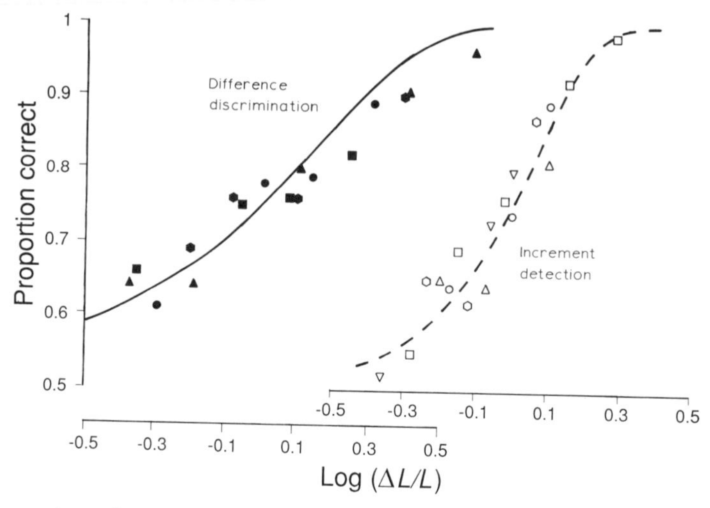

Fig. 3.6 Proportions of correct responses in 2AFC difference discriminations (filled symbols) and increment detections (open symbols) of luminance. Differently shaped symbols represent data for different standard luminances L and different stimulus durations. The data points are plotted with respect to $\log(\Delta L/L)$, arbitrarily transposed so that zero on the abscissa corresponds artificially to 75 per cent correct. The continuous curve fitted to the discrimination data is a normal integral with respect to $\Delta L/L$, and the broken curve fitted to the increment detection data is a normal integral with respect to $(\Delta L/L)^2$. Data for the same subject as in Fig. 3.3. (From *Sensory analysis* by D. Laming, p. 41. © 1986, Academic Press. Reproduced by permission.)

The final question to which Fechner's Law applies is the manner in which the difference threshold (the stimulus difference which affords 75 per cent correct in a 2AFC task) varies with the level of the base luminance L. Seventy-five per cent correct responses are achieved when d' is equal to 0.95; that is, when, according to the normal model,

$$\Delta L / L = 0.95\sigma, \tag{3.7}$$

which is Weber's Law (eqn 1.1). The conformity of the difference thresholds from the experiment by Leshowitz *et al.* (1968) to this relation has already been examined on p. 33 (Fig. 3.3).

This detailed examination of the properties of difference discriminations has one other benefit. Luce and Edwards (1958) criticized Fechner's derivation of his measure of sensation (eqn 3.1) from Weber's Law on the grounds that a 'just-noticeable difference' exists only as a finite difference and it is illegitimate to replace it, as Fechner did, by a differential. The finite difference equation relating ΔL to L admits other solutions besides and, for any relation except the special case of Weber's Law, Fechner's method actually gives the wrong result. But in the present examination of difference discriminations the threshold has been recast as a statistical abstraction from d', and d' is a continuous variable. It can be estimated by experiment for any stimulus difference δL. Suppose, now, a measure of internal sensation to be constructed by cumulating values of d'. If a just-noticeable difference be taken to correspond to d' equal to 0.95 (that is, to 75 per cent correct, 2AFC), then the d' scale of sensation agrees with Fechner's cumulation of jnds at a lattice of points separated by that amount. But the limiting ratio $d'/\delta L$ as δL tends to zero (Fechner's differential) is now well defined (though it is not necessarily equal to the quotient $d'/\Delta L$ calculated at $d' = 0.95$ as Fechner assumed). It is now legitimate to substitute the limiting value of $d'/\delta L$ in Fechner's argument, which now gives the *correct* result. Luce and Edwards' objection is specific to the classical notion of the threshold as a limit of perceptibility, measured by the method of adjustment.

3.5 INTERIM CONCLUSIONS

At this half-way stage in this experimental critique of Fechner's Law it is clear that the normal model (eqn 3.2) provides a very satisfactory account of difference discriminations. For two separate stimuli presented in silence, not only does the threshold conform satisfactorily to Weber's Law down to about the absolute threshold, but so also do the discriminability function and the signal-detection characteristic. The magnitude of the standard stimulus with respect to which comparison is made scales all statistical properties of a difference discrimination. A stronger statement can be made of Weber's Law than at first appeared: briefly, the discrimination of two separate stimuli of magnitudes L and $L + \Delta L$ depends only on the quotient $\Delta L/L$.

That strong form of Weber's Law can be rephrased as 'depends only on the quotient $(L + \Delta L)/L$' or, what is also equivalent, 'on the difference $\ln(L + \Delta L) - \ln L$'. This last form of the statement predicates a model in which different stimuli on the continuum are represented by probability distributions differing only in location (the normal model, eqn 3.2), the locations varying as the logarithm of the physical stimulus magnitude. In short, Fechner's law emerges as the relation between stimulus magnitude and the operational parameter in a model which accurately represents the complete statistical properties of difference discriminations on an entire stimulus continuum (except for the region below absolute threshold).

So far as difference discriminations are concerned, Assertion 1 on p. 28 holds good. But whether the operational parameter in the normal model also describes the magnitudes of internal sensations (Assertion 2) is quite another matter. Happily, the question posed by Assertion 2 can be circumvented by examining further experimental findings which show that the normal model is not unique. In the next chapter I introduce another model (the χ^2 model) which describes the phenomena of difference discriminations just as accurately and just as concisely as does the normal; but the operational parameter in this second model is a power function of the stimulus magnitude, not logarithmic. The question posed by Assertion 2, whether the logarithmic transform can be taken as a measure of subjective sensation, then depends on whether one of these two models can be shown to describe the state of nature better than the other and, if so, which. It will turn out that the χ^2 model is able to accommodate a much wider range of experimental phenomena than the normal. The survival of Fechner's Law has, in fact, depended on confining attention to an unnecessarily narrow range of phenomena within the field of sensory discrimination.

4 A reinterpretation of sensory discrimination—the χ^2 model

The normal model (eqn 3.2) in the preceding chapter provided an accurate and concise description of the statistical properties of difference discriminations and it might appear, on that account, that Fechner's Law is justified, at least as the relation between physical stimulus magnitude and the operational parameter of a viable description of the psychophysics of a sensory continuum. That would be too hasty a conclusion, because the normal model is not unique.

In this chapter I show that numerical predictions, nearly identical to those from the normal model—certainly so close that direct experimental discrimination is impossible—may be obtained from a χ^2 model, analogous to eqn 3.2. In this model each stimulus is represented by a χ^2 distribution of fixed number of degrees of freedom 2ν multiplied by (some power of) the stimulus magnitude. The precision of discrimination is set by the parameter ν (analogous to σ^2 in the normal model) and the very close equivalence to the normal model obtains because, for typical values of 2ν (say 50), the logarithm of a χ^2 variable is closely approximate to the normal in distribution.

The choice between Fechner's Law on the one hand, and a power law relation of unspecified exponent on the other, therefore turns on which of these two models can be shown to afford the more comprehensive description of the state of nature. Examination of further experimental findings shows that the χ^2 model accommodates much the wider range of phenomena.

4.1 THE χ^2 MODEL

Suppose as an alternative to the normal model (eqn 3.2) that each stimulus on a continuum is represented by a χ^2 variable scaled by L^k. Instead of a set of normal distributions of common variance translated by various amounts with respect to log stimulus magnitude, there is now a set of χ^2 distributions of common degrees of freedom 2ν, fanning out from a common origin. Each distribution is expanded about that common origin by a different scale factor L^k. Figure 4.1 shows two of these χ^2 distributions combined in a signal detection model analogous to Fig. 3.2.

The structure of the diagram in Fig. 4.1 indicates that this χ^2 model may be used in exactly the same way as the normal model in Fig. 3.2 to generate predictions for all three kinds of experiment exemplified in Figs 3.3, 3.5, and 3.6. The only problem is what those predictions might turn out to be; it admits a simple solution.

The immediate prediction from the model in Fig. 4.1 is the pair of shaded areas α and β under the density curves to the right of the criterion χ^2_C. These are the predicted probabilities of a false positive and of a correct detection for that particular location of the criterion and those particular values of the stimulus magnitudes. As the criterion sweeps across the abscissa in Fig. 4.1, so the point (α, β) describes an operating characteristic in the unit square (as in Fig. 3.5(a)). That operating characteristic is the entire empirical content of the model. It is easy to see that the areas α and β must be invariant under any transformation of the abscissa which preserves the order of the different values of the decision variable χ^2. The logarithm is such an order-preserving transformation. So, exactly the same numerical predictions would be obtained from a model expressed in terms of $\ln \chi^2$ (rather than χ^2 itself) as decision variable.

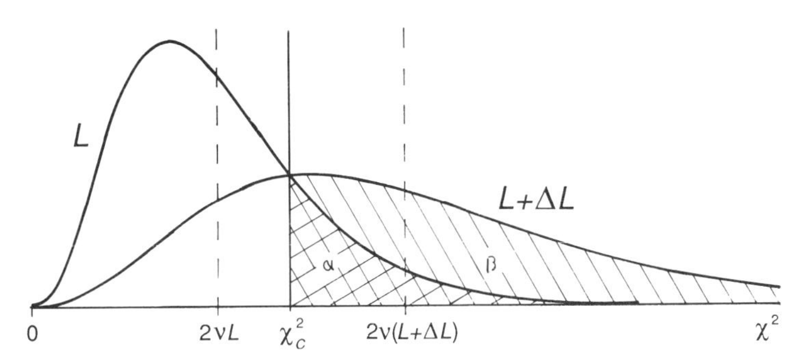

Fig. 4.1 A statistical decision model composed of two χ^2 distributions, each with 2ν degrees of freedom. In this diagram 2ν has been set equal to 8 and the luminance ratio $(L + \Delta L)/L$ to 2. These values have been chosen purely for illustrative purposes; they afford approximately threshold resolution and, at the same time, bring out the asymmetry of the model distributions. (Figure adapted from *Sensory analysis* by D. Laming, p. 74. © 1986, Academic Press. Reproduced by permission.)

Now Johnson (1949, p. 165) has shown that the logarithm of a χ^2 variable is approximately normal, much nearer to the normal in distribution than is χ^2 itself. To be precise, the natural logarithmic transform of $L^k\chi^2$ has[1]

$$\text{mean} = k \ln L + \ln 2 + \text{constant} \tag{4.1a}$$

and

$$\text{variance} \approx \nu^{-1}. \tag{4.1b}$$

So approximate predictions for the χ^2 model may be calculated from a normal model with mean varying as $k \ln L$ and fixed variance ν^{-1}, that is, from the model (eqn 3.2) with $\sigma = k/\sqrt{\nu}$. Figure 4.2 shows how accurate this approximation is. The value $2\nu = 50$ was chosen for expository purposes, but corresponds to the precision of discrimination typically obtained with difference discriminations in primary attributes like luminance, sound intensity, pressure, taste and smell (see Laming 1986, pp. 76–7). For 2ν as great as 50 the operating characteristics calculated exactly in Fig. 4.2 are almost indistinguishable from those calculated from the normal approximation. It follows that the χ^2 model provides as accurate an account of the experiments in Figs 3.3, 3.5, and 3.6 as does the normal.

That account, as accurate as the normal model, is delivered without any assumption of a logarithmic transform. To be sure, a logarithmic transform is involved in the *approximate*

[1] The constant is actually the digamma function with argument ν^{-1}; see Jeffreys and Jeffreys (1966, p. 465).

evaluation; but it forms no part of the χ^2 model itself, it does not enter into the exact calculation and requires no psychological interpretation. This prompts two considerations:

1. The empirical support for Fechner's Law is equally support for a linear law (k could be set equal to 1 in eqn 4.1a) which would measure the intensity of sensation exactly in terms of the physical magnitude of the stimulus eliciting it. Which of these two laws is to be preferred? I shall resolve this question by increasing the range and variety of experimental results to be accommodated within the one model. The particular experimental findings introduced below, parallel in volume to those already considered, can be readily accommodated by the χ^2 model, but not by the normal.

2. The experiments with difference discriminations to which attention has so far been directed do not tell us what the value of the parameter k in eqn 4.1 needs to be; that parameter is still free, undetermined. For this reason one might be tempted to cite the χ^2 model as equivalent support for Stevens' Power Law. That would be a mistake, as will also appear below.

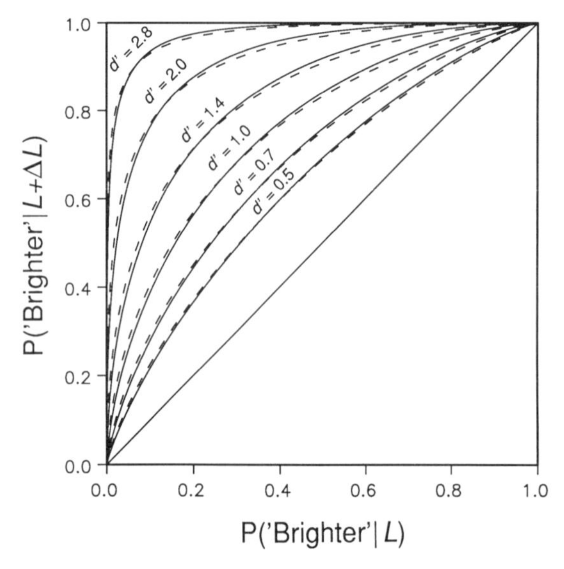

Fig. 4.2 Operating characteristics calculated exactly from the χ^2 model (Fig. 4.1, but with 2ν equal to 50; broken curves) compared with approximations calculated from the normal model (Fig. 3.2, continuous curves).

4.2 INCREMENT DETECTION

I draw a careful distinction between a discrimination between two separate stimuli presented in silence (difference discrimination) and the detection of an increment added briefly to a continuous background (increment detection). All the experiments so far examined concerned difference discriminations; increment detection shows a different set of psychophysical properties, as I now explain.

Figure 3.5(b) (p. 38) is another experiment from Nachmias and Steinman (1965) with the same subject as Fig. 3.5(a). In fact, these two experiments differ in only one particular. As before, one stimulus was a uniform flash of light of either 52 or 230 ms duration filling a circular field 1° in diameter. But in this second experiment the other stimulus, the signal to be detected, was a fine bright line, 1.9 min arc in thickness, added to the uniform field. The line was 18.2 per cent brighter than the surrounding field. After each presentation of a stimulus the subject reported her posterior confidence, on a six-point scale as before, that the bright line had been superimposed on the uniform field. Two sets of data are shown in Fig. 3.5(b), one for each duration of the stimuli. These data differ from those for the difference discriminations of the same durations in Fig. 3.5(a) in that the operating characteristic for detection of an increment is clearly asymmetric, being slewed towards the bottom left-hand corner of the unit square. This asymmetry is generally found with increment detection and always in the same direction; further examples may be found in Watson *et al.* (1964; detection of tone in noise) and Gescheider *et al.* (1971; detection of 60 Hz vibration).

The open symbols in Fig. 3.6 (p. 40) are data from the experiment by Leshowitz *et al.* (1968), this time for the detection of an increment in luminance. These data were recorded from the same subject as the discrimination data (filled symbols) and under exactly comparable conditions. This was accomplished by presenting the luminance L continuously over the same 1° field as before and superimposing an increment ΔL for 32 ms during either the first or the second of two designated observation intervals. The subject's task was to report in which of the two temporal intervals the increment had been presented. The proportions of correct responses in this increment detection task are shown by the open symbols in Fig. 3.6. These data have been plotted in the same way as the difference discrimination data, again with respect to $\log(\Delta L/L)$ as abscissa. It is immediately apparent that the increment detection data have a steeper trend than the difference discrimination data. In fact, the broken curve drawn through these data has exactly twice the gradient of the continuous curve. Now, gradient with respect to a logarithmic abscissa transposes into exponent with respect to a linear abscissa. So, whereas the continuous curve is a normal integral with respect to $\Delta L/L$, the broken curve is a normal integral with respect to the *square* of $\Delta L/L$.

This different shape of the detectability function is also a general finding. Other examples from other sensory modalities of detectability functions which approximate a normal integral with respect to the square of the Weber fraction may be found in the data of Hanna *et al.* (1986), McBurney *et al.* (1967), Stone and Bosley (1965), and Laming and Marsh (1988).

The increment thresholds from this experiment, some of them estimated by interpolation from the detection data in Fig. 3.6, have already been displayed as the open circles in Fig. 3.3. The two-segment structure of the increment threshold characteristic was explained on p. 35, as also was its generality with respect to other sensory modalities.

The experimental comparisons in Figs 3.3, 3.5, and 3.6 show that the detection of an increment has statistical properties distinct from those of the discrimination of a difference between two separate stimuli. These differences are summarized in Table 4.1. The question now is whether the different properties of increment detection can be better accommodated by the normal model (eqn 3.2) or by the χ^2 model or equally by both.

Table 4.1 Psychophysical properties of different stimulus configurations

Experimental measure	Difference discrimination	Increment detection
Operating characteristic	Symmetric, normal with equal variances	Asymmetric, non-central χ^2
Psychometric function	Normal integral with respect to ΔL	Normal integral with respect to $(\Delta L)^2$
Threshold characteristic	Weber's Law, down to absolute threshold	Weber's Law at high luminances; square root law at low luminances

From 'Some principles of sensory analysis' by D. Laming, *Psychological Review*, **92**, 464. © 1985, American Psychological Association. Reprinted by permission.

4.3 DIFFERENTIAL COUPLING

The different statistical properties of difference discriminations and increment detection are sufficient to establish that sensory analysis must be differentially coupled to the physical stimuli; and the argument which demonstrates this point is also the quickest route to showing that the normal model cannot accommodate the properties of increment detection, essentially because it implicitly assumes a direct coupling between stimulus and sensory analysis.

The first step in the argument characterizes the notion of *direct coupling*. Suppose that a stimulus of magnitude L generates some internal pattern of excitation of mean level $f(L)$. That pattern of excitation is a random process, being the aggregation of many independent components, all of comparable size, derived from different primary neural discharges or, in vision, from different quantal absorptions in the retina. The level $f(L)$ may be taken to be the mean of an approximately normal distribution, possibly of the representative distribution in the signal detection model in Fig. 3.2. 'Direct coupling' means that the internal excitation is a *direct* transform of the physical pattern of stimulation. So, an increase in the magnitude of the stimulus generates a corresponding increment in the internal pattern, and $f(L)$ increases strictly with L. This notion is illustrated in Fig. 4.3(a) where $f(L)$ is taken, for the sake of illustration, to be a logarithmic function ($\mu(L)$ in eqn 3.2), though, in fact, no specific form need be assumed. 'Differential coupling', on the other hand, means that $f(L)$ is constant, independent of L, so that the *mean* level of excitation plays no part in the discrimination. This is the assertion that is to be proved.

Suppose, now, an increment ΔL to be added to the physical stimulus magnitude. This increases the internal excitation to a mean level $f(L+\Delta L)$, and the physical increment will be detected if the internal increment $\Delta f(L)$ is of sufficient size relative to those fluctuations in activity that occur by chance. I assume that $f(L)$ is sufficiently well behaved as a function of L that it can everywhere be expanded in a Taylor series:

$$f(L+\Delta L) = f(L) + \Delta L f'(L) + \tfrac{1}{2}(\Delta L)^2 f''(L) + O\{(\Delta L)^3\}. \tag{4.2}$$

Then

$$\Delta f(L) = f(L+\Delta L) - f(L)$$

$$= \Delta L f'(L) + O\{(\Delta L)^2\}, \tag{4.3}$$

and this is the increment BC in Fig. 4.3(a). Since ΔL is small, terms in $(\Delta L)^2$ and higher powers can be neglected; this is equivalent to approximating BC with B′C in that figure, and B′C is strictly proportional to ΔL. So it must follow that, for each fixed L, d' is proportional to ΔL and the discriminability and detectability functions are both approximately normal integrals with respect to ΔL.

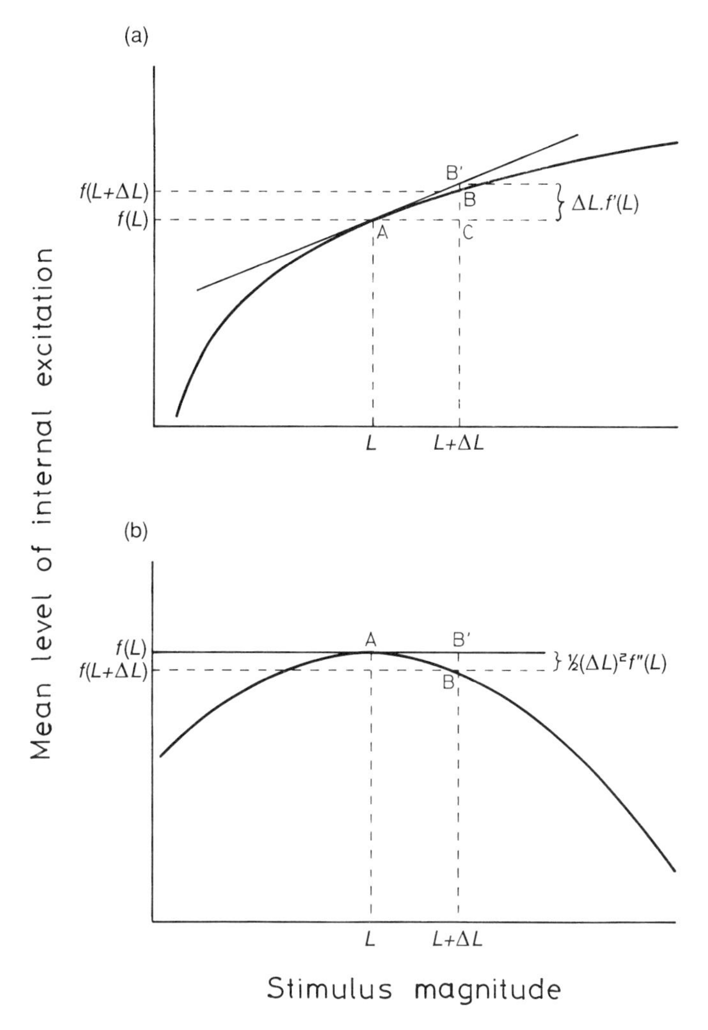

Fig. 4.3 Diagrams to illustrate the argument demonstrating differential coupling. In the upper diagram (a) an increase in stimulus magnitude from L to $L + \Delta L$ produces an increase CB in mean internal excitation, which is approximately proportional to ΔL. That is, d' should increase in proportion to ΔL, and this is so for difference discriminations. However, for increment detection d' increases approximately as $(\Delta L)^2$, so that a configuration is required like that in the lower diagram (b). Here C and B′ coincide, and BB′ is approximately proportional to $(\Delta L)^2$. But this can happen only if the tangent at A is horizontal. (From *Sensory analysis* by D. Laming, p. 62. © 1986, Academic Press. Reproduced by permission.)

Although this assertion is true of discriminability functions, Table 4.1 records that it does not hold for increment detection. A detectability function is approximately a normal integral with respect to $(\Delta L)^2$, that is, with respect to BB′. This is possible only if BB′ is the same as BC; that is, if the points B′ and C are coincident as in Fig. 4.3(b), which has the tangent at A horizontal. But this means that $f'(L)$ in eqn 4.3 is zero at the point A, and since the detectability function has the same shape for all stimulus magnitudes L, $f'(L)$ must be zero everywhere. That is, the shape of the detectability function requires the function $f(L)$ to be constant and, without loss of generality, we may put

$$f(L) \equiv 0. \tag{4.4}$$

The argument now stands as follows. Discriminability functions are nicely compatible with Fig. 4.3(a), that is, with direct coupling, while detectability functions are not. Detectability functions require $f(L)$ to be constant ($f'(L) = 0$ as in Fig. 4.3(b)), that is, require differential coupling. The shape of detectability functions is incompatible with direct coupling. But it is the same sensory system which both discriminates between two flashes of light, L and $L + \Delta L$, and detects an increment ΔL added to a background luminance L. Direct coupling as depicted in Fig. 4.3(a) cannot therefore be correct. The coupling must be differential, and the discrimination of differences between separate stimuli must depend on some property of the sensory process other than the difference $\Delta L f'(L)$ in Fig. 4.3(a).

The reason for the different psychophysical properties of increment detections and difference discriminations is explained in Fig. 4.4. A difference discrimination (a) involves two separate stimuli which, after differentiation, present two pairs of transients (shown by broken lines) to further analysis, transients of sizes proportional to L and to $L + \Delta L$, respectively. Increment detection (b), on the other hand, involves only one stimulus of size ΔL which is added to the continuous background of level L during either Interval 1 or Interval 2. After differentiation only one pair of transients is presented to further analysis. This pair is of size proportional to ΔL and needs to be distinguished from those random perturbations of the background L which occur by chance. In this way differential coupling transforms these two kinds of stimulus configuration into qualitatively different sensory-analytic discriminations and thereby provides the essential element in the explanation of their different properties.

The normal model (eqn 3.2) invokes a (direct) logarithmic transform of the stimulus magnitude. It leads to Fig. 4.3(a). It delivers the same predictions, except possibly for the value of a parameter specifying the sensitivity, for both difference discriminations and for increment detection. This is contrary to observation. The normal model (and hence Fechner's Law) happens to work for difference discriminations because, for that configuration of the stimuli to be distinguished, it provides a good numerical approximation to the χ^2 model. That is the sum total of its significance.

The χ^2 model, on the other hand, is nicely compatible with a differentiation of sensory input, as I now show.

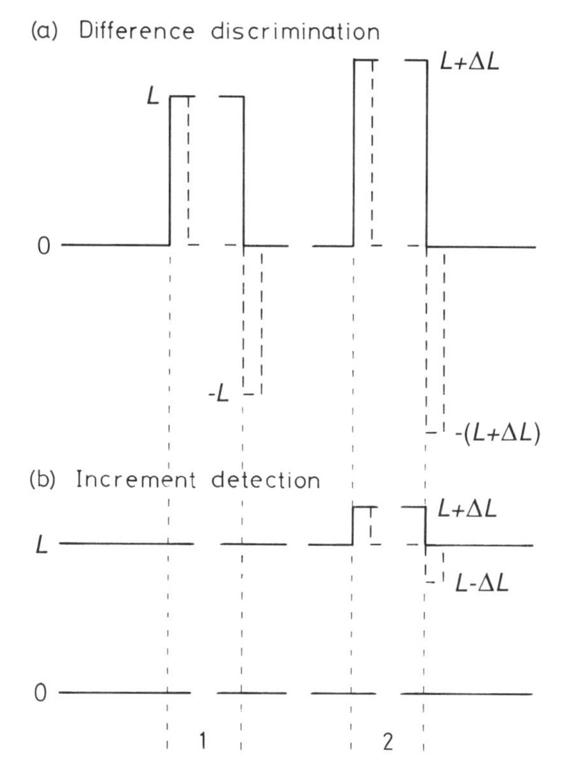

Fig. 4.4 A diagrammatic comparison of difference discriminations and increment detection. The broken lines show the effect of a differentiation of sensory input. A difference discrimination (a) presents two pairs of transients of sizes L and $L + \Delta L$, respectively, to further analysis, while increment detection (b) presents only a single pair of size ΔL to be distinguished from those perturbations of a uniform background L which occur by chance. (From *Sensory analysis* by D. Laming, p. 68. © 1986, Academic Press. Reproduced by permission.)

4.4 PHYSIOLOGICAL REALIZATION OF THE χ^2 MODEL

At the physical level of description a visual stimulus is exactly a Poisson process of density proportional to the luminance. Suppose, now, the difference be calculated between two statistically independent copies of such a stimulus (see Laming 1986, p. 80, Fig. 6.1). The mean input, directly proportional to the luminance, cancels; but the fluctuations about the mean combine orthogonally, because they are derived from statistically independent copies of the stimulus. Those fluctuations approximate a Gaussian noise process and have a power density again proportional to the luminance, because the variance of a Poisson variable is equal to its mean. The χ^2 distributions describe the energy in samples of that Gaussian noise (Chapter 6 in Green and Swets 1966).

Physical stimuli of Poisson structure are found only in vision; but in other senses such a structure is introduced, approximately, in the process of sensory transduction. In hearing, the pure tone stimulus is a small sinusoidal oscillation of air pressure about the atmospheric mean and it produces small sinusoidal displacements of the basilar membrane about *its* mean. Most primary auditory neurons are innervated by a single inner hair cell whose electric potential varies periodically with the displacements of the basilar membrane. The neuron discharges preferentially at a particular phase of this period, but with a probability that is less than one. If transitory refractory effects be ignored, that probability is constant from cycle to cycle of the stimulus giving a geometric discharge process (see Sellick and Russell 1980; Kiang *et al.* 1965; Rose *et al.* 1967). Each single neuron discharges (usually only once) on only a proportion of the cycles of the stimulus; but, because different neurons discharge on different cycles, in aggregate they present a volley of action potentials in response to every cycle of the stimulus, locked to a specific phase. The volley varies randomly in size from cycle to cycle and has Poisson-like properties.

Talbot *et al.* (1968) have demonstrated somewhat similar properties in several different kinds of primary afferents in the skin. Now, although any one primary discharge train may show regular properties, uncharacteristic of a Poisson process, when similar trains from independent neurons are superposed, the aggregated activity comes to resemble a Poisson process more and more (see Khintchine 1960, Chapter 5; Cox 1962, Chapter 6; McGill 1967), essentially because of increasing uncertainty from which neuron the next discharge will come. Finally, stimulation in taste and smell is a molecular process which itself introduces the randomness characteristic of the Poisson. So, the idea of differential coupling as a finite differencing between statistically independent copies of the stimulus is of general applicability.

The obvious site for this differential coupling (there is no other candidate) is the neural receptive field. Centre/surround receptive fields have been known to exist in the retina for 40 years (Kuffler 1953) and subsequent research has shown that kind of neural organization, albeit with more elaborate dispositions of the excitatory and inhibitory regions, to be widespread in the visual areas of the brain. Similar neural organizations have been demonstrated in the skin (Mountcastle and Powell 1959). What needs to be added is that, in view of the psychophysical evidence, the excitatory and inhibitory inputs are balanced. Notwithstanding that quite a few visual physiologists have realized that the visual system is differentially coupled to its stimulus (e.g. Rushton 1969; Westheimer 1972; Krauskopf 1967; Arend *et al.* 1971), there has been a curious reluctance to put the two observations together. Possibly this has been because the maintained discharge of retinal ganglion cells has seemed to present compelling evidence to the contrary. But that maintained discharge admits an alternative interpretation (below; see also Laming 1989b) which is entirely compatible with the hypothesis of differential coupling.

4.5 THE SQUARE-LAW TRANSFORM

The receptive field combining both excitatory and inhibitory inputs constitutes one fundamental principle of (visual and somaesthetic, at least) neural organization. The other fundamental principle, even more widespread, is the transmission of neural activity, over any appreciable distance between units, by all-or-none action potentials. There is only one kind of action potential, and only one polarity of signal (excitation) can be transmitted. I model this second fundamental principle by a half-wave rectification of the differentially coupled input to each neural unit. Output therefore reflects only the positive-going excursions of the combined inputs. If those combined inputs approximate a Gaussian noise process, as will happen when the input is a steady background luminance, the output will approximate the positive excursions of the noise and will appear as a continuing discharge (see especially Laming 1986, p. 86, Fig. 6.5). This is the reason why the maintained discharge, however compelling it might appear to the contrary, provides no valid evidence against the hypothesis of differential coupling.

Modelling the square-law transform which accounts for the different shapes of detectability and discriminability functions requires one further idea beyond the half-wave rectification of a differentially coupled input. That further idea produces a square-law compression of small signals, small with respect to the background level of noise in the sensory analytic channel. The idea is expounded in detail in Laming (1985, 1986, Chapter 6); a brief summary must suffice here.

If, as in Fig. 4.4(a), the perturbations of the sensory process due to differentiation of the stimulus input are large in relation to the background noise, then the positive transient is transmitted unattenuated and the negative one entirely suppressed. That circumstance obtains in a discrimination between two separate stimuli and the statistical properties of difference discriminations derive from the information afforded by the unattenuated positive transient. But if the stimulus is small enough (as it has to be in the threshold detection of an increment) to produce perturbations of order comparable to the background noise level, both positive and negative transients are transmitted, but as differently attenuated modulations of the maintained discharge of the sensory neuron. Suppose those small perturbations, positive and negative, are intermingled in the receptive field of some superior neuron so that they cannot thereafter be disentangled. They will not cancel exactly, because they are of slightly different sizes, but will leave a resultant which calculation shows (Laming 1986, p. 88) to vary as the *square* of the increment ΔL to the physical stimulus.

This square-law transform of small stimuli provides a quantitative account of the different statistical properties of increment detection:

1. The aggregate perturbation modifies the distribution of the energy in the signal. The transmitted signal is now equivalent to a sample from the Gaussian noise background with a sinusoid (the aggregate perturbation) embedded in it and has a non-central χ^2 distribution (Green and Swets 1966, pp. 169–71; Laming 1986, Appendix A) with a non-centrality parameter (the aggregate perturbation again) exactly proportional to $(\Delta L)^2$. The appropriate signal detection model for the detection of an increment therefore consists of a χ^2 and a non-central χ^2 distribution with a common number of degrees of freedom (e.g. Jeffress 1964). It has an asymmetric operating characteristic slewed towards the bottom left-hand corner. The characteristics in Fig. 3.5(b) were calculated from just such a model; Laming (1986, p. 94) presents further examples.

2. An analysis of this asymmetric non-central χ^2 model analogous to that in Fig. 3.2 gives an expression for d' increasing as the non-centrality parameter, that is, in proportion to $(\Delta L)^2$ (see Laming 1986, pp. 256–60). Transposing this expression into terms of the proportion of correct responses in a 2AFC task gives the relation shown by the broken curve in Fig. 3.6, a normal integral with respect to $(\Delta L)^2$.

3. An increment becomes detectable when the non-centrality parameter (proportional to $(\Delta L)^2$) exceeds a certain size in relation to the power density (proportional to L) of the Gaussian noise process. For this reason ΔL varies as $\sqrt{L}$ at the increment threshold as indicated by the broken line in Fig. 3.3. The reason why that trend does not continue throughout the range of luminances studied, however, is much more complicated than can even be summarized here, and for further analysis of the properties of the non-central χ^2 model Laming (1986, Chapters 6–9) must be consulted.

4.6 FECHNER'S 'INNER' AND 'OUTER' PSYCHOPHYSICS

For Fechner, *outer psychophysics* concerned the relation between physical variables, such as stimulus magnitude, and sensation. 'Inner' psychophysics concerned the like relation between physiological variables and sensation. Fechner saw this distinction as a possible way of accommodating apparent discrepancies between Weber's Law and psychophysical observation.

> While Weber's Law is only of limited validity with respect to stimulus and sensation in the area of outer psychophysics, it probably has unlimited validity in the area of inner psychophysics, if transposed to the relationship of sensation to kinetic energy or to some other specific function of the underlying psychophysical processes. This conclusion is reached since all deviations from this law, which may be observed when external stimuli give rise to sensations, are probably due to the fact that only under normal or average conditions does the stimulus release kinetic energy proportional to the amount of internal activity directly underlying sensation. We might foresee, therefore, that once we have succeeded in making this transformation to psychophysical processes in an exact way, this law will take on for the field of mind–body relations just as general and fundamental a meaning as the law of gravitation in the field of celestial movement. (Fechner, in Adler 1966, pp. 56–7)

Fechner conceived of the process of stimulation as a transfer of energy, subject generally to the Law of Conservation of Energy. He did not have the idea of the stimulus releasing stored potential energy, nor the much more modern idea of it transmitting information. But his intuition that the deviations from Weber's Law occur at the transition from the physical to the physiological domains has a curious modern resonance.

At the physical level of description the Poisson structure of a visual stimulus enables increments to be detected when they exceed a certain fraction of the square root of the luminance (because the Poisson standard deviation increases as the square root of the mean). This is the behaviour of physical light detectors and is the basis of the de Vries–Rose law (de Vries 1943; Rose 1948; see Fig. 3.3 here). Where that law obtains, the threshold is 'information limited'. Since the difference threshold for luminance increases faster than the square root, it cannot be information limited at the physical level of description.

A Poisson process of level $L + \Delta L$ affords two discriminative statistics by which it might be distinguished from a similar process of level L: there is (a) the difference of mean, ΔL, which generates the de Vries–Rose Law and (b) the difference of variance (see Laming 1986, pp. 169–72). Provided the luminance L is sufficiently great that the Poisson distribution can be approximated by the normal, discrimination based on that difference of variance is accurately described by the χ^2 model and Weber's Law is obtained instead. Weber's Law is therefore observed when the more informative cue supplied by the Poisson mean is blocked by differential coupling to the physical stimulus. Weber's Law thereby emerges from the transformation from 'outer' to 'inner' psychophysics, although not in the way Fechner envisaged.

4.7 CONCLUSIONS

So long as attention is confined to difference discriminations, not only difference thresholds, but also discriminability functions and signal-detection characteristics, are accurately described by the normal model (eqn 3.2). Fechner's Law emerges as the relation between physical stimulus magnitude and the operational parameter in that model. That relation provides a reinterpretation of Fechner's law which evades all problems associated with the meaning of the word 'sensation'. However, the χ^2 model provides an alternative account of the statistical properties of difference discriminations, just as accurate, just as succinct, but with a power relation substituted for Fechner's logarithmic law. Which model to choose?

Examination of the statistical properties of increment detection has revealed a similar volume of experimental findings which the χ^2 model can accommodate (by adding a non-central χ^2 distribution to the model), but which the normal model cannot. To put the reason for that failure succinctly: the normal model posits a direct (though logarithmic) relation (i.e. Fechner's Law) between physical stimulus magnitude and internal activity. Comparison of the different properties of difference discriminations and increment detection show that relation to be differential. Differentiation of visual input or of primary neuron activity in other sensory modalities delivers a process approximating to Gaussian noise, and the χ^2 model works, where the normal model fails, because the χ^2 variable may be identified with the energy in a sample of that Gaussian noise.

The special significance of the argument in this chapter is that Fechner's Law not only lacks experimental support, but is actually contrary to observation. Set aside the consideration that Assertion 2 on p. 28—that all just-noticeable differences are subjectively equal—is no more than fiat. If Fechner's Law is to be a plausible candidate as the measure of sensation, it must be seen to play a fundamental role somewhere in the formulation of psychophysical theory, in this case, in the theory of sensory discrimination. What this chapter has shown is that within the field of sensory discrimination an even more fundamental role accords to a power function of unspecified exponent in combination with the χ^2_C model. Fechner's Law enters in only as a part of an excellent approximation to that χ^2 model as applied to difference discriminations. Exit Fechner's Law.

Finally, in the absence of any comment to the contrary, it might be supposed that the exponent k in eqn 4.1 is at our disposal, so that the χ^2 model is at least *compatible* with Stevens' Power Law. That would be premature. Weber's Law transforms into itself under any power law transform of the stimulus magnitude; that is, if

$$\Delta L/L = \Theta, \tag{4.5}$$

then

$$(L + \Delta L)/L = (1 + \Theta), \tag{4.6}$$

and

$$(L + \Delta L)^k/L^k = (1 + \Theta)^k, \tag{4.7}$$

so that the value of the exponent is undetermined. This is so for as long as attention is restricted to difference discriminations. But when the range of phenomena is extended to incorporate increment detection as well, the scale on which stimulus magnitude is measured becomes of material importance. This is best shown in my critique of the energy detection hypothesis of auditory detection (Laming 1973, pp. 145–8; Laming 1986, pp. 46–52). I show there that the results from a variety of auditory signal detection experiments are most succinctly described by taking the psychological measure of the auditory stimulus to be *amplitude*, not energy. In the analysis of detection data it matters how the stimulus magnitude is measured, and existing analyses suggest, in every case, a particular natural physical measure of the stimulus. That is to say, the exponent k can always be taken to be 1, and the phenomena of sensory discrimination do not lend support to any measure of sensation distinct from the physical measure of the stimulus.

Of course, the experimental methods developed by S.S. Stevens and his colleagues might provide quite a different sort of justification for some measure of sensation or other, and to an examination of that large body of experiment and data we must now turn.

5 Stevens' Power Law

S.S. Stevens' involvement with the measurement of sensation began in the 1930s. At that time he specialized in the study of hearing, and that specialization brought him into contact with the problem faced by acoustic engineers in explaining the implications of acoustic measurements to their (lay) clients. His involvement with that problem led to the development of the sone scale (Stevens 1936). About 1953 Stevens returned to the problem of the measurement of sensation, interested now in all kinds of sensory attributes. He developed new experimental methods, of which magnitude estimation is the best known and most widely used, and with these methods obtained some striking new results. This chapter introduces his methods and surveys his principal results.

At certain points in later chapters the argument will turn on the particular way in which Stevens carried out his experiments. In preparation for such arguments, I look carefully here at his recommended procedure for magnitude estimation, with special attention to what it is that the subject is asked to judge.

5.1 MAGNITUDE ESTIMATION

As an introduction to his recommended procedure, Stevens (1956b) describes one magnitude estimation experiment in especial detail:

> The stimulus-tone was 1000~ whose intensity was controlled by *E*. *O* sat before a pair of push-type switches, one of which served to produce the standard loudness and the other the variable loudness. To suppress switching transients, the tone was passed through a narrow band-pass filter after which it went to a pair of earphones . . .

The task can best be described by means of the instructions:

> *Instructions.* The left key presents the standard tone and the right key presents the variable. We are going to call the loudness of the standard 10 and your task is to estimate the loudness of the variable. In other words, the question is: if the standard is called 10 what would you call the variable? Use whatever numbers seem to you appropriate—fractions, decimals, or whole numbers. For example, if the variable sounds 7 times as loud as the standard, say 70. If it sounds one fifth as loud, say 2; if a twentieth as loud, say 0.5, etc.

Try not to worry about being consistent; try to give the appropriate number to each tone regardless of what you may have called some previous stimulus.

> Press the 'standard' key for 1 or 2 sec. and listen carefully. Then press the 'variable' for 1 or 2 sec. and make your judgment. You may repeat this process if you care to before deciding on your estimate. (Stevens 1956b, p. 3)

The results which Stevens (1956b, Fig. 1) presents from this experiment conform nicely to the sone scale,

$$\text{Loudness} \propto E^{0.3}, \tag{5.1}$$

where E is the energy (per s) in the stimulus tone, or, what is equivalent,

$$\text{Loudness} \propto A^{0.6}, \tag{5.2}$$

where A is the amplitude.

Figure 5.1 presents the results from another similar experiment in which the initial standard and its modulus were omitted. In this experiment the stimuli were again 1 kHz tones of eight different amplitudes spaced at intervals of 10 dB presented twice each to 32 subjects in a different random order to each subject. Each subject gave the first tone heard any number he considered appropriate. Thereafter he continued with the instructions: 'Try to make the ratios between the numbers you assign to the different tones correspond to the ratios between the loudnesses of the tones. In other words, try to make the numbers proportional to the loudness, as *you* hear it' (Stevens 1956b, p. 20). Of course, some subjects used larger numbers than others; so Stevens scaled the judgments from each subject in this experiment to make the geometric means of each different subject's scaled judgments equal, a practice he called 'modulus equalization'. The data points in Fig. 5.1 represent the geometric means of the 64 scaled judgments (differently scaled for each subject) of each stimulus and the vertical bars show the extent of the interquartile intervals. If N be used generically to denote a number uttered by a subject, the scaled mean judgments conform nicely to the equation

$$N = 0.043A^{0.6}. \tag{5.3}$$

In the same article Stevens (1956b, pp. 5–6) proffers some unusually detailed advice how to do magnitude estimation experiments:

... let me say that the success of the foregoing experiment was achieved only after much trial and error in the course of which we learned at least some of the things *not* to do. On the positive side, in experiments involving a fixed standard, some of the things that should be done appear to be these:

(1) Use a standard whose level does not impress the O as being either extremely soft or extremely loud, i.e. use a comfortable standard—one that O can 'take hold of'.
(2) Present variable stimuli that are both above and below the standard.
(3) Call the standard by a number, like 10, that is easily multiplied and divided.
(4) Assign a number to the standard only, and leave the O completely free to decide what he will call the variables. For example, do not tell O that the faintest variable is to be called '1', or that the loudest is to be called some other number. If E assigns numbers to more than one stimulus, he introduces constraints of the sort that force O to make judgments on an interval rather than on a ratio scale.
(5) Use only one level of the standard in any one session, but use various standards, for it is risky to decide the form of a magnitude function on the basis of data obtained with only one standard.
(6) Randomize the order of presentation. With inexperienced *Os* it is well, however, to start with loudness ratios that are not too extreme and are, therefore, easier to judge.

(7) Make the experimental sessions short—about 10 min.
(8) Let *O* present the stimuli to himself. He can then work at his own pace, and he is more apt to be attending properly when the stimulus comes on.
(9) Since some estimates may depart widely from those of the 'average' *O*, it is advisable to use a group of *O*s that is large enough to produce a stable median.

Reading between these lines of Stevens' advice, it is evident that even he found it easy to fail to get good power law data. If one or another of Stevens' specific recommendations is disregarded, the mean magnitude estimates will depart in varying degrees from the desired empirical relation. Poulton (1968) has listed many examples of deviations from the power law obtained in this way.

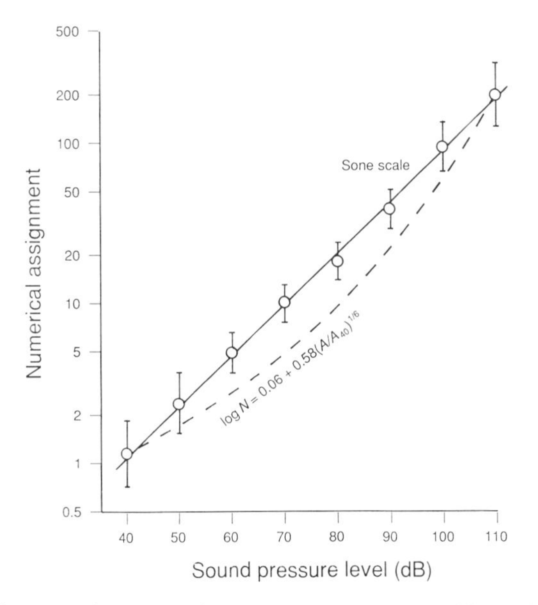

Fig. 5.1 Numerical magnitude estimates from Stevens (1975, p. 28) of the loudness of a 1 kHz tone by 32 observers judging each stimulus twice only. The vertical bar through each data point shows the inter-quartile range of the 64 constituent judgments, corrected for differences in scale between subjects. The continuous straight line is the sone scale and the broken curve shows calculations from a hypothetical relation (see later, Chapter 8) between the power law exponent and the Weber fraction.

One series of magnitude estimation experiments which have departed systematically from Stevens' (1956b) advice have been carried out by R.D. Luce, D.M. Green, and their colleagues at Harvard University. Some of these experiments will feature prominently in Chapter 10. Typically, these experimenters have used slightly smaller ranges[1] of stimuli than in Fig. 5.1, with the different stimulus values much more closely spaced, e.g. 40–90 dB in Baird *et al.* (1980) in 2.5 dB steps. Even more relevant is their practice of presenting the data from individual subjects, a rather larger number of trials from each individual than from the

[1] After about 1965 human subject committees in America would not ordinarily allow experimenters to exceed 95 dB SPL.

entire panel of subjects represented in Fig. 5.1. The earliest of these studies by Luce and Mo (1965) presented 18 weights in the range 30–1600 g 100 times each to six individual subjects and 20 1 kHz tones in the range 43–90 dB to a further six. Although the mean magnitude estimates show a generally linear trend on a log-log plot (Luce and Mo 1965, pp. 166–7, Figs 1 and 2), there are some obvious kinks in the trend, different kinks from different subjects, signifying idiosyncratic deviations from the power law. Moreover, these deviations are hardly the result of an inadequate number of responses. It is likely that aggregating data from a panel of subjects is actually necessary to obtain good power law data.

The same claim has previously been made by Pradhun and Hoffman (1963). Their experiment had six subjects make 20 estimates each of a range of nine weights under six different conditions comprising wide (10–506 g) and narrow (240–306 g) ranges and five different spacings of individual weights within the wide range. Twenty-one out of 36 regressions of log estimate on log weight for individual subjects in individual conditions proved significant at the 0.05 level. However, the data averaged over all subjects and all conditions conformed rather well to a power law (Pradhun and Hoffman 1963, p. 539, Fig. 3).

Notwithstanding that Stevens and his colleagues have repeatedly obtained magnitude estimates that bear a nice power law relation to the physical stimulus magnitude (once they had discovered the recipe), that result seems to be the very opposite of robust.

5.2 STEVENS' POWER LAW

Using the method of magnitude estimation substantially as I have described it, Stevens and his colleagues established subjective scales for many different stimulus attributes. Some two dozen of the attributes they explored are listed in Table 5.1, together with the exponent values which Stevens cited as typical. Those exponents vary from 0.33 for the luminance of a 5° field to 3.5 for electric shock. In each experiment the mean numerical estimates conformed to a power law like eqn 5.3, i.e.

$$N = cX^{\beta}, \tag{5.4}$$

where the exponent β varied from one attribute to another. This relation I call *Stevens' Power Law.*

It is not the case, however, that *all* stimulus attributes display this power law relation in a magnitude estimation experiment; there are some exceptions. In the light of these exceptions, Stevens (1957b) distinguished two classes of perceptual continua, distinguished according to the manner in which the corresponding physical stimulus attribute was measured:

1. *Prothetic continua.* Variation on a prothetic continuum can be effected by superposing a second stimulus on one already present. Stevens' prime example is loudness; adding one tone to another (in phase) creates a third tone of an amplitude equal to the sum of the amplitudes of the first two. More generally, a perceptual continuum is *prothetic* if the principle of superposition applies at the physical level of description, generating an additive

scale with respect to a natural measure of the stimulus magnitude. Other (perceptual) examples are apparent length, area, numerousness, duration, heaviness, lightness, and brightness.

2. *Metathetic continua.* Variation on a *metathetic* continuum involves the substitution of one stimulus in an ordered series for another. Stevens' prime example is pitch; the superposition of two tones of different frequencies does not create a third tone of a frequency equal to the sum of the first two. Metathetic continua can be scaled by direct methods such as equisection, but the result is not a power law (e.g. Stevens and Volkmann 1940). Other examples are visual position, inclination, and proportion.

Table 5.1 Typical exponents of the power function relating numerical estimates to physical stimulus magnitudes[1]

Attribute	Stimulus	Exponent
Luminance	5.7° source in darkness	0.33
Viscosity	Stirring silicone fluids	0.43
Luminance	Point source	0.50
Sound intensity, monaural	White noise	0.54
Saturation of odour	Coffee odour	0.55
Sound intensity, binaural	1 kHz tone	0.60
Visual area	Projected square	0.70
Tactual hardness	Squeezing rubber blocks	0.80
Vibration	Amplitude of 60 Hz vibration on fingertip	0.95
Cold	Metal contact on arm	1.00
Repetition rate	3 s train of clicks	1.00
Visual length	Projected line	1.00
Temporal duration	Duration of noise burst	1.10
Pressure	Static force on palm	1.10
Vocal effort	Vocal sound pressure	1.10
Luminance	Lightness of grey papers	1.20
Finger span	Thickness of blocks of wood	1.30
Weight	Weights lifted by hand	1.45
Tactual roughness	Emery cloths	1.50
Warmth	Metal contact on arm	1.60
Muscular force	Hand grip on dynamometer	1.70
Saturation	Red/grey colour mixture	1.70
Saturation	Yellow/white colour mixture	2.90
Electric shock	Current through fingers	3.50

[1] These are the 24 attributes plotted by Teghtsoonian (1971, Fig. 2); see later Fig. 11.3. Twenty-one of these exponent values were listed by Poulton (1967, Table 1); they comprised all of the values said by Stevens (1962) to be typical for which published experimental sources could be traced.

Magnitude estimation has also been applied to stimuli with no natural metric (and therefore not comprising a continuum) and, in a number of cases, compared with scale values obtained from pair comparison data of the same stimuli by Thurstone and Chave (1929). Stevens (1966a) cites attitude statements concerning the church; preferences for different wrist watches (Indow 1961); aesthetic value of handwriting (Ekman, 1958), drawings (Ekman and Künnapas 1962), and music (Koh 1965); the importance of Swedish monarchs (Ekman and Künnapas 1963a); occupational preferences (Künnapas and Wikström 1963); the pleasantness of odours (Engen and McBurney 1964); liberal–conservative preferences (Künnapas and Sillén 1964) and masculinity/femininity (Ekman and Künnapas 1963b); the seriousness of offences (Ekman 1962) and of punishments (Sellin and Wolfgang 1964); and frustration and aggression (Hamblin *et al.* 1963).

In these studies of non-metric stimuli there is, of course, no quantitative relationship of magnitude estimates to the physical stimuli to be formulated. But, at the same time, it can happen that a power law relationship emerges naturally between judgments of different aspects of the same non-metric stimuli. The following example comes from Fitzmaurice and Moreland (1995).

Fitzmaurice (1992) looked at the sums awarded as compensation for physical injury in road accidents, analysing all awards made by one insurance company in Paris during the years 1984 and 1986.[2] The amount of compensation is decided, ostensibly, in two stages. First, a doctor assesses the seriousness of the injuries suffered, scoring the extent of permanent disability resulting from the accident ('permanent partial incapacity') on a percentage scale (see later, pp. 172–3). Second, the insurance company, or judge if the case goes to court for adjudication, multiplies that assessment of permanent partial incapacity by a quantity known as the 'point' which is intended to reflect all other relevant aspects of the case. For example, a younger victim will suffer whatever permanent partial incapacity has resulted from the accident for a longer period of time and should therefore have a larger award. This is reflected in a larger 'point' score. The product of the two, permanent partial incapacity × point, gives the amount of the award in FF. In effect, each accident is subject to two assessments, the seriousness of the injuries received and the compensation awarded. Figure 5.2 displays the relationship between the two for the subset of cases decided by the courts in 1986. Each open circle represents a single case, while a filled circle represents two cases which happen to coincide in both particulars. The straight line represents a power law relationship with an exponent of 1.36.

It is to prothetic continua that Stevens' Power Law properly applies. It is interpreted as a generalization about the way in which the senses function.

It is easy to see why metathetic continua have to be excluded. If the Power Law reflects a statistical regularity in the state of nature, it must be independent (except for a multiplicative constant) of the scales on which both the physical and the subjective magnitudes are expressed. But the Power Law is essentially a mapping of ratios, physical to subjective, and it can represent a statistical regularity in nature only if those ratios are invariant under all admissible changes of scale (citing Luce 1959, Theorem 1 in reverse). Such invariance of ratios at the physical level of description is ensured only if the stimulus scale is a ratio scale with a unique zero, like length and weight. The ratio of the lengths of two lines is the same whether they be measured in inches or in centimetres. Likewise the ratio of the weights of two sacks of potatoes whether the weights be in pounds or in kilograms. Ratio scale measurement is ensured for prothetic continua by the principle of superposition; but for metathetic continua the zero point is (in most cases) arbitrary.

In practice, however, the question of how to measure the magnitude of the stimulus is more complicated than I have presented it and the distinction between prothetic and

[2] There was a significant change in French law mid-way through 1985 which made the comparison of these two years significant.

metathetic continua less clear. For example, when Gaussian noise processes are superposed the principle of superposition applies to the noise *power*, but the appropriate psychological measure of the intensity of a Gaussian noise stimulus appears to be r.m.s. amplitude (see Laming 1986, pp. 46–52) which increases as the square root of power. Another example is the saturation of red which is properly a proportion, but Panek and Stevens (1966) report that it appears to behave as a prothetic continuum. So the notion of a 'prothetic' continuum involves a certain set of psychophysical properties, of which the Power Law is one and Weber's Law is often another, which are meaningless without ratio scale measurement of stimulus magnitude. In practice, each different sensory attribute needs to be separately examined and classified on the basis of its own merits.

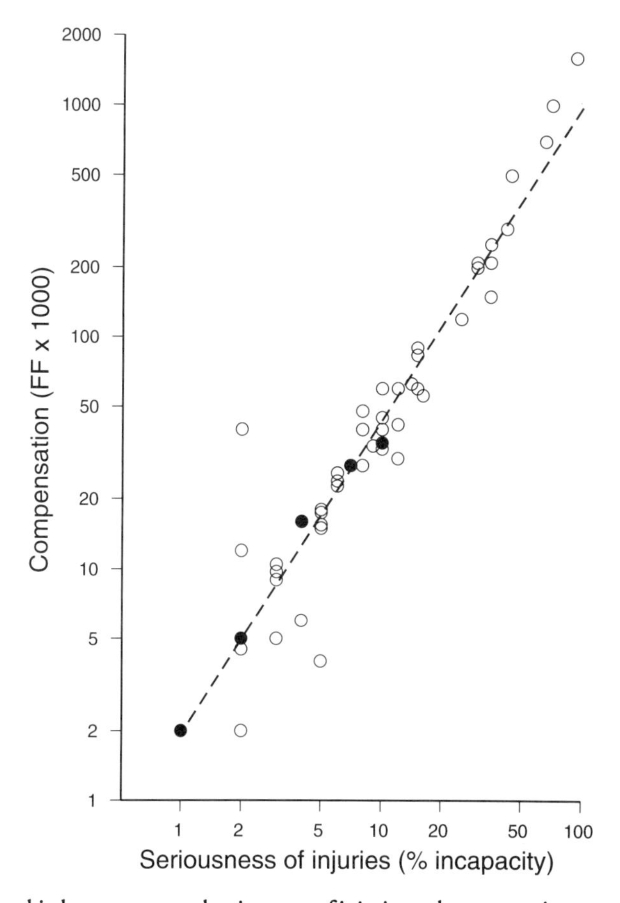

Fig. 5.2 Relationship between assessed seriousness of injuries and compensation awarded by the courts for 54 road accidents in Paris in 1986. Each open circle represents a single case, and a filled circle two cases which coincide in both particulars. The straight line is a power law with an exponent of 1.36. Data from Fitzmaurice and Moreland (1995).

Setting aside the question of exactly which stimulus continua are prothetic and which are metathetic, it can be seen that it is the former around which the controversy how to measure sensation is centred. These are the continua to which Stevens' Power Law applies and, in most cases, Weber's Law (and therefore Fechner's Law) as well. This controversy is admirably set out by Stevens (1957b). The principle of superposition endows prothetic continua with a homogeneity of structure which shows itself in a wide variety of common phenomena in addition to Stevens' and Weber's Laws (again see Stevens 1957b); some of those additional phenomena have already been described in Chapters 3 and 4. Such homogeneity is lacking amongst metathetic continua, which will scarcely concern us further.

Neither will the magnitude estimation of non-metric stimuli, which is little more than a curiosity; except that the power law relation evident in Fig. 5.2 will prove indicative when I come (pp. 171–3) to enquire how and why Stevens' Power Law arises in experimental data.

The Power Law has three simple corollaries which Stevens and his colleagues have checked out as a means of validating the original intuition. I list those corollaries below with some example experiments; they provide useful vehicles for illustrating the range of Stevens' work on the estimation of subjective sensations.

5.3 INVERSE ATTRIBUTES

In the vocabulary of subjective sensations many qualities have opposites, such as loud and soft, bright and dim, rough and smooth, saturated and pale. If subjects can assign numbers systematically to loudness, brightness, roughness, and saturation, can they also assess softness, dimness, smoothness, and paleness?

Figure 5.3 displays the mean numerical estimates from two experiments by Panek and Stevens (1966) on the estimation of redness and of paleness in a stimulus which varied in saturation on the red–white continuum. The stimulus was realized by viewing a rotating cylinder covered with red and grey papers in such a way as to provide a linear gradient of colorimetric purity. A small part of the cylinder was viewed through a reduction tube; and the red and grey fused because the cylinder was rotating at 2000 r.p.m. The percentage of red on the abscissa of Fig. 5.3 therefore gives the saturation with respect to a red of fixed, but unknown, colorimetric purity. The different experiments presented in the figure used slightly different ranges of stimuli. There were 10 subjects in each experiment who judged each stimulus twice in different random orders. The mean estimates of redness conform nicely to eqn 5.4 with β equal to 1.7, while the estimates of paleness, though approximating the inverse gradient (0.6), show a distinct downwards concavity.

There are other studies besides which present magnitude estimates of both a subjective attribute and its inverse. The attributes scaled include the loudness and softness of tones and of noise (Stevens and Guirao 1962); the roughness and smoothness of emery cloths (Stevens and Harris 1962); the length and shortness of lines, the size and smallness of squares, and the brightness and dimness of lights (Stevens and Guirao 1963); and the hardness and softness of samples of rubber (Harper and Stevens 1964). In these experiments it is common to find the magnitude function for the inverse attribute to be slightly concave downwards (though the example I have selected for display in Fig. 5.3 shows the most extreme curvature

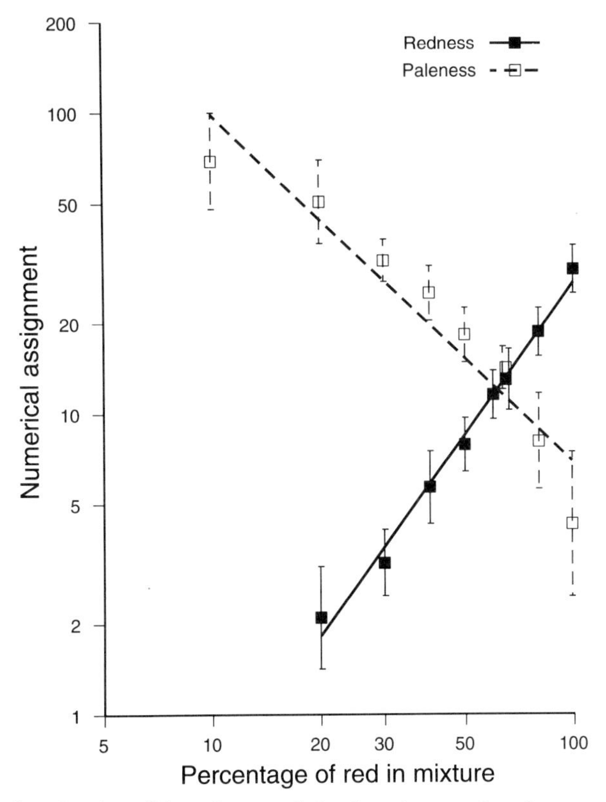

Fig. 5.3 Magnitude estimation of the redness, and also the paleness, of a red–grey mixture, the red of unspecified colorimetric purity. The vertical and horizontal lines through the data points mark the interquartile interval of the distributions of log matches. Data from Panek and Stevens (1966, p. 60, Table 1).

of all), as Stevens (1975, p. 125) acknowledged. Indeed, Stevens used this curvature to identify a particular one of each pair of subjective opposites, the one showing the greater conformity to the power law, as primary.

5.4 MAGNITUDE PRODUCTION

Since subjects can systematically assign numbers to stimuli, can they also adjust a variable stimulus to match a given number? Magnitude production, as this converse experiment is called, was first demonstrated by Reynolds and Stevens (1960). Their subjects first judged the loudness of seven different levels of broadband white noise. Then, in a second phase of the experiment, they adjusted the level of the noise to match six different numbers, the numbers being chosen to lie within the range used by the subjects in the first phase. Both the estimations and the productions conformed adequately to the Power Law (see Stevens and Greenbaum 1966, Fig. 5); but the production data required a higher exponent in eqn 5.4 than did the estimations.

Another experiment, more illuminating for our purposes, is the study of the judgment of intervals of time by Stevens and Greenbaum (1966). The duration of each interval was identified either by a white noise, presented throughout the prescribed interval, or by a red light. In the estimation experiment the subject simply assigned a number to each stimulus in proportion to its apparent duration. In the magnitude production experiment the subject pressed a key, which turned on the stimulus, white noise or red light, for a duration proportional to a given number. The data from the experiment in which the duration was marked by white noise are set out in Fig. 5.4. The open circles are geometric averages from two estimations by each of 10 subjects; the filled circles are likewise averages of two productions from each of the same 10 subjects. On this double logarithmic plot the exponent of the Power Law (i.e. β in eqn 5.4) transposes into the gradient of the data points, and it is immediately apparent that the two gradients are different. Although the trend of the data points is satisfactorily linear as the Power Law requires, the gradient (exponent) is 0.87 for the estimation data and 1.20 for the productions. The companion experiment in which the durations were marked by a red light gave similar results, the corresponding gradients being 0.93 and 1.16.

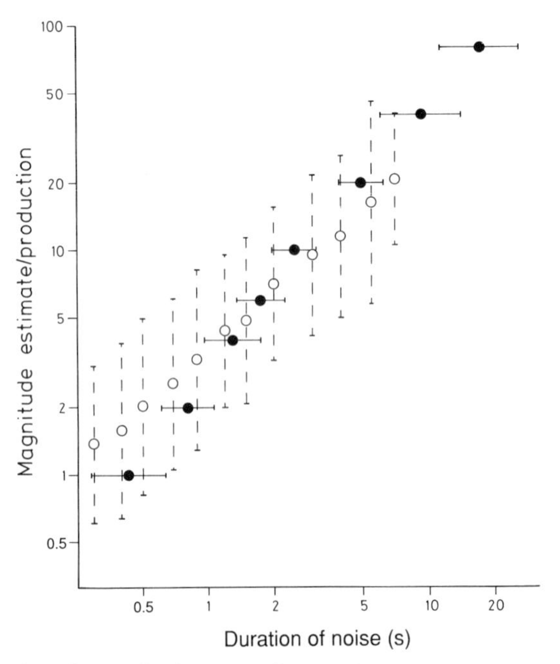

Fig. 5.4 Matching of numbers to the durations of bursts of noise. The open circles are geometric mean magnitude estimates and the filled circles magnitude productions. The vertical and horizontal lines through the data points extend to ± 1 standard deviation of the distributions of log matches. Data from Stevens and Greenbaum (1966, p. 444, Table 2).

This difference in gradient is no chance perturbation of the data. It has appeared in every experiment in which the same subjects have both assigned numbers to stimuli and adjusted stimuli to match numbers. The subjects systematically constrain their responses, be they numbers or stimulus matches, within a smaller range than that which, according to the

Power Law, is needed in the light of the range of stimuli presented for estimation or of numbers for matching: '... the observer tends to shorten the range of whichever variable he controls' (Stevens 1971, p. 426). In consequence, the gradient of the production data is always greater than that of the estimations. Stevens and Greenbaum (1966) called this the 'regression effect'.

This difference in gradient, depending on whether magnitudes are being estimated or produced, is usually small. But for the occasional individual the difference can be large. Stevens and Greenbaum (1966, Fig. 10) published the data from two individual subjects in an experiment by Stevens and Guirao (1962) on the estimation of the loudness of a band of white noise and the adjustment of the noise level to match a given number. One of those subjects yielded an exponent of 0.4 for the estimation task, but 0.9 for his productions.

5.5 CROSS-MODALITY MATCHING

Since subjects can assign numbers to stimuli and can adjust variable stimuli to match numbers, they ought, in addition, to be able to adjust a stimulus on one continuum to match another stimulus on a different continuum. Stevens and his colleagues have shown that subjects can also do this. At the same time Stevens' and Greenbaum's 'regression effect' turns out to be in no way contingent on the use of numbers either as responses or as stimuli. It occurs when one stimulus is simply adjusted to match another.

Figure 5.5 shows a further experiment from Stevens and Greenbaum in which an interval of time was marked either by a white noise or a by a red light. On each trial one of these stimuli would be presented for a certain duration, and the subject was asked to switch off the other stimulus, by pressing a key, after it had been on for the *same* duration. Figure 5.5 shows that the geometric mean matches (two matches from each of 10 subjects to each value of the stimulus presented) conform to the power law; but the gradient light/noise is less when the light is adjusted to the noise than it is when the noise is adjusted to match the light. Again, the subjects restrict the range of their chosen matches.

If numbers can be assigned to stimuli on one continuum according to the Power Law (eqn 5.4), and if stimuli on some other continuum can be adjusted to match given numbers, again according to the Power Law, then, when stimuli on the second continuum are adjusted to match given stimuli on the first, there ought to be some relationship between the three exponents. Suppose, for example, that the assignment of numbers N_x to 1 kHz tones (X) accords with the relation

$$N_x = X^{\beta_x}, \tag{5.5}$$

and assignment N_y to force of hand grip (Y) to

$$N_y = Y^{\beta_y}. \tag{5.6}$$

If Stevens' Power Law derives from real transformations inside the respective sensory systems, as Stevens believed, then when a particular force of hand grip is matched to a given tone, the number N_y assigned to the matching force of hand grip by eqn 5.6 should equate to the number N_x assigned by eqn 5.5 to the tone which is matched. This means that the force of hand grip should satisfy

$$Y^{\beta_y} = X^{\beta_x}, \tag{5.7}$$

or

$$Y = X^{\beta_x/\beta_y}. \tag{5.8}$$

That is, the matching of any attribute Y to stimuli with given magnitudes X ought to have exponent β_x/β_y. This consistency relation has been examined by Stevens (1966b).

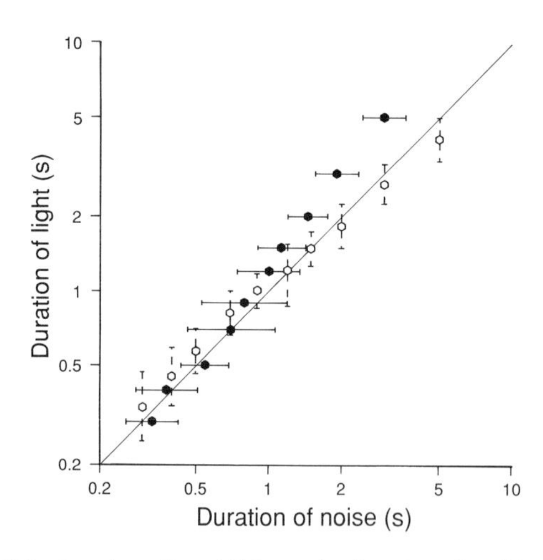

Fig. 5.5 Matching of the duration of a red light to the duration of a white noise and vice versa. The open circles are geometric mean matches of light to noise and the filled circles matches of noise to light. The vertical and horizontal lines through the data points extend to ± 1 standard deviation of the distributions of log matches. Data from Stevens and Greenbaum (1966, p. 443, Table 1).

First of all, force of hand grip, as measured with a hand dynamometer, was matched to five different attributes by J.C. Stevens *et al.* (1960); to two others as well as number (i.e. magnitude production) by J.C. Stevens and Mack (1959); and to yet two further attributes by J.C. Stevens and S.S. Stevens (1960). Stevens (1966b) brought the mean matches from all these cross-modal comparisons together in a figure which is reproduced here as Fig. 5.6. Each set of data points is reasonably linear on this double logarithmic plot, so that a good estimate of the matching relation can be obtained in each case. These estimates are set out in Table 5.2 together with predictions calculated according to eqn 5.8 from the typical exponent values in Table 5.1. The average absolute logarithmic deviation is an astounding 0.02 log units, equivalent to a ratio of observed exponent to predicted of either 0.956 or 1.046.

Stevens (1966b) also gathered together from diverse sources data on 10 different attributes (including number) that had been matched by the loudness of a band of noise. In this case Stevens used the estimated exponent from the cross-modal matching data in combination with the typical exponent for the attribute being matched to generate a prediction for the assignment of number to noise. The data have, however, been reworked in Table 5.3 in the same manner as Table 5.2, again using the typical exponents in Table 5.1 to predict the matching exponent. The average absolute logarithmic deviation is here 0.066 log units, equivalent to a ratio of observed exponent to predicted of either 0.86 or 1.16. The consistency is possibly less in this second set of matching data because of the diverse sources from which the different exponent values were drawn.

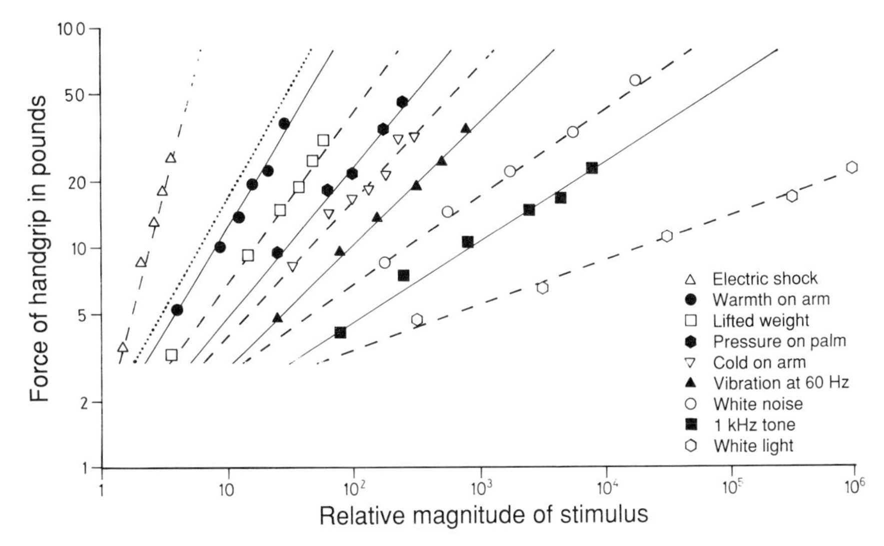

Fig. 5.6 Force of hand grip matched to values of 10 other stimulus attributes. Each set of data has been arbitrarily transposed along the abscissa for clarity of presentation. The dotted line represents a gradient of 1. (From Laming, 1994, p. 263. Figure redrawn from Stevens, 1966b, p. 5. © 1994, Routledge. Reproduced by permission.)

Table 5.2 Estimated exponents for the matching of force of hand grip to eight other stimulus attributes and to number

Attribute	Matching exponent	Predicted from Table 5.1
Luminance, 5° source	0.21	0.19
1 kHz tone, binaural	0.35	0.35
White noise, binaural	0.41	0.35
Amplitude of vibration	0.56	0.56
Cold on arm	0.60	0.59
Pressure on palm	0.67	0.65
Lifted weight	0.79	0.85
Warmth on arm	0.96	0.94
Electric current through fingers	2.13	2.06

Table 5.3 Estimated exponents for the matching of white noise to nine other stimulus attributes and to number

Attribute	Matching exponent	Predicted from Table 5.1
Luminance, 4° source	0.44	0.55
Hardness of rubber by squeezing	0.81	1.33
Length of line	1.45	1.67
Number (magnitude production)	1.45	1.67
Amplitude of vibration	1.6	1.58
Vocal effort	2.0	1.83
Force of hand grip	2.5	2.83
Saturation of redness	2.6	2.83
Tactile roughness of emery cloth	2.6	2.50
Electric current through fingers	7.5	5.83

5.6 THE PSYCHOLOGICAL SIGNIFICANCE OF MAGNITUDE ESTIMATES

When an experimental psychologist sees his data repeatedly falling into some simple pattern, he commonly fixes on an interpretation of comparable simplicity; and, the more often he replicates his original result, the more vehemently does he defend his original interpretation. This is so, notwithstanding that the replications speak only to the reliability of the original finding and say nothing about its attribution. S.S. Stevens was no exception. At many places in his writings he directly identified the numbers uttered by his subjects with the strengths of the sensations they experienced. Different expressions of this idea have been made with different levels of specificity, and I have selected three such statements to serve as foci for the coming critique:

1. *An operational characterization:* 'By a scale of subjective magnitude we mean a quantitative scale by which we can predict what people will say when they try to give a quantitative description of their impressions' (Stevens 1956b, p. 2).
2. *A definitive measure of sensation:* '. . . the sensation S is proportional to the stimulus X raised to a power β' (Stevens 1957b, p. 162, replacing Stevens' Ψ, S, and n with S, X, and β, respectively).
3. *A belief that the power law transform is realized in elementary neural function:* 'Power functions like those that govern subjective magnitude show themselves in neurelectric effects' (Stevens 1970, p. 1043).

These three statements will be examined in the next three chapters, beginning with the last and most specific.

6 The physiological basis of sensation

'Power functions like those that govern subjective magnitude show themselves in neurelectric effects' (Stevens 1970, p. 1043). S.S. Stevens believed that the power functions revealed in his magnitude estimation experiments were realized in the compressive response of primary neurons, so that, thereafter, the intensity of sensation was proportional to the level of neural activity in the sensory pathway. Consider, subjects are presented with elementary stimuli, almost entirely devoid of context. They are asked to assign numbers to the stimuli 'in such a way that they reflect your subjective impression' (Stevens 1971, p. 428). In the absence of any context with which to make comparison, what do those numbers represent? Why, the internal sensation, the intermediary between stimulus and perceptual experience! Of necessity, that intermediary is carried by the primary sensory fibres. 'Sense organs serve as the transducers that convert the energies of the environment into neural form. Like any transducer, each sense organ has its dynamic operating characteristic, defined by the input–output relation' (Stevens 1961a, p. 10). The connection between subjective magnitude and primary neural response becomes irresistible.

But a belief does not have the same force as an assertion, and it would be unfair to suggest that Stevens supposed this particular belief to be established fact. Nevertheless, he assembled all the relevant evidence that he could find to argue the case (Stevens, 1970), and I now come to a critical examination of the most pertinent of that evidence.

Although many people have been sceptical of Stevens' claims for magnitude estimates vis-à-vis sensation, the idea that the intensity of sensation corresponds to the level of activity at some (unspecified) locus within the brain is widespread, ultimately on the basis that if sensation does not reflect what is happening within the brain, what other basis can it have? This more widespread view I shall also examine. The point at issue is not whether subjective experience is, or is not, related to neural events within the brain—of course it is—but whether that relation is sufficiently simple that it is helpful to think of the intensity of sensation as reflecting some internal level of neural activity. An alternative, and quite distinct, possibility (Chapter 4) is that change in neural activity signals change in sensory input and that stimulus magnitude is inferred from a differential signal. Indeed, the relationship might be so complex overall that some quite different approach is needed.

6.1 THE POWER LAW AS A PROPERTY OF PRIMARY NEURAL RESPONSE

To support his belief that the power law transform revealed in magnitude estimation experiments was realized directly in neural response, Stevens (1970, 1971) collected together a variety of electrophysiological studies—whole nerve responses (Boudreau 1965; Teas *et al.* 1962; Borg *et al.* 1967), neuron discharge rates (Hartline and Graham 1932; Adrian and Matthews, 1927; De Valois *et al.* 1962), receptor potentials (Fuortes and

Hodgkin 1964; Dodge *et al.* 1968), cortical evoked potentials (Keidel and Spreng 1965; Ehrenberger *et al.* 1966; von Loewenich and Finkenzeller 1967)—that were consistent, to within the limits of experimental error, with a power function of low exponent. Although such an assemblage might seem compelling, a more considered appraisal suggests otherwise.

Generally, physical stimulus magnitude can be manipulated over a much wider geometric range than that over which the discharge rate of a neuron can follow. The manner in which neural discharge rate increases with stimulus magnitude is typically compressive and, bearing in mind the intrinsic variability of neural discharge, can often be described, approximately, by a logarithmic function or by a power function of exponent less than 1. Indeed, it could hardly be otherwise. The choice between the two has reflected contemporary views about the form of the Psychophysical Law. For example, Hartline and Graham (1932, p. 291, fig. 6) in a very well-known pioneering paper published both the frequency of the initial burst of firing in their recordings from single ommatidia in the eye of *Limulus* and also the rate of discharge 3.5 s after the onset of illumination. The initial rate of firing received all the attention because it increased as the logarithm of stimulus intensity; but Stevens (1970, p. 1046, fig. 2) chose to reproduce the frequency of discharge 3.5 s after onset because that fitted a power function. Other data from Matthews (1931), Tasaki (1954), and Fuortes (1959; see Rushton 1959) have also been plotted logarithmically, while more recent recordings have been read as power functions. So long as the details of the process which leads from stimulation to neural discharge are not understood quantitatively, such results testify to no more than the current state of opinion.

Two studies which I examine below have more substance to them because they compare magnitude estimations and physiological responses from the *same* subjects. They illustrate the nature of the argument and the hazards that it faces.

6.1.1 **Primary neural response to taste**

The gustatory nerve fibres from the anterior part of the tongue run through the middle ear in the chorda tympani. During middle ear surgery this nerve is often exposed and it becomes practicable to record whole nerve responses to different sapid solutions applied to the tongue. This circumstance opened the way for Borg *et al.* (1967) to conduct a more rigorous test of Stevens' belief.

The subjects in Borg *et al.*'s study were five patients undergoing middle ear surgery. Two days before their respective operations, magnitude estimation experiments were carried out with citric acid, sodium chloride, and sucrose in different concentrations. Then, in the course of their operations under light general anaesthesia, the activity of the chorda tympani was recorded in response to the same concentrations of citric acid, etc. Figure 6.1 shows the averaged values from two patients, with the vertical scales (neural response/magnitude estimate) aligned to produce the best agreement between the data points.

Although these data look convincing by themselves, they are selected as the best two sets from a small group of patients, some of whom failed to yield adequate data of one kind or the other. Now it is in the nature of primary neural activity to display a compressive saturation of discharge rate in relation to the magnitude of the physical stimulus; and it will inevitably happen from time to time that the exponent estimated from neural data will match, more or less, the value obtained from magnitude estimation. In short, the correspondence in Fig. 6.1 could be fortuitous. What is really needed is to show that the *differences* between individual magnitude estimation exponents are matched by the differences between exponents estimated from corresponding neural data. This more rigorous test of Stevens' belief is realized in the next study.

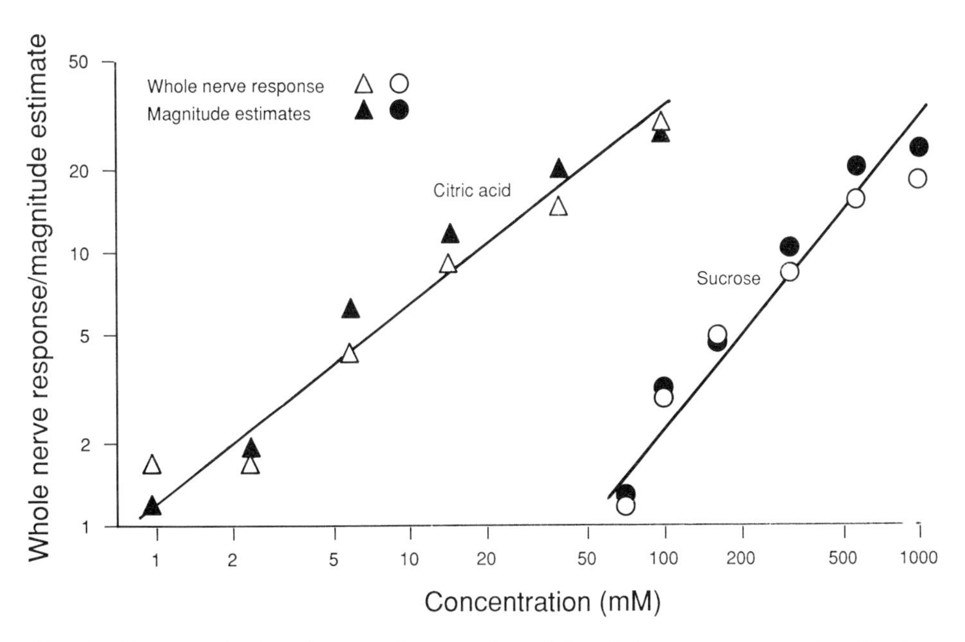

Fig. 6.1 Mean magnitude estimates and mean values of the whole nerve response plotted against molarity of citric acid and sucrose for two patients undergoing middle ear surgery. Ordinate scales have been separately chosen to yield the greatest concordance between the two kinds of data. (Redrawn from Borg *et al.* 1967, p. 17.)

6.1.2 **Primary neural response to touch**

Knibestöl and Vallbo (1980) recorded from single afferent fibres in the median or ulnar nerve of unanaesthetized human subjects. The fibres selected were slowly adapting mechanoreceptive units with receptive fields in the glabrous skin of the hand, thought to innervate Merkel discs. The number of discharges was recorded in response to indentations of various depths, up to 4 mm, in the centre of the receptive field by a probe of 1 mm^2 area, the indentation lasting for 1 s. At the same time the subject was asked to estimate the subjective magnitude of the stimulus, the very stimulus which elicited the recorded neural response.

Knibestöl and Vallbo analysed corresponding magnitude estimation and electrophysiological data from a total of 46 units in the hands of 18 different subjects. They fitted power functions to both the neural and the psychophysical data. The mean exponent estimated from the neural data was 0.72, and from the psychophysical data 1.18. This difference is highly significant. But it could still be that the primary neural response is a *component* of the psychophysical power transform. The magnitude estimate uttered by the subject depends, in part, on his particular use of numbers and Krueger (1989) has argued that numbers have subjective magnitudes of their own, related to the objective numbers by a further power transform (see later, pp. 91–2). If this be so, one might expect a systematic difference between the value of the exponent as estimated at the primary neural level and its value as evident in the magnitude estimates. At the same time, if the numerical estimates of magnitude uttered by the subjects are based on the neural discharges recorded from their median and ulnar nerves, there ought to be a substantial correlation between the two exponents estimated from the two kinds of data obtained from the same series of stimulus presentations. To exclude this last possibility Fig. 6.2 shows a scatter plot of the estimated exponents, neural versus psychophysical. There is no correlation between them.

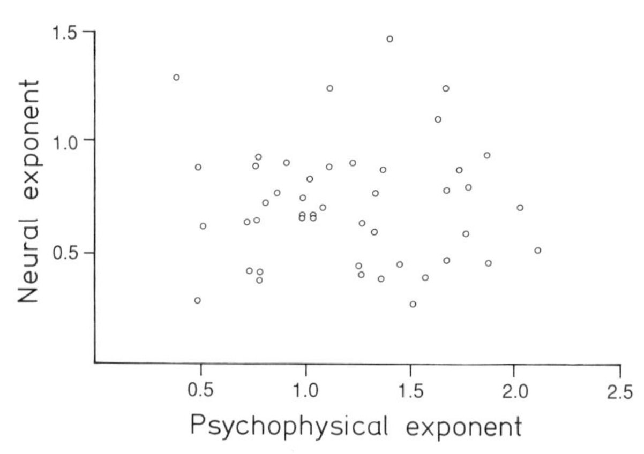

Fig. 6.2 Neural and psychophysical exponents calculated from some 46 different sets of responses (neural discharge rates and magnitude estimates) to *common* series of tactile stimuli. The correlation between the two kinds of exponent is −0.04, that is, negligible. (Data from Knibestöl and Vallbo 1980, p. 263. Figure from 'Experimental evidence on Fechner's and Stevens laws' by D. Laming, *Behavioral and Brain Sciences*, vol. 12, p. 279. © 1989, The Physiological Society. Reproduced by permission.)

The conclusion from Knibestöl and Vallbo's investigation seems to be that both primary neural discharges and magnitude estimations may be approximated by power functions, but that there is otherwise no relation between them (see also Vallbo 1995). It is not the case that variation in the magnitude estimation exponent from one subject to another is dominated by each subject's idiosyncratic use of number, the correlation with neural discharge being negligible for that reason. Quite the contrary; the geometric range of exponents estimated from the neural data (0.26–1.92) was as great as that from the magnitude estimation data (0.36–2.09). If the sizes of these particular neural discharges contribute to the magnitude estimations, they must generate most of the observed variation in the power law exponent.

It is much more likely that the particular neural recordings from single fibres made by Knibestöl and Vallbo constituted only one neural message amongst many on which the magnitude estimates were based, a point made by Wasserman (1991). The argument based on the absence of correlation in Fig. 6.2 implicitly assumes that the one fibre from which the recording was made was typical of that site in that individual and therefore of the other fibres contributing to the sensation. But since the variation of neural exponent within individual subjects appears to be as great as that between subjects (Knibestöl and Vallbo 1980, p. 257, Fig. 4), that implicit assumption cannot be justified. The contribution of the one fibre to the total sensation could have been very small, with no detectable correlation. The conclusion from Knibestöl and Vallbo's investigation must therefore be modified, from an assertion that there seems to be *no relation* between primary neural discharges and magnitude estimations, to the weaker conclusion that there is *no evidence* of such a relation between them.

But Wasserman's criticism of the initial conclusion applies equally to single unit recordings in general; that is, present techniques provide, in effect, only illustrative data with respect to the question at issue and no valid conclusion is possible about any relation between single unit activity and magnitude estimation. For such a conclusion to be valid, we should need a substantially complete understanding, first, of the quantitative manner in which physical stimuli generate primary neural discharges and, second, of the way in which those primary discharges lead to a numerical response. Present-day understanding falls far short of that requirement.

To put electrophysiological studies properly in their place, consider the conclusions that might follow if primary neural response, or some other kind of recording, were found *not* to approximate a power law. Would one conclude (a) that the power law which characterizes magnitude estimation did not, after all, apply at a neurophysiological level, or merely (b) that one had been recording from the wrong part of the sensory pathway? Briefly, *if the power law be given,* and if it also be given that the sensation which is being estimated is proportional to the level of neural activity at some suitable locus in the sensory pathway, then the physiological data address the question whether the point from which they have been recorded is prior or subsequent to the locus at which the power transform is realized. But, as a corollary of the argument, the physiological data do *not* address the question whether the power law is a valid representation of the intensity of sensation.

This point can also be put in a complementary manner. While it must necessarily be the case that the experience that I have of a stimulus is communicated in some way through my sensory nerves—nerves whose typical behaviour has been recorded at a variety of specific points in the studies mentioned above and many others besides—there is no necessity that my experience should correspond in any simple manner, especially in an isomorphic manner, to any of the particular physiological measures sampled. Unless one can identify, independently of the data, the locus in the sensory pathway at which the power law transform is realized (if it is realized at all at such a level), there is no way in which physiological data can be brought to bear on the veracity of the realization. For, if the behaviour of a particular neural unit fails to match the typical trend of magnitude estimates, it would simply be said that this particular unit is not at the appropriate level of the sensory pathway; and, by the same token, when a match between neural and psychological behaviour is judged to have occurred, there is nothing to exclude a chance coincidence.

In short, physiological data tell us nothing about the main question of interest.

6.2 THE POWER LAW AS A FUNCTION OF UNSPECIFIED PHYSIOLOGICAL PROCESSES

In the absence of a consistent and compelling correlation between the non-linear saturation of primary neural response and the magnitude estimation function, Stevens' belief that the Power Law is realized at a specifically peripheral level has no empirical support. But the less specific and more widespread idea that the intensity of sensation experienced corresponds to the level of neural activity at some (unspecified) part of the sensory pathway suggests that the Power Law might still have a physiological realization somewhere. This less specific realization of the Power Law is not, in fact, a physiological hypothesis (because the physiological measurements to which it relates are unspecified) and consequently greater subtlety is needed in its examination. However, there are certain behavioural predictions which would seem to follow, and I examine those next.

6.2.1 **The precision of estimates of the Power Law exponent**

If Stevens' Power Law has a physiological basis somewhere in the brain, then it should apply to all members of a given species with about the same value of exponent. While that value may be different for different sensory attributes (as indeed it is), it ought not to show much more than sampling variation between one experiment and another with the same attribute.

In an article surveying the methodological foundations of sensory scaling, Marks (1974) assembled some 71 independent estimates of the power law exponent for loudness vis-à-vis amplitude (or r.m.s. amplitude in the case of a noise stimulus) drawn from 26 different studies. These are values from complete experiments, averaged over groups of subjects, rather than from individuals, and so might be expected to show a lesser sampling variability than above. On the other hand, these 71 values come from different laboratories and from experiments using slightly different stimuli and might be expected to show greater variability on that account. Be that as it may, Marks' collection of loudness exponents range from 0.37 to 0.85, where Stevens' typical value is 0.6. Subsequent work has increased that range: Green *et al.* (1977) and Baird *et al.* (1980) report individual exponent values as low as 0.24 in relation to amplitude.

Eisler (1976) has collected together the results of some 111 experiments on the estimation of intervals of time. Most of those studies concern the matching of one duration with another (or the halving or doubling) to which Eisler has applied an unconventional model. But his Table 1 contains 21 experiments or conditions within experiments using Stevens' magnitude estimation procedure. The 21 estimated exponents range from 0.24 to 1.19. In addition, Poulton (1989) lists four independent studies of the sweetness of sips of sucrose solutions with widely different exponents; the exponent values reported are 0.62 (Gregson and Russell 1965), 1.03 (Marks and Bartoshuk 1979), 1.3 (Stevens 1969), and 1.5 (Ekman and Åkesson 1965).

There are, in addition, a number of studies reporting exponent values for individual subjects within the same experiment. These studies are reviewed in a different context in Chapter 11 (p. 187). For the present it is sufficient to remark that Knibestöl and Vallbo (1980), in the study described above, reported a range of values from 0.36 to 2.09 from a total of 62 individual magnitude estimation experiments (see Knibestöl and Vallbo 1980, p. 260. Fig. 7).

It is not known what range of values of estimates of a common exponent is compatible with a physiological basis for the Power Law. My own subjective feeling, for what it is worth, is that 0.24–0.85 and 0.6–1.5 for complete experiments and 0.36–2.09 for shorter series of observations with individual subjects is too great. Moreover, the study by Warren and Warren (1956), reported on p. 22, comparing the estimation of half-heaviness as a function of the relative sizes of the standard and comparison weights suggests that, if sensation does have a physiological basis, that basis cannot be realized until a late stage in the perceptual process, a stage beyond the point at which neural processes representing weight and size interact.

6.2.2 **Veridical estimation of stimulus magnitude**

Some subjects have persistently failed to provide power law magnitude estimation or ratio scaling data. Usually these have been subjects with specific professional experience in making measurements of the stimulus attribute to be judged. This was discovered in the very first experiments to be conducted. For example, Ham and Parkinson (1932) used sales personnel, accustomed to measuring noise levels, in preliminary experiments, but found that their prior experience with noise measurement influenced their judgments:

It appeared that if the responses of the observer had been properly conditioned, almost any type of result might be obtained. (Ham and Parkinson 1932, p. 513)

Laird *et al.* (1932) reported the same phenomenon and added some interesting details:

. . . in preliminary work . . . [observers] well acquainted with the audiometers and who had done considerable work in measuring noise levels were used. Erratic and misleading results were obtained from these acoustically sophisticated observers, and for an interesting reason. When the original level was sounded they would instantly identify it—with approximate accuracy—as being 60 decibels. Following this they would listen until a second stimulus was given which they estimated to be at the 30 decibel level. In other words, it was not possible for them to rule out their previous experience in identifying decibel levels and respond primarily to loudness as such. (Laird *et al.* 1932, p. 394)

Indeed, Harvey Fletcher, an experienced acoustical engineer, could write of the dB scale in 1929:

It is a well-known psychological law that equal steps on such a logarithmic scale sound *approximately* like equal loudness steps. (Fletcher 1929, p. 69)

A more recent example is provided by Rowley and Studebaker (1969), who began their work on the monaural loudness scale using graduate students in audiology:

The Audiology students were observed to use numbers that closely matched the decibel hearing levels of the presented tone, and thus produced a loudness curve that appeared to represent the dB HL scale. . . . There appeared to be such a strong attachment, on the part of audiologists, to the decibel scale that practice and repeated instructions, intended to explain the difference between the decibel and the loudness scales, did not significantly change these observers' judgments. Because of this finding, the Audiology students were excluded from the study and were replaced by other observers who were not familiar with the decibel. (Rowley and Studebaker 1969, p. 1191)

Similarly veridical judgments have also been observed in visual experiments. In an experiment on the judgment of 'half-brightness' Warren and Warren (1958) had

. . . one interesting subject whose data were not included with the others. He was (and is) a leading investigator in physiological and psychological optics, and was very familiar with photometric measurement. He . . . made judgments deviating from those of other subjects. His behavior resembled an illuminometer's: Brightness estimates were 50 per cent intensity over the entire stimulus range, despite our emphasis (and his understanding) that we were interested in 'subjective' magnitude judgments. (Warren 1981, pp. 181–2)

Likewise Mittenecker (1974) found that apprentice photographers made half-brightness matches much closer to half-luminance than did a group of trainee shopkeepers. The photographers' matches corresponded to exponents ranging from 0.55 to 0.77, whereas Stevens (see Table 5.1) claims that the typical exponent for a substantial steady light source is 0.33. Again, Kulikowski (1976), an investigator experienced in adjusting the contrast of a sinusoidal grating displayed on an oscilloscope screen, makes veridical settings of half-contrast. His other subjects did not; and Gottesman *et al.* (1981) found that magnitude estimations of contrast increased as about the 0.7 power of physical contrast.

One interpretation of these reports is that the subjects in question have fallen into Titchener's 'stimulus error', that is, they are making judgments about the physical stimulus rather than about the sensation experienced. Such a view might justify Rowley and Studebaker discarding the data from their audiology students. But I wish at this point to proffer a different view, one which will recur as further problems with the Power Law emerge.

If Plateau's intuition, cited on p. 4, is correct, that ordinarily there can be no *quantitative* assessment of a sensation, the experiments in question present a task which is, at the least, very difficult and may be impossible. In these circumstances one might expect subjects to carry out some other task (that is to say, not even naive subjects judge sensation) in which they are at the mercy of whatever extraneous constraints may be operative. This happens because the stimuli presented do not supply an adequate basis for judgment, and the Power Law obtains only when those extraneous constraints are appropriately balanced. If, however, the subject has some professional experience with physical measurements of the stimulus attribute presented for judgment, he has thereby some veridical basis for judging the stimuli themselves and cannot help but use it. No amount of instruction or remonstration can take that basis away from him. The error involved is not properly a 'stimulus error'; what is wrong is the very attempt to judge sensation.

So, a simple neural basis for the Power Law, even at some unspecified location, looks unlikely.

6.3 DIFFERENTIAL COUPLING OF SENSORY MAGNITUDES

Stevens' (1970, 1971) belief about a physiological basis for the Power Law is actually the conjunction of two propositions, either of which could be true independently of the other:

1. sensation may be identified directly with physiological response at some (possibly peripheral, but unspecified) stage of the sensory pathway; and
2. magnitude estimates measure sensation.

The studies I have just reviewed bear specifically on the hypothesis that the physiological relationship in question transposes into a power law at the behavioural level of description, that is, on the conjunction of these two propositions. It may be that the power law is wrong, but that sensation nevertheless has some simple physiological basis. The two more general propositions identified above need to be examined separately. I consider the first below; the second is postponed to the next chapter.

The idea that sensation may be identified directly with physiological response is widespread. Gescheider (1981, p. 194) expresses it in these words:

> . . . psychophysical scales of stimulus intensity reflect the operation of sensory mechanisms as they transduce and code stimulus energy into neural activity.

Hood and Finkelstein (1981) are more specific; they introduce the equation

$$R(L) = \{L^n/(L^n + \sigma^n)\}R_{\max}, \tag{6.1}$$

where $R(L)$ is the response of a vertebrate visual receptor to a flash of light of luminance L, with n, σ, and $R_{\max}$ constant. An equation of this form with exponent n between 0.7 and 1 has been found to fit the potentials recorded from the visual receptors of many different species (see Hood and Finkelstein 1979, p. 392), and in that same article these authors show that it will also accommodate their brightness estimation data from threshold upwards over a range of 3 log units with the exponent n equal to 1.

Mansfield (1981, Fig. 2), addressing the same question, presents a graphical comparison between the relative response in relation to luminance of different kinds of visual unit with magnitude estimates from Mansfield (1973). Response rates from retinal ganglion cells (Stone and Fabian 1968), from lateral geniculate neurons (Marrocco 1972), and from striate cortical neurons (Mansfield 1975) line up with the magnitude estimates on Mansfield's double logarithmic plot with a gradient (exponent) of about 1/3, while the early and late receptor potentials from rods and cones do not (cf. Hood and Finkelstein above).

The idea that the intensity of sensation experienced corresponds to the level of neural activity at some part of the sensory pathway is also implicit in many commonly received explanations of Mach's bands (Ratliff 1965; but see Laming 1988b, pp. 330–1) and other visual phenomena (see e.g. Lindsay and Norman 1977). But it will not stand up to examination, as I now show.

The experimental results examined in Chapters 3 and 4 showed that sensory discrimination was differentially coupled to the physical stimuli so that only changes in those stimuli, including those changes such as quantal fluctuations occurring by chance, were available as a basis for judgment. Information derived directly from the mean stimulus input did not contribute. That was established with respect to experiments on the discrimination of near-threshold differences between stimuli. The argument that now follows shows that substantially the same differential coupling is evident in suprathreshold estimates of brightness and other sensory qualities. The conclusion is that differential coupling is not just a simple approximation to the character of near-threshold discriminations, but is a general feature of our perceptual experience.

Remember that the point at issue is not whether subjective experience is, or is not, related to neural events within the brain, but whether that relation is sufficiently simple that it is helpful to think of intensity of sensation as reflecting some internal level of neural activity. The particular counter-examples presented below point to a differential relationship which, in the case of Land's two-colour phenomenon, transmutes differences in contrast and saturation into perceived differences in hue. They indicate, more generally, that the relationship between subjective experience on the one hand and the physiological level of description on the other is sufficiently complex that, in our present state of knowledge, thinking of sensation as some level of activity somewhere within the brain is actually counterproductive.

6.3.1 **The Craik–Cornsweet illusion**

The upper panel of Fig. 6.3 shows a sectored disc which, when spun rapidly, appears to the eye as the photograph in the middle panel. The inner disc appears darker than the annulus surrounding it; this is so, even though the centre and the periphery present the *same* time-averaged luminance. If, however, the boundary between these two areas is obscured by a thin opaque ring as in the lower panel of Fig. 6.3, the centre and the periphery appear to be equally bright. Remove the ring from the boundary (centre panel again) and the illusion is restored. This illusion was first described by Craik (1966) and related illusions have been explored by O'Brien (1958) and Cornsweet (1970, pp. 270–5).

This illusion is compelling, even when one knows why it occurs. There can, therefore, be no direct comparison of the luminances of the central disc and of the periphery. Instead, the relative brightness of these two areas is inferred from the way in which the luminance is perceived to change at the boundary. The abrupt step in luminance created by the kink in the profile of the black sector in the upper panel is easily perceptible, while the smooth ramps either side are not. So the inner disc is judged darker. But if that entire variation of luminance in the boundary region is obscured by the annulus (lower panel), one perceives just two equal steps in luminance of equal magnitude and opposite polarity. The inner disc and the periphery now appear equally bright. Only the *changes* in luminance are used as a basis for comparison.

This is a perceptual example of the differential coupling of the stimulus to sensory analysis which was established in Chapter 4 (pp. 46–8) on the basis of the different shapes of discriminability and detectability functions. Lockhead (1992, photograph p. 548) has published a more elaborate example, based on the experimental work of Arend *et al.* (1971), with several Craik–Cornsweet boundaries. The same differential coupling is evident in the perception of colour and other sensory attributes. Land (1974) has published a photograph of a coloured (red and blue) analogue of Fig. 6.3; it shows a change of hue between the

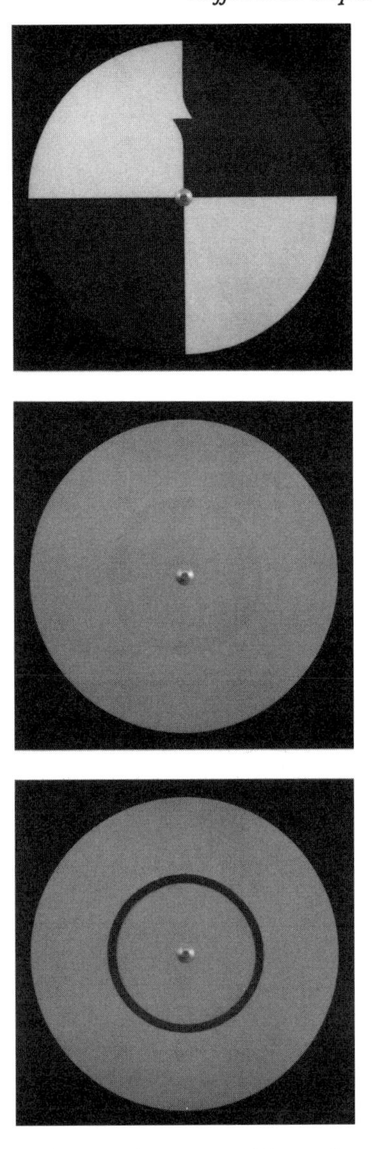

Fig. 6.3 The Craik–Cornsweet illusion. The centre and lower plates have been made from the same photographic negative which was taken while the disc in the upper plate was rotated at high speed. The inner disc has the same (time-averaged) luminance as the periphery, but it appears darker in the centre plate because at the boundary only the sharp step in luminance is perceptible. (From *Sensory analysis* by D. Laming, p. 64. © 1986, Academic Press. Reproduced by permission.)

centre and the surround. More especially, Ware and Cowan (1983) have measured the apparent colour difference between centre and surround by colour matching. Given a disc like Fig. 6.3, but with red/green or blue/yellow papers mounted on it, they equated the luminance of the two colours of each pair by adjusting the spectrum of the illumination. Then the hue of each part of the coloured disc, centre and surround, was separately matched by another disc with variable proportions of the two colours. The Craik–Cornsweet effect is strongest for achromatic discs, but is measurable also with equiluminant differences in hue.

6.3.2 **Crovitz's illusion**

Crovitz (1976) has applied the principle of the Craik–Cornsweet illusion to the graduated lengths of parallel lines. His illusion is illustrated in Fig. 6.4. The lines in the centre of Fig. 6.4(a) look shorter than those at the edges, although they are measurably of the same length. This appearance is dispelled in Fig. 6.4(b).

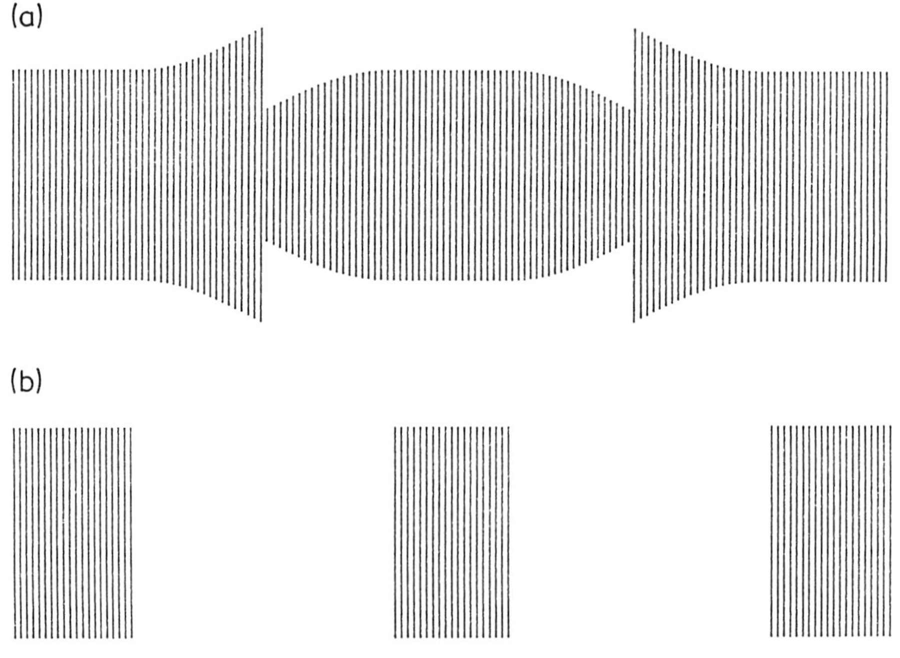

Fig. 6.4 Crovitz's illusion. (Figure (a) from *Sensory analysis* by D. Laming, p. 65. © 1986, Academic Press. Figure (b) from 'Précis of *Sensory analysis*' by D. Laming, *Behavioral and Brain Sciences*, vol. 11, p. 276. © 1988, Cambridge University Press. Both figures reproduced by permission.)

6.3.3 **MacKay's illusion**

MacKay (1973, p. 159, Fig. 1) has published a spatial frequency analogue of the Craik–Cornsweet illusion. In MacKay's display the spacing of the bars of a trapezoidal grating on an oscilloscope screen is varied in the same manner as the length of the lines in Fig. 6.4(a). The bars in the centre of the screen appear to be more widely spaced than do those at the sides, although there is no physical difference in the photograph.

6.3.4 **The Rawdon-Smith illusion**

This illusion is an auditory analogue of the Craik–Cornsweet. Figure 6.5 is a photograph of the auditory waveform (displayed on an oscilloscope) which Rawdon-Smith and Grindley

(1935) presented to their subjects. The 2 kHz tone decreases slowly in amplitude for about 7.5 s and then increases sharply to its original level. The variation of level in this record is about 3.9 dB. The subject sat in a sound-proof room, listening to this stimulus and moving a lever according as the intensity of the tone was heard to increase and decrease. The movements of the lever were recorded on a kymograph.

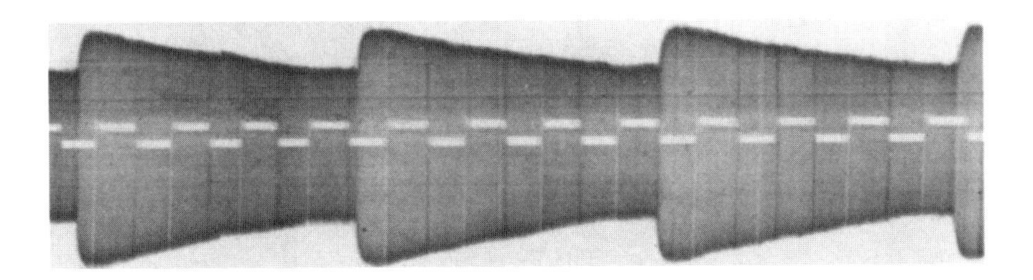

Fig. 6.5 Oscillographic record of the 2 kHz tone used to produce the Rawdon-Smith illusion. The white bars mark successive seconds of the record; the variation in intensity is about 3.9 dB. (From 'An illusion in the perception of loudness' by A.F. Rawdon-Smith and G.C. Grindley, *British Journal of Psychology*, vol. 26, facing p. 193. © 1935, The British Psychological Society. Reproduced by permission.)

Of six subjects tested under appropriate conditions, Rawdon-Smith and Grindley reported that four perceived the rapid increase in Fig. 6.5 but not the slow decrease, and therefore heard the sound to be continually increasing. An illusion of continual decrease can also be produced, but with greater difficulty. The range of variation is critical. One subject listening to 1.7 dB increases in intensity reported a progressive step-wise increase, but another listening to 4 dB increases heard the intensity to decrease as well and reported no long-term variation in average level.

In all these analogues of the Craik–Cornsweet illusion apparent differences are created between two equal levels of some stimulus attribute. That apparent difference is contingent on some subtle manipulation of the stimulus at a boundary between the two levels implicitly compared. If that boundary is obscured by, for example, the opaque annulus in Fig. 6.3(c) or by obliteration in Fig. 6.4(b), the illusory difference between the two equal stimulus magnitudes disappears. But if the boundary is subsequently restored, the illusion is restored with it. This means that the misjudgments which these illusions represent are not the products of some deception, evaporating as soon as that deception is revealed, but are consequences of the way in which our sensory apparatus analyses the stimuli presented to it. The critical property for these particular illusions is the fact that the two stimulus levels are not compared directly; rather their relative brightnesses/colours/lengths/spacings/amplitudes are inferred from the way in which the magnitude of the attribute is manipulated at the boundary between the stimuli. It is clear that the translation from physical stimulus magnitude into sensation is far from direct.

There are other phenomena arising with other sensory attributes, not being direct analogues of the Craik–Cornsweet illusion, which also suggest that sensory judgment is differentially coupled to the physical stimulus.

6.3.5 **Shepard's circular pitch paradox**

Shepard (1964) created cyclic sequences of complex tones which appeared to be always rising or falling in pitch. The components of each complex were octaves of a common fundamental, 10 components in all. The fundamental frequency was increased by a semitone from each complex to the next, so that the sequence always seemed to be rising in pitch. After 12 semitone steps, however, the fundamental frequency had risen to equal the octave of the first complex. At this point a new fundamental was added, equal in frequency to the original fundamental, so that the set of frequencies of the 10 components in the complex repeated exactly every 12 steps. In addition, the amplitudes of the different components were determined according to an envelope *fixed* in the frequency domain. This meant that the set of amplitudes also repeated exactly every 12 steps—indeed, the entire complex repeated. Figure 6.6 depicts the frequencies and amplitudes of the components of the first five complexes in the series. The fixed envelope spans 10 octaves, so that all 10 components of each complex have significant amplitudes. The changes in timbre which accompany the changes in fundamental frequency are scarcely perceptible.

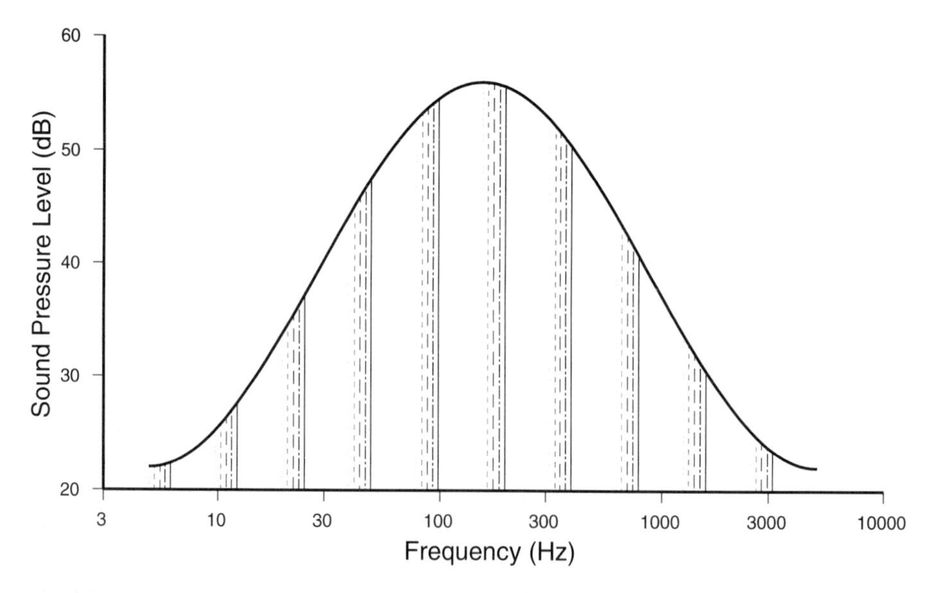

Fig. 6.6 Frequencies and amplitudes of the first five complexes in series in Shepard's circular pitch paradox. The frequencies of the components in each complex increase by octaves (shown here on a log frequency scale), but their amplitudes are determined according to a fixed envelope. Hence, every 12 semitone steps, both the frequencies and the amplitudes of the components return to their original values and the sequence of complexes, while seeming always to be increasing in pitch, cycles endlessly. (After Shepard, 1964, p. 2347, fig. 1.)

Risset (1969) has created continuous analogues of Shepard's tones—endlessly ascending or descending glissandi. The impression of change in pitch is independent of any systematic change in the physical stimulus frequency.

6.3.6 **The taste of water**

Distilled water contains no gustatory agents at all and might therefore be expected to have no taste. Although, in humans, water on the tongue appears to lead to a cessation of activity in the chorda tympani (Zotterman and Diamant 1959), it is not true that distilled water has no taste. Saliva, on the other hand, contains sodium chloride at a concentration of 0.005–0.01 M—but our mouths do not continually taste salty. The perception of taste is derived from *changes* in concentration in the oral environment. A decrease from the resting salt level in saliva to zero is just such a change and the resulting taste is attributed to the water.

This phenomenon concerns more than the relative concentrations of salt in saliva and in distilled water. If the mouth is irrigated with a salt solution, the taste of that solution disappears within 40 s or so. Thereafter, salt solutions of higher concentration taste salty, as one would expect; but weaker concentrations, including water, are variously reported to taste acid or bitter (Bartoshuk *et al.* 1964). After adaptation to sucrose, water again tastes acid or bitter; after quinine hydrochloride it tastes sweet; and after hydrochloride acid a variety of tastes (bitter, salty, and sweet) are reported by different subjects (Bartoshuk 1968).

6.3.7 **Simultaneous contrast**

Figure 6.7 reproduces a well-known illusion from Cornsweet (1970). The four small grey squares appear to be different—the grey on the white background looks darker then the grey on the black background—notwithstanding that they were all cut from the same sheet of grey paper. Hurvich (1981, p. XI, Plate 13-1) exhibits a coloured counterpart: red, purple, green, and cerise discs look to be of slightly different colours against yellow and against blue backgrounds.

Simultaneous contrast can have profound effects on the brightness of a visual stimulus; these effects are well illustrated in an experiment by Heinemann (1955). The brightness of a circular test field of 28′ diameter, exactly surrounded by an annulus (the surround) of twice the size, presented to the right eye was matched by the subject adjusting the luminance of a comparison field (of the same size and shape as the test field, but without any surround) viewed with the left eye. (Heinemann's stimulus configuration is shown later in Fig. 7.4, p. 105.) Figure 6.8 shows the average settings of the comparison luminance by one subject, as a function of the surround luminance, to match the brightness of a given test luminance. For surround luminances considerably less than the test luminance there is, typically, a small enhancement of the brightness of the test field over that brightness which it would have had in the absence of any surround; the brightness matches in Fig. 6.8 initially increase with surround luminance. But for surround luminances in excess of the test luminance, there is a dramatic depression of the test brightness; the brightness matches decrease sharply with further increase in the surround luminance. Indeed, when the surround luminance exceeds the test luminance by more than 0.1 log unit (26 per cent), the test field appears so dark that it cannot be matched by any suprathreshold luminance in the comparison field; and this is so, notwithstanding that the test field can be made to appear even darker by further increase in the surround luminance. Zero luminance in the comparison field does not generate the extreme sensation on the continuum of brightness–darkness; there are yet darker sensations that can be generated in the test field.

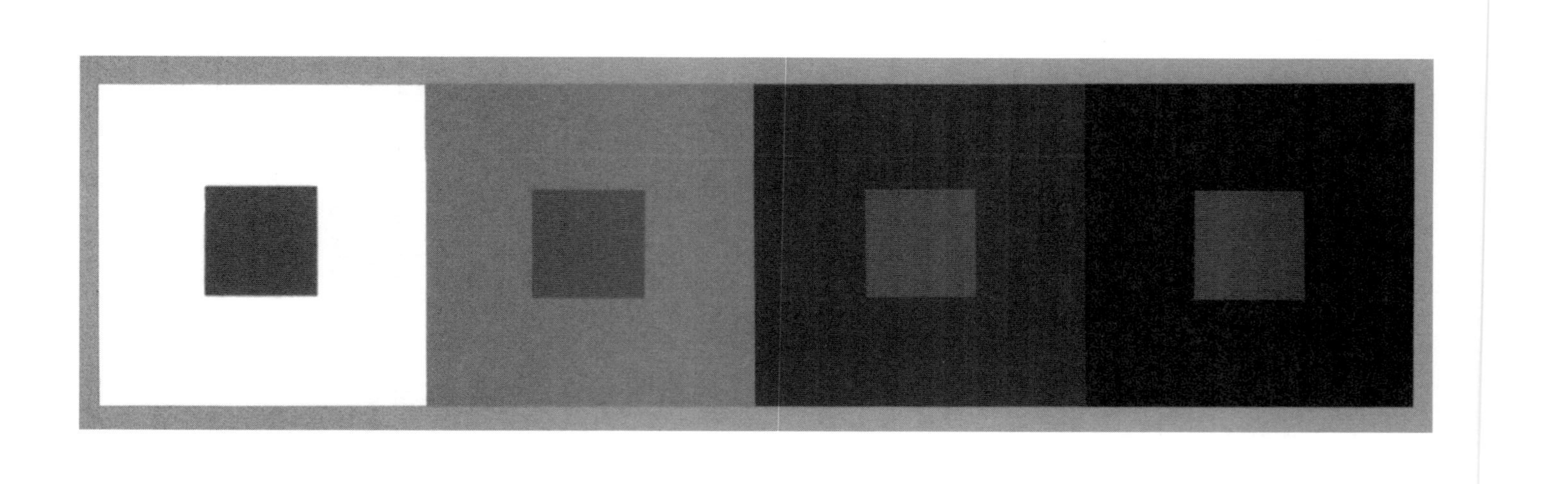

Fig. 6.7 Simultaneous contrast. The four small grey squares have all been cut from the same sheet of grey paper, but nevertheless appear to be of different greys because of the different backgrounds against which they are contrasted. (After Cornsweet, 1970, p. 279, fig. 11.7.)

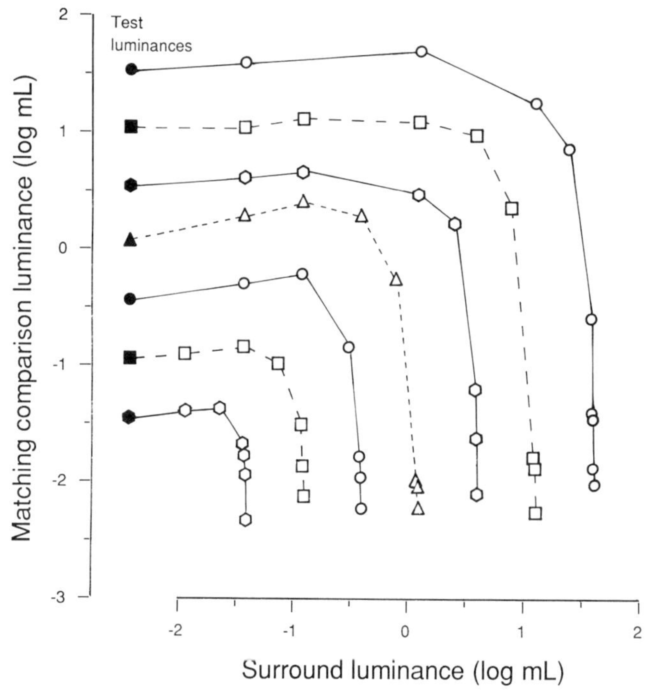

Fig. 6.8 Binocular brightness matches from Heinemann (1955). The comparison field, 28′ diameter, with no surround, viewed with the left eye, was adjusted to match the brightness of a similar test field, viewed with the right eye within a surround of 55′ diameter. The figure plots the matching comparison luminance against the luminance of the surround to the test field, for different fixed test field luminances corresponding to the filled symbols. (Redrawn from Heinemann 1955, p. 92.)

An effect in hearing analogous to simultaneous contrast in vision has been demonstrated by Pollack (1949). The subjects listened monaurally to speech which was alternately masked and unmasked for periods of 3 s by white noise of a specified level. The subjects attenuated the level of the speech in the unmasked periods (this level being analogous to Heinemann's comparison luminance) so that it sounded no louder than the masked speech. Masking noise of a level greater than the masked speech produced a sharp depression in the loudness of that speech, analogous to the depression of brightness evident in Fig. 6.8, though, in Pollack's experiment, of lesser severity. Also, if the noise and speech are presented dichotically, Egan (1948) has found that noise at an intermediate level will often *increase* the loudness of speech heard in the other ear.

These phenomena all show that the sensation of change *per se* is not derived from the perception of a difference in the absolute magnitudes of the stimuli; rather, local differences in absolute magnitude are inferred from perceived change. The relation between the intensity of the sensation experienced and the magnitude of the physical stimulus is therefore more complex than a simple mapping; and that additional complexity must be realized within the brain.

The complexity of the examples presented becomes comprehensible, in a qualitative sense at least, once it is realized that perception is differentially coupled to the physical stimulus, so that only *changes* in that stimulus, temporal and spatial, are relevant to what is seen. There is no *absolute* perception at all. This is most forcefully shown, perhaps, by Land's phenomenon.

6.3.8 **Land's phenomenon**

Two black and white photographs are taken of the same scene, one through a red filter (e.g. Wratten No. 24) and one through a green (e.g. Wratten No. 58). These two photographs are printed on a transparent medium and projected, exactly superposed, on the same screen. The photograph taken through the red filter is projected with light of the same red spectrum, while the photograph taken through the green filter is projected with white light through a neutral density filter chosen to match the attenuation of the red filter. So, every part of the combined image is illuminated with some mixture of red and white light in varying proportions. *Yet one sees a nearly full range of colours!*

Land (1959) originally demonstrated this phenomenon with a picture of a bowl of fruit. That choice arguably helps the illusion because everyone knows that bananas are yellow and that grapes are either pale green or (in Land's picture) purple-black. I demonstrate the phenomenon with Rafael's *St. George and the Dragon.* St George's armour, which is bright blue in the original, appears black in the red and white synthesis; but there is otherwise a full range of colours from green to red and brown. The colours appear desaturated relative to the original; and this ought not to be surprising because taking only *two* photographs through coloured filters implies a loss of one-third of the information that would otherwise be available in a trichromatic system. What *is* surprising is that when that information is re-presented on the screen as a mixture of red and white light, the implicit loss of information leads, not to an acute restriction of the range of colours seen, but rather to an apparent loss of saturation.

The translation from the spectrum of the light in the visual image to the colour which is seen is much more complex than one might at first suppose. Important in that translation are variations in contrast. *St. George and the Dragon* is rich in contrast, which combines with variations in the saturation of the red/white mixture of light to create the perception of a range of colours. But if the two transparencies are less than accurately focused, or if their registration is poor, the critical variations in contrast are attenuated and the demonstration fails.

In view of the complexity of the relationship between the stimulus and the percept, especially as revealed by Land's phenomenon, I do not think it helpful to think of the intensity of sensation as corresponding to any level of neural activity anywhere within the brain. If the stimulus is especially simple—a flash of light in the dark—then stimulus magnitude correlates perfectly with change in stimulus input, and neural variables can be found which appear to correlate well with brightness as experienced by a subject. As soon as the light to be matched is surrounded by another luminance, that happy correspondence fails. Brightness then depends on the relation between stimulus and surround luminances in a manner which is not at present understood, but is possibly differential. When colour varies as well, the perceptual process appears yet more complex.

Physiological studies do not illuminate the problem of measuring sensation. A different approach is needed, an exclusively psychological one. I therefore turn to a critique of the specifically psychological content of Stevens' work.

7 Scaling sensation

It is clear from the complexity of the examples cited in the previous chapter that sensation has, in the first instance, to be studied at a psychological level of description. At this level Stevens asserted '. . . the sensation S is proportional to the stimulus X raised to a power β' (Stevens 1957b, p. 162, replacing Stevens' Ψ, S, and n with S, X, and β, respectively). This assertion applies specifically to prothetic continua on which, Stevens asserted, ratios are meaningful at both the subjective and the physical level of description. On these continua the 'correct' measure of sensation is given by ratio-scaling techniques, principally magnitude estimation. With these techniques the experimenter is asking the direct question: 'How loud does this tone sound to you?' Stevens argued that we should take the subject's answer at its face value. The assertion quoted is a conclusion drawn from a large body of that kind of experimental work. In this chapter I examine its validity.

7.1 MATHEMATICAL DERIVATION OF STEVENS' POWER LAW

The empirical generalization which Stevens actually drew from his data was '. . . equal stimulus ratios tend to produce equal sensation ratios' (Stevens 1957b, p. 162). He meant, of course, equal ratios of magnitude estimates. From this generalization (together with the assumption that numbers are properly assigned to sensations in Stevens' ratio-scaling experiments) it follows that, *if a scale of sensation exists*, it must be a ratio scale related to the physical measure of the stimulus by a power function of the form of eqn 1.5. But, as will appear in the next chapter, it is not necessary that such a scale exist.

Consider two stimuli of physical magnitudes X and aX, where both a and X are at our disposal. According to Stevens' empirical generalization, these two stimuli have subjective values S and bS, with the physical stimulus ratio a always transposing into the same subjective ratio b; that is to say, the subjective ratio b depends on a, but not on X. Treating S and b as functions of the variables X and a, and taking both those variables to be continuous, the relation between the two subjective values can be expressed in the form

$$S(aX) = b(a)S(X), \qquad (7.1)$$

and it is known (Azcél 1966, Chapter 2) that the only continuous function $S(X)$ satisfying this functional relation is[1]

$$S = cX^{\beta}, \qquad (7.2)$$

[1] Put $X=1$ in eqn 7.1 so that $b(a) = S(a)/S(1)$. Then eqn 7.1 can be rewritten as

$$S(aX)/S(1) = \{S(a)/S(1)\}\{S(X)/S(1)\}.$$

Let $y(X) = \ln[S(X)/S(1)]$. Then eqn 7.1 further reduces to

$$y(aX) = y(a) + y(X).$$

Now put $u = \ln a$, $v = \ln X$, and $y(X) = f(\ln X) = f(v)$; then

$$f(u+v) = f(u) + f(v)$$

which admits only $f(v) = \beta v$ amongst continuous solutions (Azcél 1966, Chapter 2). Inverting the substitutions leads to eqn 7.2.

where c and β are constants (see also Luce 1959, Theorem 1). Substituting eqn 7.2 into 7.1 gives

$$b = a^{\beta}; \tag{7.3}$$

this makes β independent of the units of measurement at both physical and subjective levels.

Accepting Stevens' empirical generalization (which is very well supported; Stevens and Galanter (1957) reported evidence from 11 different stimulus attributes, four of them metathetic, and from several different experimental procedures, and Stevens (1975, p. 15) lists typical power law exponents for a total of 33 different continua) and accepting also the hypothesis that sensation is measurable, Stevens Power Law (eqn 7.2) follows inexorably. But it nevertheless remains to be seen whether all the implications of that equation are actually fulfilled in nature. In this chapter I examine one implication in particular.

If sensation is properly measured on a ratio scale, it has a unique zero and only the unit of measurement is at our disposal. As an example, one can weigh a sack of potatoes in pounds or in kilograms. The weight of the potatoes is the same whichever unit of measurement is used, and zero pounds (an empty sack) always equates to zero kilograms. The unique zero is obviously necessary if ratios are to be invariant under changes of scale. The ratio between the weights of two sacks of potatoes is then independent of the unit of measurement because changing from pounds to kilograms changes the numerical expressions of the two weights in exactly the same proportion.

Now it is meaningful to talk, not only about the *ratio* of the weights of two sacks of potatoes, but also about their *difference* (and at this point I need to explain that, for the time being, I specifically mean an *extensive*[2] ratio scale). Given a ratio scale of (extensive) measurement, one can not only multiply and divide, one can also add and subtract. Stevens has shown that mental multiplication and division, as revealed in the behaviour of magnitude estimates, conform satisfactorily to the dictates of his Power Law. What about addition and subtraction?

7.2 MAGNITUDE ESTIMATION OF DIFFERENCES

Beck and Shaw (1967) asked their subjects to judge the 'distance' between the loudnesses of a pair of 1 kHz tones in relation to the distance between the loudnesses of a standard pair, a distance arbitrarily called 100. The tones were presented for 1 s each with 0.5 s between the members of each pair and 2 s between the standard and the comparison pairs. The standard pair was re-presented before each comparison pair to be judged.

The particular levels of the tones that made up each comparison pair are set out in Table 7.1, together with the median magnitude estimates (of 'distance') from a group of 28 subjects who judged each pair four times each. The standard and comparison pairs were presented twice in the order <soft, loud> and twice in the opposite order <loud, soft>. The comparison pairs were selected to have loudness differences equal to 5, 10, 15, and 20 sones,

[2] Luce and Narens (1985) have shown how to construct ratio scales which *do not* represent extensive measurement, the kind of ratio-scale measurement that is familiar from the measurement of many physical quantities. The contribution which their non-extensive ratio scales might make to the measurement of sensation is considered shortly.

and each of these loudness differences was realized by four pairs of tones located respectively in the lowest, lower-middle, upper-middle, and highest part of a stimulus range that ran from 30 to 86.6 dB SPL. If Stevens' Power Law applies to the judgment of differences in loudness, then all 5 (and, respectively, 10, 15, and 20) sone pairs should elicit substantially the same numerical estimates, independent of the absolute levels of the constituent stimuli. But, as is immediately clear from Table 7.1, those stimulus pairs located at higher sound pressure levels elicited systematically smaller numerical estimates of distance.

Table 7.1 Tone pairs and median magnitude estimates of loudness distances from the experiment by Beck and Shaw (1967)

Interval in sones	Location on stimulus scale	Stimuli in dB SPL	Difference in dB	Median magnitude estimates
5	Lowest	30.0, 64.7	34.7	100
	Lower-middle	63.3, 73.3	10.0	60
	Upper-middle	79.2, 83.3	4.1	25
	Highest	83.3, 86.6	3.3	25
10	Lowest	35.8, 74.4	38.6	175
	Lower-middle	50.0, 76.0	26.0	100
	Upper-middle	73.3, 83.3	10.0	75
	Highest	79.2, 86.6	7.4	75
15	Lowest	30.0, 79.7	39.7	225
	Lower-middle	40.0, 80.1	40.1	200
	Upper-middle	50.0, 81.0	31.0	150
	Highest	73.3, 86.6	13.3	125
20	Lowest	30.0, 83.7	43.7	300
	Lower-middle	40.0, 84.1	44.1	260
	Upper-middle	58.1, 85.7	27.6	190
	Highest	63.3, 86.6	23.3	160

This experiment was repeated by Dawson (1971) using 1 kHz tones and also areas of circles presented on cards; by Curtis *et al.* (1968) with lifted weights; and by Curtis (1970) with luminous discs. Dawson asked his subjects first to estimate the subjective magnitudes of single stimuli, and then of the sums and differences of pairs of stimuli. His results are less clear than those of Beck and Shaw. In the first place the estimate of the *sum* of two sensations will tend to be dominated by whichever stimulus contributes the greater impression, and no great deviation from the Power Law is to be expected. In the second place, Dawson did not select different pairs of stimuli for judgment, as Beck and Shaw had done, that had a common calculated difference in sensation. Nevertheless, Dawson's data on the estimation of differences in visual size replicate Beck and Shaw's finding, as also does a subset of his estimates of differences in loudness, judgments of pairs corresponding to an approximately 30 sone difference selected by Stevens (1971, p. 432, Fig. 4). Stevens summed up these data in the words:

As an interval of a constant size moves up the scale of the continuum, the constant interval is judged to be smaller and smaller. (Stevens 1971, p. 431)

That is to say, the scale of sensation derived from magnitude estimates does not have extensive ratio-scale properties.

7.3 NON-EXTENSIVE RATIO-SCALE MEASUREMENT

Technically, 'measurement' means assigning numbers to the objects or entities on a continuum so that empirical relations between the objects are represented by arithmetical relations between the corresponding numbers. For example, two rods can be placed end to end to create a longer length. That operation, known as *concatenation*, is represented numerically by addition; the length of the combination is equal to the arithmetic sum of their individual lengths. Empirical concatenation can be accomplished with other continua as well. One luminance can be superposed on another, as also can two noise processes; two weights can be put into the same scale pan. In these cases the resulting scale is determined up to an arbitrary choice of unit. Length can be measured in both inches and centimetres. Changing from one unit to another simply multiplies all the numbers by a constant. A scale of measurement which is determined up to an arbitrary choice of unit is a *ratio scale* and if, in addition, concatenation is properly represented by numerical addition, it is an *extensive* ratio scale.

The point of these remarks is that Luce and Narens (1985), building on earlier results by Narens and Luce (1976) and Cohen and Narens (1979; summarized in Luce and Narens, 1983), have shown that ratio scales can be defined, up to the choice of scale unit, which do not admit arithmetic addition but, instead, incorporate some other binary operation on pairs of numbers. Such ratio scales are not extensive.

Let $f(z)$ be a strictly increasing function of z, while $f(z)/z$ is strictly decreasing. Then

$$x \oplus y = yf(x/y) \tag{7.4}$$

defines a binary operation on x and y. Under a change of scale unit, x and y become cx and cy. Substituting in eqn 7.4,

$$(cx) \oplus (cy) = cyf(cx/cy) = cyf(x/y), \tag{7.5}$$

so that the change of unit is exactly reflected in the resultant of the binary operation. The scale is a ratio scale. The double constraint on $f(z)$ ensures that the binary operation is monotone; that is, if either x or y increases, so also does their combination $x \oplus y$. But the binary operation is arithmetic addition only in the case that $f(z) = 1 + z$ (i.e. $yf(x/y) = x + y$).

Many other choices of $f(z)$ are possible for which arithmetic addition has no meaning as the combination of two numbers x and y. If loudness were measurable on one of these non-extensive ratio scales, then, although 'sums' and 'differences' of two loudnesses would still be meaningful, they would not be correctly measured by the arithmetic sum or difference of their sone values. Instead the 'difference' between two sone values s_1 and s_2 would have to be defined as that number y which satisfies

$$s_1 \oplus y = yf(s_1/y) = s_2 \tag{7.6}$$

and, depending on the choice of $f(z)$, y might decrease for constant arithmetic difference $(s_2 - s_1)$ as s_1 moves up the scale of the continuum, in accordance with Stevens' generalization quoted above. This opens the possibility that the numerical assignment of numbers to single tones and the judgment of sums and differences of loudness between two tones (Beck and Shaw 1967; Dawson 1971) might simultaneously be concordant with some ratio scale other than the well-known scale of extensive measurement.

There are, as yet, no known natural examples of quantities measurable on non-extensive ratio scales. Although there are physical continua which do not admit empirical concatenation (in the manner in which two rods can be placed end to end), measurement on those continua can be defined in other ways. For example, the temperature of the mixture of two bodies of the same fluid has a temperature equal to a weighted average of the temperatures of the constituents. Other physical measures can be defined by conjoint measurement (Luce and Tukey 1964); the rationale is very clearly explained by Narens and Luce (1986). Physical applications of such methods lead to scales equivalent to that of extensive measurement. So the non-extensive ratio scales that Luce and Narens (1985) have defined constitute a family of merely mathematical possibilities with, as yet, no natural applications.

If the numerical assignment of numbers to single sensations on the one hand and the judgment of sums and differences of sensation on the other can jointly be accommodated by some non-extensive ratio scale, then the binary operations incorporated in that scale must somehow be realized in the underlying psychophysical processes. It is not a practical proposition to determine the form of such a scale directly by multiplication of experiments comparing estimations of single stimuli with those of sums and differences, because the precision of such experimental comparisons is too poor. Such experiments are able to show that certain specific scales (e.g. the scale of extensive measurement; Beck and Shaw 1967) will not suffice; but the scale which does apply, if one exists, will have to be discovered indirectly by exploration of the underlying process. This is demonstrated in the remainder of this chapter by looking at the experimental work which followed on from the original discovery by Beck and Shaw (1967).

The initial idea to be explored is that the numbers uttered by subjects in magnitude estimation experiments are not directly proportional to the sensations they experience, but have themselves a subjective value. When a subject is asked to estimate the sum or difference of two sensations, the arithmetic addition or subtraction is realized at some intermediate stage and the result expressed as a number whose subjective value is proportional to the intermediate sum or difference. But that kind of scheme is equivalent to a particular form of function $f(z)$, with the resultant non-extensive ratio scale describing the numbers actually uttered as responses by the subjects.

7.4 THE SUBJECTIVE VALUES OF NUMBERS

Suppose that the numbers uttered as magnitude estimates are related to internal sensation by a further power law transform, that is, the numbers are values on an artificial continuum subject to its own power law with its own exponent. Stevens and his colleagues have repeatedly shown that, not only can numbers be systematically assigned to stimuli (Fig. 5.1), but equally stimuli can be adjusted to match given numbers (Fig. 5.3). If numbers behave like an artificial stimulus attribute, then magnitude estimation and production are simply species of cross-modality matching (Fig. 5.4). And if the numbers uttered by subjects have subjective values to which they are related by a power law of the form eqn 7.2, then the exponent of that power law provides an additional free parameter with which to accommodate the deviant estimates of differences in sensation. This idea was first suggested by Attneave (1962) and realized as a model for magnitude estimation by Curtis *et al.* (1968).

Suppose that attribute X with exponent β_x is matched to number N with exponent β_n. Then, rewriting eqn 5.8, the matching relation should be

$$N = X^{\beta_x/\beta_n}, \tag{7.7}$$

and the estimates of typical exponents for magnitude estimation in Table 7.1 are properly estimates of β_x/β_n. Suppose now that subjects are asked to estimate the difference between the sensations elicited by two stimuli of magnitudes X_1 and X_2. Those sensations will have values $X_1^{\beta_x}$ and $X_2^{\beta_x}$ respectively (eqn 7.2) and the difference between the sensations will be equated to the subjective value N^{β_n} of some number N. That means that

$$N^{\beta_n} = |X_1^{\beta_x} - X_2^{\beta_x}|,$$

or

$$N = |X_1^{\beta_x} - X_2^{\beta_x}|^{1/\beta_n}. \tag{7.8}$$

It is easy to see that a change in the scale unit on the physical continuum can be balanced by an equivalent change in the scale unit for the estimates N. If X is replaced by aX, then N needs to be replaced by $a^{\beta_x/\beta_n}N$; $(a^{\beta_x/\beta_n}N)^{\beta_n} = |(aX_1)^{\beta_x} - (aX_2)^{\beta_x}|$. So the scale type of N is still ratio. But it is a non-extensive ratio scale. If X_1 is assigned the number N_1, then, from eqn 7.7, $N_1^{\beta_n} = X_1^{\beta_x}$ and, substituting in eqn 7.8 (and replacing '–' by '+'),

$$N_1 \oplus N_2 = (N_1^{\beta_n} + N_2^{\beta_n})^{1/\beta_n}, \tag{7.9}$$

which is equivalent to the function (cf. eqn 7.4 above)

$$f(z) = (1 + z^{\beta_n})^{1/\beta_n}. \tag{7.10}$$

Curtis *et al.* (1968) asked the same 10 subjects to estimate both the heaviness of eight single weights spaced in approximate geometric series from 10 to 310 g, and also the difference in heaviness between each of the 28 possible pairs of those weights. The weights were suspended on lengths of fishing line below a horizontal surface which excluded them from the subjects' view. This precluded the judgments of heaviness being compromised by the size of the weights. The equations fitted to the estimates of heaviness of single weights and of differences between heavinesses were not eqns 7.7 and 7.8 above, but

$$N = X^{\beta_x/\beta_n} + c, \tag{7.11}$$

and

$$N = |X_1^{\beta_x} - X_2^{\beta_x}|^{1/\beta_n} + d; \tag{7.12}$$

that is, Curtis *et al.* had *three* additional free parameters at their disposal to fit simultaneously magnitude estimates of both single weights and of differences. Equations 7.11 and 7.12 provided a good account of their data with exponents $\beta_x/\beta_n = 0.746$ (from the heavinesses of single weights) and $\beta_x = 0.645$ and $\beta_n = 0.876$ (from the differences in heaviness between pairs of weights). These exponent values are satisfactorily consistent ($0.645/0.876 = 0.736$), but the scale of measurement now involves two degrees of freedom and is only an interval scale. There followed a series of similar experiments with other stimulus attributes by Curtis, Rule and their colleagues. The exponent values estimated from these experiments are listed in Table 7.2.

Table 7.2 Power law exponents for stimulus attributes and for number estimated by Curtis, Rule, and colleagues from comparisons of magnitude estimates for single stimuli and for differences between stimuli

Stimulus attribute	Source	β_x	β_n	β_x/β_n	
				Pred.	Obtd
Area of circles	Rule *et al.* (1970)	0.65	0.60	1.09	1.09
Area of circles[1]	Rule and Curtis (1973b)	0.39	0.60	0.66	0.67
Grey papers on	Curtis and Rule (1972)				
light background					
high standard		0.35	0.57	0.61	0.55
low standard		0.38	0.79	0.48	0.41
dark background					
high standard		0.15	0.68	0.22	0.15
low standard		0.14	0.67	0.21	0.14
Grey papers	Rule *et al.* (1974)				
lightness		0.29	0.49	0.60	0.57
darkness		−0.35	0.55	−0.64	−0.55
Luminous discs	Curtis (1970)	0.16	0.75	0.21	0.26
Roughness of emery paper[1]	Rule and Curtis (1973b)	0.71	0.57	1.25	1.26
Successive durations of red light	Curtis and Rule (1977)	1.00	0.90	1.11	1.04
Weight	Curtis *et al.* (1968)	0.65	0.88	0.74	0.75
		0.61[2]	0.93[2]	0.65[2]	0.75
Weight[1]	Rule and Curtis (1973b)	0.73	0.70	1.04	1.09

[1] Experimental data from Marks and Cain (1972).
[2] Alternative estimates from non-metric analysis by Rule *et al.* (1970).

Several different methods have been used in calculating the estimates in Table 7.2, principally least squares with weights proportional to $(\text{mean})^{-2}$ and, latterly, a non-metric analysis derived ultimately from Kruskal (1964; see Rule and Curtis 1982). Apart from the fact that the scale values are constrained by eqns 7.11 and 7.12, there is much in common with Anderson's (1970, 1972) functional measurement (see pp. 23–4). The data from the original paper by Curtis *et al.* (1968) have been analysed by both of these methods and a comparison of the two sets of estimates in Table 7.2 gives some idea of their concordance.

The estimates for β_n range from 0.49 to 0.93. To those estimates should be added the value 0.83 from Popper *et al.* (1986), derived from the estimation of loudness differences, and 0.78 from Curtis and Mullin (1975) and 1.33 from Marks (1978b; see below), both these latter two values being derived from the estimation of sums of loudnesses. The range of values of β_n is comparable to that obtained from straightforward magnitude estimation of single stimuli (see pp. 74–5), probably because the principal source of variation in the value of the exponent in either kind of experiment is the idiosyncratic use of numbers by different subjects. This is suggested by two studies. Rule and Curtis (1977) looked at the correlations between individual estimates of β_x and β_n from 30 subjects judging the difference of area between two circles and the difference of numerousness between two arrays of dots displayed within the same circular area. The two values of β_x from each subject correlated only 0.07, but the two values of β_n 0.51. Rule and Markley (1971) effectively repeated this study (though their work was published first) with the additional comparison that each of 48 subjects matched each attribute, area and numerousness, to force of hand grip as well. The correlations of β_n between attributes were 0.46 for the use of number and 0.70 for pressure of hand grip, suggesting again that the principal source of variation is the individual subject's use of the response continuum.

It needs to be emphasized also that the model implicit in eqns 7.11 and 7.12 (with '+' substituted for '–' in eqn 7.12) applies to the addition of loudnesses (and presumably to addition on other continua such as brightness) only when the two components do not fuse. A very easy experiment which might seem appropriate to test the model is binaural loudness summation. Marks (1978a) has reported such a study under conditions exactly comparable to the experiment (Marks 1978b) mentioned above. When two tones of different frequencies (2 kHz and 5 kHz) falling into different critical bands, so that they are heard as distinct components, are presented simultaneously (and also binaurally), the loudness of the combination is related to the loudnesses of the individual frequency components by eqns 7.11 and 7.12. But when two tones of the same frequency, but different SPLs, are presented simultaneously, one to the right ear and one to the left, they fuse and their combined loudness is equal to the sum of their individual loudnesses as assessed by magnitude estimation of single tones (Marks 1978a).

The concordance between the predicted and obtained values of β_x/β_n in Table 7.2 is rather good, but it needs to be emphasized that all the exponent values involved were obtained from equations (eqns 7.11 and 7.12) with the added constant. This additional free parameter appears to be necessary to achieve a satisfactory fit. Rule and Curtis (1973b) were reanalysing data from experiments by Marks and Cain (1972) which the original authors had fit with eqns 7.7 and 7.8, without the added constants. That original fit was less than satisfactory, principally because the value of β_x/β_n predicted, using eqn 7.8, from the magnitude estimation of differences (area: 0.51; roughness: 0.90; weight: 0.80) was systematically less than the corresponding value for single stimuli (0.75, 1.20, 1.11, respectively) obtained from eqn 7.7. But the inclusion of those added constants in the formulae means that we are no longer talking about power law transforms of ratio scales as advocated by Stevens (1975).

So far, the idea of a subjective scaling of number has been used simply as an excuse for introducing three additional free parameters (β_n, c, d in eqns 7.11 and 7.12) into a model which previously failed to fit the data. It may well be that eqn 7.12 reflects some systematic non-linearity in the way that people use numbers when they are called upon to use them intuitively. But it would be desirable to have collateral evidence to support that idea directly.

7.5 COLLATERAL EVIDENCE ON THE SUBJECTIVE VALUES OF NUMBERS

The idea that numbers have subjective values increasing as some non-linear compressive function of the number began with Attneave (1962, p. 626), who asked 14 behavioural scientists: 'Suppose we agree that *one* is a very small number and that a *million* is a very large number. Now: give me a good example of a medium size number.' The median reply was 100 000 and the mean 186 575. If that mean be taken as a bisection of the subjective range between 1 and 1 000 000, then the subjective value of number grows as the 0.41 power. But, of course, Attneave's demonstration might do no more than determine a numerical value for the label 'medium sized'.

7.5.1 **Conjoint scaling of number**

A more subtle technique is exemplified by Rule and Curtis (1973a). On each trial the subject first lifted a standard weight of 243 g which was called 10. The subject then lifted a comparison weight (in the range 35–243 g) and was given a number (an integer in the range 1–9) and was then asked whether the heaviness which corresponded to the number was greater or less then the heaviness of the weight. The frequencies with which each number was judged greater than each weight were put through a non-metric analysis which estimated power law exponents for both number and weight under the assumption that the frequency of judging the number greater than the weight increased monotonically with the excess of the scale value of the number over that of the weight. The non-metric analysis delivered estimates of 0.57 for weight and 0.63 for number which predict an exponent of 0.90 (= 0.57/0.63) in a conventional magnitude estimation experiment when numbers are simply matched to weights. That prediction was confirmed in a further experiment with the same subjects. It differs from the value (1.45) given in Table 5.1 because in the present experiment the weights were hidden from view (see p. 22; Warren and Warren 1956).

Similar studies scaling number with area had previously been published by Rule (1969, 1971). The data from these earlier studies was analysed with a discriminability model (case II-D of Torgerson's 1958 Law of Categorical Judgment). The first study (Rule 1969) gave a logarithmic relation between number and its subjective value over the range 1 to 10, and the second (Rule 1971) a power law with exponent 0.49. The compressive shape of those relations was confirmed in a further experiment (Rule 1972) in which subjects were given three numbers in the range 1 to 10 (e.g. 3, 5, 7) and asked whether the top (7) or bottom (3) number was 'closer' to the middle one (5). Subjects were told: 'Do not determine the answer by doing any arithmetic, but answer the questions by giving your own impression' (Rule 1972, p. 97). And the subjects obliged by saying that the top number was more often closer to the middle one than was the bottom number.

7.5.2 **Random emission of numbers**

Yet another approach to the problem of the subjective value of number is exemplified by Banks and Hill (1974) who asked subjects to utter numbers rapidly and at random, without any specific upper limit. The first 26 numbers thus uttered were recorded, rearranged in rank order, and the relationship between rank order and numerical value examined. That relationship, estimated from a group of subjects, tended to be logarithmic (so that the density of numbers uttered decreased inversely with respect to absolute numerical value), but in some circumstances it approximated a power function with exponent 0.6 or 0.67. That value of exponent agrees with the estimates from the other procedures described above; but at the same time the data recorded by Banks and Hill may be no more than another instance of Poulton's (1979, pp. 783–6) 'logarithmic bias', testifying only to the way in which subjects typically use numbers or believe they are expected to use them.

There is always the problem of distinguishing between a true subjective value that varies as some (presently unknown) function of real number and artifactual values that merely reflect the common usage of numbers or the possible failure of some premise on which the analysis rests. This problem arises because the number itself is a perfectly precise stimulus and, because of prior training in arithmetic, presents none of the uncertainties of judgment associated with real stimulus continua. Moreover, the 'natural' choice of a magnitude estimation procedure fails to resolve the issue.

7.5.3 **Magnitude estimation of number**

Suppose, for the sake of argument, the subjective size of numbers to increase as a power law with an exponent about 0.5. Then the number twice as large as 100 would have to be 400 (because $\sqrt{400} = 2 \times \sqrt{100}$); except that when the phrase 'twice as large' appears in the experimenter's instructions, it actually means 1.41 times as large. 'Twice' is a number and therefore subject to the 0.5 power law; it is equivalent subjectively to $\sqrt{2}$, and the number $\sqrt{2}$ times as large as 100 is 200 (because $\sqrt{200} = \sqrt{2} \times \sqrt{100}$). To get the number which is *subjectively* twice as large as 100 the experimenter would have to ask for the number *four* times as large (because $2 = \sqrt{4}$) and that, of course, is 400 (because $\sqrt{400} = \sqrt{4} \times \sqrt{100}$). It follows that in a conventional magnitude estimation experiment with numbers the subjective compression of the stimuli according to the presumed 0.5 power law is exactly balanced by the inverse expansion of the responses. Such an experiment ought to return the exponent to 1, and an experiment by Rosner (1965) confirms this point.

> This is an experiment to test your reactions to numbers. Whenever I say the number '37', you must respond with '83'. If I give you a number that seems 8 times larger than 37, you must respond with 664, which is 8 times larger than 83. If I say a number that seems about half as large as 37, you must say 42. In other words, you should reply with a number that bears the same proportion to 83 as the number I say bears to 37. Now I will read numbers to you very quickly. Answer just as fast as you can. You won't have time to calculate anything so do your best and don't worry about being consistent. (Rosner 1965, p. 42)

The subjects' responses gave no indication of any non-linearity; and one ought not to expect it. By the same argument, Rosner's experiment is irrelevant to the question of a subjective scale of number.

7.6 INTERIM SUMMARY

It is convenient at this point to summarize the argument so far:

1. If numerical magnitude estimates establish a valid scale of sensation, then that scale must be a *ratio scale*, because 'equal stimulus ratios tend to produce equal sensation ratios' (Stevens 1957b, p. 162), and the relation of sensation to the physical magnitude of the stimulus must be a power law.
2. If that ratio scale is extensive, not only are ratios of sensation meaningful, but *differences* as well, because an extensive ratio scale also has interval scale properties.
3. It then follows that magnitude estimates of differences in sensation should conform to the same power law as estimates of ratios. This is contrary to experimental observation.
4. Estimation of differences between sensations requires the subject to do mental arithmetic and experimental observation tells us that this arithmetic does not take place at the level of the numerical responses. It might, however, take place at some internal level intermediate between stimulus and response. That idea (eqns 7.11 and 7.12) has proved capable of accommodating the data so far with numbers having subjective values increasing as a power function with an exponent variously estimated within the range 0.49 to 0.93.
5. That exponent value is sufficiently variable from one experiment to another to require collateral confirmation. Such confirmation cannot be obtained from a conventional magnitude estimation experiment (where numbers are used as both stimuli and responses) because any non-linearity between the objective and subjective values of numbers cancels; and other less direct procedures are arguably confounded with prior bias in the use of numbers.
6. The idea that the addition and subtraction of sensations takes place at some intermediate level between the physical stimulus and the numerical response is equivalent to one instance of a non-extensive ratio scale applicable to the numerical estimates. There might be other non-extensive ratio scales able to accommodate simultaneously both estimates of single sensations and estimates of sums and differences of sensation.

There are, however, two further lines of argument which question whether the apparent success so far demonstrated in modelling the data reflects any systematic psychological reality.

7.7 SUMMATION OF SIMULTANEOUS AND SUCCESSIVE COMPONENTS

All the experiments so far examined in this chapter have asked for an estimate of the sum or difference of sensation between two component stimuli presented *successively*. Figure 7.1(a) presents diagrammatically an outline model for such experiments; it shows (eqns 7.7 and 7.8) two stimuli, X_1 and X_2, added or subtracted after a power law transform with exponent β_x, followed by a second power law transform with inverse exponent β_n to generate the numerical response. It is equivalent to a non-extensive ratio scale based on the function $f(z) = (1 + z^{\beta_n})^{1/\beta_n}$. But when the stimuli are pure tones it is a very simple matter to present them simultaneously; and when two tones of the same frequency are presented binaurally, they fuse into a single percept which is differently located in space according as the binaural components have different intensities. This is a situation where one might expect the combination rule to vary, and Marks (1978a,b, 1979a,b) has published a substantial series of experiments exploring that very issue.

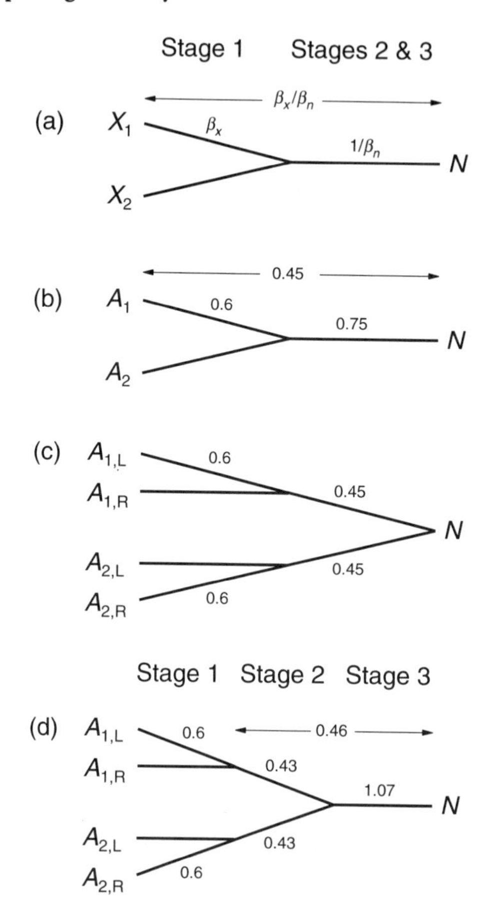

Fig. 7.1 Four diagrams setting out different models for the judgment of the sum or difference of two sensations.

If two tones are sufficiently close in frequency that they fall within the same critical band, the loudness of the two together depends only on their total energy, as though only a single tone had been presented. That result is well known (Scharf 1961; Marks 1979a) and I shall be concerned hereafter either with two tones of sufficiently different frequencies that an energy-level interaction can be discounted, or with two tones presented to different ears. Marks (1978b, Expt I) chose frequencies of 2 kHz and 5 kHz to obviate any possible interaction at the level of the critical bands. Simultaneous compounds of these two frequencies were presented binaurally for 1 s to each of 15 subjects with instructions to judge the total loudness of the compound. Extrapolating from the results reported by Curtis and Rule (Table 7.2), one would expect the appropriate equation to be

$$N = |A_1^{\beta_a} + A_2^{\beta_a}|^{1/\beta_n}, \tag{7.13}$$

with the minus sign in eqn 7.8 replaced by a plus. All 36 combinations of six different levels of the two tones were equally represented in the experiment, and since one of those levels was zero the experiment contains within itself control estimates of the loudness of each of the component tones presented by itself. Figure 7.2(a) plots the geometric mean estimates for particular levels of the 2 kHz component as a function of the level of the 5 kHz component.

The lines in Fig. 7.2(a) linking mean estimates for a common level of the 2 kHz tone tend to converge at high levels of the 5 kHz tone, indicating that the addition of constituent loudnesses does not take place at the level of the numerical estimates. By plotting the 4/3 power of the mean estimates Marks (1978b, p. 17, fig. 2) demonstrates an acceptable degree of parallelism between the transformed data, indicating additivity with respect to some intermediate subjective level. That intermediate subjective level increases as the 0.6 power of the amplitude of each constituent tone (i.e. $\beta_a = 0.6$), and the numerical estimates are related to that intermediate level as a 0.75 power, giving a combined 0.45 power for the control estimates of the loudness of single tones presented alone. All this is summarized in Fig. 7.1(b). The only difficulty in relation to previous work is that the subjective values of numbers appear here to be positively accelerated ($\beta_n = 1.33$), contrary to all previous experimental results.

If the two constituent tones are of the same frequency but of varying levels and are presented to opposite ears (note that this precludes energy-level summation within the critical band), the 0.6 power transform (β_a) is seen, but not the ensuing 0.75 ($1/\beta_n$). Marks (1978a) has demonstrated this for pure tones of 400 and 1000 Hz combined in a similar factorial array of independent levels. And if the two constituent tones of Fig. 7.2 are presented successively, rather than simultaneously, a single 0.45 power transform is seen, with addition at the level of the numerical estimates.

The data from this latter experiment (Marks 1978b, Expt III) are presented in the right-hand panel of Fig. 7.2. The experiment differed from its predecessor (left-hand panel) in only one respect: the components of each compound were presented *successively* for 1 s each with a 1 s interval between them. The same 15 subjects were used with instructions, as before, to judge total loudness. Notwithstanding this careful attention to comparability between the two experiments, the geometric mean estimates do not agree. More precisely, the control estimates of the 5 kHz tone presented alone (filled inverted triangles) *do* agree, approximately, with the similar control estimates in the left-hand panel, though the control estimates of the 2 kHz tone (other filled symbols) do not. Agreement between the two sets of estimates of the 5 kHz tones is to be expected, since the stimuli in question are identical, and suggests that the difference does not lie in a different use of number (again to be expected, since the same subjects were used). If those control estimates of the 5 kHz tone be excluded and the remaining estimates rescaled, those rescaled estimates can be shown to correspond, approximately, to the sum of the 0.45 powers of the constituent amplitudes (Marks, 1978b, p. 28, gives the exponent as 0.22 with respect to energy). Moreover, inspection of the right-hand panel suggests that the rescaling required is slight (Marks gives no exponent for this rescaling).

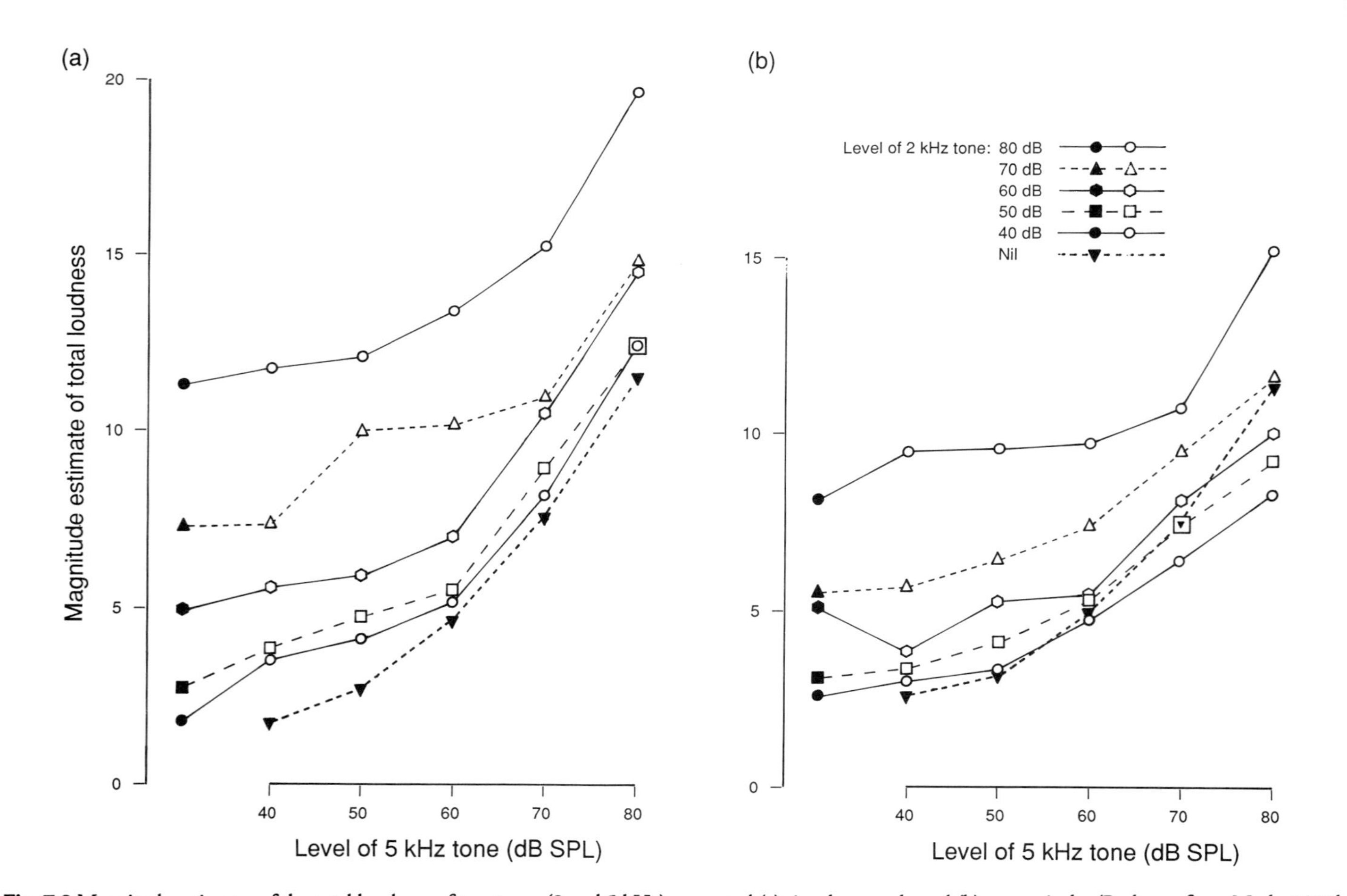

Fig. 7.2 Magnitude estimates of the total loudness of two tones (2 and 5 kHz) presented (a) simultaneously and (b) successively. (Redrawn from Marks 1978b, pp. 16 and 27.)

Finally, Marks (1979a) combines binaural combination of tones of the same frequency with differencing of successively presented components within the same experiment. Tones of 1 kHz at 15, 20, 30, 40, or 50 dB SPL were presented either monaurally or binaurally. Two such tones of 1 s duration were presented in succession with the usual 1 s interval between them and a request to estimate the difference in loudness. The experiment also included control estimates of a single tone. The results are summarized in Fig. 7.1(c). Binaural components combine as the 0.6 power of amplitude, as before (Marks 1978a), and the 0.45 powers of those binaural combinations are then differenced to give the numerical estimate. This means that successive components are differenced according to an approximate 0.27 power of amplitude, which approximates a scale proposed by Garner (1954a) based on equisection and fractionation judgments.[3]

With such profound differences as these between otherwise closely comparable experiments, introducing a subjective scale of number is no longer sufficient by itself. It is at the least necessary to distinguish between the judgment of sums and differences of sensation when the two stimuli are presented simultaneously and when they are presented successively, as Marks (1979b) does. Moreover, the difference between simultaneous and successive presentation of components is not specific to the judgment of loudness. Rule and Curtis (1985) have compared estimates of the average of two durations represented by two red lights. When the lights come on successively, with one light immediately following the other, their durations add linearly, as one would expect. But when they are presented simultaneously, either with common onset or common offset (Rule *et al.* 1983), but different durations, the combination rule has the form

$$t_{\text{ave}} = [(t_1{}^c + t_2{}^c)/2]^{1/c}, \tag{7.14}$$

with c greater than 1 (1.85, Curtis and Rule 1977; 1.51, Rule and Curtis 1985).

Marks (1978b, 1979a) has endeavoured to summarize his findings in a single model comprised of these three stages in cascade:

1. The first stage is specific to individual critical bands and individual ears; it describes the energy-wise combination of different frequency components within each critical band.
2. The second stage describes the loudness that is experienced from complex auditory stimuli with components in different critical bands and from binaural stimuli combining components from the two ears. This second stage sums the 0.3 power of the energy output from individual critical bands at the first stage (or the 0.6 power of amplitude, as in Fig. 7.1). It realizes the power law relation demonstrated by Stevens (e.g. Fig. 5.1) for magnitude estimation of the loudness of pure tones and noise. It corresponds to a non-extensive ratio scale based on the function

$$f_{\text{sim}}(z) = (1 + z^{\beta_{\text{sim}}})^{1/\beta_{\text{sim}}}, \tag{7.15}$$

where β_{sim} is estimated to be 1.33.

[3] I have simplified Marks' (1979a, pp. 277–82) account of these results. Differencing appears to be effected with respect to a 0.26 power of the stimulus amplitude, which is equivalent to following the 0.6 power transform (implicit in binaural combination) with a second transform of exponent 0.43 (see Fig. 7.1(d)). The best additivity amongst the difference scores is achieved with respect to a 0.93 power of the numerical estimates; that is to say, the estimated difference scores appear to be followed by a 1.07 power transform to give the numerical judgments. Combining the 0.43 and 1.07 power transforms gives an exponent of 0.46, very close to the 0.45 in Fig. 7.1(c).

3. The third stage describes the different power law relation that is obtained for the judgment of differences in loudness which necessarily involves the presentation of two stimuli in succession. It operates on the square root (0.45 power in Fig. 7.1) of the outputs from the second stage resulting from the different stimulus components. This third stage becomes evident when the subject is asked to perform some arithmetic with the sensations evoked by separate successive components. It corresponds to a non-extensive ratio scale based on the function

$$f_{\text{succ}}(z) = (1 + z^{\beta_{\text{succ}}})^{1/\beta_{\text{succ}}}, \tag{7.16}$$

where β_{succ} is about 0.93 (= 1/1.07, Fig. 7.1(d)).

4. These two stages assemble together as follows: the loudness of two tones presented successively is related to their individual loudnesses by

$$N_1 \oplus_{\text{succ}} N_2 = (N_1^{0.93} + N_2^{0.93})^{1.07}. \tag{7.17}$$

The loudnesses N_1 and N_2 are themselves each related to the loudnesses of monaural components by

$$N_{i,\text{L}} \oplus_{\text{sim}} N_{i,\text{R}} = (N_{i,\text{L}}^{2.17} + N_{i,\text{R}}^{2.17})^{0.46}, \tag{7.18}$$

where $\oplus_{\text{succ}}$ and $\oplus_{\text{sim}}$ denote two different binary operations defined with reference to $f_{\text{succ}}(z)$ and $f_{\text{sim}}(z)$, respectively. Combining eqns 7.17 and 7.18 into one formula gives

$$(N_{1,\text{L}} \oplus_{\text{sim}} N_{1,\text{R}}) \oplus_{\text{succ}} (N_{2,\text{L}} \oplus_{\text{sim}} N_{2,\text{R}})$$

$$= [(N_{1,\text{L}}^{2.17} + N_{1,\text{R}}^{2.17})^{0.43} + (N_{2,\text{L}}^{2.17} + N_{2,\text{R}}^{2.17})^{0.43}]^{1.07}, \tag{7.19}$$

where

$$N_{i,j} = A_{i,j}^{0.28}. \tag{7.20}$$

But the model contains an inherent arbitrariness. If the subject is judging single stimuli or compound stimuli with the components presented simultaneously, only one non-linear transform is effective giving, in the case of auditory stimuli, a loudness which grows as the 0.6 power of amplitude. But if the subject is asked to judge the difference in loudness between two successive auditory stimuli, an extra stage (Stage 3) is invoked which takes as its input the 0.5 power of the output from Stage 2. What happens to Stage 3 when only one stimulus is presented for judgment? With only a single stimulus Stage 3 should have one real input to which the additional 0.5 power transform applies and one zero input, giving an overall transform for the loudness of single stimuli of exponent 0.3 (eqn 7.20) with respect to amplitude (or 0.15 with respect to energy). So, in the judgment of single stimuli, it has to be that Stage 3 is bypassed; which is as much as to say that these two tasks, judging the sensations produced by single stimuli and judging the differences between two sensations, are carried out by two different ears. That is no explanation at all.

Note that the idea first proposed by Curtis *et al.* (1968; eqns 7.7 and 7.8) is not arbitrary in this manner. All judgments, whether of single sensations or of differences between sensations, are subject to two successive power transforms, the first pertaining to the attribute being judged, and the second specific to the numbers used as responses. The apparently divergent results obtained when subjects are asked to judge differences arise because the differencing operation is located in between these two transforms. But that model is tested in Table 7.2 only against successive presentations of the stimulus components; simultaneous presentation (Marks 1978b) gives different results.

7.8 INTRANSITIVITIES BETWEEN STIMULI AND SENSATIONS

I do not myself think that any cascade of power-law transforms, after the pattern of Fig. 7.1, can accommodate all the results from the different paradigms surveyed. Such a cascade is necessarily monotone—sensation always increases with physical stimulus magnitude—as also are all the non-extensive ratio scales identified by Luce and Narens (1985). There are now a sufficient number of counterexamples, in which an increase in stimulus magnitude generates a *decreased* estimate of sensation, that that kind of theory has to be abandoned.

7.8.1 **Summation of loudness**

I return to the experiment by Marks (1978b) in the right-hand panel of Fig. 7.2. That experiment combined six different levels, including zero, of a 2 kHz tone with the same set of levels of a 5 kHz tone, the two components being presented successively with an instruction to judge total loudness. The triangles in Fig. 7.2 are the estimated loudnesses of the 5 kHz tones by themselves, and at 60, 70, and 80 dB these estimated loudnesses exceed the judged 'total loudness' of the same 5 kHz tone in combination with a low level of the 2 kHz tone. There is also one inversion of the 2 kHz tone (at 60 dB, combined with the 5 kHz tone at 40 dB), but this may not be systematic.

In the next two chapters I examine an idea, first suggested by Torgerson (1961), that the judgment of a single stimulus in isolation is meaningless; all that can be judged is the relation between pairs of stimuli. In a conventional magnitude estimation experiment that idea must mean that each stimulus presented singly for judgment is nevertheless judged in relation to some other stimulus which is implicit in the context of the experiment; and I shall ultimately (Chapter 10) produce experimental evidence to show that the implicit context is provided chiefly by the stimulus presented on the preceding trial and the number assigned to it. In his early experiments S.S. Stevens used to present the standard stimulus as a point of reference before each variable. That provided a fixed context for each judgment, a context which materially affected the numerical estimates. Stevens (1956b, Figs 2 and 3) presents two examples, and Poulton (1968) has summarized the effects of different placements of the standard within the stimulus range as they were known at his time of writing. When, as is now common, different stimulus values are presented in sequence without any intervening standard, randomization of the order of presentation ensures that that context is substantially the same for all single stimuli (which explains why the judgments of single 5 kHz tones in Fig. 7.2(b) accord with the judgments of the same stimuli in Fig. 7.2(a)) and for all first members of successively presented pairs; but judgments of second members are carefully sorted according to the context (the first member of the pair) within which they were formulated. For that reason, judgments of successively presented pairs do not accord with judgments of single stimuli.

But if a 'pair' consists of two simultaneous auditory components, they effectively constitute a single stimulus requiring some extraneous basis for comparison like all other single stimuli. For this reason judgments of the total loudness of simultaneously presented components do not accord with judgments of the same components presented successively. Herein lies an alternative basis for accommodating, perhaps more simply than Marks (1979a), the complicated set of findings which he has published on the loudness of stimulus compounds.

7.8.2 **Binocular brightness matching**

The idea of relative judgment is further encouraged by a second intransitivity of sensation from Heinemann (1955). Figure 7.3 shows further binocular matching data from the same subject as Fig. 6.7. The brightness of a disc, 28′ diameter, exactly surrounded by an annulus of twice the size, presented to the right eye was matched to a comparison field (of the same size, but without any surround) viewed with the left eye. That stimulus configuration is shown in Fig. 7.4. The lines in Fig. 7.3 link matches of test field luminances to the same comparison luminance, but with the test field viewed against different surround luminances.

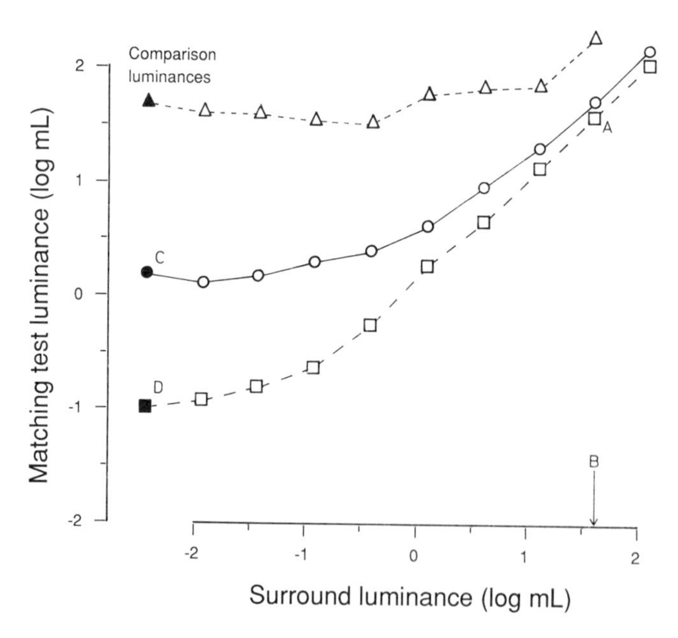

Fig. 7.3 Further binocular brightness matches from Heinemann (1955). The stimulus configuration was the same as in Fig. 6.7, but in these matches the test field luminance was adjusted to match a given comparison. The diagram plots the matching test field luminance against the luminance of the surround for three different comparison luminances. The data points A, B, C (see Fig. 7.4), and D constitute a specific intransitivity which is explained in the text. (Redrawn from Heinemann 1955, p. 93.)

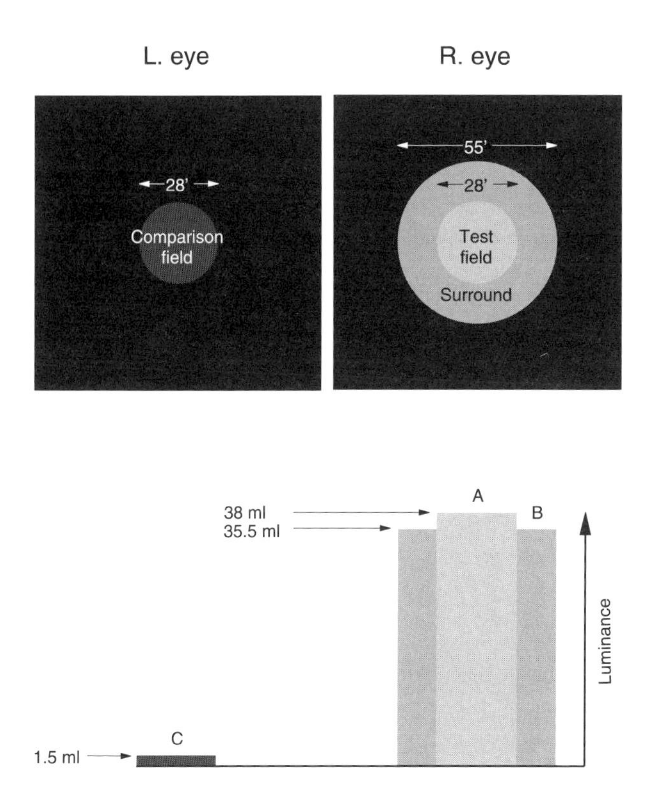

Fig. 7.4 The configuration of luminances as seen by the subject in Heinemann's (1955) experiment, with the luminances A, B, and C in Fig. 7.3 drawn to scale in the lower diagram.

As pointed out by Whittle (1994), test field luminance A has been adjusted against a surround luminance B (1.55 log mL) to match a comparison luminance D (–1 log mL) viewed without any surround. Luminance A is slightly brighter than B (by about 7 per cent). The comparison luminance D is less than the luminance C, less by more than 1 log unit. So, if C (also viewed in the dark) were to be compared with A, it would be judged much brighter (i.e. C >> A > B). But the luminance of B is more than 1 log unit above that of C and, if these two were to be compared, would be judged very much the brighter (i.e. C >> A > B >> C). These three luminances are shown drawn to scale in Fig. 7.4. The intransitivity results from the brightness of A being judged in relation to the surround luminance B, that is, inferred from the contrast between the two. This depresses the brightness of A so that it can be matched to a much lesser luminance D viewed in the dark. Context is of material importance in judging simultaneous, as well as successively presented, components.

7.8.3 **Fechner's paradox**

One final intransitivity seems to defy all rational explanation. It concerns the apparent brightness of a luminous target seen by both eyes, but with the retinal illuminance in one eye very much greater than in the other (one eye views the target though a neutral density filter). If the eye looking through the filter is closed, the total amount of light entering the eyes, one or the other, is lessened, but, for suitable values of retinal illuminance, the perceived brightness is increased.

Curtis and Rule (1980) had their subjects view two 3° diameter discs, one in each eye, through 2 mm artificial pupils and prisms so that they readily fused binocularly. For left eye luminances of 1838 and 3210 cd/m^2 the perceived brightness was at a minimum when the right eye luminance was about 10 cd/m^2, one 200th or 300th part of the left eye luminance. Perceived brightness was found to decrease as the right eye luminance was *increased* up to this value, which is about the top of the mesopic range within which both rod and cone systems are effective. The perceived brightness thereafter increased again with further increases in right eye luminance.

7.9 CONCLUSIONS

I, personally, do not think that the kinds of model surveyed in this chapter will ever support a reliable understanding of subjective sensation. The reason is that contrary results can always be accommodated by elaborating the hypothetical processing system, as Marks (1978b, 1979a; cf. Fig. 7.1) has done, and the experimental data are sufficiently imprecise that additional free parameters will usually save the cumulative body of existing ideas. So there is no way, within this framework of investigation, of asking with sufficient experimental precision whether the scales which are constructed do indeed represent fundamental entities in perceptual processing, or are merely artifacts of the particular experimental procedures from which they are derived.

What is needed are different kinds of experimental finding which apply a much greater torque to existing ideas. The three examples of the judged intensity of sensation actually decreasing as the physical stimulus magnitude increases constitute one such kind. Other such kinds of finding will come to our attention in due course; but I first sketch a radically different approach to understanding the judgment of sensation.

All the theoretical problems with which this chapter has been concerned have developed from the basic finding by Beck and Shaw (1967), since confirmed by many others, that the estimation of sums and differences of sensations do not conform to the same power law that describes the estimates of single sensations. Looking at the argument summarized above (p. 97), once the existence of a scale of sensation is accepted and identified with magnitude estimates, the conclusion follows inexorably that that scale is a ratio scale and is related to the physical stimulus values by a power law transform. If that scale is an extensive ratio scale, as Stevens (1971) and nearly all subsequent experimenters have implicitly supposed, if only by default, not entertaining any alternative possibility, then it is a corollary of the argument that sums and differences of sensations should be describable by the same power law. That corollary has proved contrary to experimental observation. If, on the other hand, the ratio scale inferred from magnitude estimation is non-extensive, then it might simultaneously accommodate both estimates of single sensations and of sums and differences; but the manner in which all those judgments might be achieved has yet to be worked out. The existing experiments exploring this issue, surveyed in this chapter, do not provide much encouragement. Problems continue, and the successes so far achieved look to be due more to the introduction of additional free parameters in the analytical model than to an increased understanding of the underlying psychophysical processes. It appears that either *sensation is not measurable* or *magnitude estimates do not measure sensation* or *both*.

Irrespective of whether sensation is measurable, the assertion with which this chapter began must be false; Stevens' Power Law cannot be sustained as a measure of sensation. That conclusion immediately poses the problem: if the Power Law does not reflect a transformation between physical stimulus magnitude and sensation, how does it arise? As an empirical finding it requires explanation.

8 Matching just-noticeable differences

'By a scale of subjective magnitude we mean a quantitative scale by which we can predict what people will say when they try to give a quantitative description of their impressions' (Stevens 1956a, p. 2). At this operational level Stevens' Power Law undeniably describes the geometric means of the responses that subjects typically give in his experiments. Examination of the theoretical possibilities in previous chapters has shown that the Power Law does not have any simple basis in physiological function, nor is it tenable as a ratio-scale measure of sensation. But Stevens' experimental results still require explanation. In this chapter I examine one alternative idea of astonishing simplicity.

At the beginning of Chapter 3 I expressed Fechner's Law as two independent assertions. The first of those assertions concerned the representation of the phenomena of sensory discrimination within a logarithmic stimulus metric; and after a detailed examination spread through Chapters 3 and 4 it emerged that a linear metric, the natural measure of physical stimulus magnitude, provided an even better foundation for the formulation of sensory discrimination than the logarithmic. In the event the truth or falsity of the second assertion seemed neither here nor there. But, rephrase that second assertion in its more conventional form—all just-noticeable differences are subjectively equal—and apply it literally, not just to differences within the one continuum, but to differences on different stimulus continua. Take number to be an artificial continuum with similar properties to a natural stimulus continuum (cf. pp. 91–2), so that magnitude estimation and production are treated simply as cross-modal matches with respect to the number continuum. Fechner's dictum then has some unexpected consequences of which the chief is Stevens' Power Law.

8.1 MATCHING JUST-NOTICEABLE DIFFERENCES

In a brief letter to the *Psychological Review* Auerbach (1971) made this elementary point: suppose S_x and S_y are two stimulus continua which both conform to Weber's Law with Weber fractions Θ_x and Θ_y, respectively. Suppose further that a pair of stimuli (Y_1, Y_2) on S_y matches a pair (X_1, X_2) on S_x when the two stimuli in each pair are equally discriminable from each other, that is, when both pairs correspond, say, to d' just-noticeable differences (a just-noticeable difference being defined, as a matter of convenience, by $d' = 1$) . That matching condition may be written

$$X_2/X_1 = (1 + \Theta_x)^{d'} \qquad (8.1a)$$

if, and only if,

$$Y_2/Y_1 = (1 + \Theta_y)^{d'}; \qquad (8.1b)$$

or

$$\ln (X_2/X_1) = d' \ln (1 + \Theta_x) \qquad (8.2a)$$

on continuum S_x, if, and only if,

$$\ln(Y_2/Y_1) = d' \ln(1 + \Theta_y) \tag{8.2b}$$

on continuum S_y.

The condition of equal discriminability means that it is the same d' in both eqns 8.2 and, eliminating that parameter, gives

$$\ln(Y_2/Y_1) \ln(1 + \Theta_y) = \ln(X_2/X_1)/\ln(1 + \Theta_x) \tag{8.3}$$

as the matching relation. But eqn 8.3 can also be written as

$$Y_2/Y_1 = (X_2/X_1)^{\beta}, \tag{8.4}$$

where

$$\beta = \ln(1 + \Theta_y)/\ln(1 + \Theta_x) \tag{8.5a}$$

$$\approx \Theta_y/\Theta_x. \tag{8.5b}$$

This matching of equally discriminable pairs of stimuli is an exact application of Fechner's dictum. At the same time the matching of ratios (eqn 8.4) which follows from it is exactly the generalization that Stevens (1957b, p. 162) drew from his experiments with magnitude estimation. In fact, eqn 8.4 is Stevens' Power Law for cross-modality matches and eqn 8.5 relates the exponent of the cross-modal matching relation to the Weber fractions on the two continua.

Suppose now that the numbers uttered by subjects in magnitude estimation experiments are values on some artificial stimulus continuum. Suppose further that that artificial continuum conforms to Weber's Law, possibly because of people's prior experience with numbers or possibly consequent on instructions from the experimenter. In such a case magnitude estimation and production tasks are simply (artificial) species of cross-modality matching. Equation 8.4 applies:

$$N_2/N_1 = (X_2/X_1)^{\beta_x}, \tag{8.6}$$

with

$$\beta_x \ln(1 + \Theta_x) = \text{constant}, \tag{8.7}$$

independent of the continuum S_x. Now eqn 8.4 describes the matching of stimulus pairs on continuum S_x by pairs on continuum S_y with exponent β. If that exponent be rewritten as β_{xy}, then substituting eqn 8.7 into 8.5a gives

$$\beta_{xy} = \beta_x/\beta_y, \tag{8.8}$$

which is the consistency relation examined by Stevens (1966b; see pp. 65–8).

In this way Fechner's dictum can generate all of the principal findings from Stevens' ratio-scaling methods. Indeed, it explains more than the scale of sensation which Stevens proposed. It explains:

1. why Stevens' Power Law is a power law (essentially by tying Stevens' findings to other well-established experimental results on sensory discrimination);

2. why Stevens' Power Law holds substantially for those (prothetic) continua which also conform, at least approximately, to Weber's Law (it depends on matching log stimulus magnitude on one continuum to log stimulus magnitude on another (cf. eqn 8.4), an idea previously proposed by MacKay 1963);

3. why, at a qualitative level at least, the exponent of the power law may be changed by certain factors, for example simultaneous contrast (Stevens 1966c), which also change the Weber fraction (see Craik 1938; Kern 1952; Whittle 1986; the two quantities are related by eqn 8.7); and

4. why Stevens' Power Law does not generalize to the estimation of differences in sensation.

The last of these points is not obvious and turns on a subtle, but fundamental, difference between this present idea and the scale of sensation proposed by Stevens. A just-noticeable difference is a relation between a *pair* of stimuli. So what is now presumed to be matched is the relation between a pair of stimuli on one continuum and another pair of stimuli on some other continuum. These pairs of stimuli are matched according to their discriminabilities which, in principle, are measurable. There is no need to introduce any subjective substructure to support that matching.

However, a single stimulus in isolation does not generate any kind of difference, noticeable or not, and, within this new scheme of things, *the matching of a single stimulus on one continuum to a single stimulus on some other continuum is meaningless.* (The distance between London and Edinburgh is 400 miles. What is the distance between London?) Accordingly, in those experiments such as magnitude estimation in which stimuli are presented one at a time for judgment, there is presumed to be some implicit reference stimulus from which the stimulus presented for judgment differs by so many jnds. There must also be some implicit reference on the response continuum, and the response actually assigned to a single stimulus equates the numbers of jnds on the two continua with respect to these implicit reference points. For this reason eqns 8.1–8.4 and 8.6 are all expressed it terms of *ratios* of stimulus values.

When the subject is asked to estimate differences in sensation, however, a reference point on the stimulus continuum is explicitly supplied by the experimenter. There is no reason why the matching relation generated from the magnitude estimation of single stimuli when the point of reference is essentially uncontrolled should generalize to the estimation of differences in sensation when the reference point is explicitly supplied.

To support this point, Table 7.1, which lists the levels of the stimuli in each pair presented for judgment in the experiment by Beck and Shaw (1967), also gives the dB difference between the stimuli. This dB difference is (20 times) the logarithm of the ratio between the physical stimulus amplitudes presented for judgment which, in turn, is the quantity in parentheses on the right-hand side of eqn 8.6. On the left-hand side of that equation N_1 is the implicit numerical reference and N_2 is the numerical response uttered by the subject. So the magnitude of the estimate, on this view of the matter, ought to increase as a power function of the stimulus ratio. The data are set out in Fig. 8.1 where it can be seen that, except for the two smallest differences, the median magnitude ratio increases roughly as the 0.3 power of stimulus amplitude ratio. The analysis is suggestive.

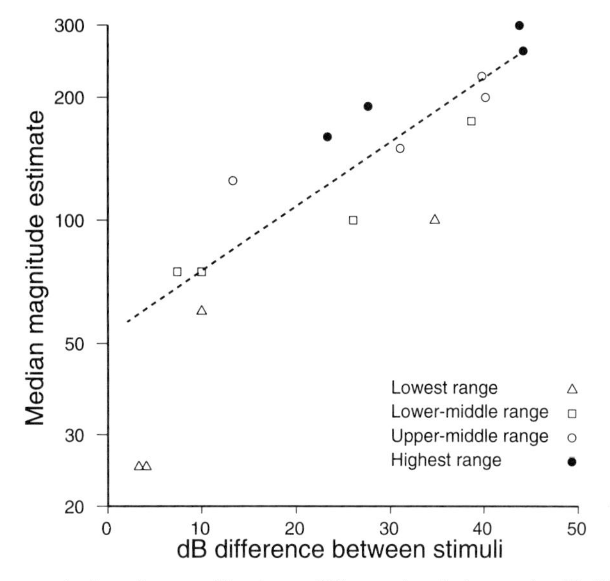

Fig. 8.1 Median magnitude estimates of loudness difference in relation to the dB differences between the pairs of stimuli in the experiment by Beck and Shaw (1967; cf. Table 7.1).

It looks at this point as though the matching of just-noticeable differences in the manner first formulated by Auerbach (1971) promises to accomplish a very great deal by way of explanation, and to accomplish it, moreover, *without invoking any underlying scale of sensation.* In addition, it promises a much sought after rapprochement between the results of the ratio-scaling procedures developed by Stevens and the much older tradition of work on sensory discrimination. But all this is subject to the empirical relation 8.7 between the power-law exponent and the Weber fraction. That relation I shall evaluate shortly.

8.2 A COMMON SCALE OF SENSORY MAGNITUDE

Auerbach's (1971) letter came as a brief comment on a then recently published article by Teghtsoonian (1971) who had derived eqn 8.7 from more elaborate premisses. As an interpretation of data which I come to in Chapter 11, Teghtsoonian proposed that there was a common scale of sensory magnitude, common to all sensory attributes. Magnitude estimates are values on this common scale, and the Power Law describes the manner in which different sensory continua are mapped onto the common subjective scale. Since different continua differ greatly in their physical (logarithmic) ranges (see Table 11.1, p. 179 below), so their respective power law transforms have to effect different degrees of compression to fit each one into the common subjective range.

Not only magnitude estimates, but other kinds of sensory operation such as threshold discriminations are also realized on the common scale of subjective magnitude. It follows that, once a stimulus continuum has been transformed by the appropriate psychophysical function, it assumes a common set of discriminative properties with respect to the subjective level of description, common to all (transformed) physical continua. In particular, an analogue of Weber's Law is presumed to apply at the subjective level of description with a subjective Weber fraction that is independent of the attribute being judged. This means that if the physical stimulus attribute satisfies Weber's Law, the Weber fraction at the physical level of description must be related to that common fraction through the transform prescribed by Stevens' Power Law. Equation 8.7 expresses this relation.

8.3 EKMAN'S LAW

The analogue of Weber's Law at the subjective level of description was named 'Ekman's Law' by Stevens (1966a). It states that the error of judgment in subjective units increases in proportion to the subjective magnitude and gives substance to a conjecture by Brentano (1874; see p. 68 of the 1974 translation). For a stimulus attribute that satisfies both Weber's Law and Stevens' Power Law, Ekman's Law follows as an immediate consequence because Weber's Law (eqn 1.1) transforms into itself under any power law transform of the stimulus measure; only the Weber fraction is changed. So, if Weber's Law and Stevens' Power Law are both given, Ekman's Law does not make any additional empirical statement.

Some studies (e.g. the data from J.C. Stevens and Tulving, 1957, as presented by Stevens, 1971, p. 441, Fig. 8) have reported that magnitude estimates have a log normal distribution; in consequence, the standard deviation of raw estimates grows in proportion to their mean (see also Eisler 1962, 1963a,b). If that were generally true (I do not examine its validity here), it would amount to an analogue of Weber's Law for magnitude estimates and it would transpose under a power law transform into a similar relation at the subjective level of description. It might appear, at first sight, that application to the very judgment of sensation would make Ekman's Law an independent empirical statement; but, in reality, its application to sensation is not distinct from the application of Weber's Law to just-noticeable differences in physical stimulus magnitude. The relation which is posited at the subjective level of description is no more than the reflection through the power law transform of the prior relation, if it exists, between the standard deviation and the mean of numerical estimates (cf. Teghtsoonian 1974).

However, Ekman (1956) was not proposing any particular shape of distribution of responses at the objective level. Rather, he described a simple graphical method of transposing measures of variability expressed in physical stimulus units into measures expressed on the subjective scale, followed by a graphical plot of standard deviation (in subjective units) against mean. Although Ekman's (1956, pp. 237–41) published examples were no more than tests of Weber's Law using certain existing data, his graphical procedure can be applied to any relation between the mean and standard deviation at the physical level (Weber's Law is not assumed . . .) and any transform to the subjective (. . . nor is the Power Law). Where the threshold measured at the physical level deviates from Weber's Law, Ekman's Law would seem to imply a corresponding deviation from the psychophysical power law, so that once the transformation to the subjective level has been effected, Weber's Law holds exactly. This idea is found in Fechner's distinction between outer and inner psychophysics (see Adler 1966, pp. 56–7) and it is also implicit in Teghtsoonian's (1971) scenario. It, at last, gives Ekman's Law independent empirical substance in the form of a functional relationship between deviations from Weber's Law, where they occur, and corresponding deviations from Stevens' Power Law. Discrimination between the amplitudes of two pure tones (below) provides an opportunity to test this empirical element of Ekman's Law.

8.3.1 **The subjective Weber fraction**

One crucial test of Teghtsoonian's scenario turns on the alleged constancy of the fraction in Ekman's Law. Briefly, the estimate of the subjective Weber fraction obtained by combining an estimate of the physical Weber fraction with an estimate of the Power Law exponent according to eqn 8.7 ought to be the same (to within reasonable limits of experimental error) for all continua for which the calculation can be carried out. Table 8.1 is the summary table of data which Teghtsoonian cited to support his thesis. What limits of experimental error one ought to tolerate in this comparison is a matter of opinion. My own opinion, for what it is worth, is that the very close agreement of all the subjective Weber fractions in Table 8.1 is too good to be true; one ought to expect a noticeably greater variation amongst independent determinations of a Weber fraction than is apparent in the rightmost column of that table, even from one subject to another in the same experiment, to say nothing of the variability to be expected between independent determinations of a power law exponent.

Table 8.1 Calculated values of the subjective Weber fraction for nine continua

Continuum	Weber fraction	Power Law exponent	Subjective Weber fraction
Brightness	0.079	0.33	0.026
Loudness	0.048	0.60	0.029
Finger span	0.022	1.30	0.029
Heaviness	0.020	1.04	0.030
Length	0.029	1.04	0.030
Taste, NaCl	0.083	0.41	0.033
Saturation, red	0.019	1.70	0.033
Electric shock	0.013	2.50	0.033
Vibration			
60 Hz	0.036	0.095	0.034
125 Hz	0.046	0.067	0.031
250 Hz	0.046	0.64	0.029
Mean			0.031
Grand mean for nine continua			0.030

From 'On the exponents in Steven's Law and the constant in Ekman's Law' by R. Teghtsoonian, *Psychological Review*, vol. 78, p. 75. © 1971, American Psychological Association. Reprinted by permission.

I comment on three of Teghtsoonian's comparisons:

1. *Heaviness.* Teghtsoonian's Weber fraction (0.020) is estimated from half the interval of uncertainty, calculated according to Urban's method, in Experiment II by Oberlin (1936). In that experiment, using the traditional method of constant stimuli, the subjects were allowed to respond either 'heavier', 'lighter', or 'equal'. Much more appropriate, according to modern understanding of sensory discrimination, is Oberlin's Experiment I in

which 'equal' responses were not allowed. Half the interquartile interval in that experiment gives a fraction of 0.052 (the data are re-presented in Laming, 1986, fig. 1.4, where, if an additive constant (66 g) be added to the physical values of the stimuli, the Weber fraction reduces to 0.043; Laming, 1986, eqn 1.7) and use of the analogous *precision* (h) in Experiment II gives 0.046. Using the middle of these three Weber fractions, the estimate of the subjective fraction rises to 0.067.

2. *Brightness.* Teghtsoonian's Weber fraction (0.079) is averaged over five experiments for the detection of *increments* added to uniform backgrounds (Teghtsoonian 1971, table 2). The power law exponent, on the other hand, is estimated from judgments of single stimuli of about 5.7° diameter presented for 2 s in darkness (J.C. Stevens and S.S. Stevens 1963), and the appropriate Weber fraction for comparison must relate to a discrimination between two *separate* stimuli similarly presented. Cornsweet and Pinsker's (1965) data, corrected for the particular threshold criterion they used, give a Weber fraction of 0.210 (Laming 1986, p. 76, table 5.1), which transposes into a recalculated subjective fraction of 0.065.

3. *Vibration.* A similar criticism applies to the estimates calculated for tactile vibration. Teghtsoonian has taken his Weber fractions from the very early study by Knudsen (1928) who measured increment thresholds. Difference thresholds are much greater. Craig's (1974) threshold measurements for discrimination between two separate 200 ms bursts of 160 Hz vibration applied to the tip of the index finger give a Weber fraction of 0.245 (see Laming 1986, p. 141, fig. 8.3). This transposes into a subjective Weber fraction estimated to be 0.158 and 0.151 for 125 and 250 Hz vibration, respectively.

The high degree of consistency in the calculated estimates of the subjective Weber fraction in Table 8.1 is deceptive and does not stand up to critical examination.

8.4 THE EMPIRICAL RELATION BETWEEN THE WEBER FRACTION AND THE POWER LAW EXPONENT

This relation has previously been examined in a qualitative manner by Stevens (1961b). Stevens' stance was that measures of resolving power (e.g. the Weber fraction) have nothing to do with measures of sensation (such as magnitude estimates) and he therefore argued against any inverse correlation between the Weber fraction and the Power Law exponent (eqn 8.7). As counterexamples he claimed, amongst other findings, that the threshold for luminance may vary as much as 50-fold with change in the area of the stimulus (referring to Hunt 1953), while such corresponding change as exists in the Power Law exponent (from 0.5 for a point source to 0.33 for a 5.7° diameter stimulus) is in the *wrong* direction. Again, the Weber fraction for the amplitude of a pure tone varies with its frequency to such a degree that the subjective size of a just-noticeable difference cannot possibly be the same for all frequencies (citing Newman 1933). But the same difficulties arise with Stevens' counter-examples as were previously encountered with Teghtsoonian's collection of measures. The estimates of the power function exponents were obtained from judgments of single stimuli presented in silence, while the estimates of the Weber fractions relate to increment thresholds, not difference discriminations. The thresholds which Stevens cited from Hunt (1953) concerned the detection of an increment added to a uniform luminance; and Newman (1933) was relying on the thresholds for auditory amplitude measured by Riesz

(1928) using single-sideband amplitude-modulated tones. This technique presents the subject with a combination of two continuous tones close together in frequency (3 Hz in Riesz's experiments) and the measured thresholds relate to the detection of the beats produced thereby. More recent work by Jesteadt *et al.* (1977b), using a discrimination between two separate tones presented in silence, found no significant variation of the Weber fraction with frequency, on which Stevens' argument depended.

Figure 8.2 presents my own collection of some 32 pairs of Weber fractions and power law exponents, and Tables 8.2 and 8.3 list the sources. Brief notes on the experiments are set out in Appendix A. In compiling this collection of data I have paid careful attention, as careful as may be, to the comparability of the stimuli presented in the two experiments in each pair. In particular, all the Weber fractions relate to difference discriminations between two separate stimuli; many have been taken from Laming (1986, pp. 76–7, table 5.1). In some cases (listed in Table 8.3 and represented by filled symbols in Fig. 8.2) the two quantities have been obtained from the same experimenter, usually from different experiments employing the same apparatus and published in the same paper. In these cases one might expect to see a clearer relationship, but, in fact, the scatter of the data points is just as great. The triangles indicate those stimulus attributes surveyed by Teghtsoonian (1971) and listed in Table 8.1, but not necessarily the same measures as Teghtsoonian cited. Some of those attributes are represented more than once. The thick broken line shows eqn 8.7 with the constant set equal to 0.053, which is the median of the calculated estimates. It does not match any trend in the data; except that there happen not to be any instances of a small Weber fraction (fine discrimination) paired with a low exponent.

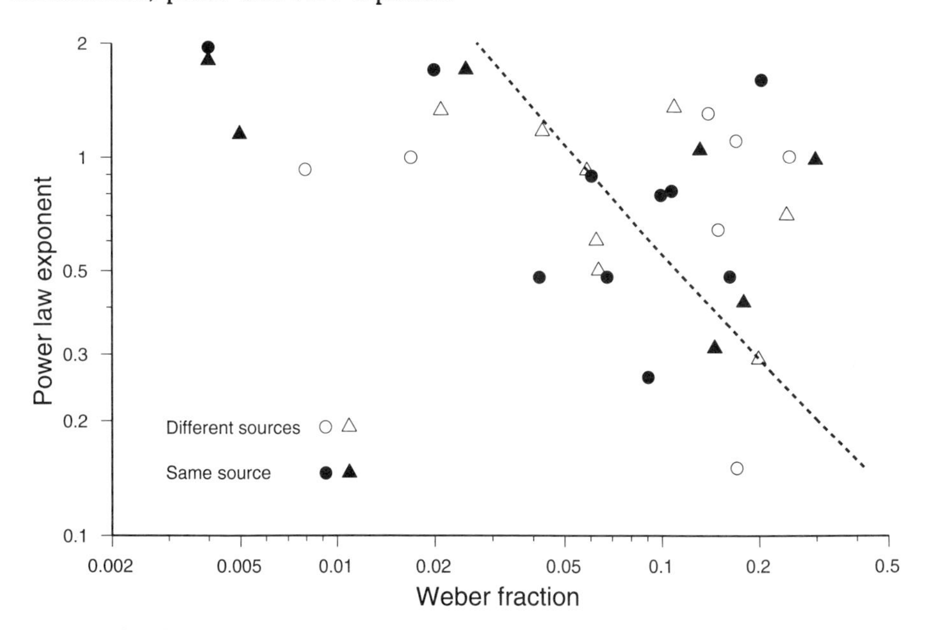

Fig. 8.2 Weber fractions and Power Law exponents from 32 pairs of experiments. Filled symbols indicate those pairs where both quantities have been obtained from the same experimenter; triangles the stimulus attributes surveyed by Teghtsoonian (1971, see Table 8.1), though not necessarily the same values. The continuous line is eqn 8.7 with the constant set to 0.053.

Table 8.2 Weber fractions and Power Law exponents

Stimulus attribute	Weber fraction	Source of discrimination data	Power Law exponent	Source of estimation data	Subjective Weber fraction
Amplitude of Gaussian noise[1]	0.064	Harris (1950)	0.50	Stevens and Guirao (1962)	0.031
Amplitude of 1 kHz tone[1]	0.063[2]	Jesteadt *et al.* (1977b)	0.60	Stevens (1956b)	0.037
Amplitude of vibration[1]	0.245	Craig (1974)	0.70[3]	Stevens (1959a)	0.153
Contrast of grating	0.150[4]	Legge (1981)	0.64	Gottesman *et al.* (1981)	0.089
Finger span[1]	0.021	Gaydos (1958)	1.33	Stevens and Stone (1959)	0.028
Lifted weight[1,5]	0.059	Fechner (1860)	0.92	Rule and Curtis (1976)	0.053
	0.043	Oberlin (1936)	1.17	Stevens and Galanter (1957)	0.049
Luminance[1]	0.200	Leshowitz *et al.* (1968)	0.29	Onley (1960)	0.053
Pressure on skin	0.171	Gatti and Dodge (1929)	1.1	J.C. Stevens and Mack (1959)	0.174
Smell	0.170	Stone *et al.* (1962), Stone (1963), Stone and Bosley (1965)	0.15[6]	Berglund *et al.* (1971)	0.024
Taste, 'sip and spit'					
Bitter	0.250	Schutz and Pilgrim (1957)	1.00		0.223
Common salt[1]	0.110		1.35	Stevens (1969)	0.141
Sucrose	0.140		1.30		0.170
Temperature, cold	0.017	Johnson *et al.* (1973)	1.00	J.C. Stevens and Stevens (1960)	0.017
Visual separation	0.008	Volkmann (1863)	0.93	M. Teghtsoonian and Teghtsoonian (1971)	0.007

1 Surveyed by Teghtsoonian (1971), possibly citing different measures.
2 At 80 dB SL.
3 Adjusted to 160 Hz by reference to Stevens (1968).
4 At 0.06 contrast.
5 Two pairs of studies over different ranges of weight.
6 Median exponent from accumulated studies on 26 different odours.

Table 8.3 Weber fractions and Power Law exponents from the same source

Source	Stimulus attribute	Weber fraction	Power Law exponent	Subjective Weber fraction
Cain (1977a, b)	Odour of			
	n-amyl alcohol[2]	0.163	0.48	0.072
	n-butyl alcohol[2]	0.068	0.48	0.032
	n-amyl butyrate[3]	0.091	0.26	0.023
	n-butyl alcohol[3]	0.042	0.48	0.020
Graf *et al.* (1974)	Luminance[1]	0.146	0.31	0.042
Indow and Stevens (1966)	Colour: red/yellow	0.004	1.95	0.008
	Colour: green/yellow	0.020	1.70	0.034
Indow (1967)	Saturation of colour: red/white[1]	0.004	1.80	0.007
Krueger (1984)	Numerousness	0.108	0.81	0.083
McBurney (1966)				
McBurney *et al.* (1967)	Common salt[1]	0.180	0.41	0.068
Merkel (1888)	Luminance[1]	0.132	1.04[4]	0.129
Merkel (1889a)	Pressure on skin	0.1	0.79[4]	0.075
Merkel (1889b)	Intensity of noise[1]	0.3	0.98[4]	0.257
Merkel (1894)	Visual length[1]	0.005	1.15[4]	0.006
Panek and Stevens (1966)	Saturation of colour: red/white[1]	0.025	1.70	0.042
Taves (1941)	Numerousness	0.205	1.59[4]	0.297
Treisman (1963)	Temporal duration	0.061	0.89	0.053

[1] Surveyed by Teghtsoonian (1971), possibly citing different measures.
[2] Stimuli presented in a glass vessel.
[3] Stimuli presented by means of an air olfactometer.
[4] Exponent estimated from halving/doubling of sensation.

Figure 8.2 shows that eqn 8.7 does not obtain in nature. Although there is a negative correlation between the Weber fraction and the Power Law exponent as required by that equation (the Spearman rank correlation coefficient is −0.44, which is significant at 0.01 on a one-tailed test), the scatter of the data points about the predicted relation is much, much greater than can be attributed to experimental error. Indeed, if there is *any* fundamental relation between sensory discrimination and the estimation of subjective magnitudes, as Teghtsoonian suggested, there must also be *some* corresponding empirical relation between estimates of the Weber fraction and the Power Law exponent. Figure 8.2 shows that no precise relation of that kind exists.

Two studies have looked for such a relation, not between different stimulus attributes, but between the Weber fractions and Power Law exponents for different subjects within the same pair of experiments. Graf *et al.* (1974) compared the discrimination of different luminances. The stimuli were two 1° diameter discs, 3° apart vertically, presented for 4 s each. Difference thresholds were measured at both a low (0.035 ft-L) and a high luminance (111 ft-L); and the same stimuli were used for magnitude estimation with, again, either a low or a high standard. Two groups of 24 subjects were tested with either simultaneous presentation of the two stimuli to be compared, or successive, the two 4 s presentations being separated by a 10 s readaptation period. There were substantial correlations (+0.20 to +0.62) amongst each group of 24 subjects between Weber fractions measured at the low and at the high level and between the Power Law exponents measured with respect to the corresponding standards. But analogous correlations between the Weber fractions and the exponents were negligible (−0.25 to −0.01).

Krueger (1984) used computer printouts bearing a number of Xs randomly arranged within a 25 × 35 matrix to study the judgment of numerousness. In the magnitude production task subjects thumbed quickly (without counting) through an ordered sequence of printouts to find one with 25, 50, 100, or 200 Xs. In magnitude estimation they were asked to estimate the number of Xs on each of a series of 12, randomly ordered printouts. Difference thresholds were measured by the method of constant stimuli, comparing standards of 25, 100, and 400 with a range of eight comparison printouts. There was a highly significant correlation (+0.39) between the exponents for magnitude production and estimation from the 100 subjects; but the correlations between the Weber fractions and the exponents from both production and the two halves of the estimation task were small (−0.09, −0.15, and +0.01). Equation 8.7 does not hold even for individual subjects within a common pair of experimental tasks where comparability is maximal.

8.5 ESTIMATION OF LOUDNESS OF 1 KHZ TONES

A substantial body of careful experimental work has shown that discriminations between the amplitudes of two pure tones deviate from Weber's Law and conform instead to the approximate relation

$$\Delta A \approx aA^{5/6}. \tag{8.9}$$

The experimental findings have been summarized by Laming (1986, pp. 13–15).

This variation of resolving power with amplitude affords another way to examine the possibility of some relation between sensory discrimination on the one hand and the estimation of subjective magnitudes on the other, because the principle of matching just-noticeable differences means that a deviation from Weber's Law at the physical level of description should be matched by a corresponding deviation of magnitude estimates from Stevens' Power Law.

To see what form that deviation ought to take, note that if

$$f(A) = \exp\{A^{(1-\alpha)}\ln(1+\Theta)/a(1-\alpha)\}, \tag{8.10}$$

then, when ΔA satisfies eqn 8.9 with α equal to 5/6,[1]

$$f(A+\Delta A)/f(A) = 1+\Theta. \qquad (8.11)$$

So, if the level of a pure tone were to be measured, not according to its natural physical measure (amplitude of pressure oscillation), but instead according to $f(A)$, it would (with respect to this substitute measure) conform accurately to Weber's Law. Then, according to the principle of matching equally discriminable pairs of stimuli, numerical estimates of loudness should increase as some power of $f(A)$; that is,

$$\log \text{mag. est.} = c + \beta\{A^{(1-\alpha)}\ln(1+\Theta)/a(1-\alpha)\}, \qquad (8.12)$$

where c is a constant which reflects the scaling of the numerical estimates and α, for this particular attribute, is about 5/6.

Equation 8.12 should be compared with

$$\log \text{mag. est.} = c + \beta \ln A, \qquad (8.13)$$

which results from taking logarithms in eqn 5.4 (Stevens' Power Law). Since $A^{(1-\alpha)}$ increases faster than $\log A$ for any α less than 1, the message from the comparison is that log magnitude estimates of the loudness of pure tones ought to increase faster at high levels than the linear increase prescribed by eqn 8.13. A decreasing Weber fraction ($\Delta A/A \propto A^{-1/6}$) should transpose according to eqn 8.7 into an increasing exponent (increasing as $A^{1/6}$).

The broken curve in Fig. 5.1 shows the best agreement (except for an arbitrary vertical shift) between eqn 8.12 and Stevens' (1975, p. 28, Fig. 10) data for estimation of the loudness of a 1 kHz tone. For α equal to 5/6, log magnitude in eqn 8.12 increases as $A^{1/6}$ and the curve in Fig. 5.1 (p. 57) has equation

$$\log N = 0.06 + 0.58(A/A_{40})^{1/6} \qquad (8.14)$$

where A_{40} is the amplitude of a 40 dB SPL tone. There is substantial curvature in eqn 8.14 which is not matched by the data; in those logarithmic coordinates a straight line (the sone scale) provides a much better fit. The loudness of 1 kHz tones was, in fact, the first stimulus attribute to be studied with ratio-scaling methods and has, in consequence, been very much studied. No one has ever suggested that the underlying relation between log estimate and stimulus magnitude is positively accelerated as the broken curve in Fig. 5.1. On the

[1] Equation 8.10 gives

$$f(A+\Delta A)/f(A) = \exp\{[(A+\Delta A)^{(1-\alpha)} - A^{(1-\alpha)}]\ln(1+\Theta)/a(1-\alpha)\}. \qquad (*)$$

When $\Delta A \ll A$, the expression in square brackets is approximately

$$\begin{aligned}[(A+\Delta A)^{(1-\alpha)} - A^{(1-\alpha)}] &= A^{(1-\alpha)}[(1+\Delta A/A)^{(1-\alpha)} - 1] \\ &= A^{(1-\alpha)}[(1-\alpha)\Delta A/A + O\{(\Delta A/A)^2\}] \\ &\approx (1-\alpha)A^{-\alpha}\Delta A \\ &= a(1-\alpha)\end{aligned}$$

on substitution from eqn 8.9 with α equal to 5/6. Equation 8.11 now follows from substitution in (*).

contrary, two recent studies (Hellman *et al.* 1987; Zwislocki and Jordan 1986) have demonstrated conclusively that there is no relation between discrimination of amplitude and the slope of the loudness function.

However, other experiments (but not Stevens', 1975, data) which have examined the precision achieved by individual subjects in the estimation of the loudness of 1 kHz tones have found that such estimates are *relatively more accurate* at higher stimulus levels. For example, Baird *et al.* (1980, p. 282, fig. 5) report that the coefficient of variation calculated from magnitude estimates given by three individual subjects decreased by factors of about 3.7, 3 .1, and 1.8 respectively as the stimulus level increased from 40 to 90 dB SPL. Over this same range eqn 8.9 implies that there should be an improvement in relative discriminability (i.e. in the difference threshold, not necessarily in the variability of magnitude estimates) of 2.61 (linear measure), which matches to within the limits of experimental error.

So, for this particular attribute, amplitude of a 1 kHz tone, the deviation from Weber's Law, which is now well established, is not reflected in a corresponding deviation from Stevens' Power Law. But it might be that the improving accuracy of sensory discrimination as the stimulus magnitude increases leads to a similar improvement in the *precision* of the magnitude estimates.

8.6 THE PRECISION OF MAGNITUDE ESTIMATES

If the estimation of subjective sensation were closely related to sensory discrimination, the respective precisions with which each kind of judgment is made ought to be comparable. The ways in which the two kinds of judgment are expressed are different—discrimination experiments commonly use a two-alternative forced-choice paradigm, while magnitude estimation offers a notionally continuous range of response alternatives. But the precisions of the two kinds of judgment can nevertheless be compared by transposing each into a variability expressed in terms of the (square of) the stimulus metric which *is* common to both. I offer six particular comparisons as examples.

1. *Loudness of pure tones.* Figure 5.1 presents Stevens' (1975) accumulated data on the estimation of the loudness of 1 kHz tones and shows in addition the interquartile ranges of the estimates of each stimulus level. These ranges relate to two judgments of each stimulus by each of 32 subjects who, with no standard or prescribed modulus, might scale their numerical estimates at any arbitrary level. The interquartile ranges in Fig. 5.1 have been adjusted for intersubject differences in the following manner: each subject's judgments have been multiplied by whatever factor is necessary to make the geometric mean estimate, averaged over all 16 judgments, assume a fixed value, the same value for all subjects (Stevens 1971, p. 428). The corrected standard deviations are tabulated by Stevens (1971, p. 442, table 1); they reflect only the variability *within* subjects. The corrected standard deviation is a minimum (0.17 log units) at 80 dB. This is equivalent to a probable error of 0.11 log units expressed in terms of the scale of magnitude estimates, or 0.19 log units at the physical level of description after reflection through the 0.6 power law in inverse direction. A probable error of 0.19 log units is, in turn, equivalent to a Weber fraction of 0.55. By way of comparison, Jesteadt *et al.* (1977b), in a comprehensive set of measurements of difference

thresholds for the amplitudes of pure tones, reported the Weber fraction for a 1 kHz tone of 500 ms duration at 80 dB to be 0.06 (corrected to 75 per cent correct responses and expressed in amplitude units). The difference is an order of magnitude in linear measure or two orders in terms of variance.

2. *Loudness of Gaussian noise.* J.C. Stevens and Tulving (1957) recorded magnitude estimates from a class of 70 naive subjects making their very first judgments of loudness. Eight different samples of white noise of about 3 s duration were presented in a common order with no prior standard or modulus. The judgments from each subject were scaled in the manner described above to remove any contribution to the variance from differences of scale between different subjects. The distributions of the 70 scaled numbers assigned to each stimulus were approximately log-normal. To demonstrate this property Stevens (1971, p. 441, fig. 8; see Fig. 10.3, p. 154) published the cumulative distributions in a plot with a normal probability scale on the ordinate and log magnitude estimate on the abscissa, fitting a straight line to each set of data. The standard deviations can be estimated from such a plot by measuring the gradient of the fitted lines. Those standard deviations are set out in Table 10.1 (p. 154); they have an asymptotic value of 0.17 log units. That is the same value as the minimum standard deviation of the judgments of the loudness of pure tones above and is equivalent, as before, to a Weber fraction of 0.55. In comparison, the data from Harris (1950; see Laming 1986, p. 11, fig. 1.9, and p. 76, table 5.1) give a value of 0.064 for the Weber fraction for bursts of Gaussian noise. The difference in terms of the variance of the judgments is again about two orders of magnitude.

3. *Saturation of colour: red–white.* Figure 5.3 presents magnitude estimates from Panek and Stevens (1966) of the redness of a red–grey mixture. The typical probable error of these estimates is 0.1 log units (Panek and Stevens 1966, p. 60, table 1). After transposition to the physical level of description by reflection through the Power Law (exponent 1.7) in inverse direction, this probable error becomes 0.06 log units, equivalent to a Weber fraction of 0.15. Direct measurement of the discriminability function (Panek and Stevens 1966, p. 64, Fig. 4) reveals that for an 80 per cent red mixture the difference threshold is about 4 per cent, equivalent to a Weber fraction of 0.05. This is a lesser difference than that revealed above, but is nevertheless about one order of magnitude in terms of variance.

4. *Temporal duration.* Stevens and Greenbaum (1966, p. 444, table 2; see Fig. 5.4 here) have published the standard deviations of their magnitude estimates of temporal durations. The minimum deviation (in the middle of the stimulus range) for estimating the duration of a white noise is 0.34 log units. When this value is reflected through the Power Law (exponent 0.87) in inverse direction, it equates to 0.39 log units with respect to physical time, equivalent to a Weber fraction (84 per cent correct) of 1.46 (*sic*). Treisman (1963), on the other hand, using an auditory stimulus to define temporal intervals of similar durations reported a standard deviation (equivalent to 84 per cent correct) from the method of single stimuli that varied from 0.066 to 0.174 of the mean at different temporal durations. The relative difference is again a whole order of magnitude in linear measure or two orders in terms of variance.

5. *Numerousness.* In the study by Krueger (1984) described above the mean intrasubject standard deviation for estimating the apparent numerousness of 100 Xs is 0.17 log units (Krueger 1984, p. 539, fig. 3), equivalent to a probable error of 0.115 log units or an interquartile interval (77, 130). The Weber fraction is only 0.117 with respect to the

standard of 100, so that the probable error of the magnitude estimates is greater by 2.58 (or nearly 7 when expressed as a ratio of variances). The corresponding calculation on the magnitude productions gives a variance ratio of 9.

6. Luce and Mo (1965). This investigation, described earlier (p. 58), is the one study to include an explicit comparison between the precision of magnitude estimation and of recognition in a two-alternative forced-choice paradigm. Interspersed between the magnitude estimation sessions there was one block of 100 trials on a two-choice recognition task employing two fixed stimuli only (weights or 1 kHz tones) from the magnitude estimation set. Each trial in this recognition task was followed by immediate knowledge of results. Using a model developed by Luce and Galanter (1963), Luce and Mo calculated the dB difference between magnitude estimation stimuli (that is, stimuli as they were judged in the magnitude estimation task) that would have generated the actual proportions of errors observed in the recognition task. Their model may be characterized as follows. There is a distribution of magnitude estimates assigned to each stimulus, the distributions being estimated from the actual numbers uttered by the subject. Given two such distributions, one for each of the stimuli in the recognition task, one can calculate the probabilities of correct identification of each of those stimuli (assuming only their magnitude estimates to be available as a basis for identification) after the manner of Tanner and Swets' (1954) signal-detection model. Those probabilities of identification will depend on the choice of stimuli, and that choice is adjusted (calculations are now based on distributions of magnitude estimates that are interpolations between those distributions estimated from the magnitude estimation data) until the two calculated probabilities match the probabilities of correct identifications actually observed in the recognition task. Comparing the dB differences calculated in this way with those actually used in the recognition task, Luce and Mo (1965, p. 173) claim that the prediction of the recognition data from the magnitude estimation data is 'poor' for one subject, 'fair' for four more, and 'relatively good' for the remaining seven. However, there is reason to doubt the representativeness of the recognition trials relative to conventional threshold measurements. For the six subjects estimating heaviness the equivalent Weber fraction (75 per cent 2AFC) estimated from the recognition trials ranged from 0.085 to 0.34, whereas Oberlin's (1936; see Laming 1986, p. 7) fraction was 0.043; and for the six subjects presented with 1 kHz tones the equivalent Weber fraction (71 per cent correct, 2AFC, expressed as an amplitude ratio) ranged from 0.125 to 0.27, whereas the fraction interpolated in the data of Jesteadt *et al.* (1977b) at 60 dB is only 0.08 (again as an amplitude ratio). It looks as though the subjects may, to some extent, have carried a distinctive mode of judgment from the prior magnitude estimation trials over to the recognition trials, achieving a lesser degree of recognition accuracy in consequence.

8.7 COMMENTARY

It is clear from the first five examples that magnitude estimates are typically more variable than are the judgments implicit in the measurement of a difference threshold—very much more variable, by one to two orders of magnitude in Stevens' experiments. Although difference discriminations and magnitude estimates of the same stimuli are, of necessity, based ultimately on the same sensory process, magnitude estimation must involve some *additional* psychological process beyond that involved in threshold discrimination. I call that additional process *sensory judgment.* The sensory part of the whole, as reflected in sensory discrimination, contributes 1–10 per cent only of the variance; that is to say, 90–99 per cent of the variability of magnitude estimates is due to the factors subsumed under 'sensory judgment'. When that additional process is invoked, it completely dominates the outcome.

The sixth example is different. What needs to be emphasized is that Luce and Mo (1965) generally disregarded the suggestions from Stevens (1956b), reproduced here on pp. 56–7, how to conduct a magnitude estimation experiment. They reported the data from individual subjects; those subjects each contributed a large number (about 2000) judgments; the individual sessions were long (60–90 min); the stimulus values were spaced perhaps four times as densely as Stevens would have spaced them. Probably as a consequence, Luce and Mo failed to generate good power law data. Although mean estimates for individual subjects generally increased as a power of the stimulus magnitude, idiosyncratic variations were imposed on that general trend. The possibilities must therefore be considered, first, that close conformity to the power law is an artifact of the averaging of data, often from different subjects; and second, that, in practice, the data incorporates an implicit randomization over a variety of contextual factors which greatly increases the variability.

The idea that there ought, nevertheless, to be some simple relation between sensory discrimination and magnitude estimation is misconceived. Stevens (1971, p. 440) claimed 'If the data can be appropriately averaged, it does not matter how widely the variability may range, provided the number of independent measurements can be increased.' That is so provided one *knows* that the variability being averaged is of the nature of 'errors of measurement', independent of that which is being measured. That is not known to be so in magnitude estimation and other ratio-scaling methods. The possibility has to be considered that what was averaged in Stevens' experiments was the net effect of those other judgmental factors which contributed more than 90 per cent of the variability, the specifically sensory contribution being overwhelmed in the averaging. To assume, as Stevens did, that, because the outcome of that averaging was a nice conformity to the Power Law, so those other factors did not bias the sensory contribution, entirely begs the question.

There is no prior reason at all why there should be any particular relationship between sensory discrimination and sensory judgment and, empirically speaking, there is no close relationship to be seen. So, while the idea of matching pairs of stimuli with equal discriminabilities on different continua initially promised much, it is found on careful examination to be incompatible with the state of nature. The comparison between the variabilities of difference discriminations on the one hand and magnitude estimations on the other is, in fact, a profound result for two reasons.

1. Many people have looked for some empirical relationship between sensory discrimination and magnitude estimation—Krueger (1989) is but the latest. There is no systematic relationship to be found.
2. The empirical problem which especially needs to be studied is why magnitude estimation has such a greatly increased variability over that which is naturally contributed by the stimuli presented for judgment.

9 Judging relations between sensations

The suggestion by Auerbach (1971), that subjects in cross-modality matching experiments match a pair of stimuli on one continuum to an equally discriminable pair on another, is a simple and interesting example of a *relation* theory. In a relation theory each judgment expresses the relation between a *pair* of stimuli or a pair of sensations. The notion of judging a single sensation by itself, independently of its relation to any other sensation, is, on this view, meaningless. In those experiments such as magnitude estimation which present stimuli one by one for judgment, some implicit reference, the sensation produced by some implicit standard, has to be assumed.

9.1 RELATION THEORIES

The notion of a *relation theory*, as a generic class of models for sensory judgment, was first characterized by Krantz (1972), drawing on ideas in an earlier unpublished paper by Shepard dating from 1968. Shepard's paper set out the psychological issues raised by this notion and was subsequently published in a much revised form (Shepard 1981). Shepard (p. 40) points out that what Stevens and his colleagues have actually shown is that 'to a first approximation, *it is equal ratios of physical magnitude that are psychologically equivalent*'. Equality of ratios is not sufficient, by itself, to establish a scale of sensation; the argument set out on pp. 87–8 required, in addition, the assumption that such a scale, assigning a subjective value to each single stimulus, actually existed.

Krantz (1972) contrasts relation theories with *mapping theories*, in which each single stimulus X on a continuum is mapped onto a unique sensation S on a subjective continuum. The parameters of such a mapping have to be set up before any assignments can be made, and this is what the experimenter is presumed to accomplish when he initially presents the subject with a standard stimulus and assigns it a modulus. Thereafter the judgment of single stimuli is simple, though the judgment of relations between pairs of stimuli and even more between tetrads (e.g. Birnbaum 1978, 1982a) demands some mental gymnastics on the part of the subject.

The essential difference between the two kinds of theory can be expressed in this manner: in a mapping theory all the necessary points of correspondence between stimulus and sensation, the zero point, the exponent, and the scale unit, are assumed to be fixed, realized somehow inside the subject. Any single stimulus presented for judgment can be evaluated absolutely, that is, in relation to these fixed internal standards according to a mapping of the form

$$X_i \rightarrow N_i. \tag{9.1}$$

In a relation theory, on the other hand, the scale unit is missing, unless it is obtained by reference to some other stimulus, either a standard explicitly supplied or one implicit in the context of the judgment. In this case the mapping has the form

$$(X_i, X_j) \rightarrow N_{ij}. \tag{9.2}$$

To put this issue in another, more immediate, way: Stevens interpreted his experimental findings to imply that '. . . the sensation S is proportional to the stimulus X raised to a power β'(Stevens 1957b, p. 162, replacing Stevens' Ψ, S, and n with S, X, and β, respectively). As an equation this proposition assumes the form

$$S = cX^{\beta}. \tag{9.3}$$

It is widely supposed that the exponent β is characteristic of the stimulus attribute and therefore fixed. But c also has to be fixed, if eqn 9.3 is to deliver a measure of the subjective value of any single stimulus. The constant c sets the unit of measurement on the subjective scale and that unit may be different for different subjects; that is Stevens' justification of his practice of 'modulus equalization' described above on p. 56. But the scale unit has to be consistent, that is to say, c has to be constant for each and every subject, if the power law is to be realized.

Suppose now that only relative judgment is possible. Each judgment relates to a pair of stimuli, X_1, X_2, and eqn 9.3 is replaced by

$$S_2/S_1 = (X_2/X_1)^{\beta}. \tag{9.4}$$

from which the constant c has disappeared. There is now no unit of measurement; its place in the measurement of X_2 is taken by X_1. Consequently differences in sensation cannot be judged, at least, not directly. Only ratios can be judged directly, and this distinction provides a possible way of accommodating the present incompatibilities between magnitude estimations of single stimuli and of differences in Chapter 7.

It might appear, at first sight, that the many magnitude estimation experiments which have been reported, concerning the judgment of *single* stimuli, testify to the falsity of the relational idea. Shephard's idea is that the primary judgment concerns the sensation ratio between a pair of stimuli and that magnitude estimations of apparently single stimuli are, in reality, judgments of ratio with respect to some implicit X_1. I show later that that is indeed so. If that X_1 be taken, as Krantz (1972, p. 184) takes it,[1] to be the standard or the first stimulus presented, then the difference with respect to mapping theory turns out to be no more than cosmetic. But if the implicit X_1 should vary from trial to trial (and I show later that it does), then the variability of magnitude estimates will be increased thereby. Herein lies a possible way of relating the greatly increased variance of magnitude estimates to the much lesser variability of threshold judgments.

The distinction between relation and mapping theories is potentially confusing because, although Krantz (1972) is writing at an abstract axiomatic level, he nevertheless includes sufficiently powerful assumptions in his treatment as to readily generate all the standard

[1] To be precise, Krantz's (1972, pp. 184–6) Axiom 3 ensures that the initial stimulus and the number assigned to it are reflected throughout the sequence of judgments.

results from Stevens' laboratory, including the Power Law for single stimuli. Falmagne (1985, pp. 311–12) shows how quickly those results may be derived from Krantz's formulation. As a consequence, Krantz's relation theory is equivalent at a purely empirical level to Stevens' ratio-scale formulation (eqn 9.3), and what the argument is really about is merely how that agreed set of experimental results should be formulated in mathematics and axiomatized. Ultimately, that choice is no more than a matter of theoretical style and, from an empirical standpoint, uninteresting.

At Krantz's time of writing the incompatibility between magnitude estimations of single stimuli and of differences was only beginning to be studied, and the greatly increased variance of magnitude estimates had yet to receive attention (though some were aware of the problem, e.g. Luce and Mo, 1965); so Krantz does not address those problems. But, since then, those two problems have created severe difficulties of interpretation for the traditional view of sensation, and relation theories, generically speaking, have become important as offering an alternative approach. I present three examples to clarify the distinction further.

9.1.1 **The subjective values of numbers**

Stevens took the numbers uttered by his subjects to be directly proportional to the magnitude of the sensations they experienced; only the scale unit, the overall size of the numbers selected, was (allegedly) at the subject's disposal. If this is so, the numbers uttered constitute a scale of sensation, and that scale has to be a ratio scale (see p. 87 above). Curtis *et al.* (1968; see also p. 92), on the other hand, envisaged that real numbers might form an artificial stimulus continuum with properties like any other stimulus continuum, and that the subjective size of a number might be related to its numerical value by a power function, as happens with real stimulus attributes. On this view (but taking no account of magnitude estimations of differences), the numbers uttered as magnitude estimates are related to the sensations experienced by an unknown power law transform (representing the relation of a number to its subjective value), and sensation is measurable only on a logarithmic interval scale.

A logarithmic interval scale is defined by the assertion that the logarithm of the scale measure has interval scale properties, with arbitrary zero and scale unit. If S in

$$S = c_x X^{\beta_x} \tag{9.5}$$

is measured on a logarithmic interval scale, then $\ln S$ in

$$\ln S = \ln c_x + \beta_x \ln X \tag{9.6}$$

has interval scale properties. Those interval scale properties are preserved under any linear transformation (substitution of different values for $\ln c_x$ and β_x in eqn 9.5) and this is equivalent to a power law transformation of S in eqn 9.6. If S can be reported only through the medium of a further power law transform of unknown exponent (to objective numbers), then neither the value of β_x nor c_x in eqn 9.5 can be determined and a log interval scale is the most precise measurement that can be made.

To see that this is so, note that the matching between number and physical stimulus magnitude can be reformulated in terms of their logarithms as

$$\ln N = \ln (c_x/c_n) + (\beta_x/\beta_n) \ln X. \qquad (9.7)$$

The combined coefficients c_x/c_n and β_x/β_n can be estimated from experimental data, but thereafter one would have no way of knowing how large a part of each coefficient related to the regression of log number on log sensation, and how much to the similar regression of log sensation on log stimulus magnitude. The most that could be discovered about sensation S comes from the comparison of pairs of stimuli. Equation 9.4 eliminates the unknown constant c_x and tells us that 'equal stimulus ratios tend to produce equal sensation ratios' (Stevens 1957b, p. 162). If two stimulus magnitudes stand in some physical ratio r, their respective sensations will stand in some other, but unknown, ratio s. If the measure of sensation were subject to an arbitrary power transform (e.g. when expressed as a numerical response), the ratio s would be different, but would be the same 'different' ratio for all instances of the physical ratio r. Stevens (1957b, pp. 175–7) was aware of the fragile foundation of such a measurement of sensation.

All this is so, of course, only so long as attention is restricted to judgments of single stimuli; Curtis *et al.* (1968) sought to resolve that uncertainty by asking for magnitude estimations of differences in sensation as well.

9.1.2 **Physical correlate theory**

Warren (1958, p. 676) proposed that 'judgments of sensory magnitudes are based upon experience with the manner in which sensory excitation is correlated with the amount of some physical attribute associated with the stimulus.' But the physical attribute on which the judgment is based may not be the one which the experimenter uses as a measure of stimulus magnitude. For example, the intensity of illumination varies inversely as the square of the distance from a point source of light. If, when requested to halve or double the intensity of illumination, subjects actually doubled or halved the distance of the source (metaphorically speaking), a power law with exponent 0.5 would be observed for judgments of brightness. A similar argument applies to judgments of loudness.

This is an unambiguous relation theory which says nothing about sensation *per se*. It has an obvious application to doubling or halving the intensity of a light or sound, and leaves the estimation of a single brightness or loudness, with no comparator, meaningless. It has received a re-presentation and a thorough critical review (Warren 1981) and can be succinctly evaluated as follows. Physical correlates of stimulus variables are invariably related to those variables by simple dimensional laws involving exponents of low integer or simple fractional value (e.g. the inverse square law for luminance and sound energy). The exponents obtained from magnitude estimation experiments typically do not take the simple integer or fractional values that physical correlate theory dictates (cf. Tables 3.1, 8.2, and 8.3). At the same time the complex of physical relationships actually obtaining in any practicable experiment is never so simple as theory supposes and, in general, is too complex to allow of any practical predictions being calculated.

Because previous stimuli presented for judgment are known to bias later estimates,

Warren and his colleagues (e.g. Poulton *et al.* 1965, 1968; Warren, 1965; Warren and Poulton, 1960, 1962, 1966) have tended to focus on the very first judgments made by large groups of naive subjects. That disposes of bias due to previous experimental experience. When such a naive subject is asked to judge the lightness of a grey paper, for example, it would not be surprising if the bias that is generated in other experiments by previous trials is now replaced by a similar bias resulting from previous everyday experience with judgments of light and dark. To that extent it may well be that some physical attribute associated with the stimulus comes to play a role, but a very minor role and virtually impossible to demonstrate. The difficulty is that the variability of estimates of exponents of magnitude estimates is such that even if one did obtain a simple integer or fractional value under certain specific conditions, there would be no way of knowing whether that value reflected the role of some physical correlate or was merely due to chance. It would be necessary to obtain such values *routinely* to establish Warren's hypothesis, and the intrinsic variability of magnitude estimates precludes that ever happening.

Warren's arguments rest chiefly on work with brightness (Warren 1969) and loudness (Warren 1977), for which the corresponding physical variables are subject to an inverse square law. But many people have contributed the criticism that magnitude estimation seems to work equally well with other stimulus attributes which appear not to have any readily associated correlate (e.g. Dorfman, 1981: sweetness, the pleasantness of sucrose solutions, non-metric stimuli). At the same time an experiment by Garner (1954b; see later, pp. 169–70) suggests that even where a physical correlate exists, subjects do not use it. Garner's subjects appeared to have no idea how loud a sound, half as loud as a given 90 dB standard, should sound. Subsequent work (Garner 1958, 1959) showed that whatever prior idea subjects brought with them to the experiment, from everyday experience, was entirely overwhelmed by intervening experimental experience within the space of 20 trials. The possible influence of a physical correlate is weak indeed.

9.1.3 **The common scale of subjective magnitude**

As I have already explained, Auerbach's (1971) suggestion is a particular relation theory that leads to eqn 8.5a as an empirical prediction. Teghtsoonian's (1971) proposal that there is a common scale of subjective magnitude onto which all stimulus continua are mapped is a mapping theory that leads to the same prediction. For so long as attention is confined to the judgment of ratios of sensations, these two models are empirically equivalent. They differ, however, as soon as attention is turned to the judgment of sums and differences.

9.2 CORRELATION OF SUCCESSIVE MAGNITUDE ESTIMATES

Notwithstanding that Krantz (1972, p. 177) was sceptical about there ever being any single critical experiment sufficient to discriminate between relation and mapping theories, I show, in the remainder of this chapter, first, that magnitude estimates are relative judgments (so that a relational formulation is mandatory) and, second, that subjects appear able to distinguish at least two distinct relations between two stimulus magnitudes (so that Krantz's particular formulation will not suffice). All this turns on experimental results published since Krantz's time of writing.

The first assertion, that magnitude estimates are relative judgments, follows from the pattern of correlation between successive log estimates. This pattern is shown convincingly in a study by Baird *et al.* (1980). The stimuli were 21 1 kHz tones presented binaurally for 500 ms each; their levels ranged from 40 to 90 dB SPL in steps of 2.5 dB. Three subjects each made a total of about 2500 judgments in blocks of 100 trials spaced over a period of a week, different stimuli being selected at random for judgment. These arrangements, of course, violate Stevens' (1956b) dicta reproduced on pp. 56–7. Figure 9.1 shows the correlation between successive log magnitude estimates, that is, between $\log N_{n-1}$ and $\log N_n$ (where N_n is the number uttered on trial n), as a function of the difference between the logarithms of the corresponding stimulus magnitudes (in dB). When a stimulus value is repeated to within ± 5 dB, this correlation is about +0.8; though it tails away to nothing for large differences between successive stimuli.

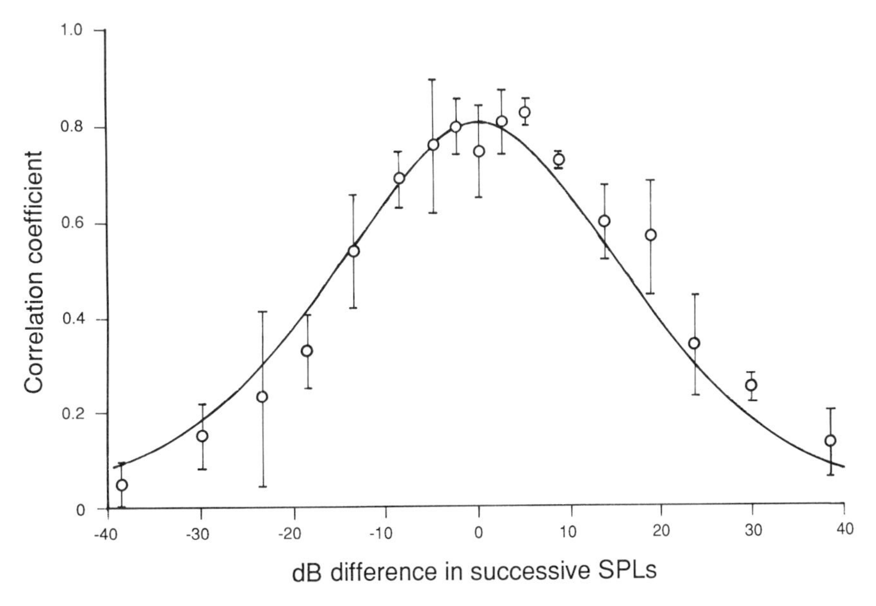

Fig. 9.1 Coefficients of correlation between the logarithms of successive numerical estimates of loudness in relation to the ratio of successive amplitudes of 1 kHz tones. The circles represent the mean correlation averaged over three subjects and the vertical bars extend to ± 1 standard deviation. The continuous curve is eqn 10.40. (Redrawn from Baird *et al.* 1980, p. 286.)

The calculation of the correlations in Fig. 9.1 (these details will prove important later, p. 160) was carried out in this manner: each of the 21 different stimuli could appear, independently, on some trial $n-1$ and on trial n, giving a matrix of 21×21 possible combinations. The correlation between $\log N_{n-1}$ and $\log N_n$ was calculated separately for each cell of this matrix (i.e. for each stimulus pair) before averaging over cells of like or similar dB difference. Because the extreme differences in log stimulus magnitude are represented by fewer cells in the 21×21 matrix, there was some further grouping of average correlations for narrow ranges of these extreme differences. This means that the correlations in Fig. 9.1 are uncontaminated with the variation of $\log N$ with stimulus level, a variation which would otherwise have contributed a strong positive correlation (see Baird *et al.* 1980, pp. 285–6). The correlation of +0.8 when a stimulus value is repeated therefore means that two-thirds of the variability ($0.8^2 = 0.64$) of the second judgment is inherited from the first, which must therefore have been used as a point of reference.

This is the pattern when S_n differs by not more than 5 dB from S_{n-1}. It implies a particular procedure on the part of the subject in choosing his numerical response. The log number uttered on trial n is selected as bearing the kind of relationship to $\log N_{n-1}$ that $\log S_n$ is perceived to bear to $\log S_{n-1}$. If $\log N_{n-1}$ happens to be relatively high, relative to its overall distribution, so also is $\log N_n$, and vice versa. But since the subject cannot know until he has formulated his judgment what size of stimulus has been presented to him, the procedure followed cannot depend on the stimulus value to be judged. That is to say, the relative absence of correlation following a large stimulus difference does not mean that the judgment was not relative in the same way; instead, it means that the judgment was much more variable (in consequence of the large stimulus difference) and the correlation low for that reason. I leave the quantitative variation of the correlation coefficients with stimulus difference and the derivation of the theoretical curve in Fig. 9.1 until Chapter 10 (pp. 160–2).

This striking pattern of correlation of log magnitude estimates was discovered by Jesteadt *et al.* (1977a) in the course of a moderately routine regression analysis of $\log N_n$ on $\log S_n$, $\log S_{n-1}$, and $\log N_{n-1}$, intended to test the response ratio hypothesis of Luce and Green (1974). Green *et al.* (1977) then showed that the same pattern appeared in magnitude production of loudness (1 kHz tones again) as well as in magnitude estimation. Luce and Green (1978) showed that the maximum degree of correlation was reduced (to +0.5–0.6) in an experiment where the frequency of the tone changed (1 to 4 kHz) from one trial to another. Baird *et al.* (1980) have reported a similar pattern of correlation for the area of random geometric shapes (Fig. 10.6) and an attenuated pattern (maximum correlation +0.37) for cross-modality matching of loudness to area (Fig. 10.7). Further correlations have been contributed by Ward (1979) for the separation between two dots on a screen and for the matching of duration to separation.

It needs to be recorded that the typical instructions in these experiments 'emphasize[d] that perceived ratios among stimulus intensities should be preserved in the . . . responses' (Baird *et al.* 1980, p. 285). Such instructions might have accentuated the pattern exhibited in Fig. 9.1. Nevertheless, two conclusions follow. First, when successive stimuli are similar in level, each estimate is relative to the preceding stimulus and the number assigned to it. But a subject cannot know until judgment has been made whether the present stimulus is similar in level to its predecessor or not, so the same relative mode of judgment must apply irrespective of the relation between successive stimuli. That is to say, widely spaced stimuli must also be judged in relation to their predecessors, even though there is no corresponding correlation between successive responses (see later, pp. 160–2). Second, the point of reference varies from trial to trial, and the variability of magnitude estimates is increased thereby.

9.3 JUDGMENTS OF RATIOS AND JUDGMENTS OF DIFFERENCES

Notwithstanding the clear implication of the correlations in Fig. 9.1, there is a further experimental test needing to be carried out because it provides an independent basis for discrimination between the two generic classes of theory, mapping and relation.

A mapping theory assigns a subjective scale value to each individual stimulus. So when a pair of stimuli are presented, estimation of the ratio, of the sum, and of the difference, of the sensations which they evoke are three different mental operations with three distinct outcomes. The experimental evidence presented in Chapter 7 showed that at this point mapping theories, in general, proved inadequate because the ratio scale of sensation which is uniquely identified by judgments of ratios will not also accommodate the judgments of sums and differences. To put the matter succinctly, subjects seem unable to perform all those mental gymnastics which mapping theories say should be possible, to formulate all those judgments of the different relations which can be defined between an arbitrary pair of sensations.

If, however, the psychophysical primitive is the judgment of a relation between a *pair* of sensations, there is no psychological basis for distinguishing between the different kinds of relation (between the two sensations) that one might define between the physical magnitudes of the stimuli. In case this sounds counterintuitive: at the physical level of description length is a primitive property of a line. Given two lines, one can talk meaningfully about the ratio, the sum, and about the difference between their lengths. But given only one line, there is only one length that can be measured. There is no ratio, sum, or difference because there is only one length. What holds for a single line at the physical level of description (one might think of *length* as a relation between two points) holds, in a relation theory, for a *pair* of lines at the subjective level. The psychophysical primitive is the relation between that pair. There is no more primitive definition in a relation theory of the sensation of length evoked by a single line, so that, at the subjective level of description, only one relation can be identified between two lines (notwithstanding the transitory oversight of the originator of the idea; Krantz 1972, p. 196). This relation may be called a 'ratio' or a 'difference' or any other name one pleases, depending on the kind of scale one wishes to construct. To avoid biasing the subsequent discussion, I shall refer to it as the *psychophysical primitive.*

It is nevertheless the case that subjects give different numerical responses when asked to judge the 'ratios' of pairs of sensations to those that they give when asked to judge 'differences'. In any relation theory two sensations define only one psychophysical primitive, so that judgments of 'ratios' and judgments of 'differences' must have the same sensory foundation and ought to bear some simple relation, at least a monotonic relation, to each other.

This idea, that there might be a common sensory basis to the judgment of both ratios and differences, was first proposed by Torgerson (1961), but for a reason quite unconnected with the notion of a relation theory. Prior to the development of Stevens' (1956b) method of magnitude estimation, subjective sensation was conventionally scaled by assigning stimuli to categories separated by 'equal sense distances'. Plateau's (1872b) experiment, described on p. 3, was a very early example of this genre. Category judgment has received very little attention so far in this book because of the historical accident that when magnitude estimation was established as an experimental method and it became apparent that category scales were curvilinear with respect to magnitude estimates, Stevens (1957b) and Stevens and Galanter (1957) rejected category scales as 'biased'. But, subsequently, Galanter and Messick (1961) suggested, on the basis of an experiment in which the same subjects judged the same 20 levels of noise under both category and magnitude estimation instructions, that category scales might typically be a logarithmic function of magnitude (estimate) scales. In which case, they could well have a common sensory basis, with category judgments conforming to Fechner's Law and magnitude estimates to Stevens' Power Law. Torgerson was suggesting that if judgments of ratios (basically, magnitude estimates) and differences (category judgments) did indeed have a common sensory basis, then the controversy, at that time relatively fresh, between Fechner's Law and Stevens' Power Law might be unresolvable on empirical grounds. The difficulty is that, if judgments of sensation (either ratios or differences) can be formulated in terms of a power function, they can be formulated with equal precision in terms of a log function. This is the relation between eqns 2.1 and 2.2 on p. 24. A possibility of empirical discrimination between the two laws would exist only if judgments of 'ratios' revealed a different set of psychological values to judgments of 'differences'; and Torgerson cited data from Garner (1954a) to suggest that bisections of the *difference* between two stimuli (i.e. the 'arithmetic mean') seemed to yield the same stimulus value as an adjustment which formed equal ratios (i.e. the 'geometric mean'). It happens that the question, whether such a possibility of empirical discrimination between Fechner's and Stevens' Laws exists, also constitutes a critical test of relation theories, at least as they have been formulated by Krantz (1972). I enquire now whether the idea of a common sensory basis for both judgments of 'differences' and judgments of 'ratios' holds up under careful experimental study.

Birnbaum and Veit (1974) studied the judgment of relations between pairs of weights. Their weights were contained in identical plastic cylinders, to be lifted by the subject, weighing 50, 75, 100, 125, 150, 175, and 200 g. Some 36 different subjects were asked to judge, in different blocks of trials, both the differences and the ratios between each of the 49 possible pairs of weights, differences on a nine-point category scale, ratios on a numerical scale. They hypothesized that mean judgments could be simply related in this manner: if W_i and W_j are the scale values of weights i and j, then the judgment of difference

$$D_{ij} = c(W_i - W_j) + d, \tag{9.8}$$

while the judgment of ratio

$$R_{ij} = a \exp\{b(W_i - W_j)\}. \tag{9.9}$$

In these equations a, b, c, and d are constants, but the scale values W_i and W_j are the same.

Birnbaum and Veit (1974) proposed eqn 9.8 as a typical representation of judgments of differences, while eqn 9.9 was said to be typical of judgments of ratios. If now the same subject is asked to make both judgments (in separate experiments) with respect to the same pairs of stimuli, the logarithms of his ratio judgments

$$\begin{aligned} \ln R_{ij} &= b(W_i - W_j) + \ln a \\ &= (b/c)(D_{ij} - d) + \ln a \end{aligned} \tag{9.10}$$

should be linearly related to his difference judgments. Since the models for both difference and ratio tasks can be expressed in terms of differences between psychological scale values, those models can be supported by a relation-theoretic interpretation.

Compare all this with the model advocated by Curtis and Rule (1972; cf. Chapter 7, p. 92) which develops the ideas of Curtis *et al.* (1968). Once the domain of attention is broadened to include the judgment of differences as well as ratios, the spectrum of experimental findings is sufficiently varied to support a mapping-theoretic interpretation. If sensation is related to physical stimulus magnitude according to eqn 7.7, it follows that judgments of the ratios of sensations are given by

$$R_{ij} = (X_j/X_i)^{\beta_x/\beta_n} \tag{9.11a}$$

or[2]

$$\ln R_{ij} = (\beta_x/\beta_n)(\ln X_j - \ln X_i). \tag{9.11b}$$

Judgments of differences, on the other hand, are given by eqn 7.8 as

$$D_{ij} = (X_j^{\beta_x} - X_i^{\beta_x})^{1/\beta_n}. \tag{9.12}$$

Envisage, now, a complete orthogonal experiment, such as the one by Birnbaum and Veit (1974), with a fairly small set of stimuli in which every stimulus is paired equally often with every other stimulus (including itself) for judgment of both the difference and the ratio of the corresponding sensations. Equation 9.11b tells us that the average of the logarithms of the ratio judgments will be

$$\ln R_{\cdot j} = (\beta_x/\beta_n)\ln X_j - \bar{r}, \tag{9.13}$$

and the average difference judgment will be approximately

$$D_{\cdot j} \approx X_j^{\beta_x/\beta_n} - \bar{d}, \tag{9.14}$$

so that

$$\ln R_{\cdot j} \approx \ln (D_{\cdot j} + \bar{d}) - \bar{r}. \tag{9.15}$$

In these equations $\bar{r}$ and $\bar{d}$ are, respectively, the average values of $(\beta_x/\beta_n) \ln X_i$ and $X_i^{\beta_x/\beta_n}$. It can be seen that $\ln R_{\cdot j}$ is here (eqn 9.15) a *logarithmic* function of $D_{\cdot j}$, whereas Birnbaum's preferred model makes it a linear function (eqn 9.10).

Birnbaum (1980) brought together the data from Birnbaum and Veit (1974) and from six similar experiments by himself and his colleagues to discover which relation between $\ln R_{\cdot j}$ and $D_{\cdot j}$, the linear relation of eqn 9.10 or the logarithmic one of eqn 9.15, best described the empirical relation between judgments of (log) ratios and judgments of differences of sensation. The experiments which Birnbaum reanalysed are listed in Table 9.1 and the results of his reanalysis are plotted in Fig. 9.2. The relation between $\ln R_{\cdot j}$ and $D_{\cdot j}$ in eqn 9.15 is non-linear and for common scale values (that is, equating W in 9.8 and 9.9 with $X_j^{\beta_x}$ in 9.13 and 9.14) will depend on β_n. Birnbaum calculated the curvilinear predictions in Fig. 9.2 on the basis of $\beta_n^{-1} = 1.47$, since that was the average of the values summarized by Rule and Curtis (1982).

[2] The use of the symbols X_i, X_j for physical stimulus magnitudes will distinguish equations relating to Curtis *et al.*'s model from those relating to Birnbaum's.

Birnbaum's own model, which supposes a common sensory basis to both kinds of judgment, gives, of course, the straight line predictions in Fig. 9.2, and it is clear that every one of the seven experiments examined by Birnbaum accords more closely with the straight line predictions from his own model than with the curvilinear alternative derived from the model of Curtis and Rule. That conclusion was confirmed by a least squares analysis of each set of data with respect to each model. In addition, a straightforward plot of estimated ratios against estimated differences (Birnbaum 1980, p. 313, Fig. 4) showed rather few reversals with respect to a common rank order. Since then there have been two further experiments supporting the same conclusion. Birnbaum (1982a, p. 420) has reported an otherwise unpublished replication of the experiment by Hagerty and Birnbaum (1978), and Mellers *et al.* (1984) have reported another which will concern us below.

Table 9.1 Experiments reanalysed by Birnbaum (1980; cf. Fig. 7.1)

Stimulus attribute	Source	Number of stimuli	Stimulus range
Lifted weights	Birnbaum and Veit (1974)	7	50–200 g (linear spacing)
Frequency of tones, 78 dB SPL	Elmasian and Birnbaum (1984)	9	191–844 Hz (log spacing) 191–3730 Hz (log spacing)
Darkness of dot patterns	Birnbaum (1978)	7	8–90 dots (log spacing)
Amplitude of 1 kHz tones	Birnbaum and Elmasian (1977)	9	42–90 dB (log spacing)
Darkness of grey papers	Veit (1978) (Expt 1)	7	0.063–0.572 reflectance
Likeableness of adjectives	Hagerty and Birnbaum (1978)	7	'cruel'—'sincere'
Easterliness and westerliness of US cities	Birnbaum and Mellers (1978)	7	San Francisco–Philadelphia Philadelphia–San Francisco

From 'Comparison of two theories of 'ratio' and 'difference' judgments' by M.H. Birnbaum, *Journal of Experimental Psychology: General*, vol. 109, p. 310. © 1980, American Psychological Association. Reprinted by permission.

So far the evidence favours the proposal that there is a common sensory basis to judgments of both ratios and differences, and that idea is essential to any relation theory. But there is an alternative interpretation of Birnbaum's reanalysis. Equations 9.11–9.15 relate the *mean* judgments of log ratios and of differences to the subjective scale values of the stimuli. In any realizable experiment the judgments are scattered at random about their means, so that, in Birnbaum's reanalysis with respect to the model preferred by Curtis and Rule (eqns 9.11–9.15), there is an unpleasant mixture of non-linear transforms between scale values and mean judgments and averaging of data—a mixture which invariably tends to smooth out non-linearities in the empirical predictions. If the random contributions to the judgments are small, so that eqns 9.13 and 9.14 are adequate approximations even to the raw observations, this mixture of non-linear transformation and averaging matters little. But the examples cited on pp. 120–2 indicate that the precision of magnitude estimates is

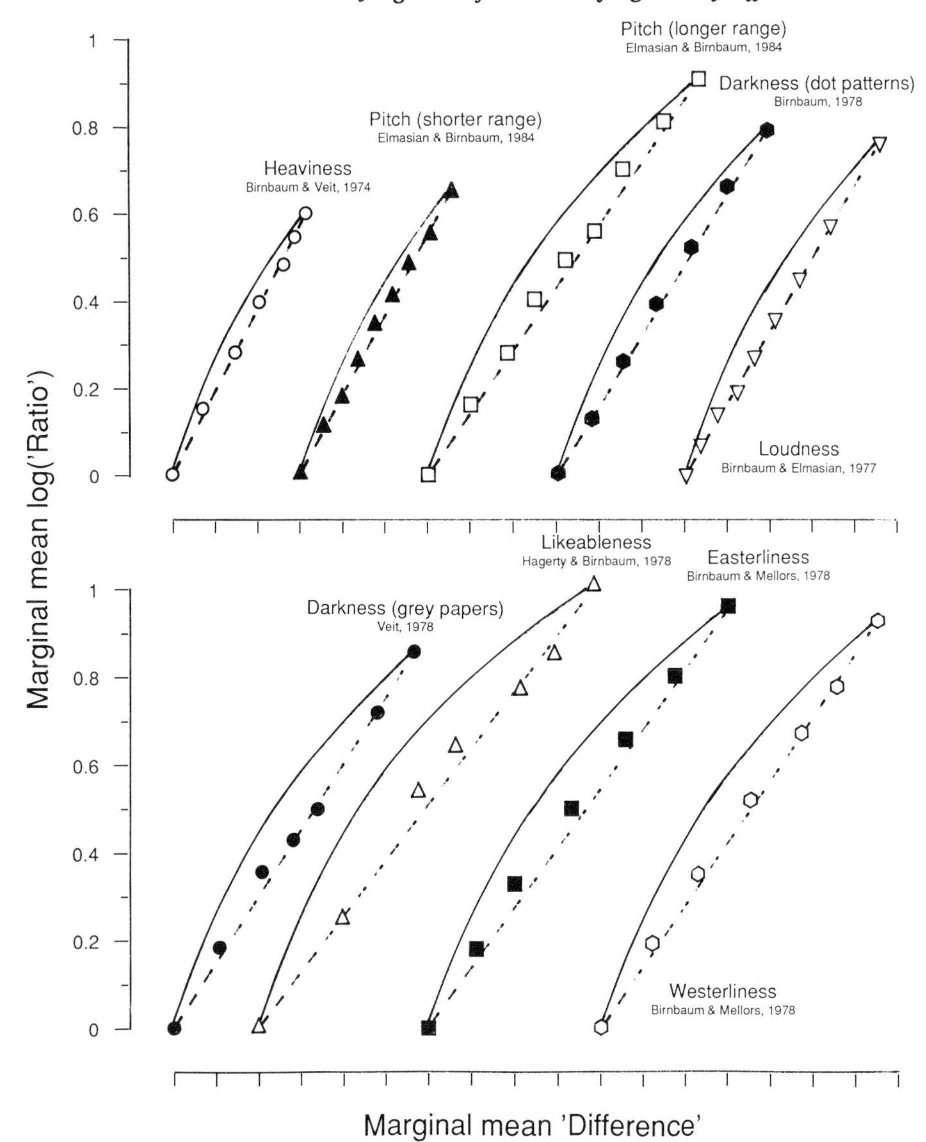

Fig. 9.2 Relation of marginal mean log 'Ratio' to marginal mean 'Difference' in the nine experiments listed in Table 9.1. The continuous curves represent eqn 9.15 with β_x/β_n in eqn 9.13 set to 1.47; while the broken straight lines are eqn 9.10. Different sets of data points have been shifted vertically to make the minimum log ratio in each case equal to zero and the 'difference' judgments are subject to an arbitrary linear transformation to make the configurations of the different sets of data comparable. (Redrawn from Birnbaum 1980, p. 311.)

unexpectedly poor and, presumably, the precision of the more complicated judgments required in the experiments reanalysed by Birnbaum poorer still. It is therefore questionable whether the reanalysis presented by Birnbaum (1980) adequately addresses the discrimination between the two hypotheses of interest.

9.4 A CRUCIAL EXPERIMENT?

It is, in fact, unexpectedly difficult to devise an experiment to effect that discrimination with sufficient precision. Such an experiment will typically present all possible pairs of stimuli from a small set equally often for judgment, asking on different occasions for an estimation of the ratio and of the difference between them. While specific models, one an example of mapping theory and the other a relation model, may be found to generate distinguishable predictions for the two kinds of judgment, it needs to be shown that an outcome that favours one model over the other does so because the sensory basis of the two kinds of judgment is, or is not, the same, rather than because of specific assumptions added into the models to generate quantitative predictions. That requirement can really be satisfied only if the predictions tested against the experimental data are, as it were, assumption-free—predictions about the rank orders of the two kinds of judgment, for example. Now, within the totality of pairs of stimuli drawn from a small fixed set, those pairs which display a large difference in magnitude will tend also to exhibit a large ratio between their magnitudes. So one must ordinarily expect to find a positive correlation between the rank orders of judgments of differences and of ratios. Indeed, combining that positive correlation with the typical imprecision of sensory judgment makes it plain that some extraordinary ingenuity is needed to obtain data from a complete orthogonal experiment that discriminates reliably between the class of mapping theories on the one hand and relation theories on the other. That extraordinary ingenuity has been displayed by Rule *et al.* (1981).

Rule *et al.* selected a set of eight weights: 20, 35.04, 56.18, 84.48, 120.97, 166.66, 222.66, and 290 g. The cube roots of these values differ by equal increments. The weights were suspended on nylon fishing lines passing through holes in a horizontal surface so that they were hidden from the subjects' view and the subjects' judgments of heaviness were unconfounded with the visual appearance of the weights. If, now, the subjective scale of heaviness be taken to be a power function of physical weight with an exponent of 0.7 (when this value is multiplied by $\beta_n^{-1} = 1.47$ in eqn 9.11 it gives 1.03, which is a typical value for the exponent obtained from magnitude estimation when the physical weights are hidden from sight; cf. Warren and Warren 1956, and p. 95 here), the differences between the subjective values of adjacent pairs of weights *increase* with scale value, while the ratios of those subjective values *decrease*. Moreover, a similar pattern of contrary variation obtains for pairs of weights separated by 2, 3, 4, 5, and 6 places in the sequence set out above. Rule, Curtis, and Mullin asked 80 subjects to judge the ratios of the heavinesses of pairs of weights; 10 subjects were assigned to each weight as standard and judged the ratio of each weight (including the standard itself) to their assigned standard five times, with the different pairs presented for judgment in random order. A further 15 different subjects estimated the difference in heaviness between all 28 pairs of (different) weights four times each.

Now a relation theory—any relation theory—says that while judgments of differences and of ratios may be related in some unspecified manner, that relation must be monotone. These two kinds of judgment have (it is asserted) a common sensory basis. If that basis generates an increase in one of the two kinds of judgment, it must *always* generate a corresponding increase in the other kind. So, to resolve the present controversy, it will be sufficient to examine just the *order* of the geometric mean judgments. The rank orders of the means of each kind of judgment are plotted in Fig. 9.3. Subsets of stimulus pairs separated by 1 (respectively 2, 3, 4, 5, 6 and 7) places in the sequence set out above are represented by different symbols and linked by different kinds of line. It can easily be seen that judgments of 'differences' and of 'ratios' between pairs of stimuli separated by 1 (respectively 2, 3, 4, 5, and 6) places in the sequence show contrary ordinal trends, correlating in the ordinal sense with a coefficient approaching -1. In short, in this present experiment with its cunningly conceived set of stimulus values, it seems that the two kinds of judgment, of differences in sensation and of ratios between sensations, cannot possibly be based on a common psychophysical primitive. Over the totality of stimulus pairs, judgments of differences and of ratios are positively correlated, as one would expect; but within the particular subsets deliberately created in the design of this experiment that correlation is clearly negative, contrary to prediction.

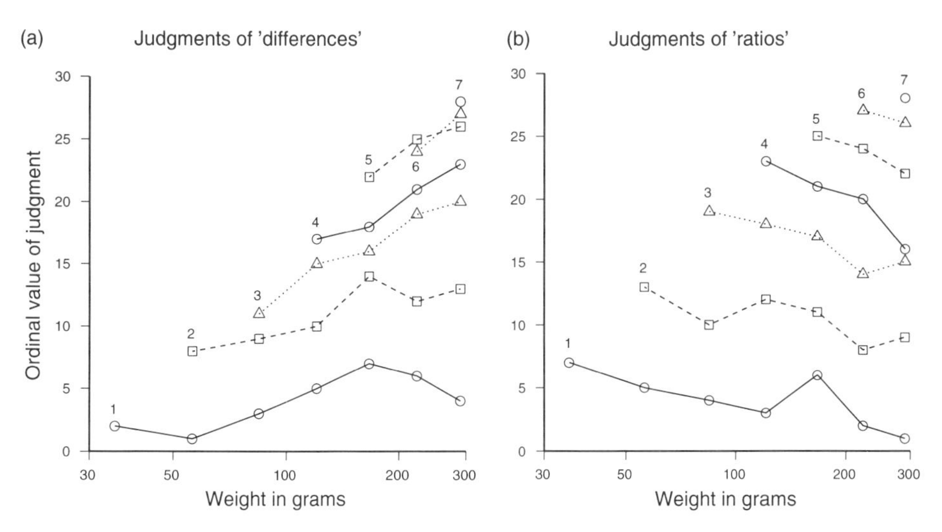

Fig. 9.3 Rank order of judgments of 'differences' and of 'ratios' for subsets of stimuli separated by 1 (respectively 2, 3, 4, 5, 6 and 7) places in the stimulus sequence in the experiment by Rule *et al.* (1981). Rank orders are plotted against the greater weight in each pair as abscissa. (Redrawn from Rule *et al.* 1981, p. 463.)

This experiment has been repeated by Mellers *et al.* (1984, Expt 1). Their replication is exact, even to minor details, except for the instructions to the subjects and the overall experimental plan. That plan differed in that all subjects contributed an equal number of judgments of both ratios and differences of all 64 pairs of weights, the different tasks, judgment of ratios, and judgment of differences being interleaved in different blocks of trials. But, notwithstanding the care taken to repeat the experiment exactly, the results from Mellers *et al.* were quite different. The pattern of mean log 'ratio' judgments, as a function of the two weights being compared, was very similar to the pattern of mean 'difference' judgments, in nice conformity with the model espoused by Birnbaum (1980; eqns 9.8–9.10 above); and the inversion of rank order between difference and ratio estimates within the subgroups of comparisons selected by Rule *et al.* (Fig. 9.3) was entirely lacking.

Looking at the differences between these two experiments in more detail, Mellers *et al.*'s (1984) mean log 'ratios' differ rather little from the pattern of means published by Rule *et al.*

(1981). Both sets of mean 'ratio' judgments are shown in Fig. 9.4 against a logarithmic ordinate. The data from Rule *et al.* are shown by open symbols (of the same shape as the corresponding symbols in Fig. 9.3). Those means contributed by a common group of subjects (10 different subjects were assigned to judge with respect to each standard) are linked by a broken line. The data from Mellers *et al.* are shown by filled symbols of the same shape as the corresponding data points from Rule *et al.* Mellers *et al.*'s subjects spread their ratio judgments a little less widely than Rule *et al.*'s subjects, but otherwise the similarity of numerical values is what one would expect from a meticulous replication. Indeed, the difference is sufficiently small that it could even have resulted from a difference in the way the means had been calculated: Mellers *et al.* used the same group of subjects to make all the ratio judgments; Rule *et al.* used a different subgroup of subjects to judge ratios with respect to each standard. That is therefore not a material difference between the two experiments.

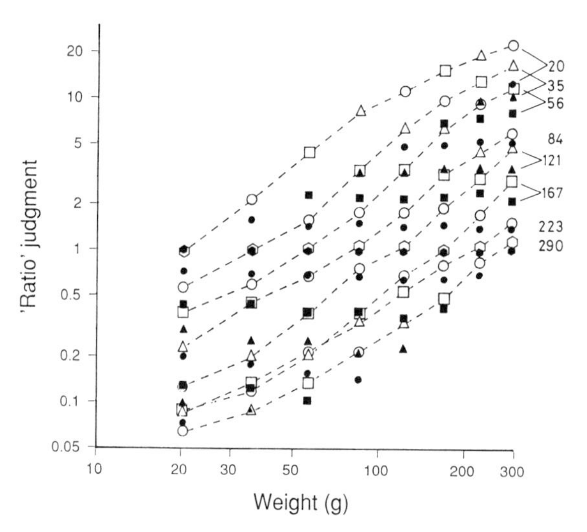

Fig. 9.4 'Ratio' judgments from the experiments by Rule *et al.* (1981; open symbols) and Mellers *et al.* (1984; filled symbols). The shape of the open symbols is the same as the corresponding data points in Fig. 9.3, and the shape of the filled symbols is the same as the corresponding open symbols here. The judgments contributed by different subgroups of subjects in Rule *et al.*'s experiment are linked by broken lines, with the weight of the standard indicated to the right. (Redrawn from Rule *et al.* 1981, p. 463, and Mellers *et al.* 1984, p. 220.)

Mellers *et al.*'s (1984) pattern of difference judgments also looks, at first sight, much like the pattern of data from Rule *et al.* (though Mellers *et al.* exhibit means for all 64 pairs of stimuli instead of the 28 comparisons only by Rule *et al.*). That similarity can be seen in Fig. 9.5, which is organized in the same manner as Fig. 9.4, but now in two separate panels with the ordinate scales adjusted to give approximately the same gradient to the data points. The similarity of the two patterns of data is striking—except that the data from Rule *et al.* (left-hand panel) are plotted against a logarithmic ordinate, while Mellers *et al.*'s data are plotted against a linear ordinate! That is to say, *the two experiments differ by an exponential transform of the difference judgments* from Mellers *et al.* to Rule *et al.* This is substantially the difference between eqns 9.10 and 9.15.

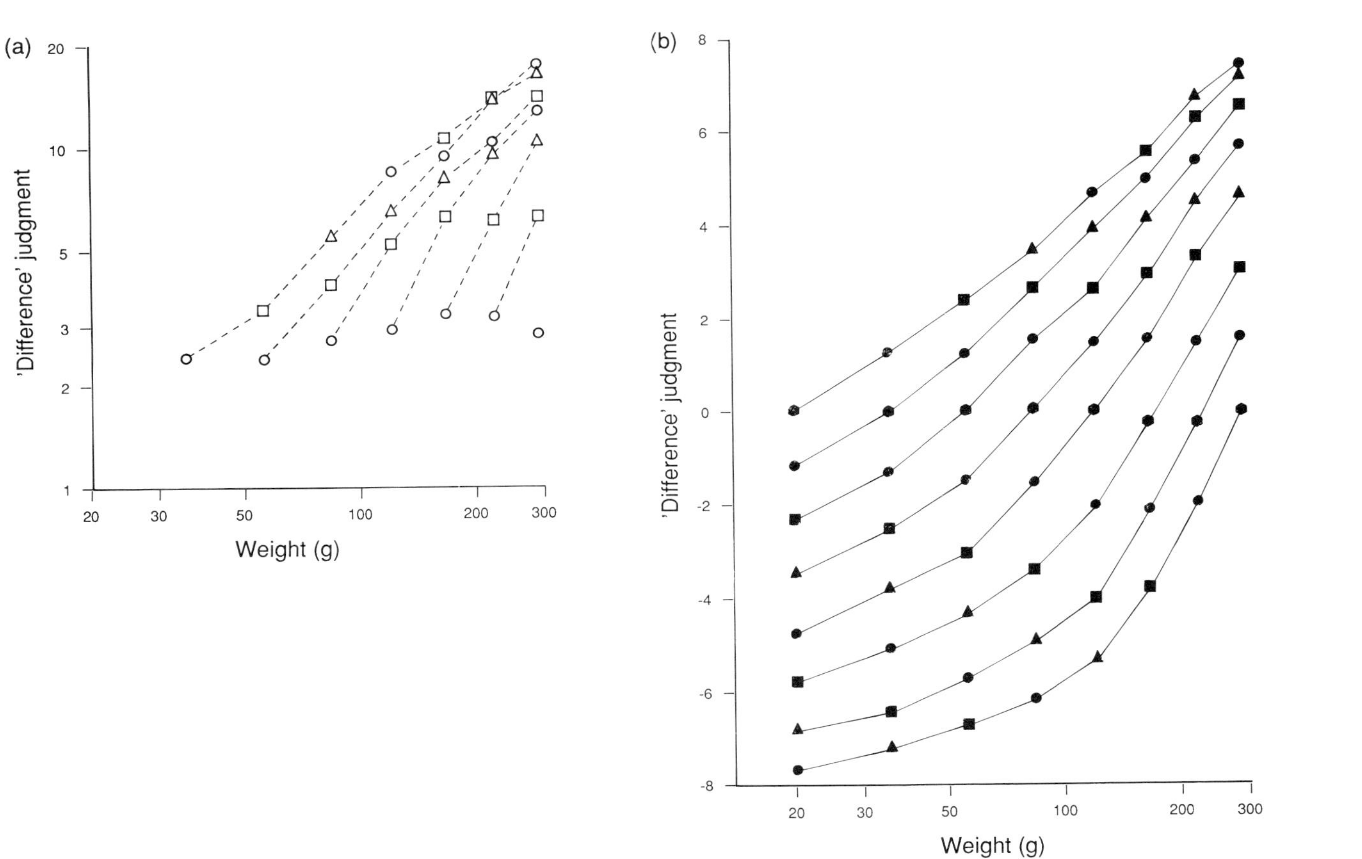

Fig. 9.5 'Difference' judgments from the experiments by Rule *et al.* (1981) (a) and Mellers *et al.* (1984) (b). As in Fig. 9.4, the shapes of the open symbols in (a) match the corresponding data points in Fig. 9.3, and the shapes of the filled symbols match the corresponding open symbols. The means of judgments with respect to a common standard (the same values as in Fig. 9.4) are linked by lines. (Redrawn from Rule *et al.* 1981, p. 463, and Mellers *et al.* 1984, p. 220.)

I emphasize that a meticulous replication of the original experiment by Rule *et al.* has given quite a different result. The difference between the original and the replication corresponds nicely to the difference in theoretical stance between the two groups of investigators. The two different results are in accord with the other experimental findings from each group, and the total pattern of reported results is reminiscent of the controversy over 'imageless' thought (e.g. Woodworth 1938, pp. 787–9). I conjecture that there is some critical difference between the two experiments which has not even found its way into the small print. I presume that neither set of authors is aware of that critical difference or, at most, they deem it to be quite insignificant.

Two possible resolutions of the conflict come to mind. One resolution says that Birnbaum and his colleagues have developed a way of instructing their subjects which induces most of them to present (very approximately) the exponentials of difference judgments as judgments of 'ratios' (or the logarithms of ratio judgments as judgments of 'differences'—one cannot tell which). This interpretation is suggested by the spontaneous report of one exceptional subject (who was omitted from the analysis) in the experiment by Mellers *et al.*

> This subject . . . voluntarily reported during the course of the experiment that he decided there were exactly eight weights. He informed the experimenter that he had assigned the numbers 1 through 8 to the successive weights, calculated a numerical difference or ratio depending on the task, and gave the computed number as his response. (Mellers *et al.* 1984, p. 221)

This strategy is exactly the model used by Rule *et al.* (1981, p. 462) to exemplify their theory, and their results (but not Mellers *et al.*'s) accord rather closely to it.

The second resolution suggests that subtle differences between the administration of the two experiments allowed Rule *et al.*'s subjects to identify the particular weight they were lifting with uncomfortably high accuracy and with artificial consequences. It is patent from Fig. 9.3 that Rule *et al.*'s subjects were judging two quite distinct relationships between the pairs of stimuli as 'differences' and as 'ratios'. This second possible resolution of the matter turns on the suggestion that their stimulus presentations provided cues sufficiently informative to support a perception of the different weights approaching the veridical (the subjects were allowed to lift the two weights in turn as often as they wished before making a judgment), in which case Rule *et al.*'s experiment does not bear on the question at issue.

If the question of one basis for both judgments or two separate bases is to be resolved with experiments such as these, it will be necessary to have collateral observations which tell us more about the subjects' internal mental processes. However, in the next chapter I present a different approach to the same problem. That approach shows that there is, after all, only one basis for judging a relation between a pair of attribute values.

9.5 COMMENTARY

The pattern of correlation between successive log magnitude estimates reported by Green, Luce, and their colleagues from several different experiments tells us that magnitude estimates are relative, relative to the stimulus and the number assigned to it on the preceding trial. Setting aside the possibility that the particular procedures in those experiments generate a fundamentally different kind of behaviour to that in magnitude estimation experiments elsewhere (similar patterns of correlation have been independently reported by Ward, 1979), magnitude estimation and, presumably, sensory judgments in general, need to be formulated within a relation theory.

As relation theories have been formulated by Krantz (1972), all judgments of a pair of stimuli, whether of the 'ratio' or of the 'difference' between the pair or whatever, are based on the same psychological primitive and should therefore, except for chance variation of the responses, show an ordinal correlation of +1.0 with each other. That happens because in a relation theory there can be only one psychological primitive derived from each pair. The body of experimental work summarized by Birnbaum (1980) accords nicely with that requirement, as also does the experiment by Mellers *et al.* (1984). But the original of that experiment by Rule *et al.* (1981) manifestly does not. What should one conclude?

Notwithstanding that Rule *et al.* (1981, p. 459) could conclude, quite correctly, that 'the judgments [in their experiment] were based on two perceived relations that are ordinarily consistent with arithmetic operations of ratios and differences', their experiment is not thereby incompatible with a relation theory. Consider this scenario.

In their experiment each subject lifts a sequence of weights, W_1, W_2, W_3 . . . Suppose that each weight is compared with its predecessor (i.e. W_n with W_{n-1} as in a relation theory) to estimate its *physical* weight. A (possibly notional) number $N(W_n|W_{n-1})$ is assigned to that estimate of physical weight, generating a sequence of numbers

$$N(W_{n-2}|W_{n-3}),\ N(W_{n-1}|W_{n-2}),\ N(W_n|W_{n-1}),\ N(W_{n+1}|W_n),\ N(W_{n+2}|W_{n+1})\ \ldots \qquad (9.16)$$

If the subject is asked to judge differences, he reports the difference between the two numbers assigned to the estimates of the corresponding weights, i.e. $\{N(W_n|W_{n-1}) - N(W_{n-1}|W_{n-2})\}$. If he is asked to judge ratios, he reports the ratio of the two numbers, i.e. $\{N(W_n|W_{n-1})/N(W_{n-1}|W_{n-2})\}$. If the stimulus values are chosen with sufficient cunning, as Rule *et al.* certainly did, selected subsets of judgments will exhibit an inverse correlation between the rank orders of judgments of ratios and of differences. But it is still the case that each weight is judged only in relation to its predecessor. There is no absolute judgment of heaviness as a mapping theory requires.

With this scenario in mind I return to the experiment by Marks (1978b) described in Chapter 7 (pp. 98–100), especially the data for successive presentation of the two tones in Fig. 7.2. The problem with those data is that the total loudness of a 5 kHz tone at 60, 70, and 80 dB was judged greater than that of an equal 5 kHz tone plus a low-level 2 kHz tone, the 2 kHz tone being presented equally often before and after its 5 kHz partner. This is frankly counterintuitive. Envisage that the loudness of each single tone is estimated, as it is presented, in relation to its predecessor—generating a sequence like

$$N(A_{n-2}|A_{n-3}),\ N(A_{n-1}|A_{n-2}),\ N(A_n|A_{n-1}),\ N(A_{n+1}|A_n),\ N(A_{n+2}|A_{n+1})\ \ldots \qquad (9.17)$$

To obtain a judgment of total loudness the numbers notionally assigned to the two tones in the pair are added together, i.e. $\{N(A_n|A_{n-1}) + N(A_{n+1}|A_n)\}$. The pairs of tones are presented in random order, so that when the 5 kHz tone is presented by itself it is preceded equally often by all of the 10 different tones (five levels of 2 kHz tone and five of 5 kHz). When, however, that same tone is presented as a member of a pair, it is preceded half of the time by its 2 kHz partner. There is therefore an implicit comparison between

1. $N(A_n^{(5)}|A_{n-1})$, where A_{n-1} is randomized over all the single tones employed in the experiment; and
2. $\{N(A_n^{(2)}|A_{n-1}) + N(A_{n+1}^{(5)}|A_n^{(2)})\}$, where A_{n-1} is randomized as before, but $A_n^{(2)}$ is always a 2 kHz tone of specific level.

Cross (1973), working in Stevens' laboratory, reported a magnitude estimation experiment with six levels of noise presented in such an order that each level was preceded equally often by every other level, including itself. His results may be succinctly summarized in the equation

$$\log N_n = 0.585 \log A_n + 0.055 \log A_{n-1}; \tag{9.18}$$

that is to say, the level of the immediately preceding noise biased the judgment of the present stimulus, creating thereby an incomparability between the two components in the comparison from Marks (1978b) set out above. Whether the bias in eqn 9.18 (coefficient 0.055) is powerful enough to have a noticeable effect (but Cross's reanalysis of data from a very similar experiment by Ward 1973, using 1 kHz tones, gave a coefficient of 0.177), and whether that bias may be extrapolated, just so, to Marks' experiment is unknown. But it is conceivable that in particular circumstances the lack of balance in respect of their predecessors between components 1 and 2 above could produce a reversal of their judged magnitudes. Herein lies a possible explanation of the anomaly. It is pertinent that no counterintuitive reversals occurred for pairs of tones.

The arguments and the experimental evidence presented in this chapter show that a theory of sensory judgment has to be a relation theory. What, then, is the nature of the relation between two stimuli on which numerical and category assignments are based? That is the natural next question.

10 The psychophysical primitive

Birnbaum (1978), surveying the experiments by himself and his colleagues which occupied part of the previous chapter, believes that the psychological primitive is a sensation difference, ratio judgments being an exponential function of that difference. The alternative, which he rejects, is a sensation ratio, difference judgments being a logarithmic function of that ratio. Birnbaum's conclusion rests on experiments involving quartets of stimuli and the judgment of such extravagant quantities as differences of ratios and ratios of differences. Those more elaborate experiments receive a brief mention below.

It is not clear whether Birnbaum's conclusion is intended to be absolute—'sensation difference' as the definitive primitive—or merely to state that the results of the experiments by himself and his colleagues are most simply formulated in terms of 'sensation difference'. If Birnbaum's conclusion is interpreted in an absolute sense, a certain difficulty arises. Judgments of sensation differences would be immediate, but judgments of ratios would require some mental arithmetic. Surely, subjects would know the difference—judgment of ratios would be noticeably more difficult and take longer, a matter which could be checked by measuring the response time—and there would be no need for the judgment of elaborate four-term relationships. But that increased difficulty has nowhere been reported. If, as is more reasonable, Birnbaum's conclusion is taken merely as expressing a preference how existing experimental results should be viewed, then the possibility is recognized of other formulations encompassing yet wider spectra of experimental findings.

In this chapter I present a third proposal for the psychological primitive which has the virtue that it accommodates, in addition, many existing results on the variability of sensory judgments.

10.1 ORDINAL JUDGMENT

Twelve years ago I proposed the following scheme (Laming 1984). Suppose the stimulus S_n presented on the nth trial has physical magnitude X_n and is *perceived* as having (physical) magnitude x_n. The physical magnitude X_n is a determinate value chosen by the experimenter, but the perceived magnitude x_n is an unobservable random variate internal to the subject. The difference between X_n and x_n models the error or variability of perception. The perceived magnitude x_n of the stimulus S_n is compared with the (perceived) magnitude x_{n-1} of the stimulus presented on the preceding trial with *five* possible qualitative outcomes:

$$\left.\begin{array}{l}
\text{(i) } \log x_n \text{ is very much greater than } \log x_{n-1}\ (\log x_n \gg \log x_{n-1});\\[1ex]
\text{(ii) } \log x_n \text{ is greater than } \log x_{n-1}\ (\log x_n > \log x_{n-1});\\[1ex]
\text{(iii) } \log x_n \text{ is equal to } \log x_{n-1}\ (\log x_n = \log x_{n-1});\\[1ex]
\text{(iv) } \log x_n \text{ is less than } \log x_{n-1}\ (\log x_n < \log x_{n-1});\\[1ex]
\text{(v) } \log x_n \text{ is very much less than } \log x_{n-1}\ (\log x_n \ll \log x_{n-1}).
\end{array}\right\} \qquad (10.1)$$

Since x_{n-1} provides only a single point of comparison, one might expect only *three* of these outcomes to be possible, (ii), (iii), and (iv), or even only two, (ii) and (iv). But a large number of experiments on the amount of information transmitted in category judgments, experiments which have been repeated with many different stimulus attributes, show that subjects are able to assign stimuli reliably to up to five distinct categories, but not more than five (see Garner 1962, Chapter 3; Laming 1984, p. 155, table 4). I therefore suggested that subjects are sensitive to the degree of difficulty experienced in comparing x_n with x_{n-1}, an idea previously suggested by Plateau (1872b; see p. 4 above). On some trials that difference may be so great that it is immediately obvious that S_n is (very much) greater than S_{n-1} (outcome (i)). On other trials that may become apparent only after some sensible time and effort spent in examination of the stimulus, in which case outcome (ii) (rather than (i) or (iii)) obtains. Depending on the perceived relation between S_n and S_{n-1} the subject selects a numerical response (magnitude estimate) N_n which bears a similar relation to N_{n-1}, the number uttered on trial $n-1$; specifically,

$$\left.\begin{array}{l}\text{(i) If } \log x_n \gg \log x_{n-1}, \text{ then } \log N_n \gg \log N_{n-1};\\ \text{(ii) If } \log x_n > \log x_{n-1}, \text{ then } \log N_n > \log N_{n-1};\\ \text{(iii) If } \log x_n = \log x_{n-1}, \text{ then } \log N_n = \log N_{n-1};\\ \text{(iv) If } \log x_n < \log x_{n-1}, \text{ then } \log N_n < \log N_{n-1};\\ \text{(v) If } \log x_n \ll \log x_{n-1}, \text{ then } \log N_n \ll \log N_{n-1};\end{array}\right\} \quad (10.2)$$

and so on.

This scheme of assignment is set out in Fig. 10.1, which presents a 'model' in the sense in which Poulton (1968, 1979, 1989) uses that term. The abscissa ($\log x_n / x_{n-1}$) is divided into five regions according as x_n <<, < , =, >, or >> x_{n-1}. The boundaries between those regions are not precise. The notion of what pairs of x_n and x_{n-1} may be taken to be equal (or 'very much less than', 'less than', 'greater than', or 'very much greater than') may vary from time to time during an experiment, and certainly from subject to subject if data are aggregated from a cohort of subjects before analysis. When S_n is judged to be the same as S_{n-1} (dark grey region), it is given the same number ($\log N_n / N_{n-1} = 0$). When, instead, S_n is judged to be greater (or less) than S_{n-1} (mid-grey regions), it is given a number N_n greater (or less) than N_{n-1}. Subjects' preference for round numbers means that N_n usually bears some simple integer ratio to N_{n-1}, and the horizontal lines in the figure correspond to the ratios 5/4, 3/2, 2, 5/2, and 3 (4/5, 2/3, 1/2, 2/5, and 1/3). The actual choice of numerical ratio will depend on the previous value of N_{n-1} (to make N_n a round number), but not (within the mid-grey region) on $\log x_n / x_{n-1}$. In the same way, when S_n is judged to be very much greater (or very much less) than S_{n-1} (pale grey regions), it is given a number N_n very much greater (or very much less) than N_{n-1}; the horizontal lines in the diagram now correspond to the ratios 5/2, 3, 4, 5, and 6 (2/5, 1/3, 1/4, 1/5, and 1/6). The total range of numerical judgments (1 : 36) represented in the diagram has been chosen to be close to the typical range of responses (see Figs 11.5 and 11.7) discovered by Teghtsoonian (1971) in his analysis of range effects amongst S.S. Stevens' data.

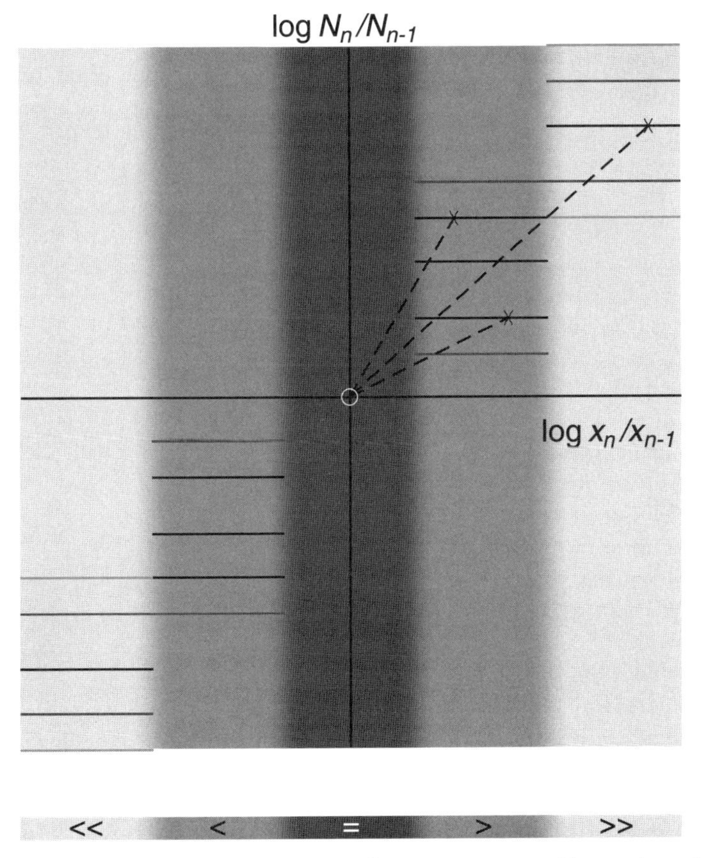

Fig. 10.1 A diagram to illustrate the ordinal scheme of assignment 10.2. Different values of $\log x_n/x_{n-1}$ are divided into five categories (<<, <, =, >, and >>) separated by fuzzy boundaries. When S_n is judged to be the same as S_{n-1} ($\log x_n/x_{n-1} \approx 0$), it is given the same number; that response is represented by the filled circle at the origin. Otherwise the choices of number for a given category of relationship may vary. The asterisks represent three particular assignments and the broken lines connecting those assignments to the fixed point at the origin correspond to a ratio scale with a random scale unit.

The ratio between successive numerical assignments (i.e. N_n/N_{n-1}) will vary from one trial to another, even though the pair of stimuli (the stimulus to be judged and its predecessor) are the same. But the logarithm of that ratio can always be divided by the actual value of $\log x_n/x_{n-1}$ to give a gradient B_n, which will vary randomly from trial to trial. The overall scheme of assignment amounts to a ratio scale with a random scale unit.

In view of the kinds of ideas generated within signal detection theory (see Green and Swets 1966; Macmillan and Creelman 1991), one might well ask why this scheme cannot be specified more precisely than it is. An analogy with the dynamics of a roulette wheel will explain why. The roulette wheel spins inside a bowl. The croupier propels the ball along the rim of the bowl where, after perhaps two revolutions, it begins to descend, through loss of speed, down the wall of the bowl and onto the wheel, which is spinning all the while. There the ball is deflected by contact with one or more of the wheel's spoilers and eventually finishes in one of the numbered pockets. The entire process is governed by the physical dynamics of elastic bodies and, *in principle*, the ultimate destination of the ball should be calculable from initial conditions. But, *in practice*, the calculations are much too complex to be carried out with that kind of accuracy and the initial conditions are never known with sufficient precision. Instead, any calculations concerning the outcome of the game of roulette have to make do with a very simple probabilistic model of the wheel which says that at each play all pockets are equally likely as the ultimate destination of the ball. In like manner, one might imagine some quite elaborate mental operations intervening between the presentation of a stimulus and the production of a judgment. But, in the present state of knowledge, it is not possible to say what those mental operations might be, or even to make an intelligent guess, and the simple ordinal scheme of assignment set out in eqns 10.2 and Fig. 10.1 is as precise as it is feasible to be at this point in time.

By means of this assignment the numbers uttered as magnitude estimates increase and decrease in a *qualitative* sense, according as the stimuli are perceived to do likewise. The idea 10.2 was based on my reading (Laming 1984) of the category judgment experiments summarized by Garner (1962, Chapter 3) and especially the studies by Pollack (1952, 1953). At that time of writing I had yet to discover the intuition by Plateau (1872b, quoted above on p. 4) which is realized exactly in this scheme. Merely ordinal judgment in Stevens' 'direct' methods has also been suggested by Mashhour (1965). It will be explained later (see eqn 10.3) how this ordinal scheme of assignment can nevertheless be harnessed to deliver quantitative predictions for particular experiments.

In the experiments by Birnbaum and his colleagues, comparing judgments of differences of sensation with judgments of ratios, subjects were offered the usual continuum of numerical responses, as in any magnitude estimation experiment, for expressing their judgment of a ratio. The scheme set out above can be applied as it stands, with but one modification. Since judgment is requested of the ratio between successive stimuli S_n and S_{n-1}, the numerical response should correspond to N_n/N_{n-1}. For the judgment of differences, on the other hand, Birnbaum's subjects were offered a category scale (a nine-point scale in Birnbaum and Veit, 1974). The same scheme will suffice if a category assignment C_n is substituted for $\{\log N_n - \log N_{n-1}\}$. The typical relationship of judgments of 'ratios' to judgments of 'differences' can thereby be seen to reflect the mathematical relation between the different scales on which subjects are asked to give their responses. Each judgment of a 'difference' is represented by a shift, either a large shift or a small shift, outwards from the centre of an equal interval scale (1, 2, 3, . . . 9), and each judgment of a 'ratio' by some multiple or fraction, either a large multiple or a small, of a neutral point (100) on the real number scale. It is not clear that judgments of 'ratios' and judgments of 'differences' differ in any other respect.

There is, however, one problem needing comment. Birnbaum (1978) based his argument for sensation difference as the psychological primitive on experiments by Veit (1978) and by Hagerty and Birnbaum (197b) which compared four different four-stimulus tasks, judgment of, respectively, ratios of ratios, ratio of differences, difference of ratios, and difference of differences. Without going into details, all these four tasks appeared to give distinctive results in the sense that their data could not be reduced to an expression of the same intermediary on different numerical response scales (as with 'ratios' and 'differences' above). Such distinctive results appear intuitively to require a more precise basis for judgment than could be afforded by the simple ordinal scheme set out in 10.1 and 10.2.

No details have been published of the precision of the judgments in any of Birnbaum's experiments. In view of the accumulated evidence from category judgment experiments mentioned above, one would expect that precision to be limited to an accuracy equivalent to an assignment to at most five distinct categories; and such a limit is built into the scheme I have set out. If that were true of the judgment of basic 'differences' and 'ratios', it is difficult to see how the more elaborate four-stimulus judgments could be so distinctive. There is, however, an alternative, if speculative, possibility. If, as with the exceptional subject in Mellers *et al.*'s (1984) experiment, the stimulus cues afforded a near-veridical perception of stimulus pairs, that is, of ratios/differences, then the distinctive results for the more elaborate four-stimulus judgments would fall into place. But, as with the experiment by Rule *et al.* (1981) above, they would not then address the question of interest.

In addition to the foregoing explanation of the typical relation between judgments of 'ratios' and of 'differences' found by Birnbaum and his colleagues, the scheme I proposed in 1984 also offered quantitative explanations of the following phenomena, of which the first four are amplified below:

1. The increase in the variability of absolute identification in proportion to the geometric range of the stimulus set (Laming 1991b; see Fig. 10.2).
2. The increase of variability of successive log numerical estimates from trial to trial, as in J.C. Stevens and Tulving (1957; see Fig. 10.3).
3. The variation of the interquartile intervals in Stevens' (1975; see also Stevens 1971, p. 442, and Fig. 10.4) loudness estimation data with relative position within the stimulus set.
4. The autocorrelation of log magnitude estimates from Baird *et al.* (1980; see Fig. 9.1), including the variation of the correlation coefficient with stimulus dB difference.
5. The limit to the amount of information transmitted in absolute judgments (equivalent to the use of at most five categories without error); though the 'five' is assumption, not explanation.
6. The variation in the precision of category judgment when the stimuli are presented in a constrained, only partially random, sequence (Luce *et al.* 1982).

I comment that a scheme which is able to relate such a number and diversity of previously unrelated experimental findings probably does so by capturing some essential characteristic of the underlying psychological process rather than by mere chance. In the remainder of this chapter I set out a simple model which encapsulates my scheme and then apply it to the first four of the phenomena listed above. This exercise will explain by illustration.

10.2 A MODEL FOR 'ABSOLUTE' JUDGMENT

The scheme of ordinal assignment 10.2 maps differences between successive log perceived stimulus magnitudes onto differences between successive log numerical assignments. The variables N_n and N_{n-1} are actual numbers uttered as responses by the subject, and the variables x_n and x_{n-1} are interpreted as stimulus magnitudes, but stimulus magnitudes as they are perceived by the subject, that is, subject to errors of perception. The quantities $\log x_n$ and $\log x_{n-1}$ are sample values from the normal model of eqn 3.2 (p. 32) with means

$\log X_n$ and $\log X_{n-1}$ and common variance σ^2. But because the scheme of assignment of $(\log N_n - \log N_{n-1})$ to $(\log x_n - \log x_{n-1})$ is little better than ordinal, the quotient $(\log N_n - \log N_{n-1})/(\log x_n - \log x_{n-1})$ varies at random from trial to trial. The asterisks in Fig. 10.1 represent three such numerical assignments. It is convenient to formulate the scheme of assignment as a ratio scale with a random scale unit

$$\log N_n - \log N_{n-1} = B_n(\log x_n - \log x_{n-1}), \tag{10.3}$$

where B_n, the gradient of a line drawn from the origin to the point of assignment (i.e. to an asterisk in Fig. 10.1) is a positive *random* coefficient taking independent values on successive trials. The scheme can also be expressed in the form

$$(N_n/N_{n-1}) = (x_n/x_{n-1})^{B_n}. \tag{10.4}$$

Equation 10.3 has the form of a regression equation; but it needs to be emphasized that the randomness intrinsic to the ordinal scheme 10.2 cannot be adequately represented by an *additive* error term (as is conventional in regression analysis). The ordinal assignment has a fixed point at $\log x_n - \log x_{n-1} = 0$ (the open circle in inverse contrast at the origin in Fig. 10.1) and its intrinsic randomness concerns the *scale* of the assignment about that fixed point. That dictates a random coefficient whose variation will prove instrumental in the explanation of a wide variety of phenomena.

Equation 10.3 means, immediately, that there can be ***no absolute judgment*** of stimuli; every stimulus is judged in relation to its predecessor. It is unequivocally relation-theoretic. It means also that there can be no absolute judgment of *ratios* of stimulus magnitude (differences in log magnitude) either. This is not immediately obvious because it looks, in view of the way the equation is written, as though the increment in log estimate $(\log N_n - \log N_{n-1})$ is strictly proportional to the increment in perceived log magnitude $(\log x_n - \log x_{n-1})$. This is not, in fact, so.

If the mapping from physical stimulus magnitude to numerical estimate is a ratio scale, there must be two fixed points, internal to the subject, to fix the zero and the unit of the mapping. That view, implicit to Stevens' Power Law, cannot accommodate the accumulated spectrum of experimental findings. It is clear from the pattern of autocorrelation (Fig. 9.1) that one point of the mapping is contributed by the stimulus presented and the response made on the preceding trial. Such a point of comparison is not fixed, internal to the subject; instead, it varies from trial to trial and predicates a relation theory of magnitude estimation. That variable point of comparison defines a zero for the comparison, and the critical question which now presents itself is whether there is an internal unit for the assessment of relations between stimuli. Briefly, is there an internal scale for the estimation of differences in log stimulus magnitude, or ratios of magnitude, from one trial to the next?

It is common to suppose that there is such an internal scale unit. For example, Krantz's (1972) choice of relational axioms ensures that there is a representation of the stimulus dimension (a scale) such that one stimulus ratio is judged greater than another if (and only if) the ratio of the corresponding scale values is greater (Krantz 1972, p. 186, Theorem 2). This only differs at a philosophical level from a straightforward mapping theory. Luce and Green (1974) introduce errors of perception in their response ratio hypothesis, but accompanied by a curious device. Each stimulus is assumed to generate *two* independent random variables to support the judgment process; call them x_n and x_n^*. The numerical estimate on trial n is related to that on trial $n - 1$ according to

$$N_n/N_{n-1} = cx_n/x_{n-1}^*, \tag{10.5}$$

where c is a constant representing a drift of the numerical responses. Thus, one quantity x_n enters into the judgment of the stimulus presented on trial n; the other independent quantity x_n^* provides the comparator for the judgment on the next trial $n + 1$. This use of two independent random variables to model each trial looks odd, but is necessary to preserve the relational character of the model. If there were only one intermediate variable proposed (i.e. if $x_n^* = x_n$), then eqn 10.5 would reduce to

$$N_n/N_{n-1} = cx_n/x_{n-1},$$

which implies

$$N_n/N_0 = c^n x_n/x_0; \tag{10.6}$$

that is, all judgments would be effectively referred to the initial standard and its modulus, and any properties of the model specific to the judgment of ratios would disappear. But that disappearance happens only if the judgment of ratios is treated as an arithmetic matter with respect to a fixed scale unit.

What is specifically different in eqn 10.3 is that the coefficient B_n of the mapping of differences in log stimulus magnitude onto differences in log numerical estimate is *random*. Not only does the judgment on the preceding trial provide a variable point of comparison, it provides the *only* such point. Equation 10.3 formulates a *rough correlation* only between the two sets of variables, not an exact proportionality. The assignment of numbers to stimuli is basically an *ordinal* operation. This is represented in eqn 10.3 by a *random* scale 'unit'.

The dramatic effect of making B_n a *random* coefficient can hardly be over-emphasized. It is most readily brought out by calculating the variances on each side of eqn 10.3. Taking expectations,

$$E\{\log N_n - \log N_{n-1}\} = \beta(\log X_n - \log X_{n-1}), \tag{10.7}$$

where β is the mean of B_n. Equation 10.7 is a relation-theoretic expression of Stevens' Power Law (though not an explanation; that problem is postponed until the next chapter) and β is the exponent. Writing $\beta + \delta_n$ for B_n and $\log X_n + \varepsilon_n$ for $\log x_n$, where δ_n and ε_n are independent error variables of zero expectation, eqn 10.3 becomes

$$\log N_n - \log N_{n-1} = (\beta + \delta_n)(\log X_n - \log X_{n-1} + \varepsilon_n - \varepsilon_{n-1}). \tag{10.8}$$

Subtracting eqn 10.7, squaring each side, and taking expectations of the squares now gives

$$\mathrm{Var}\{\log N_n - \log N_{n-1}\} = E\{\delta_n^2\}(\log X_n - \log X_{n-1})^2 +$$

$$\beta^2 E\{(\varepsilon_n - \varepsilon_{n-1})^2\} + \mathrm{E}\{\delta_n^2\}^2 \mathrm{E}\{(\varepsilon_n - \varepsilon_{n-1})^2\}$$

$$= \sigma_\beta^2(\log X_n - \log X_{n-1})^2 + 2\beta^2\sigma^2 + 2\sigma_\beta^2\sigma^2, \qquad (10.9)$$

in which σ_β^2 is the variance of δ_n and σ^2 the common variance of ε_n and ε_{n-1}. In this equation the two terms $2\beta^2\sigma^2$ and $2\sigma_\beta^2\sigma^2$ represent respectively errors of perception and their interaction with the judgment process, and I shall abbreviate them with the single term v_0:

$$v_0 = 2\beta^2\sigma^2 + 2\sigma_\beta^2\sigma^2. \qquad (10.10)$$

But what is especially important in eqn 10.9 is the component of variability on the right-hand side proportional to the *square* of the log stimulus difference $(\log X_n - \log X_{n-1})$. This term enters the equation precisely because B_n is random, that is, because σ_β^2 is greater than zero.

10.3 THE VARIABILITY OF ABSOLUTE IDENTIFICATION

The most immediate confirmation of the model comes from an absolute identification (category judgment) experiment (Braida and Durlach 1972, Expt 4). In this application log numerical judgment ($\log N_n$) in eqn 10.3 is replaced by category assignments (C_n) to give

$$C_n - C_{n-1} = B_n(\log x_n - \log x_{n-1}). \qquad (10.11)$$

The possible values of B_n are now constrained so as to make the left-hand side of eqn 10.11 an integer. Alternatively, one might conceive of the right-hand side of eqn 10.11 as a continuous variable which is rounded to the nearest integer to determine C_n in relation to C_{n-1}, the rounding being ignored in the calculations which follow. Present knowledge of the subject's mental processes is insufficient to indicate any more elaborate idea (cf. pp. 146–6 above) and either interpretation of eqn 10.11 is sufficiently approximate in relation to the precision of existing experimental data.

Braida and Durlach (1972, Expt 4) presented 1 kHz tones of 500 ms duration and of various levels, one at a time, for identification. There were tones of 10 different levels spaced, in different sessions, at ¼, ½, 1, 2, 3, 4, 5, and 6 dB intervals. The highest level was always 86 dB, so that the range of stimuli presented for identification was 83.75–86 dB in one extreme case and 32–86 dB in the other. On each trial one of these tones, selected at random, was presented to the subject for identification. The responses were the numbers 1 to 10, and after each response the subject was told the correct answer. This means that while the actual category assignment C_{n-1} on trial $n-1$ may have been in error, the correct assignment is known without error before it has to be used as a point of reference for the assignment on trial n. Any variability attaching to C_{n-1} in eqn 10.11 should therefore be disregarded in calculating the variance of C_n, which is equal to

$$\mathrm{Var}\{C_n - C_{n-1}\} = \sigma_\beta^2(\log X_n - \log X_{n-1})^2 + v_0, \qquad (10.12)$$

rewriting eqns 10.9 and 10.10.

In the experiment the stimuli S_n and S_{n-1} were chosen independently and at random from a set of 10, equally spaced on the dB scale. The amplitude ratio of the highest stimulus to the lowest defines a geometric range $\mathscr{S}$, and the logarithmic range ($\log \mathscr{S}$) plays an important part in the argument which follows through its contribution to the average value of $(\log X_n - \log X_{n-1})^2$ in eqn 10.12. But since that average will be needed later in the analysis of several further experiments, it is worth developing a general formula here.

Suppose there are k stimuli spaced evenly over the logarithmic range $\log \mathscr{S}$. There are $k - 1$ equal spaces between those stimuli (there being one stimulus at each end of the range) and each space is equal to

$$\Delta = (\log \mathscr{S})/(k - 1). \tag{10.13}$$

The average value of $(\log X_n - \log X_{n-1})^2$ is now

$$k^{-2}\Sigma_{ij}(\log X_i - \log X_j)^2,$$

where i and j vary independently over the range $(1, \ldots k)$,

$$= k^{-2}\,\Sigma_{ij}[(\log X_i - \log \overline{X}) + (\log \overline{X} - \log X_j)]^2,$$

where $\log \overline{X}$ is the average of the $\log X_i$,

$$= k^{-2}\Sigma_{ij}[(\log X_i - \log \overline{X})^2 + (\log \overline{X} - \log X_j)^2],$$

because the cross-product terms sum to zero,

$$= 2\,k^{-2}\,\Sigma_i\,(\log X_i - \log \overline{X})^2$$

$$= 2k^{-1}\sum_{i=1}^{k}[i - \tfrac{1}{2}(k + 1)]^2\Delta^2,$$

by setting $\log X_1$ equal to 0 and $\log X_i$ equal to $(i - 1)\Delta$

$$= (k^2 - 1)\Delta^2/6$$

$$= \{(k + 1)/6(k - 1)\}(\log \mathscr{S})^2, \tag{10.14}$$

on substituting from eqn 10.13. In particular, the average value of $(\log X_n - \log X_{n-1})^2$ for 10 equally spaced stimuli is $11(\log \mathscr{S})^2/54$. So, approximately,

$$\mathrm{Var}\{C_n\} = \sigma_\beta^2(\log \mathscr{S})^2/5 + v_0. \tag{10.15}$$

The data from each session consist of a 10×10 matrix of stimulus-response frequencies which may conveniently be analysed by means of a Thurstone Case V model (i.e. eqn 3.2; see Torgerson 1958, Model 1D). In applying this model it is customary to set the standard deviations of the discriminal dispersions to unity and estimate the best fitting means for the stimuli, and when this is done the stimulus means increase roughly as the logarithms of the physical stimulus magnitudes (i.e. linear with respect to dB; see Kornbrot 1984, p. 195, fig. 5). But the particular analysis I present here is different. The stimulus means were set equal to their decibel values (i.e. at equal intervals on the scale of log physical magnitude) and a common variance estimated in dB^2, the same variance for all the stimuli within any one set, but an independent variance for each stimulus spacing. These estimates of variance show how the variability of judgment varies with the logarithmic range of the stimulus set.

The results of the calculation for three different subjects are shown in Fig. 10.2. It is clear that the model variance increases approximately in proportion to the square of the stimulus spacing (the abscissa of Fig. 10.2 is scaled in proportion to the *square*) or, what is equivalent, the square of the log stimulus range. This is the immediate consequence of the involvement of the log stimulus range in eqn 10.15 which, in turn, results from the coefficient B_n in eqn 10.11 being random. The straight line represents the regression of estimated variance (dB^2) on the square of the stimulus spacing (again dB^2). It has a gradient of 0.486 and a small positive intercept on the abscissa equal to 1.52 dB^2. This is an estimate of the quantity v_0 introduced in eqn 10.10.

If one asks what kind of experiment would employ a zero stimulus range, the nearest equivalent is the measurement of a difference threshold between two separate tones. Jesteadt *et al.* (1977b) reported a Weber fraction of 0.43 dB (71 per cent correct, 2AFC) at 80 dB SL. This is equivalent to 0.79 dB at 84 per cent correct (which is equivalent to one standard

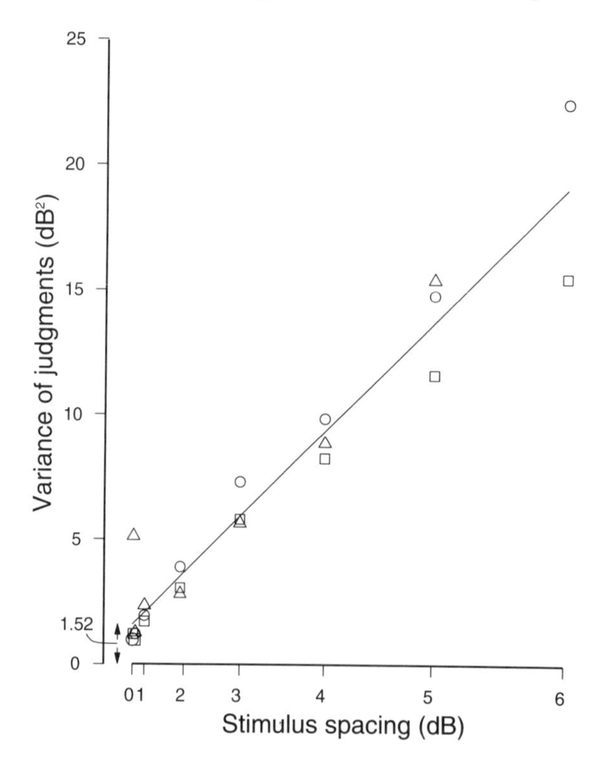

Fig. 10.2 Estimates of the variance of identification judgments in each condition (different stimulus spacings) in Experiment 4 by Braida and Durlach (1972). Differently shaped symbols show estimates from three different subjects. The straight line is eqn 10.15.

deviation in the normal integral model of the discriminability function) and to 1.12 dB when nominal allowance is made for the difference between a 2AFC paradigm (Jesteadt *et al.* 1977b) and a single stimulus presentation (Braida and Durlach 1972). The corresponding variance from Jesteadt *et al.* is therefore 1.25 dB^2.

10.4 THE VARIANCE OF LOG MAGNITUDE ESTIMATES

I am concerned next, not with the excessive variance of magnitude estimates relative to threshold judgments (cf. pp. 120–2), but, first, with the increase in the variability of log estimates from trial to trial in the experiment by J.C. Stevens and Tulving (1957) and, second, with the asymptotic variation of the interquartile interval with respect to position within the stimulus set in Stevens' (1975) data on loudness.

10.4.1 **Trial-to-trial increase in variability**

J.C. Stevens and Tulving (1957, Expt I) recorded magnitude estimates from a class of 70 naive subjects making their very first judgments of loudness. Eight different samples of white noise of about 3 s duration were presented in a common order with the instructions: 'Try to make the ratios between the different noises [*sic*] correspond to the ratios between the loudnesses of the noises. In other words try to make the number proportional to the loudness as you hear it' (J.C. Stevens and Tulving 1957, p. 601). The intensity levels of the successive samples of noise are shown in Fig. 10.3 together with the cumulative distributions of the 70 numbers assigned to each. The estimates uttered by different subjects have been normalized according to the procedure described on p. 56 and the distributions shown reflect only *intra*subject variability.

Magnitude estimates have an approximately log-normal distribution; accordingly the data in Fig. 10.3 are plotted against a logarithmic abscissa and a normal probability ordinate. This makes the cumulative distribution function appear as a straight line of gradient proportional to the inverse of the standard deviation (with respect to $\log N$). Straight lines have been fitted to the samples of magnitude estimates in Fig. 10.3, from which their respective standard deviations and variances may be estimated. Those estimates are set out in Table 10.1 where it can be seen that the variance of the estimates *increases* over the first three or four stimuli to an asymptotic value of about 0.030 square log units. This is the trial-to-trial increase in variability requiring explanation.

Special care was taken to avoid suggesting any particular number to be assigned to the first sample of noise. But, since the data in Fig. 10.3 have been normalized, it is reasonable to introduce a notional standard stimulus X_0 and modulus N_0. Then the (adjusted) first estimate is, from eqn 10.8,

$$\log N_1 - \log N_0 = (\beta + \delta_1)(\log X_1 - \log X_0 + \varepsilon_1 - \varepsilon_0) \qquad (10.16)$$

and its variance, from eqn 10.9,

$$\mathrm{Var}\{\log N_1\} = \sigma_\beta^2(\log X_1 - \log X_0)^2 + 2\beta^2\sigma^2 + 2\sigma_\beta^2\sigma^2, \qquad (10.17)$$

it being taken for granted that the (notional) modulus N_0 is fixed.

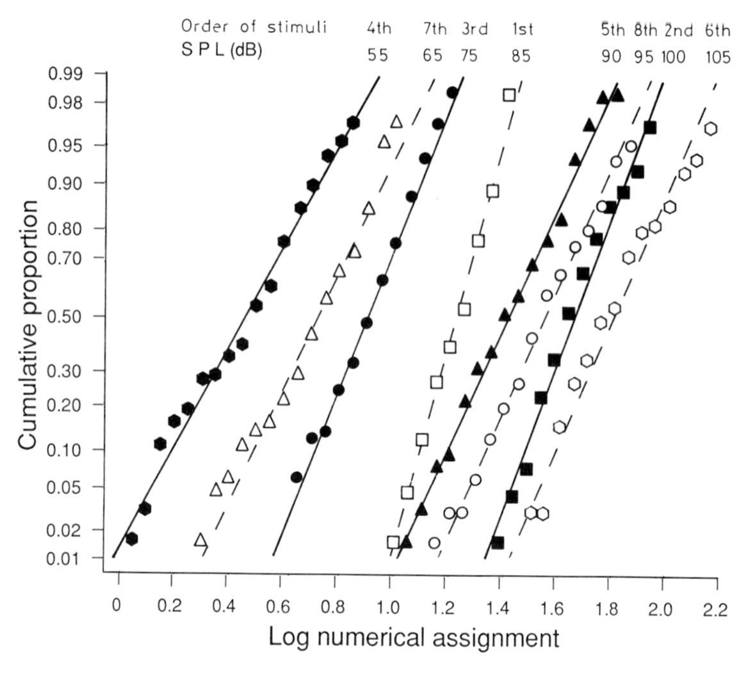

Fig. 10.3 Cumulative distributions of numerical estimates of loudness by a group of 70 subjects making their very first judgments. The gradient of the distribution function decreases from one judgment to the next, indicating a progressive increase in variance up to an asymptotic limit (see Table 10.1). (Data from J.C. Stevens and Tulving (1957). Figure from 'The relativity of "absolute" judgements' by D. Laming, *British Journal of Mathematical and Statistical Psychology*, 1984, vol. 37, p. 166. © 1971, American Psychological Association. Reproduced by permission.)

Table 10.1 Standard deviations and variances of the successive distributions of magnitude estimates in Fig. 10.2

Trial no.	Stimulus level (dB SPL)	Standard deviation	Variance
1	85	0.10	0.010
2	100	0.14	0.020
3	75	0.15	0.023
4	55	0.21	0.043
5	90	0.17	0.031
6	105	0.17	0.028
7	65	0.18	0.033
8	95	0.17	0.029

From 'The relativity of "absolute" judgements' by D. Laming, *British Journal of Mathematical and Statistical Psychology*, **37**, 166. © 1984, British Psychological Society. Reprinted by permission.

In magnitude estimation there is, of necessity, no immediate knowledge of results. So the second estimate may be determined in relation to the first according to (eqn 10.8 again)

$$\log N_2 - \log N_1 = (\beta + \delta_2)(\log X_2 - \log X_1 + \varepsilon_2 - \varepsilon_1), \tag{10.18}$$

whence, adding eqn 10.16,

$$\log N_2 - \log N_0 = \beta(\log X_2 - \log X_0 + \varepsilon_2 - \varepsilon_0) +$$

$$\delta_1(\log X_1 - \log X_0 + \varepsilon_1 - \varepsilon_0) + \delta_2(\log X_2 - \log X_1 + \varepsilon_2 - \varepsilon_1), \quad (10.19)$$

with

$$\mathrm{Var}\{\log N_2\} = \sigma_\beta^2\{(\log X_2 - \log X_1)^2 + (\log X_1 - \log X_0)^2\} + 2\beta^2\sigma^2 + 4\sigma_\beta^2\sigma^2. \quad (10.20)$$

It can readily be seen that without some additional assumption, the variance increases at each trial in proportion to $\sigma_\beta^2(\log X_n - \log X_{n-1})^2 + 2\sigma_\beta^2\sigma^2$, ultimately increasing beyond all bounds. While such an increase appears over the first three or four trials in Fig. 10.3, the variance then tends to a stable limit, and some additional idea is required to impose such a limit on the increase of the variability of judgment.

I have previously suggested (Laming 1984, p. 163) that only a proportion of the error implicit in the assignment of N_{n-1} to the stimulus on trial $n-1$ is transmitted to the judgment on trial n. One might usefully think of eqn 10.8 as generating a candidate number which is then modified according to the subject's prior idea of what kinds of numbers would be suitable as numerical responses. Certain experiments, reviewed in the next chapter (pp. 183–5), show how subjects discover from the numerical examples used to illustrate their instructions what kinds of numbers those are. Subjects do not utter implausible numbers like 10^{-6} or 1 000 001, and the variance of log N_n, which would otherwise continue to increase according to eqn 10.9, tends to an asymptotic limit which I write as V_{lim}.

Let V_{n-1} be the variance of $\log N_{n-1}$. The particular approach to the limit does not need to be specified precisely—existing data are not precise enough to discriminate between alternatives—and I write here (simpler than in Laming 1984)

$$V_n = (1-\theta)\,V_{n-1} + \theta\mathrm{Var}\{\log N_n - \log N_{n-1}\}$$

$$= (1-\theta)\mathrm{V}_{n-1} + \theta\sigma_\beta^2(\log X_n - \log X_{n-1})^2 + \theta v_0, \quad (10.21)$$

where θ is a parameter between 0 and 1. In the limit, $V_n = V_{n-1} = V_{\mathrm{lim}}$; hence

$$V_{\mathrm{lim}} = \sigma_\beta^2 E\{(\log X_n - \log X_{n-1})^2\} + v_0. \quad (10.22)$$

In Table 10.1 that limit appears to be about 0.03 log units and is reached in perhaps four trials, and I note for future reference that the variance contributed on the first trial is about 1/3 of that asymptotic value. But it would be unwise to read anything more into the statistics in Table 10.1 because the model analysis set out above supposes all subjects to begin from the same notional standard stimulus and modulus whereas, in reality, what has been equated between subjects is their geometric average estimate over the whole eight trials of the experiment. Such modulus equalization cannot but interact with the growth of variance over those trials.

10.4.2 **Variability within the stimulus set**

Stevens' (1956b) data on the estimation of loudness have already been presented in Fig. 5.1

and are shown again in Fig. 10.4 to illustrate the variation in the variability of (log) magnitude estimates between different positions within the set of stimuli. The interquartile intervals at the *extremes* of the stimulus range are greater then those in the *middle* by a factor of 1.82 (see Stevens 1971, p. 442, table 1).

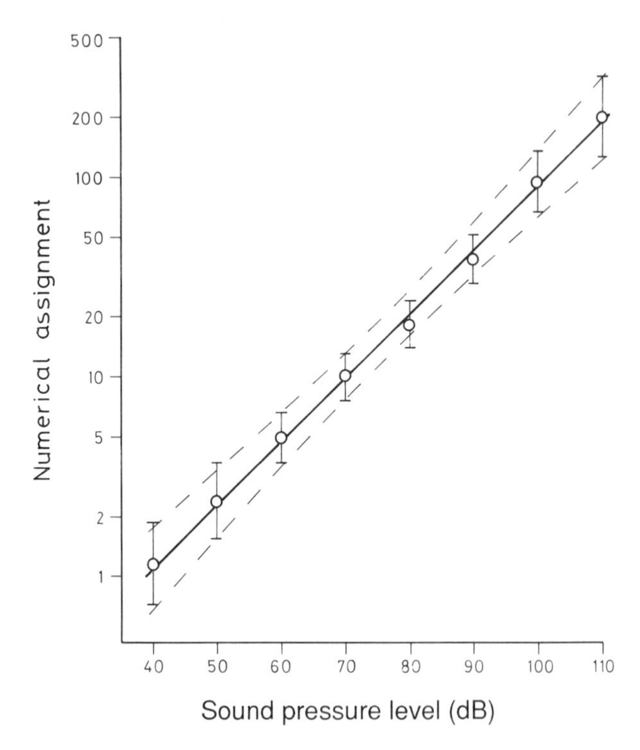

Fig. 10.4 Numerical magnitude estimates of the loudness of a 1 kHz tone by 32 observers judging each stimulus twice only. The vertical bar through each data point shows the interquartile range of the 64 constituent judgments. The broken curves represent predictions from eqn 10.26 for those interquartile ranges. (Data from Stevens (1975, p. 28). Figure from 'The relativity of "absolute" judgements' by D. Laming, *British Journal of Mathematical and Statistical Psychology*, 1984, vol. 37, p. 167. © 1975, John Wiley & Sons, Inc. Reproduced by permission of John Wiley & Sons, Inc..)

As a preliminary to an approximate calculation, the manner in which this variation in the size of the interquartile intervals arises is illustrated graphically in Fig. 10.5. The ordinal scheme set out in Fig. 10.1 means that the variability of a particular numerical assignment (specifically a particular $\{\log N_n - \log N_{n-1}\}$) increases in proportion to (the square of) the perceived log ratio x_n/x_{n-1}. That is shown by the broken lines fanning out from the origin. Those lines are reproduced in Fig. 10.5 to show that the variability of a log numerical estimate of 80 dB SPL, to take a particular example, depends on the preceding stimulus. When 80 dB is preceded by itself, the white open circle in inverse contrast shows that the preceding numerical estimate is usually repeated. When it is preceded by 70, 60, 50, and 40 dB SPL, the numerical estimates spread progressively wider, in proportion to the dB difference. But 80 dB can never be preceded (in Stevens', 1956b, experiment) by any stimulus more remote than 40 dB SPL—at most a 40 dB difference. An extreme stimulus, 110 dB SPL on the other hand, can be preceded by a stimulus (40 dB SPL) differing by as much as 70 dB; this is shown by the wider spread of the shading at the extremes of the stimulus range.

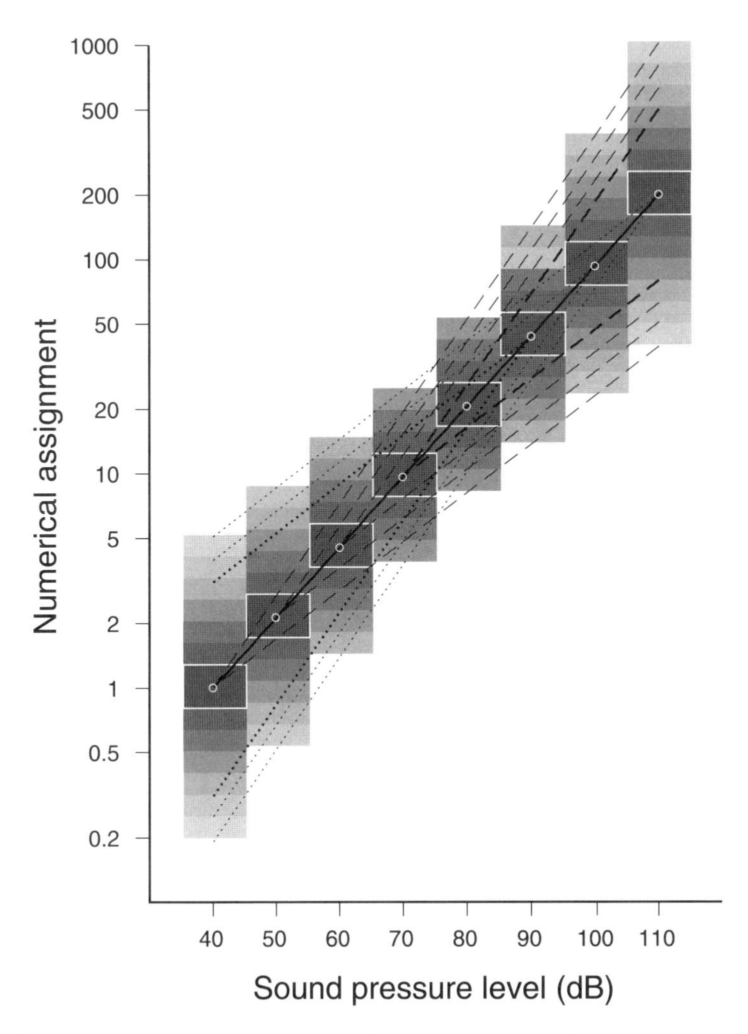

Fig. 10.5 A diagram to illustrate the source of the differences in the variability of magnitude estimates at different positions within the stimulus set. The variability of any particular log numerical assignment increases with the square of the dB distance from the preceding stimulus. That increase is shown (for numerical assignments to 80 dB SPL) by the fans of broken lines and (generally) by the shaded areas above and below each mean. The spread of the shading is greatest at the extreme stimulus values because the preceding stimulus might sometimes be 70 dB distant at the opposite end of the stimulus set. The diagram also illustrates the source of the correlation between successive log numerical assignments when the dB distance between successive stimulus values is small. A difference of only 10 dB confines the spread of responses to the darkest area (outlined in white) which is only a small part of the total spread. In that case successive responses are highly correlated.

The calculation which follows is chiefly concerned with that distribution of dB distances between each stimulus and its possible predecessors, different for different positions within the stimulus set, and the consequent different spreads of numerical estimates. But there is a further complication resulting from the transmission of error from more remote judgments via the use of the preceding judgment (x_{n-1}, N_{n-1}) as a point of reference.

In Stevens' (1956b, pp. 19–22) experiment there were eight stimulus values, equally spaced on the dB scale, presented in quasi-random order for judgment, so that, substituting for k in eqn 10.14, the average value of $(\log X_n - \log X_{n-1})^2$ is $3(\log \mathscr{S})^2/14$. Substituting this value in eqn 10.22,

$$V_{\text{lim}} = 3\sigma_\beta^2(\log \mathscr{S})^2/14 + v_0. \tag{10.23}$$

This is the limit for purely random choices of S_n and S_{n-1}, but what is required is a variance for a particular choice of S_n with S_{n-1} random as before. In what follows the subscript n will continue to denote the nth trial, while the subscript i will indicate the ith stimulus in the stimulus set. Suppose, now, that S_i is presented on trial n. The variance of the log estimate on that trial, which will be denoted by V_i, is given for a particular S_{n-1} by putting X_n equal to X_i in eqn 10.21,

$$V_i = (1 - \theta)\, V_{n-1} + \theta\sigma_\beta^2(\log X_i - \log X_{n-1})^2 + \theta v_0. \tag{10.24}$$

The preceding stimulus S_{n-1} is unspecified and, in a random sequence, X_{n-1} may take any value within the stimulus set with equal probability. So V_{n-1} can be equated with V_{lim} (eqn 10.22) and, for given X_i,

$$E\{(\log X_i - \log X_{n-1})^2\} = (\log X_i - \log \overline{X})^2 + E\{(\log \overline{X} - \log X_{n-1})^2\}, \tag{10.25}$$

where $\overline{X}$ is the geometric mean stimulus magnitude. The average value of $E\{(\log \overline{X} - \log X_{n-1})^2\}$ is $3(\log \mathscr{S})^2/28$, half the value entered in eqn 10.23. Hence,

$$\begin{aligned} V_i &= (1 - \theta)\, V_{\text{lim}} + \theta\sigma_\beta^2[(\log X_i - \log \overline{X})^2 + 3(\log \mathscr{S})^2/28] + \theta v_0 \\ &= V_{\text{lim}} + \theta\sigma_\beta^2[(\log X_i - \log \overline{X})^2 - 3(\log \mathscr{S})^2/28]. \end{aligned} \tag{10.26}$$

This is a symmetric quadratic relation between V_i and relative location within the stimulus set.

The standard deviation of the log magnitude estimates uttered in response to S_i is equal to the square root of V_i and multiplication by 0.6745 gives half the interquartile interval.[1] The deviation of that quantity $(0.6745\sqrt{V_i})$ about the mean, as calculated from eqn 10.26, is indicated by the broken curves in Fig. 10.4. The concordance of the quadratic expression with the reported interquartile intervals is good, especially since the chief discrepancies are discrepancies in the *means* with respect to the Power Law (eqn 5.2), not in the variances. However, no constraint has been placed on the coefficients of eqn 10.26, and subsidiary

[1] 0.6745 is the *probable error* of a normal distribution, half the minimum interval about the mean, in units of standard deviation, which contains half the weight of the distribution.

calculations show that the actual variation between the interquartile intervals in the centre of the range and those at the extremes (a ratio of 1.82 in linear measure or 3.31 in variance) is slightly greater than eqn 10.26 can reasonably accommodate.

Now the interquartile intervals plotted in Fig. 10.4 have been adjusted by Stevens' 'modulus equalization' (see p. 56) which purports to remove the intersubject component of group variance, correcting individual estimates for the different ranges of numbers uttered by different subjects. It may well be that modulus equalization removes, in addition, some component of variability which is properly intrinsic to the individual. Even if different subjects all begin from the same prescribed modulus, uttering numbers of the same order, the process of assignment specified by eqn 10.2 would cause their numerical judgments to diverge absolutely, generating different overall geometric means—differences which are nevertheless removed with 'modulus equalization'.

10.5 CORRELATION OF SUCCESSIVE MAGNITUDE ESTIMATES

The experiment by Baird *et al.* (1980) has already been described in the previous chapter (p. 129) and the correlations between successive estimates of loudness exhibited in Fig. 9.1 in relation to the dB difference between the stimuli. The argument that follows explains how those correlations arise and derives an expression for the variation of the coefficient with the dB difference.

The gist of the argument, however, can be explained by reference to Fig. 10.5. When a stimulus value is repeated, the number assigned to it on the previous trial is usually also repeated—this is represented by the open circles in inverse contrast in the figure—except that errors of perception may sometimes lead to some small variation. When a stimulus is preceded by an adjacent value, the numerical assignments spread a little more widely. This spread, relative to the response on the preceding trial, is represented by the darkest innermost rectangles (bordered with white) in Fig. 10.5 and, for a stimulus of 80 dB SPL preceded by 70 dB (or 90 dB), is further indicated by a pair of broken (or dotted) lines. But, when the preceding stimulus is more remote, it can be seen (looking again at the broken and dotted lines, now of lighter weight, in relation to judgments of 80 dB) that the spread of the assignment is proportionately increased. So the variance of numerical assignments to 80 dB is much greater overall than the variance following 70 (or 90) dB, whence two successive assignments to adjacent stimuli must be highly correlated. Looking ahead to eqn 10.27, $\mathrm{Var}\{\log N_n\}$ and $\mathrm{Var}\{\log N_{n-1}\}$ correspond to the complete column of shaded rectangles, $\mathrm{Var}\{\log N_n - \log N_{n-1}\}$ to the darkest rectangle only, bordered in white. There has to be a substantial covariance term to balance the equation.

As the preceding stimulus value becomes more remote from 80 dB, so the spread of numerical assignments becomes ever wider. This relationship is indicated by successive pairs of broken lines in Fig. 10.5, which also indicate that the spread of responses increases in proportion to the dB distance between successive stimuli. This means that the *variance* of the assignments, strictly speaking, the variance of $(\log N_n - \log N_{n-1})$, increases as the *square* of the dB distance, leading to a quadratic expression (eqn 10.40 below) for the correlation coefficient.

Now to the algebraic derivation. The variance of the increment in log magnitude estimate from trial $n-1$ to trial n can be written as

$$\mathrm{Var}\{\log N_n - \log N_{n-1}\} = \mathrm{Var}\{\log N_n\} + \mathrm{Var}\{\log N_{n-1}\} - 2\mathrm{Cov}\{\log N_n, \log N_{n-1}\}. \quad (10.27)$$

An expression for the variance on the left-hand side of eqn 10.27 has already been given as eqn 10.9,

$$\mathrm{Var}\{\log N_n - \log N_{n-1}\} = \sigma_\beta^2(\log X_n - \log X_{n-1})^2 + 2\beta^2\sigma^2 + 2\sigma_\beta^2\sigma^2. \quad (10.28)$$

The right-hand side of eqn 10.28 is substantially less than $\mathrm{Var}\{\log N_n\} + \mathrm{Var}\{\log N_{n-1}\}$ because the cumulated error which is transmitted from trial $n-1$ to trial n by the use of the stimulus and judgment on trial n as a point of reference is excluded from the difference variable, $(\log N_n - \log N_{n-1})$. For this reason, the covariance term on the right hand side of eqn 10.27 is far from negligible and $\log N_n$ and $\log N_{n-1}$ are positively correlated.

In the estimation of that correlation from numerical data (see pp. 129–30 above), the variances $\mathrm{Var}\{\log N_n\}$ and $\mathrm{Var}\{\log N_{n-1}\}$ are the variances conditional on the stimulus on trial n having one prescribed value, say X_i, and the stimulus on trial $n-1$ another, X_j, where $(\log X_i - \log X_j)$ is equal to the prescribed dB ratio. The data points in Fig. 9.1 are averaged correlation coefficients, averaged over all pairs of stimuli differing by the given dB ratio. But here, in the interests of simplicity, I shall first take an average over the variances $(\mathrm{Var}\{\log N_n\} + \mathrm{Var}\{\log N_{n-1}\})$ conditional on stimulus X_i on trial n and stimulus X_j on trial $n-1$, where $(\log X_i - \log X_j)$ is equal to the given dB ratio, averaged over all admissible X_j (eqn 10.32 below), and then calculate the correlation. The averaged variances, of course, depend on the dB ratio (eqn 10.33 below).

In this present experiment with 21 2.5-dB-spaced stimuli, the average value of $(\log X_n - \log X_{n-1})^2$ is, from eqn 10.14, $11(\log \mathcal{S})^2/60$ (where, as before, $\mathcal{S}$ is the geometric range of the stimulus set) and, adapting eqn 10.23,

$$V_{\lim} = 11\sigma_\beta^2(\log \mathcal{S})^2/60 + v_0. \quad (10.29)$$

So, adapting eqns 10.24–6 in the same way,

$$\begin{aligned}
&\mathrm{Var}(\log N_{n-1} | X_{n-1} = X_j) \\
&= (1-\theta)\,V_{n-2} + \theta\sigma_\beta^2[(\log X_j - \log \overline{X})^2 + E\{(\log \overline{X} - \log X_{n-2})^2\}] + \theta v_0, \\
&= V_{\lim} + \theta\sigma_\beta^2[(\log X_j - \log \overline{X})^2 - 11(\log \mathcal{S})^2/120], \quad (10.30)
\end{aligned}$$

after taking expectations with respect to $\log X_{n-2}$ over the complete set of stimuli and writing $V_{\lim}$ for V_{n-2}. Also from eqn 10.21,

$$\begin{aligned}
&\mathrm{Var}(\log N_n | (X_{n-1} = X_j) \cap (X_n = X_i)) \\
&= (1-\theta)\mathrm{Var}(\log N_{n-1} | X_{n-1} = X_j) + \theta\sigma_\beta^2(\log X_i - \log X_j)^2 + \theta v_0 \\
&= V_{\lim} + (1-\theta)\theta\sigma_\beta^2(\log X_j - \log \overline{X})^2 + \\
&\theta\sigma_\beta^2(\log X_i - \log X_j)^2 - (3-\theta)\theta[11\sigma_\beta^2(\log \mathcal{S})^2/120]. \quad (10.31)
\end{aligned}$$

Hence,

$$\text{Var}(\log N_n|(X_{n-1}=X_j)\cap(X_n=X_i))+\text{Var}(\log N_{n-1}|X_{n-1}=X_j)$$
$$=2V_{\text{lim}}+(2-\theta)\theta\sigma_\beta^2[(\log X_j-\log\overline{X})^2-11\sigma_\beta^2(\log\mathscr{S})^2/120]$$
$$+\theta\sigma_\beta^2[(\log X_i-\log X_j)^2-11\sigma_\beta^2(\log\mathscr{S})^2/60]. \qquad (10.32)$$

Suppose now, for the sake of argument, that $X_i \geqslant X_j$ and put

$$\log X_i - \log X_j = \log Y. \qquad (10.33)$$

Because the coefficients in Fig. 9.1 are averaged over all pairs of stimuli with a given dB difference, the sum of variances (Var{$\log N_n$} + Var{$\log N_{n-1}$}) needed in eqn 10.27 is the expectation of eqn 10.32 with respect to all admissible values of $\log X_j$. Now $\log X_j$ may assume any value within the set of stimuli from $(\log\overline{X} - \tfrac{1}{2}\log\mathscr{S})$ (i.e. the bottom of the stimulus range) up to $(\log\overline{X} + \tfrac{1}{2}\log\mathscr{S} - \log Y)$, but cannot exceed this limit else X_i would be greater than the top of the stimulus range. So $\log X_j$ is a random selection from the restricted range $(\log\overline{X} - \tfrac{1}{2}\log\mathscr{S}, \log\overline{X} + \tfrac{1}{2}\log\mathscr{S} - \log Y)$ and has mean $(\log\overline{X} - \tfrac{1}{2}\log Y)$.

Suppose there are k' stimuli available within this restricted range. It spans a logarithmic range $(\log\mathscr{S} - \log Y)$ and this must comprise $(k'-1)$ spaces between stimuli, whereas the full range $(\log\mathscr{S})$ comprises $(k-1)$ (cf. eqn 10.13). Hence,

$$(\log\mathscr{S} - \log Y)/(k'-1) = (\log\mathscr{S})/(k-1). \qquad (10.34)$$

The average value of $(\log X_j - \log\overline{X})^2$ in eqn 10.32 is therefore

$$k'^{-1}\sum_{j=1}^{k'}(\log X_j - \log\overline{X})^2$$
$$= k'^{-1}\sum_{j=1}^{k'}[(\{\log X_j - (\log\overline{X} - \tfrac{1}{2}\log Y)\} - (\tfrac{1}{2}\log Y)]^2$$
$$= k'^{-1}\sum_{j=1}^{k'}[(\{\log X_j - (\log\overline{X} - \tfrac{1}{2}\log Y)\}^2 - (\tfrac{1}{2}\log Y)^2]$$

because the cross-product terms disappear,

$$= \{(k'+1)/12(k'-1)\}(\log\mathscr{S} - \log Y)^2 + (\tfrac{1}{2}\log Y)^2,$$

substituting half the value of eqn 10.14 for the first component of the summation,

$$= (\log\mathscr{S} - \log Y)^2/12 + \{2/(k'-1)\}(\log\mathscr{S} - \log Y)^2/12 + (\tfrac{1}{2}\log Y)^2,$$
$$= (\log\mathscr{S} - \log Y)^2/12 + (\log\mathscr{S} - \log Y)(\log\mathscr{S})/6(k-1) + (\log Y)^2/4, \qquad (10.35)$$

on substituting from eqn 10.34. When, as in the present experiment, $k = 21$, the average value of $(\log X_j - \log\overline{X})^2$ in eqn 10.32 becomes

$$(\log\mathscr{S} - \log Y)^2/12 + (\log\mathscr{S} - \log Y)(\log\mathscr{S})/120 + (\log Y)^2/4. \qquad (10.36)$$

Substituting this value and eqn 10.33 in eqn 10.32,

$$E\{\mathrm{Var}(\log N_n) + \mathrm{Var}(\log N_{n-1}) | \log X_n - \log X_{n-1} = \log Y\}$$

$$= 2V_{\mathrm{lim}} + (2-\theta)\theta\sigma_\beta^2[(\log \mathcal{S} - \log Y)^2/12 + (\log \mathcal{S} - \log Y)(\log \mathcal{S})/120 +$$

$$(\log Y)^2/4 - 11(\log \mathcal{S})^2/120] + \theta\sigma_\beta^2[(\log Y)^2 - 11(\log \mathcal{S})^2/60]. \qquad (10.37)$$

In an earlier examination of the correlation coefficients in Fig. 9.1 (Laming 1984) I set θ (which corresponds to θ^2 in that earlier article) to 2/3 on the basis of an independent examination of the growth of variance in the experiment by J.C. Stevens and Tulving (1957; see Table 10.1). The value of this parameter is far from precisely determined and is not critical. If it is now set to 0.7, the coefficient of $(\log Y)^2$ in eqn 10.37 is approximately σ_β^2 and the left-hand side reduces approximately to

$$E\{\mathrm{Var}(\log N_n) + \mathrm{Var}(\log N_{n-1}) | \log X_n - \log X_{n-1} = \log Y\}$$

$$\approx 2V_{\mathrm{lim}} + \sigma_\beta^2[(\log Y - (\log \mathcal{S})/12)^2 - 0.135(\log \mathcal{S})^2]. \qquad (10.38)$$

This equation has been derived on the basis that $X_i \geqslant X_j$. If $X_i \leqslant X_j$, eqn 10.38 must have $-\log Y$ substituted for $\log Y$ (so that this quantity is always non-negative). The expression on the right-hand side of eqn 10.38 may be substituted generally for $\mathrm{Var}\{\log N_n\} + \mathrm{Var}\{\log N_{n-1}\}$ in the right-hand side of eqn 10.27 provided $\log Y$ is replaced with $|\log X_n - \log X_{n-1}|$. Rewriting eqn 10.27,

$$\mathrm{Var}\{\log N_n - \log N_{n-1}\} = (\mathrm{Var}\{\log N_n\} + \mathrm{Var}\{\log N_{n-1}\})(1-\rho), \qquad (10.39)$$

where ρ is the desired correlation coefficient. Substituting now from eqns 10.9 and 10.38,

$$\rho = 1 - \frac{\sigma_\beta^2 |\log X_n - \log X_{n-1}|^2 + v_0}{2V_{\mathrm{lim}} + \sigma_\beta^2[(|\log X_n - \log X_{n-1}| - (\log \mathcal{S})/12)^2 - 0.135(\log \mathcal{S})^2]} \qquad (10.40)$$

$$= 1 - \frac{[|\log X_n - \log X_{n-1}|^2 + A}{[|\log X_n - \log X_{n-1}| - (\log \mathcal{S})/12]^2 + B}$$

where

$$A = v_0/\sigma_\beta^2 \qquad (10.41a)$$

and

$$B = 2V_{\mathrm{lim}}/\sigma_\beta^2 - 0.135(\log \mathcal{S})^2. \qquad (10.41b)$$

The curve fitted to the data points in Fig. 9.1 has the form of eqn 10.40. Just two parameters have been estimated from the data, A and B (eqns 10.41). It demonstrates that the simple scheme of ordinal judgment set out in 10.1 and 10.2 can accommodate the pattern of correlation reported. The derivation of eqn 10.40 involves several approximations at different stages of the derivation, but these are not out of keeping with the limited precision of the data in Fig. 9.1.

10.5.1 **Estimation of apparent area**

Beside the experiment on the estimation of loudness described in the previous chapter, Baird *et al.* (1980) also reported experiments on the estimation of area and on the matching of loudness to area. For the estimation of area the stimuli were random outline shapes displayed on a television monitor for 500 ms. The areas of the figures varied in 21 geometric steps from 0.381 to 76.35 cm^2. The same three subjects each made a total of about 2500 judgments of these stimuli, in blocks of 100 spaced over a period of a week. As before, different stimuli were selected at random for judgment. Figure 10.6 shows the correlation between successive log estimates of apparent area as a function of the logarithms of the ratio between the areas of the corresponding stimuli with the standard deviation of each correlation coefficient indicated by a vertical bar. When that ratio is near unity (stimuli of similar area, but not necessarily of the same outline shape), this correlation is as high as +0.7, but it again tails away to nothing for large ratios between successive areas. Equation 10.40 is again fitted as the continuous curve to these data.

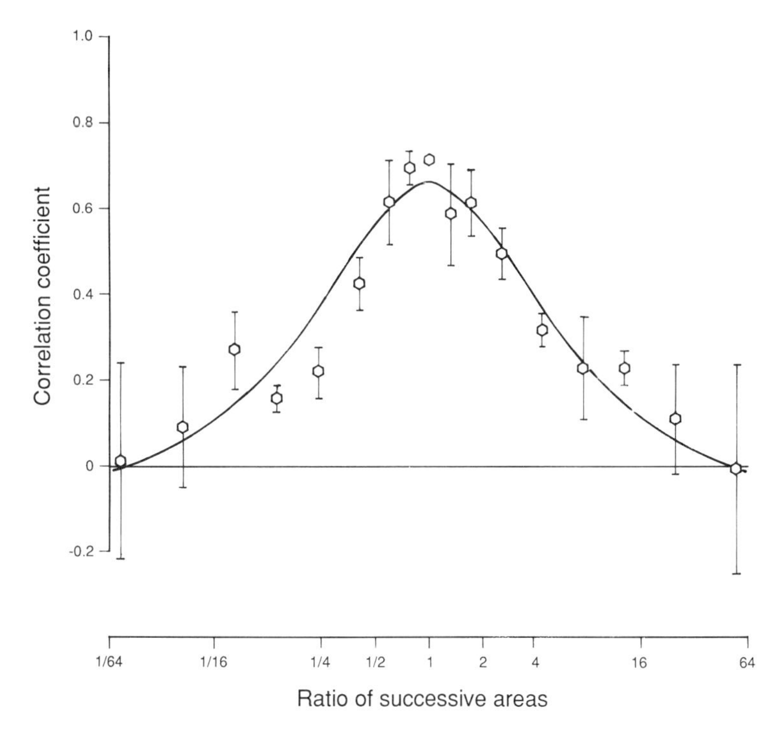

Fig. 10.6 Coefficients of correlation between the logarithms of successive numerical estimates of area in relation to the ratio of successive stimulus areas. The hexagons represent the mean correlation averaged over three subjects and the vertical bars extend to ± 1 standard deviation. The continuous curve is eqn 10.40. (Redrawn from Baird *et al.* 1980, p. 286.)

10.5.2 **Cross-modal matching of loudness to area**

Both stimulus continua were used in the cross-modal matching task. The 'stimuli' were the same set of outline geometric shapes as before, but now presented on the television monitor for as long as the subject needed to select his response. The 'response' was a chosen level of a 1 kHz tone presented repeatedly, 500 ms on, 100 ms off. The initial level of the tone from which the subject began his adjustment was chosen at random on each trial somewhere in the range 40–90 dB, in 1 dB steps. The subject could raise or lower the level of this tone by pressing buttons on a control box until a level which seemed to match the area was achieved. The same three subjects again made a total of about 2500 matchings of loudnesses to outline figures over a period of a week, this time in blocks of 50. As before, different stimuli were selected at random for matching. Figure 10.7 shows the correlation between successive log amplitudes of the matching tone (in dB) as a function of the logarithms of the ratio between the areas of the corresponding outline figures. That pattern of correlation can again be described by eqn 10.40.

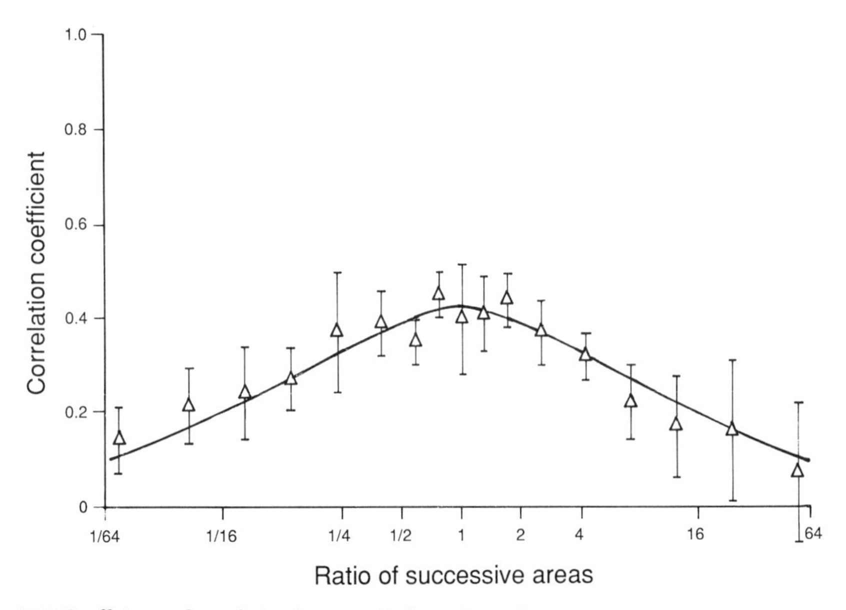

Fig. 10.7 Coefficients of correlation between the logarithms of successive settings of the amplitude of a 1 kHz tone in relation to the ratio of successive stimulus areas in cross-modal matching. The triangles represent the mean correlation averaged over three subjects and the vertical bars extend to ± 1 standard deviation. The continuous curve is eqn 10.40. (Redrawn from Baird *et al.* 1980, p. 287.)

10.6 THE STRUCTURE OF CROSS-MODAL MATCHING

When the ratio of successive geometric areas is near unity, the correlation between successive log matches is about +0.4, whereas the corresponding correlations for numerical estimates in Figs 9.1 and 10.4 are about +0.8. These different degrees of correlation provide a certain insight into the nature of the judgment processes in magnitude estimation and cross-modality matching.

According to eqn 10.40, the maximum correlation between successive log numerical estimates is achieved when the stimulus is repeated. In that case there is no constraint on the choice of $\log X_{n-1}$ and $\mathrm{Var}\{\log N_{n-1}\} = V_{\mathrm{lim}}$. Equation 10.32 thereby simplifies to

$$\mathrm{Var}(\log N_n|(X_{n-1} = X_i) \cap (X_n = X_i)) + \mathrm{Var}(\log N_{n-1}|X_{n-1} = X_i)$$
$$= 2V_{\mathrm{lim}} - 11\theta\sigma_\beta^2(\log \mathcal{S})^2/60. \tag{10.42}$$

The maximum correlation is approximately

$$\rho_0 = 1 - v_0/[2V_{\mathrm{lim}} - 0.128\sigma_\beta^2(\log \mathcal{S})^2], \tag{10.43}$$

in which the denominator depends chiefly on the subject's notion what range of numbers he is expected to utter. Indeed, this is why a limit exists to the variability of (log) magnitude estimates. It is expressed in terms of the square of the log stimulus range $(\log \mathcal{S})^2$ multiplied everywhere by σ_β^2, the variance of the 'exponent' B_n. The maximum correlation therefore varies between different estimation experiments, if it varies at all, because of different values of v_0, the irreducible error of perception, pertaining to different stimulus continua.

Cross-modality matching involves the adjustment of some physical stimulus, in the present case the amplitude of the 1 kHz tone, and it is necessary to consider how correlations between successive adjustments of such a stimulus might be related to those between successive estimates of magnitude. There is a useful comparison to be made here with the magnitude production task of Green *et al.* (1977) which evidently used the same apparatus. Each production trial began with the matching tone set somewhere at random within the range 40–90 dB (which was the range used in Fig. 9.1). The subject could raise or lower the level in large steps (4, 5, or 6 dB at random) by pressing one of two buttons and by small 1 dB steps by pushing one of two other buttons. When the tone was judged to match the given number, a fifth button recorded the match. It is common practice in magnitude production to select both the numbers to be matched and the range over which the physical stimulus attribute might be adjusted in the light of the corresponding ranges in a comparable estimation experiment. Accordingly, one might expect to see similar values of both v_0 (because the stimulus continuum is the same) and of V_{lim} (because of the matching of numerical and stimulus ranges), and this appears to be so in the experiment by Green *et al.* (1977). Their fig. 4 (p. 455) reveals a similar pattern to Fig. 9.1 here with a maximum correlation of about +0.8. It is therefore reasonable to suppose that the correlations in Fig. 9.1 and the corresponding values of v_0 and V_{lim} apply also to the matching of some intermediary with amplitude in the cross-modal matching in Fig. 10.7. That premiss can be codified by rewriting eqn 10.43 as

$$\rho_a = 1 - v_a/[2V_{\mathrm{lim}} - 0.128\sigma_\beta^2(\log \mathcal{S})^2], \tag{10.44a}$$

for the maximum correlation between successive numerical estimates of area, and

$$\rho_t = 1 - v_t/[2V_{\mathrm{lim}} - 0.128\sigma_\beta^2(\log \mathcal{S})^2], \tag{10.44b}$$

for the maximum correlation between successive matches of an intermediary with a tone.

Equation 10.44b applies to magnitude production when a specific number is given, a number known without error. But, in cross-modal matching, the intermediary (which, for convenience, I think of as a number) is itself an estimate with, in the present case, a minimum variability v_a. That variability transposes into an equivalent additional variability of the matching tone, giving for the maximum correlation between successive cross-modal matches,

$$\rho_{at} = 1 - (v_a + v_t)/[2V_{lim} - 0.128\sigma_\beta^2(\log \mathcal{S})^2]. \qquad (10.45)$$

Combining eqns 10.44 and 10.45,

$$1 - \rho_{at} = (1 - \rho_a) + (1 - \rho_t)$$

or

$$\rho_{at} = \rho_a + \rho_t - 1. \qquad (10.46)$$

Equation 10.46 relates the correlations obtained when a stimulus value is repeated. In Fig. 9.1 ρ_t for a repeated stimulus is 0.74, and in Fig. 10.6 ρ_a is 0.72. Entered into eqn 10.46, these values give ρ_{at} as 0.46. The value obtained in Fig. 10.7 is 0.40.

The gist of this argument is that ρ_{max} is limited by the irreducible error of perception, of the stimulus in magnitude estimation and of the adjusted response variable in magnitude production. In cross-modality matching there are two irreducible errors of perception; eqn 10.46 is the natural consequence. It is not necessary to the argument that there be a numerical estimate as intermediary (though it helps in formulating it). What does follow, however, is that number is truly an artificial response continuum in the sense that it involves, of course, no error of perception.

10.7 COMMENTARY

It seems to me unlikely that a simple idea such as the ordinal scheme of assignment set out in relations 10.2 should be able to accommodate so many and so diverse a set of experimental results without being a passable approximation to the underlying state of nature. It follows that the psychological primitive cannot be more precise than that ordinal scheme. Birnbaum (1978) considered both sensation differences and sensation ratios as possible, and possibly alternative, primitives. If subjects were able to judge stimulus pairs on an interval scale (i.e. differences) or on a log interval scale (ratios), sensory judgment would be more precise than it is. For example, the maximum number of categories that could meaningfully be used would hardly be limited to five (Garner 1962), and the variability of absolute identifications would not be so closely tied to stimulus range. The point to be made is that sensory judgments, whether of 'differences' or of 'ratios', are subject to error. The attendant errors need to be incorporated into the formulation of the scheme of judgment; and when that is done the most appropriate scheme appears to be no better than ordinal.

That merely ordinal nature of the comparisons which underlie human judgment can be seen in an experiment by Pollack (1953). A tone of a frequency selected at random from nine fixed values within the range 100–8000 Hz is presented for 2.5 s. The subjects' task is to identify the tone. Notwithstanding the very fine sensitivity which most people show when distinguishing between the frequencies of two tones, the accuracy of identification of the frequency of a single tone (by subjects without perfect pitch) is limited to about five categories (at most 2.3 bits of information; Pollack 1952). That low limit may be exceeded if the tone to be identified is preceded by a known reference tone, one of the nine fixed frequencies in Pollack's (1953) experiment, of 2.5 s duration, with a further gap of 2.5 s before the tone to be identified. The maximum improvement in information transmitted was 1 bit (which is what one would expect from a single binary reference point). But that improvement is limited to frequencies neighbouring the known reference tone; it did not propagate to the rest of the frequency scale.

A second implication of the preceding analysis is that there is only one psychological primitive, as required by a relation theory. If there were an alternative mode of judgment available to the subject, the metric of judgment would have to be at least interval or log interval and would show in judgments of greatly increased precision. At a purely ordinal level there can be only one primitive.

I envisage that the ordinal scheme I have outlined may need revision, especially its outworkings in experimental models. It may well admit a more elegant and precise formulation, but I think it will remain substantially the same idea. It is time to state two implications.

1. There is no absolute judgment of stimulus magnitude and, equally, there is no absolute judgment of *differences* in (log) magnitude or of *ratios.*
2. Sensory judgment is no better than ordinal. For that reason it can be adequately formulated in terms of a natural physical measure of stimulus magnitude. Sensory judgment provides no basis for any scale of sensation distinct from that natural physical measure.

(To be sure, if the observations to which ordinal judgment is applied have a suitable physical structure, some stronger scale of measurement might emerge. Ordinal comparisons of weights in a scale pan or of lengths laid alongside a ruler permit ratio scale measurement. The point needing emphasis is that there is nothing analogous to a scale pan or ruler intrinsic to the observer. Again, some distinction seems to be needed between judgments where 'the difference between them [two sensations] is great or small' (Plateau 1872a, p. 377). I envisage such a distinction being related to the limit to discrimination as reflected in threshold measurements. That, as was shown in Chapter 4, can also be formulated in terms of a natural physical measure of stimulus magnitude.)

One task remains. Stevens and his colleagues have published many experiments showing a nice conformity to a power law. That oft repeated result still requires explanation and that is the subject of the next chapter.

11 Why Stevens' Law is a power law

Stevens and his colleagues have published many experiments, magnitude estimation, magnitude production, and cross-modality matching, in which the averaged responses show a nice conformity to a power law. That oft repeated result has yet to receive explanation, and that explanation is the subject of this chapter.

Stevens (1957b) proposed that '... the sensation S is proportional to the stimulus X raised to a power β' (Stevens 1957b, p. 162, replacing Stevens' Ψ, S, and n with S, X, and β, respectively). While that statement relates the results from the three procedures to each other by means of the consistency relations (eqns 5.5–5.8) between different exponents, it does not provide any further element of explanation; it does not relate those averaged responses to any other finding from any other kind of experiment, not even to the variability of the responses in the present experiments. And the interpretation in terms of sensation is entirely gratuitous.

It was shown in Chapter 7 that such a mapping of individual stimuli onto a scale of sensation will not do because the mapping onto an extensive ratio scale which accommodates direct judgments of individual sensations does not generalize to the judgment of sums and differences of sensations. Although such a generalization can be accommodated by a mapping onto certain non-extensive ratio scales, a mapping which might correspond, for example, to the additional assumption that the numbers uttered as magnitude estimates are actually values on an artificial stimulus dimension, related by its own power law transform to a subjective domain where the addition and subtraction of sensations actually takes place, that idea does no more than inject an extra free parameter into the model applied to the data. Further elaborations of the judgment, even so mild an elaboration as a judgment of the loudness difference between pairs of tones presented binaurally, compared with control judgments of the loudness difference of identical pairs presented monaurally (Marks 1979a), generate a need for further free parameters to accommodate the data. The 'processing system' is getting out of hand.

The correlations between successive log magnitude estimates in Fig. 9.1 show what is wrong. Stimuli are not judged absolutely, in isolation, with respect to the same fixed scale. Instead, each stimulus is compared with its predecessor, and the number assigned to that predecessor forms an essential point of reference. A relation theory is plainly required, and this kind of theory circumvents the most immediate of the problems above; judgments of single stimuli need no longer tally with judgments of sums and differences of sensation. Within a relation theory the judgment of a single stimulus is meaningless and, in practice, each stimulus presented by itself is actually judged in relation to its predecessor. That predecessor is ordinarily uncontrolled, except for the second member of a pair of stimuli which is judged in relation to the first, and the lack of comparability between predecessors means that there is no necessary relation between the magnitude estimates of single stimuli and of the sums and differences of pairs.

However, the relational view implies that there is only one relation, one psychological primitive, between each pair of stimuli on which a judgment of 'ratio' or of 'difference' might be based. In consequence, judgments of different arithmetical relations ought to be montonically related, being based on a common sensory relation. The direct evidence on that is equivocal. But indirect evidence in the previous chapter, especially from the analysis of variability of sensory judgments of all kinds, tells us that the psychological primitive is no better than ordinal. If the basic comparison of one stimulus with another is purely ordinal, how do Stevens and his colleagues get their power law results?

In this chapter I offer an explanation of Stevens' Power Law based on the assumption that the specifically sensory contribution to judgments of subjective magnitude is exceedingly weak, so that the responses are dominated by contextual biases implicit in the design of the experiment and in the order in which the stimulus values are presented. Poulton (1968, 1979, 1989) has shown by collecting many examples that a wide variety of such biases are operative. But the assumption that I need is stronger than that, specifically that the biases on judgment actually *dominate* the outcome. I first justify this stronger assumption.

11.1 GARNER'S EXPERIMENTS

Garner (1954b) has created one of those simple and elegant experiments which go straight to the heart of the matter. This experiment deserves to be much better known; I reproduce the data in Fig. 11.1.

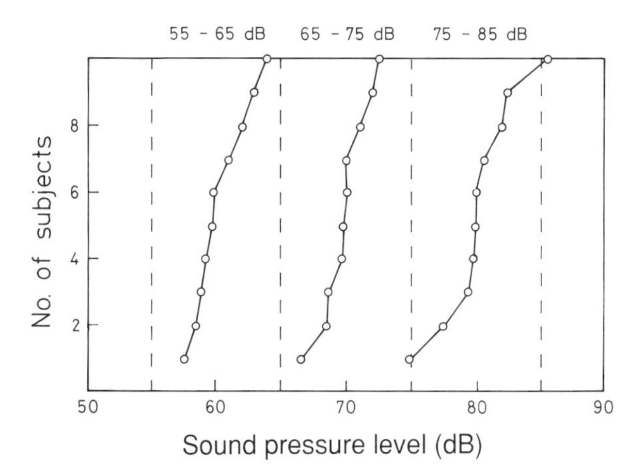

Fig. 11.1 Cumulative distributions from Garner (1954b) of sound pressure levels judged to be half as loud as 90 dB. (Figure from 'Reconciling Fechner and Stevens?' by D. Laming, *Behavioral and Brain Sciences*, 1991, vol. 14, p. 190. © 1954, American Psychological Association. Reproduced by permission.)

Garner determined the sound pressure level of that 1 kHz tone that sounded half as loud as 90 dB in the following manner. On each of 600 trials the subject heard first the 90 dB tone and then a comparison tone, and was asked simply whether the second tone sounded more or less than half as loud as the first. The number of 'more than half as loud' judgments increased systematically with the level of the comparison tone, approximately as a normal probability integral, so it was a simple matter to estimate a half-loudness point for each subject by interpolation. Figure 11.1 plots the cumulative distributions of those half-loudness points for three groups of 10 subjects. Of those three groups of subjects, one heard comparison tones spaced at intervals of 2 dB from 75 to 85 dB; a second heard comparison tones between 65 and 75 dB; and the third between 55 and 65 dB. For each subject the estimated half-loudness point falls within the range of comparison levels presented for judgment. Only the first group heard comparison tones lying above as well as below 80 dB, which, according to the sone scale, is the level half as loud as 90 dB; so all the subjects in the other two groups should have protested that the tones they heard were all less than half as loud as the standard. Only one subject did in fact protest. She said that all the comparison tones from 65 to 75 dB were *more than half as loud* as the standard; she was happily reassigned to the 55–65 dB group.

Garner's experiment opens up the question of subjective sensation with a simplicity and directness unmatched by any other extant experiment in the field. To *a first approximation* Garner's subjects had no idea how loud a sound half as loud as 90 dB would sound, and their judgments were driven by context alone. The experiment made no sense unless the comparison tones presented for judgment extended both above and below the half-loudness point and the results obtained follow directly from this implicit assumption on the part of the subjects. Obviously, for the range of stimuli presented for judgment to have any effect on those judgments, the subjects must learn what that range is. In a subsequent experiment Garner showed how quickly such learning is accomplished.

In a near-replication of his 1954 experiment, Garner (1958, 1959) had 135 subjects perform the same task as before with respect to narrow ranges of comparison tones varying by ± 2 dB about a central level situated, for different groups of subjects, at 55, 60, 65, 70, 75, 80, and 85 dB. For the very first judgment made by each subject the comparison tone was set exactly at one of these values. Those very first judgments, of course, were entirely uninfluenced by the range of tones yet to be presented and reflect only the contextual background that subjects bring with them from everyday life. Analysis of those very first judgments by themselves showed a systematic increase of 'more than half as loud' with stimulus level, with a 50 per cent point at 77.6 dB and a 0.05 confidence interval from 75.4 to 79.9 dB (Garner 1958). Further analyses combining the first two, the first 10, and finally the first 20 judgments (Garner 1959, p. 215, fig. 2) showed the effect of that initial everyday context to be quickly overtaken by the experience of the experimental stimuli. The proportion of 'more than half as loud' judgments made by the different groups of subjects tends towards a stable level independent of the location of the range of comparison stimuli actually presented. That stable level was well established within 20 trials.

Garner's experiments do not actually show that there is *no* facility for absolute judgment of loudness—indeed, the main experiment to which the 20 trials summarized above were merely preliminary appears to establish the contrary—but the contribution of that facility to the responses uttered is very slight. There are, of course, a multitude of other experiments implicitly addressing the same point. But they are all of them less incisive than Garner's, and none of them contradict the assertion that their results are chiefly due to a particular balancing of contextual constraints. This means that Stevens takes, as the determinant of judgments of subjective magnitudes, a factor which actually has at most a small effect and ignores, by default, the much larger contributions from the context in which the judgments are made. One can now see why mapping theories and also relation theories (certainly as formulated by Krantz 1972) both run into problems; why good power law data from Stevens' method of magnitude estimation are so dependent on minor details of the procedure (cf. pp. 55–7); and why the variability of magnitude estimates is so much greater than can be attributed to sensory factors.

The inferences I have drawn from Garner's experiment are approximate rather than exact; but they are sufficient to show that beginning with a hypothetical measure of sensation is a strategic error. In order to attain a well-founded scientific understanding of sensory judgment it is necessary to direct analytical models first at the principal determinants of the judgments, that is, at the contextual biases. Such a theoretical study is beyond the scope of this present work, but a simple assumption—briefly, that good power law data depend on a certain balance between the different biases, a balance which may be achieved by careful randomization—leads to a simple explanation of Stevens' Power Law.

11.2 CONTEXTUAL CONSTRAINTS ON MAGNITUDE ESTIMATES

Stevens' Power Law holds typically for those stimulus continua which also conform to Weber's Law, that is, for attributes for which a just-noticeable difference ΔX satisfies

$$(X + \Delta X) = (1 + \Theta)X. \tag{11.1}$$

On such a continuum a series of stimuli of magnitudes

$$X_0,\ (1 + \Theta)^{n}X_0,\ (1 + \Theta)^{2n}X_0,\ (1 + \Theta)^{3n}X_0 \ldots \tag{11.2}$$

increase in steps of exactly n jnds and all pairs of adjacent stimuli are equally discriminable. In order to exclude differences in the discriminability of different pairs of adjacent stimuli as a material factor in magnitude estimation, a geometric series of magnitudes such as 11.2 is the natural choice, with a large number of jnds separating adjacent pairs. This kind of choice is also made with attributes which do not quite satisfy Weber's Law. Stevens' (1975) data for the estimation of the loudness of 1 kHz tones in Fig. 5.1 also relate to a set of stimulus values selected according to this principle. The spacing of those tones is 10 dB which is equivalent to over 20 jnds at 80 dB (cf. Jesteadt *et al.* 1977b, p. 176, table B-II). At such a wide spacing any specifically sensory confusion is truly negligible.

It is usual to plot the results of magnitude estimation experiments with respect to the logarithm of the stimulus variable. In such a logarithmic metric the geometric series 11.2 becomes the arithmetic series

$$\ln X_0,\ \ln X_0 + n\ln(1 + \Theta),\ \ln X_0 + 2n\ln(1 + \Theta),\ \ln X_0 + 3n\ln(1 + \Theta) \ldots, \tag{11.3}$$

uniformly spaced on the logarithmic scale. Suppose now that subjects are induced to select their responses in like manner, distributed approximately geometrically on the continuum of real numbers. There is a very common tendency to use *round* numbers: 1, 2, 5, 10, 20, 50, 100, 200, . . . and so on which means that each decade of the real number scale gets used about equally often (cf. Baird *et al.* 1970). This contributes to a logarithmic bias (Poulton 1979, pp. 783–6), which is enhanced by instructing the subjects to make judgments on the basis of apparent ratios (as Stevens 1971, p. 428, did; see also p. 55 here). Then the distribution of numbers uttered, aggregated over all the different stimuli, will also be uniform, approximately so, with respect to the logarithmic metric.

This is easier to achieve than one might suppose. In her study of monetary compensation awarded for accidental injury, Fitzmaurice (1992) collected all the awards made by one insurance company to victims of road accidents in Paris during 1984 and 1986, a total of 790 cases. The principal basis for compensation was the seriousness of the injuries, measured by the degree of permanent partial incapacity as assessed by a doctor on a percentage scale. Figure 11.2 shows the frequency of different percentage assessments in the sample of 790 cases. The dotted curve is a negative exponential which decreases by 0.5 for every increase of 10 percentage points along the abscissa. It points up that the distribution of numbers over the lower half of the range is approximately geometric—it would be approximately uniform on a logarithmic scale—except that, superimposed on that geometric distribution, certain numbers (5, 8, 10, 12, 15, 18, 20, 25) are used rather more frequently than their immediate neighbours.

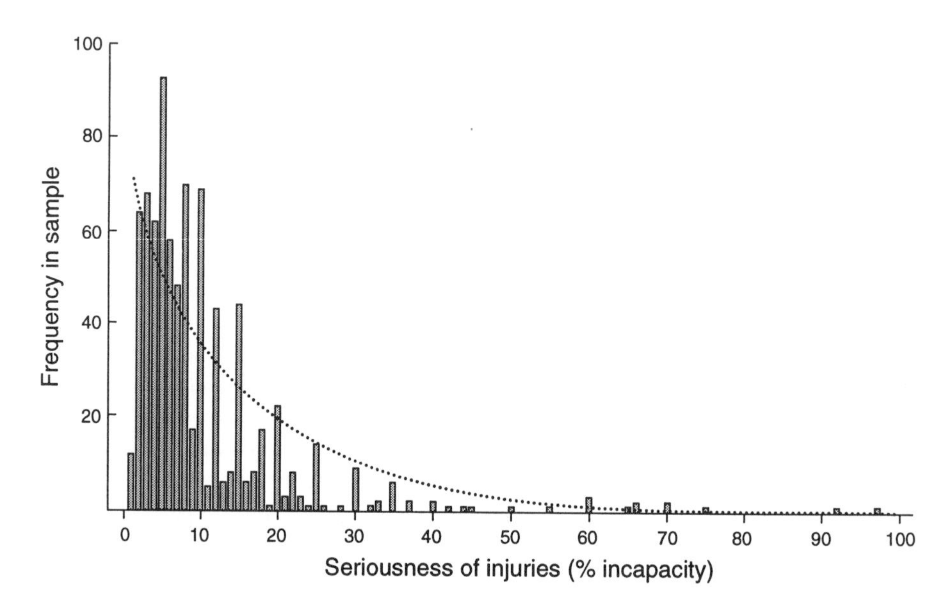

Fig. 11.2 Frequency of different assessed degrees of permanent partial incapacity in the 790 road accident cases studied by Fitzmaurice (1992).

The use of certain preferred numbers shows up even more clearly in the amounts of compensation actually awarded in those 790 cases. The frequencies of different monetary amounts are shown in Fig. 11.3. Those amounts cluster (with respect to a logarithmic abscissa) around 10 000 FF. Fitting a normal probability density to the data, Fitzmaurice

(1992) found, first, that certain specific values of compensation projected well above the normal density function and, second, that these preferred amounts of compensation could be fitted pragmatically into ascending series such as

4000, 5000, 6000, 7500, 9000;
8000, 10 000, 12 000, 15 000, 18 000;
20 000, 24 000, 30 000, 36 000, 48 000, 60 000[1]

in which successive terms increased by 20–25 per cent. This periodicity of the preferred amounts was confirmed by a formal Fourier analysis (Fitzmaurice and Moreland 1995).

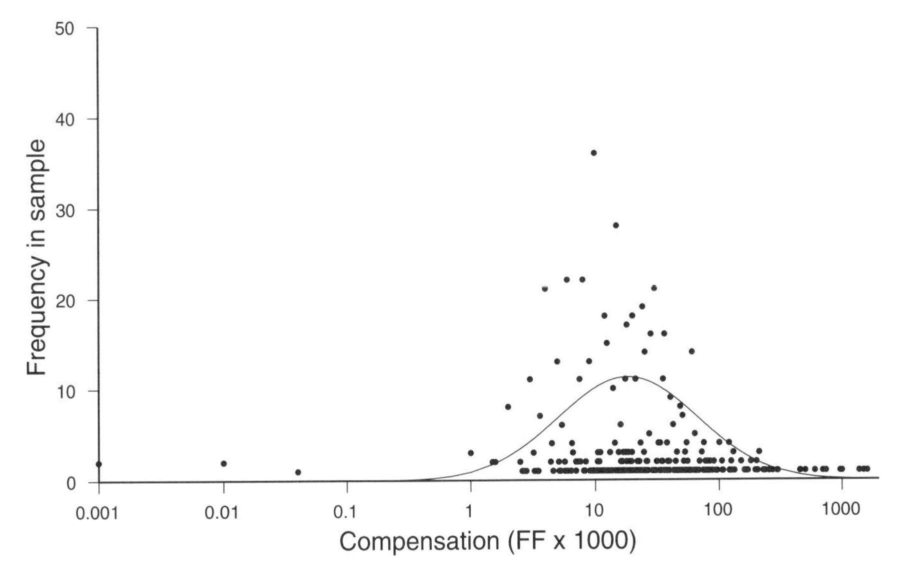

Fig. 11.3 Frequency of different amounts of compensation awarded in the 790 road accident cases studied by Fitzmaurice (1992). The normal density function identifies those preferred amounts which occur more frequently than would otherwise happen by chance.

The compensation awarded tends to a preferred value because, in most cases, the 'correct' amount is only imprecisely indicated; and the geometric spacing of those preferred amounts points to a natural logarithmic use of numbers. To represent a noticeable increase in compensation, the award has to be increased by 20 per cent or so, whatever the initial amount. But the actual sum awarded is frequently constrained to be a 'round number' and the proportionate increase to a simple integer ratio. The percentage increase varies slightly for that reason.

I emphasize that this selection of preferred numbers in both Figs 11.2 and 11.3 is a feature of the judgments of ordinary people. It means that inducing Poulton's (1979) 'logarithmic bias' in specially instructed laboratory subjects is only too easy.

[1] The first two series are abstracted from Fitzmaurice (1992, pp. 261 and 262), but the third is based on my own reading of her data.

To complete a model for magnitude estimation some procedure is now needed for assigning particular numbers to individual stimuli. It does not matter to the present argument what that procedure is, whether it reflects an underlying facility for absolute judgment of subjective magnitude or not, provided only that it is unbiased with respect to the logarithmic metrics of both the stimuli and of the responses and therefore supports a linear mapping of the one onto the other. The ordinal scheme (eqns 10.2) set out in the previous chapter will certainly do. All that is needed is for the subject to 'throw' his numbers at the stimuli; the idea is illustrated in Fig. 11.4. Individual assignments might be temporarily biased; but, since the stimuli are presented in random order, those individual biases cancel in the aggregate. In the absence of systematic bias, log numerical assignment regresses linearly onto log stimulus magnitude, because both variables are uniform with respect to a logarithmic metric. The regression equation takes the form

$$\log N = \log c + \beta \log X, \tag{11.4}$$

which is simply the logarithmic transform of Stevens' Power Law (eqn 5.4).

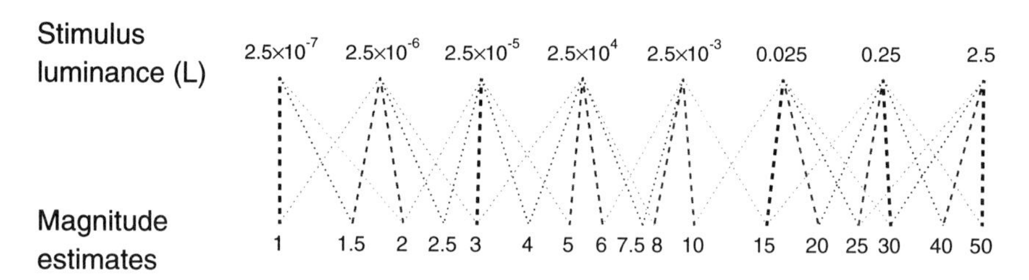

Fig. 11.4 Diagram to illustrate the (partially random) assignment of numbers to stimuli in magnitude estimation. The stimulus magnitudes and the response range have been borrowed from J.C. Stevens and Stevens (1963, fig. 3).

This regression of log number onto log stimulus magnitude can be seen to be operative in a study by Baird *et al.* (1971). There were 10 horizontal lines, ¼ inch wide and 0.81 to 25.12 inches long, projected, one at a time, onto a screen. Eight groups of subjects were asked to estimate the length of each line relative to the shortest line as standard, which was given modulus 1. The lines were presented five times in random order. Not surprisingly, the estimates were nearly veridical, with exponents (β) ranging from 0.86 to 1.02. In the second phase of the experiment seven of the groups were given a specific number to assign to the longest line, different numbers for different groups, in addition to the unit modulus for the shortest. Although one might have expected two prescribed values to impose a linear transform on the near-veridical judgments of the first phase, a different linear transform for each group, the actual results were quite different. For five of the seven groups the geometric mean judgments approximated a power law with exponents ranging from 0.71 to 2.55, while the eighth (control) group continued to give veridical judgments.

The lengths of the different lines were in approximate, though not exact, geometric series and the first phase of the experiment induced the subjects (university undergraduates) to use their numbers likewise. In the second phase the adjustment of an extended or contracted range of numbers to the existing range of stimuli took place in a logarithmic, not a linear, metric, notwithstanding the near-veridical judgment of length. It is likely that the implicit logarithmic metric derived from the near-geometric spacing of the line lengths, a spacing which becomes uniform on a logarithmic scale.

This explanation of Stevens' Power Law depends on the stimulus values constituting a geometric ladder like 11.2. So, if the stimuli were to deviate sufficiently from that geometric arrangement, a corresponding distortion of the magnitude estimates (vis-à-vis the power law) should be observed.

J.C. Stevens (1958) inserted a group of closely spaced (2 dB) noise levels within a wider spaced (10 dB) series (40–100 dB SPL) so that, for different groups of subjects, one or another of the 10 dB intervals in the wider series was filled at 2 dB intervals. Closely spaced stimulus values produced, locally, a steeper increase in log magnitude estimate as a function of noise level relative to the judgments of a control group who were asked to judge the widely spaced (10 dB) series alone. Locally the gradient (power law exponent) increased from 0.31 (for the control group) to 0.55, 0.44, and 0.43 for additional stimuli inserted at the bottom, middle, and top end, respectively, of the wider series. (J.C. Stevens 1958, fig. 3).

J.C. Stevens (1958, fig. 1) has also compared geometric (5 dB; 45–90 dB SPL) spacing with 'equal loudness spacing' over the same range. The 'equal loudness' noise levels were chosen to be equally spaced (in an arithmetic series) on the subjective magnitude scale estimated from the previous judgments of the geometric ladder of stimuli by the same subjects. The difference between the two sets of stimuli does not stand out from the intrinsic variability of the experiment. Comparison between geometric and *linear* spacing has not, to my knowledge, been attempted.

A more striking demonstration comes in an experiment by Mellers and Birnbaum (1982) who asked subjects to judge the darkness of random dot patterns. The patterns consisted of 1 mm dots, 12 to 90 in number, randomly arranged within a 25 mm square. The subjects were asked to estimate the 'ratio' of the darkness of each stimulus to a standard (12 dots, the lightest pattern) which was given the modulus 100. The task was carried out with two different sets of stimuli. Six patterns with 12, 18, 27, 40, 60, and 90 dots, respectively (a geometric series), were common to both sets. Each set contained five additional patterns, at the light end (14, 15, 16, 21, and 23 dots) of one set and at the dark end (47, 51, 70, 74, and 77 dots) of the other. The mean estimates for the six common stimuli calculated from judgments embedded in the two different stimulus sets exhibit quite different relationships to the stimulus variable. For example, the square with 40 dots was judged about 5.5 times as dark as the standard when the stimulus set was loaded at the light end, but only 3.5 times if the additional stimulus values were located at the dark end (Birnbaum 1982b, p. 37). Indeed, judgments of stimuli embedded in the set with a predominance of dark patterns increase as an approximately logarithmic function of the number of dots (see Mellers and Birnbaum 1982, p. 587, fig. 4, in which mean magnitude estimates are approximately linear on a log-linear plot).

The effect of varying the scale values of the stimuli can be very subtle. Schneider and Parker (1990) conducted a magnitude estimation experiment with six levels of a 2.5 kHz tone, spaced at about 10 dB intervals, and four levels of a 500 Hz tone, randomly intermixed. In one condition the four levels of the 500 Hz tone approximated the lowest four levels of the 2.5 kHz tone, and in another they approximated the four highest levels. One might therefore think of the six levels of the 2.5 kHz tone as defining a pragmatic scale of loudness, and the experiment as studying the loudness, relative to that scale, of the four levels of the 500 Hz tone. Although the mean estimates of the six levels of the 2.5 kHz tone were substantially the same in both conditions, the estimates of the 500 Hz tone, the two middle levels being common to both conditions, were not. Briefly, the apparent loudness of a fixed level of the 500 Hz tone depends on whereabouts on the stimulus continuum the other three levels are placed. The complementary result was obtained for six levels of the 500 Hz tone combined with four levels of the 2.5 kHz tone.

A similar argument explains why a power law should fit the data in Fig. 5.2 for the relation between seriousness of injury and amount of compensation awarded, notwithstanding that the stimulus variable has no natural metric. Doctors on the one hand and judges on the other judge the same set of cases of accidental injury. They do not assess the same features of those cases. The doctors are concerned with the degree of permanent partial incapacity and the judges with the amount of compensation to be awarded. But if two geometric arrays of numbers are assigned to the same set of (non-metric) stimuli, one by the doctors, the other by the judges, a power law relationship is generated between them. The amount of compensation awarded is supposed to be calculated according to this formula:

$$\text{amount of compensation} = \text{degree of permanent partial incapacity} \times \text{point}, \quad (11.5)$$

the 'point' score representing those relevant facets of the case other than the injuries sustained; and the medical assessment of the seriousness of the injuries would, of course, have been available to the judge in making his decision. If the amount of compensation really were calculated according to formula 11.5, one would expect an exponent of 1 in Fig. 5.2. The exponent of 1.36 suggests, instead, that the judge decides the compensation directly and the 'point' is then calculated from formula 11.5 by division.

To sum up, it is apparent that good power law data depend on a geometric spacing of the stimulus values. In combination with the balance of contextual constraints implicit in a random sequencing of the stimulus presentation, this effects a regression onto log stimulus magnitude. If the stimulus spacing is other than geometric, the implicit regression is realized with respect to some other metric and a power law may not be obtained.

11.3 THE POWER LAW EXPONENT

The preceding argument explains:

1. why Stevens' Power Law is a power law;
2. why it holds substantially for those stimulus attributes which also conform to Weber's Law; and
3. why its validity appears to be dependent on fine details of the experimental method by which the judgments are collected;

but it leaves unexplained

4. how the value of the exponent is determined.

It can be seen from Table 5.1 that the exponent β takes different values for different stimulus attributes, allegedly characteristic of the attribute.

The exponent β is estimated by regression of log N onto log X in eqn 11.4. The greatest precision in the estimation of the regression coefficient is obtained by choosing the widest practicable range of the independent variable, that is, the widest practicable log stimulus range. I presume this is what experimenters do when they are principally interested in the value of β. The maximum practicable stimulus range varies greatly from one attribute to another, and differences in the geometric range employed turns out to be the principal factor determining differences in β.

Let X_{max} be the greatest stimulus magnitude presented and X_{min} the least; then the geometric range of the stimulus values is

$$\mathcal{S} = X_{max}/X_{min}.$$

When magnitude X_{max} is presented, it elicits a mean numerical estimate $\overline{N}_{max}$ prescribed by eqn 11.4; likewise X_{min} elicits a mean estimate $\overline{N}_{min}$. Let

$$\mathcal{R} = \overline{N}_{max}/\overline{N}_{min}$$

denote the geometric range of the mean numerical estimates. Then it follows from eqn 11.4 that

$$\beta = \log \mathcal{R}/\log \mathcal{S},$$

and this equation presents an alternative, if slightly less accurate, method of estimating β.

If the subjects in magnitude estimation experiments are simply 'throwing' a geometric array of numbers at a geometric array of stimuli, substantially the same array of numbers at different arrays of stimuli, then β, the exponent, should vary simply as the reciprocal of $\log \mathcal{S}$.

Figure 11.5 speaks to this point. Each of the 24 experiments from which the exponent values listed in Table 5.1 were obtained is represented in this figure by a single point. That

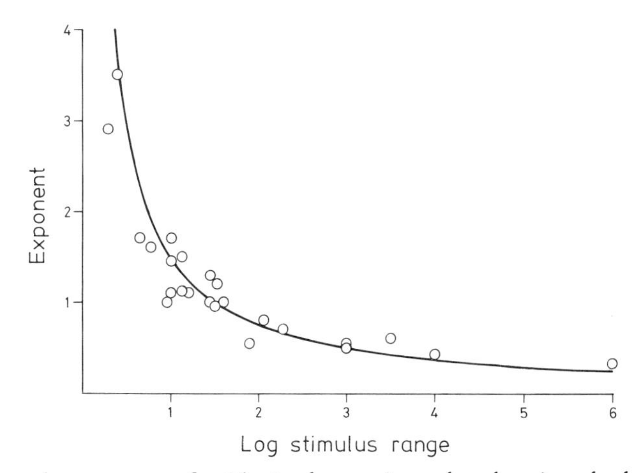

Fig. 11.5 Power law exponents for 24 stimulus continua plotted against the logarithms of the geometric ranges of stimulus values in the experiments from which the exponent values were estimated. The numerical data are listed in Table 5.1 and the continuous curve is the rectangular hyperbola $\beta = 1.48/\log_{10} \mathcal{S}$. (After Teghtsoonian 1971, p. 73, fig. 2.)

point has ordinate equal to the estimate of the exponent and abscissa equal to the base 10 logarithm of the geometric range of the stimulus values employed. (Further details of these experiments, specifically the stimulus and mean response ranges (cf. Fig. 11.7 below) are set out in Table 11.1.) The continuous curve is a rectangular hyperbola with equation $\beta = 1.48/\log_{10} \mathscr{S}$. This is the relation that would be obtained if in every experiment the subjects had used numbers covering a geometric range equal to 1 : 30. It is clear that much the greater part of the variation in the value of the exponent from one attribute to another is contributed by the different geometric ranges of stimulus values.

This relation was discovered by Poulton (1967) who scrutinized the experimental foundations for the estimation of 21 of some 27 exponent values cited by Stevens (1962) as typical of their respective sensory continua—all those of Stevens' exponents, in fact, for which adequate experimental data had been published. Poulton (1967, p. 312) claimed that the rank correlation (Kendall's τ) between the value of the exponent and the logarithmic range of stimuli employed in the experiment from which it was estimated was −0.60. In fact, as Teghtsoonian (1971, footnote to p. 73) pointed out, Poulton had misinterpreted the dB stimulus range in three of the 21 experiments. When that misinterpretation had been corrected, the correlation (now Pearson r between the reciprocal of the exponent and the log stimulus range) was increased to 0.935. This relation was first presented in the diagrammatic form of Fig. 11.5 by Teghtsoonian (1971, fig. 2) who also added three further stimulus continua to the collection. These additional stimulus continua generally increased the spread of the data points along the two limbs of the rectangular hyperbola, and the Pearson r for the full 24 experiments is 0.956.

In a subsequent analysis Teghtsoonian (1973) presented the collections of cross-modality matching data assembled by Stevens (1966b; see pp. 65–8 here) in similar form. Teghtsoonian's figures are reproduced below as Fig. 11.6 and the corresponding details of the experiments are set out in Tables 11.2 and 11.3. The rectangular hyperbolas in those figures indicate that when Stevens' subjects matched various continua with force of hand grip (Fig. 11.6(a)), they selected a geometric range of forces equivalent to 1 : 6.2. It is likely that that range was constrained by the mechanics of the hand grip dynamometer which the subject manipulated to record his responses. The Pearson correlation for the data in Fig. 11.6(a) is 0.98. Figure 11.6(b) presents a second set of data in which subjects adjusted the loudness of a noise to match subjective magnitudes on seven other continua.[2] In this case the logarithmic range of noise levels amounts to 45 dB; the Pearson correlation is again 0.98.

These results are very nearly consistent with the assertion that the geometric range of responses, numerical estimates or stimulus magnitudes produced in a matching task, is independent of the range of stimuli presented for judgment. To show the extent to which this generalization is only approximate, I examine the results collected in Fig. 11.5, which yields the poorest of the three correlations (0.956), in more detail.

[2] Three of the continua, length of line, vocal effort, and force of hand grip, in Table 5.3 have been omitted here because the data relate to the matching of those continua to given samples of noise and are therefore not appropriate to the present analysis (Teghtsoonian 1973, footnote 4).

Table 11.1 The magnitude estimation experiments represented in Figs 11.5 and 11.7

Stimulus attribute	Source	Stimulus range	Stimulus units	Response range	Exponent
Luminance, 5.7° source	J.C. Stevens and Stevens (1963)	2.5×10^{-6}–2.5	Lamberts	1–50	0.33
Viscosity	Stevens and Guirao (1964)	10–105	Centipoises	2.3–125	0.44
Luminance, point source	Stevens and Galanter (1957)	10^{-2}–10	Lamberts	2–60	0.50
Sound intensity, monaural	Reynolds and Stevens (1960)	40–100	dB	1.3–40	0.54
Saturation of coffee odour	Reese and Stevens (1960)	0.0075–0.6	Relative concentration	3–35	0.55
Sound intensity, binaural	Stevens (1956b)	40–110	dB	0.6–83	0.60
Visual area	Stevens and Guirao (1963)	17.5–3300	cm^2	2.5–80	0.70
Tactual hardness	Harper and Stevens (1964)	8.3–970	Relative force/ indentation	2–68	0.80
Amplitude of vibration	Stevens (1959a)	10–40	dB SL	1.2–30	0.95
Cold	J.C. Stevens and Stevens (1960)	3.3–30.5	°C below physiological zero	3.1–28	1.00
Repetition rate	J.C. Stevens and Shickman (1959)	1–40	Clicks/s	1.1–40	1.00
Visual length	Stevens and Galanter (1957)	4–111	cm	1.5–45	1.00
Temporal duration	Stevens and Galanter (1957)	0.25–4	s	0.5–6.1	1.10
Pressure on the palm	J.C. Stevens and Mack (1959)	0.5–5	lb wt	2–30	1.10
Vocal effort	Lane *et al.* (1961)	2–27	dB (arbitrary ref. level)	2.4–30	1.10
Luminance (grey papers)	Stevens and Galanter (1957)	3×10^{-4}–10^{-2}	Lamberts	1–90	1.20
Finger span	Stevens and Stone (1959)	2.3–63.7	mm	4.4–200	1.30
Lifted weight	Stevens and Galanter (1957)	19–193	g	0.7–20	1.45
Tactual roughness	Stevens and Harris (1962)	24–320	Grit no.	0.95–34	1.50
Warmth	J.C. Stevens and Stevens (1960)	2.5–14.7	°C above physiological zero	1.8–31	1.50
Force of hand grip	J.C. Stevens and Mack (1959)	4–40	lb wt	1.5–55	1.70
Saturation of red	Panek and Stevens (1966)	0.2–0.9	Relative saturation	1.5–19.8	1.70
Saturation of yellow	Indow and Stevens (1966)	0.5–1.0	Relative saturation	2.7–20	2.90
Electric current	Stevens *et al.* (1958)	0.33–0.84	mA	1.2–48	3.50

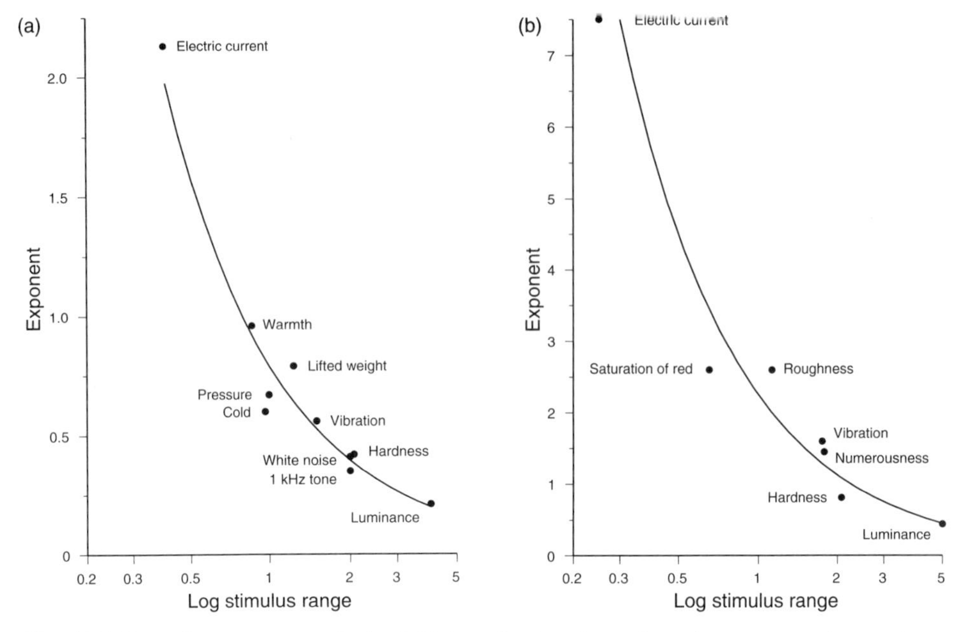

Fig. 11.6 Power law exponents obtained (a) by adjusting force of hand grip to match stimulus magnitudes on nine other continua, and (b) by adjusting the loudness of a band of noise to match stimuli on seven other continua, plotted against the logarithms of the geometric ranges of stimulus values in the experiments from which the exponent values were estimated. The numerical data are listed in Tables 11.2 and 11.3 and the continuous curves are again rectangular hyperbolas: (a) $\beta = 0.79/\log \mathcal{S}$, and (b) $\beta = 2.25/\log \mathcal{S}$. (After Teghtsoonian, 1973, p. 8.)

Table 11.2 Cross-modal matches to force of hand grip summarized in Fig. 11.6(a)

Stimulus attribute	Source	Stimulus range	Stimulus units	Response range (lb wt)	Exponent
Luminance, 5.7° source	J.C. Stevens *et al.* (1960)	4×10^{-2}–400	mlamberts	4.5–23	0.21
Sound intensity, 1 kHz tone	J.C. Stevens *et al.* (1960)	47–87	dB SPL	4–22.5	0.35
Sound intensity, white noise	J.C. Stevens *et al.* (1960)	55–95	dB SPL	8.5–57	0.41
Tactual hardness	Harper and Stevens (1964)	8.3–970	Relative force/ indentation	6–43	0.42
Amplitude of vibration	J.C. Stevens *et al.* (1960)	17–47	dB SL	4.7–35	0.56
Cold	J.C. Stevens and Stevens (1960)	3.3–30.6	°C below physiological zero	8.2–32	0.60
Pressure on the palm	J.C. Stevens and Mack (1959)	0.5–5	lb wt	9.3–46	0.67
Lifted weight	J.C. Stevens and Mack (1959)	28–480	g	3.2–30	0.79
Warmth	J.C. Stevens and Stevens (1960)	2.0–14.5	°C above physiological zero	5–36	0.96
Electric current	J.C. Stevens *et al.* (1960)	0.29–0.72	mA	3.5–25	2.13

Table 11.3 Cross-modal matches to level of white noise summarized in Fig. 11.6(b)

Stimulus attribute	Source	Stimulus range	Stimulus units	Response range (dB)	Exponent
Exponent					
Luminance, 4° source	J.C. Stevens and Marks (1965)	10^{-2}–1000	mlamberts	37–83	0.44
Tactual hardness	Harper and Stevens (1964)	8.3–970	Relative force/ indentation	58.5–92.5	0.81
Numerosity	Stevens and Guirao (1962)	1.25–75	–	33–84	1.45
Amplitude of vibration	Stevens (1959a)	10–45	dB SL	29.5–85	1.60
Tactual roughness	Stevens and Harris (1962)	24–320	Grit no.	36–92.5	2.60
Saturation of red	Panek and Stevens (1966)	0.2–0.9	Relative saturation	53–86	2.60
Electric current	Stevens (1959a)	0.33–0.74	mA	36–77	7.50

11.4 THE RANGE OF RESPONSES

A deeper insight into the results in Fig. 11.5 is provided by a direct examination of the relation between the stimulus and response ranges in eqn 11.8. The mean numerical responses to X_{max} and to X_{min} were read off from the graphical presentations of the data in the original published reports of the 24 experiments; and the sources, the stimulus and response ranges, and the exponents estimated therefrom have already been listed in Table 11.1. The logarithms of the geometric ranges of mean numerical estimates are plotted against the logarithms of the geometric ranges of stimulus values in Fig. 11.7. It can be readily seen that $\log_{10}\mathscr{R}$ varies from one experiment to another over a range of about 1 log unit, while $\log_{10}\mathscr{S}$ varies over 6 log units. If, instead of regarding the exponent β as a fixed parameter of the sensory processing system, it is treated purely empirically as the quotient of the logarithmic ranges of numbers and stimuli that happen to have been used in the experiment, then its estimate can be seen to be dominated by the logarithmic range of the stimulus values. But it is not exactly true that the geometric range of numerical responses is independent of that range. The regression line in Fig. 11.7 has equation

$$\log_{10}\mathscr{R} = 1.213 + 0.124\log_{10}\mathscr{S}, \tag{11.9}$$

so that the response range increases roughly as the eighth root of the stimulus range.

Equation 11.9 might well be taken to imply that there is some low level of sensitivity on the part of subjects to the absolute (geometric) range of the stimuli presented for judgment; but this is not necessarily so. Conventionally, the stimuli are treated as independent variables and the responses as dependent, in which case the (geometric) mean response is an unbiased estimate. But the view I am espousing here makes the numerical responses, collectively, an independent variable, and the experiment is, as it were, a sorting out of a fixed collection of numerical responses with respect to the stimuli. It will help to consider how this might come about.

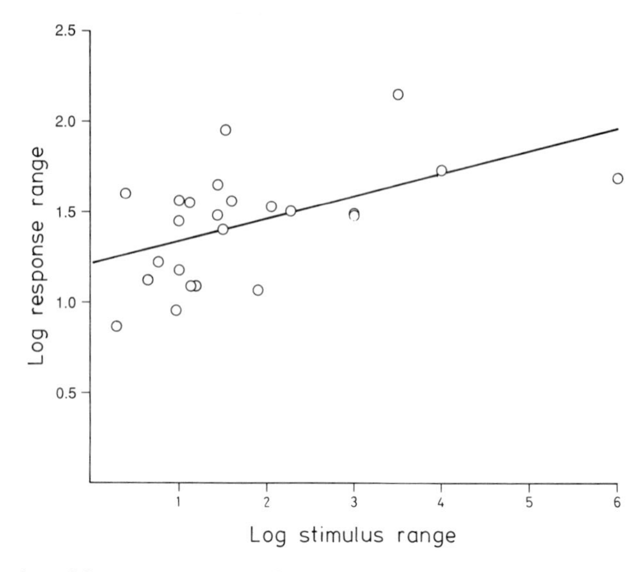

Fig. 11.7 Logarithm of the geometric range of mean numerical estimates plotted against the logarithm of the geometric range of stimulus values for the same 24 experiments as Fig. 11.5. (After Poulton 1979, p. 795, Fig. 10.)

Suppose the subject has some fixed idea what the maximum and minimum estimates are which might reasonably be uttered. Suppose, further, that those maximum and minimum estimates function like the bounds of a category scale. If a subject is asked to assign a series of stimuli to one of nine categories labelled 1, 2, . . . 9, he does not use Category 0, nor Categories 10, 11, 12, . . . If a stimulus seems so much less than its predecessor that the appropriate response is 'Category 0' (according to the scheme of assignment in eqn 10.2), it is assigned to Category 1; and if it seems so much greater that 'Category 10' or '11' or '12' seems required, it is assigned to Category 9. Magnitude estimates could be kept within implicit bounds in similar manner. It will appear below that those maximum and minimum bounds are suggested by the experimenter through the medium of the numerical examples used to illustrate his instructions to the subject. And when the experimental task is matching stimulus values with force of grip on a hand dynamometer or with the loudness of a band of noise, physical limits are imposed on the range of possible responses by the mechanics of the dynamometer and by the range of the potentiometer by which the subjects adjust the noise. Those physical limits are common to all subjects and it is pertinent that the correlation between power law exponent and inverse log stimulus range is even greater in the collections of cross-modal matching experiments (Fig. 11.6) than in the magnitude estimation data of Fig. 11.5.

If now the different stimulus values are widely spaced, so that there are a relatively large number of occasions when one stimulus is judged to be 'very much greater' or 'very much less' than its predecessor, the implicit bounds will be exceeded (and the actual estimate uttered set at the maximum or the minimum) the more often; and the mean estimates will migrate outwards towards those implicit bounds. In this way wider spacing of the stimulus values can lead to wider spacing of the mean estimates, especially the means for the smallest and largest stimuli, within the implicit bounds of acceptable numerical estimates. It is also conceivable that, on those continua with stimulus values spread over wide geometric ranges, it is easier to distinguish one stimulus value from another, leading to more judgments of 'very much greater' or 'very much less' (cf. eqn 10.1). That increased accuracy of assignment will then translate into an increased geometric mean response range. This is not, however, a suggestion that can be checked except by a detailed examination of the individual responses.

While the hypothesis of a fixed overall distribution of numerical responses clearly accounts for much the greater part of variability amongst exponents, explanation is still needed why the range of numerical estimates should vary so little from one experiment to another, at least in the experiments reported by Stevens and his colleagues.

11.4.1 **Instructions to the subjects**

To begin with, there is sometimes a difficulty in explaining the task of assigning numbers in proportion to one's subjective experiences of stimuli. Stevens (1966a) advises:

> Because not everyone is familiar with the concept of proportionality, it has sometimes proved helpful to start off with an experiment on apparent length of lines. The lines, six to ten in number, should cover a wide range of lengths—say, a ratio of about 50 to 1. After judging such lines in irregular order, most observers seem to achieve a reasonably firm grasp on the concept of assigning numbers proportional to magnitude. (Stevens 1966a, p. 531)

That sounds like training one's subjects to use numbers covering a range of 1 to 50, because the typical exponent for length is, as one would expect, 1.0 (Table 5.1). Stevens (1971) replies:

> Untrained, inexperienced college subjects seem to do as well at the matching tasks as those who have had many years of practice. Hence, there is no need to 'train' the subjects. Indeed, since there is no right or wrong to the subjects' responses, it is not clear what would be meant by training. Under some circumstances, the nature of the task may profitably be clarified by allowing the subjects to begin by matching numbers to an easier continuum, such as the apparent length of lines, or the apparent size of circles. (Stevens 1971, p. 428)

Stevens' recommended instructions to subjects are not neutral. It is possible for an experimenter to influence the range of numbers used by including numerical examples in his instructions; in fact, where an experimenter explicitly tries to do so, he (or she) usually succeeds. Robinson (1976) reported two magnitude estimation experiments, the first utilizing the frequency of 1 ms pulses from an oscillator (pulse frequencies ranging from 1.662 to 31.542 per s) and the second with the amplitude of a square-wave which provided a sound of rich harmonic structure at a fundamental frequency of 926 Hz (amplitudes ranging from 59 to 94 dB). Each comparison stimulus was presented for 10 s and the comparison amplitudes varied over a range approaching 10 to 1000 with respect to a standard to which the number 100 was assigned. The subjects were divided into two groups, A and B, and the instructions to Group A read as follows:

> As you read this you are hearing a series of pulses of a constant frequency. For this experiment assign the number 100 to this frequency which will be called the Reference Frequency. It will be present

between each trial. I am going to present you with a number of Comparison Pulse Frequencies with one occurring on each of the following 10 trials. Your task will be to try to estimate the frequency of each Comparison Pulse Frequency relative to the Reference Frequency you now hear. For example, if on a particular trial the Comparison Pulse Frequency seems 1½ times the Reference Frequency, assign the number 150 to it: if it is ½ the Reference Frequency, assign the number 50 to it. (Robinson 1976, p. 81)

The instructions to Group B were identical in wording and word position to those above except that the numbers '1½', '150', '½' and '50' were replaced by '7½', '750', '¼', and '25', respectively. The same instructions were given to the two groups in the second experiment except that 'frequency' and 'pulse frequencies' were replaced by 'loudness' and 'loudnesses', respectively.

The different numerical examples in their instructions constituted the *only* difference between the two groups in these experiments. That difference was sufficient to make the subjects in Group B spread their numerical estimates more widely. The different response ranges and the exponents estimated for each group in these two experiments, and in two replications, are set out in Table 11.4. The differences are all significant.

Table 11.4 Geometric mean estimates of the smallest and largest stimuli in the experiments by Robinson (1976)

Experiment	Groups A		Groups B	
	Response range	Exponent	Response range	Exponent
Pulse frequency				
Initial expt	21–240	0.871	19–650	1.29
Replication	20–230	0.893	26–1000	1.33
Loudness				
Initial expt	10.6–190	0.729	9–450	1.039
Replication	8.6–200	0.768	8.2–350	0.955

Another example of the influence of the experimenter's instructions comes from the second experiment by Veit (1978, cited by Birnbaum 1980, p. 315). The stimuli were pairs of 5 cm squares of neutral colour and various reflectances; the ratios of the physical reflectances within a pair varied from 1/9 to 9. Subjects were instructed to judge the ratio of the greyness of the upper square to the greyness of the lower square. If the greynesses of the two squares appeared equal, the response was to be 100. If the upper square appeared twice as dark as the lower, 200; four times as dark, 400; with 50 and 25 being cited as additional examples. For this group of subjects the largest mean ratio judgment was 5.31, equivalent to a power law exponent of 0.76. A second group of subjects were given an additional pair of examples in their instructions. If the upper square appeared eight times as dark, 800; if only one-eighth as dark, 12.5. For this second group the maximum mean ratio judgment was 7.35, equivalent to an exponent of 0.90.

A third example is provided by Mellers and Birnbaum (1982) in the experiment described above (p. 175) There were two different sets of instructions given to different subjects. One set of instructions included the following examples: 100 = equal in darkness to the standard, 150 = 1½ times as dark, 200 = 2 times, 250 = 2½ times, and 300 = 3 times as dark. In the other set of instructions the examples were: 100 = equal in darkness to the standard, 300 = 3 times as dark, 500 = 5 times, 700 = 7 times, and 900 = 9 times as dark. With the first set of instructions, mean estimates ranged from 100 up to about 350; with the second set of instructions, but the same stimulus values, they ranged up to 700 and 800 for the six values common to both stimulus sets.

Finally, Hardin and Birnbaum (1990) asked subjects to estimate the relative prestige of one occupation over another for 49 pairs of occupations arranged in a factorial design. Half of the subjects (in the 'ratio-4' condition) received a page of printed examples going up to 'four times as prestigious'. That group judged a physician to be '4 times' as prestigious as a trash collector. The other subjects ('ratio-64' condition) received illustrative examples up to '64 times as prestigious'. This second group judged the physician to be '64 times' as prestigious as the trash collector.

Evidently the subjects in these experiments were sufficiently uncertain how to estimate frequency or loudness or darkness or greyness that they were open to guidance how widely they should spread their estimates and thereby to the subtle suggestions implicit in the experimenter's choice of numerical examples. When, in the last experiment, the stimuli had no quantitative element at all, the suggestions incorporated in the experimenter's instructions proved irresistible. The numerical examples actually supplied to the subjects, in all but the last experiment, related to the *same* (notional) response scale; all that differed was the spread of the example values on that scale. It is evident that subjects need some prior idea, not about the relationship of stimuli to numbers, but about what kinds of numbers, absolutely, to utter. The experiments just cited demonstrate one source of that idea.

Another source, of course, is prior experience from having served in a similar experiment previously. This leads to a bias that Poulton (1979) labels simply:

Transfer From the Range of Numbers Used in a Previous Investigation

S.S. Stevens and his colleagues use the same members of the departmental staff and graduate students for more than one investigation (S.S. Stevens, 1959). From the evidence just reviewed on the transfer of ranges of numbers, it is almost certain that there is transfer of the range of numbers from one investigation to the next. (Poulton 1979, p. 800)

It is clear that subjects develop some prior idea about the range of numbers they think they should use. The manner in which such a prior idea interacts with the ordinal scheme of judgment 10.2 is illustrated, schematically, in Fig. 11.8. This figure reproduces the division of the abscissa into five regions corresponding to the judgments 'very much less than', 'less than', 'about the same as', 'greater than', and 'very much greater than' which was set out in Fig. 10.1 (except that the abscissa is now $\log X_n/X_{n-1}$, the log ratio of successive stimulus magnitudes, instead of $\log x_n/x_{n-1}$, the log ratio as perceived by the subject) and the allocation of numerical assignments to those regions. But the extreme regions '<<' and '>>' are now extended to larger ratios of successive stimulus values without there being any change in the range of numbers allocated to them. So long as the ratios between successive stimulus values remain small (regions '<', '=', and '>'), the range of numbers used might be expected to increase in proportion to the range of the stimulus values. But as the stimulus range increases, that cannot continue. Although the numerical range will continue to increase, that increase must be less than proportionate to the increase in the stimulus range, leading to a generally S-shaped relation (sketched as a dotted line in Fig. 11.8) between the average value of ($\log N_n - \log N_{n-1}$) and the log stimulus ratio ($\log X_n/X_{n-1}$) (ignoring, now, any errors of perception). This possibly explains, in a qualitative sense, the weak relationship between response range and increasing stimulus range in Fig. 11.7.

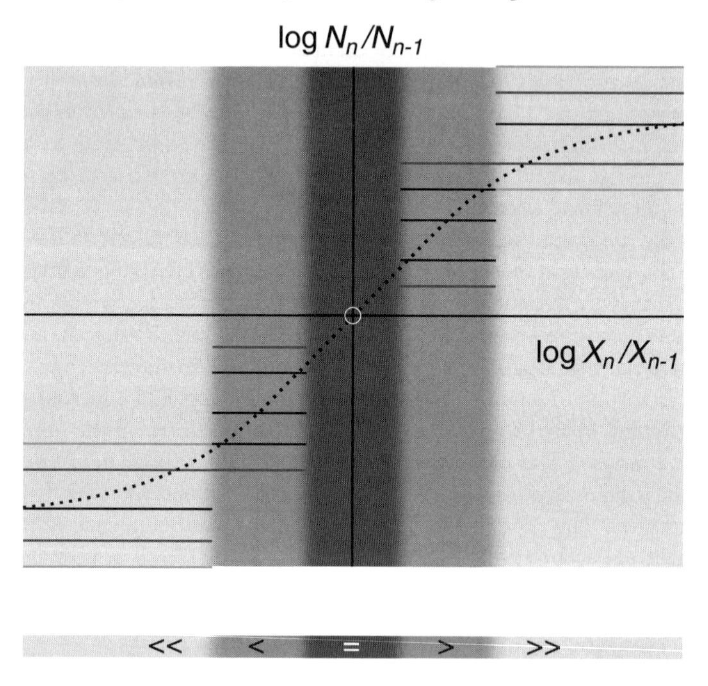

Fig. 11.8 The interaction of a limited range of numerical responses with the ordinal judgment scheme. If the categories '<<' and '>>' are extended sufficiently (by using a wider geometric range of stimulus values; cf. Fig. 10.1), the range of numbers assigned to the stimuli cannot continue to increase in proportion. The dotted S-shaped curve sketches the approximate effect of a limited range of numerical responses.

It should be noted that although Fig. 11.8 exhibits a roughly sinusoidal perturbation of an otherwise linear relationship between log stimulus ratio and log response ratio, the idea set out in that figure is quite distinct from the principle advanced by Teghtsoonian *et al.* (1995) as an explanation of the minor perturbations of the Power Law seen in the data of Luce and Mo (1965), Green and Luce (1974), and elsewhere. Teghtsoonian *et al.* propose that an otherwise exact power law relation between stimulus magnitude and numerical assignment is distorted by subjects' preferences for round numbers. The distortion occurs because the numbers that subjects actually use are not distributed exactly logarithmically and, in addition, the assignment of numbers to stimuli is (assumed to be) locally biased thereby. Although the idea in Fig. 11.8 produces superficially similar distortions, it depends on subjects being willing to use only a limited range of numbers which have to be allocated in some way to the five-way ordinal classification of the ratios between successive stimulus magnitudes.

11.4.2 **Individual differences**

There are individual idiosyncrasies in the use of numbers which show most obviously in the use of 'round' numbers. If the range of numbers uttered in a magnitude estimation task is determined by an internal transform from the values of the stimuli presented, those individual idiosyncrasies ought not to obtrude. But if, as I suggest here, the collection of numbers used is *effectively* an independent variable in the experimental design (and one which varies widely from subject to subject), then one should expect to see wide variation in the values of exponents estimated from the data of different individual subjects. Stevens' practice of aggregating the data from groups of observers, typically a group of 10, who each judge each stimulus twice only in different random orders, has the effect of hiding such idiosyncrasies. But other experimenters, especially those outside Stevens' coterie who do not follow Stevens' (1956b) detailed recommendations, have revealed wide individual variation.

Knibestöl and Vallbo (1980), in the study described earlier in Chapter 6 (pp. 71–2), reported a mean exponent of 1.0 from a total of 62 individual magnitude estimation experiments; this mean compares well with the 1.10 in Table 5.1 for static force on the palm of the hand. But the values of the 62 individual exponents from which that average was calculated ranged from 0.36 to 2.09 (see Knibestöl and Vallbo 1980, p. 260, fig. 7). In the estimation of heaviness Pradhan and Hoffman (1963) obtained individual exponents ranging from 0.42 to 1.98; these are the extreme values from a total set of 40 estimates obtained from six subjects estimating the heaviness of weights ranging from 10 to 506 g with various spacings of the nine stimuli. (For comparison, the value in Table 5.1, from Stevens and Galanter (1957), is 1.45). Employing the same attribute Luce and Mo (1965) obtained estimates of the exponent ranging from 0.71 to 1.24, one estimate from each of six subjects judging the heaviness of 18 weights from 20 to 1600 g; and likewise obtained exponents ranging from 0.30 to 0.68 from a further six subjects judging the loudnesses of 20 1 kHz tones from 43 to 90 dB SPL. Green and Luce (1974) reported six individual exponents ranging from 0.30 to 1.1 (0.15 to 0.55 re stimulus energy) in an experiment with 20 1 kHz tones from 32.5 to 80 dB SPL, with a standard at 55 dB called 100, and a further six ranging from 0.36 to 0.70 in a replication of the experiment without the designated standard. Finally, in Stevens' own laboratory J.C. Stevens and Guirao (1964) obtained exponents for the estimation of loudness ranging from 0.4 to 1.1 from 11 individual subjects.

Variation of this order in the estimation of individual exponents from a wide range of stimulus values is too great to be attributed simply to experimental error. Some part of this variation, at least, must be intrinsic to the subject; and the question now arises whether these intrinsic differences are of a perceptual nature, and therefore specific to the attribute being judged, or arise from the subject's idiosyncratic use of numbers, and are therefore general to magnitude estimation as an experimental procedure. Ekman *et al.* (1968) addressed this question by asking 21 subjects to serve on successive days in magnitude estimation experiments with weight, area, concentration of salt, roughness of sandpapers, luminance, and aesthetic preference for children's drawings of a tree. There were seven values of each stimulus attribute, and the subject estimated the ratio of the magnitudes for each of the 21 different pairs four times each. The range of stimuli employed in each of the five metric tasks was chosen so that the mean numerical estimates covered approximately the same range as in the aesthetic preference task; this was desirable in order that intrasubject correlations between the use of numbers in the different tasks should not be compromised by absolute differences in the ranges of numbers uttered. Correlations between the power law exponents for different attributes now reduce to correlations between the ranges of numbers uttered (Ekman *et al.* 1968, table 3). All such correlations were positive except for a zero correlation between estimations of heaviness and of aesthetic preference, and seven correlations out of the total of 15 were significant at 0.05 (two-tailed). There is, therefore, an intrasubject consistency in the use of numbers in judging different attributes; though in Ekman *et al.*'s study, which yielded pairwise correlations around 0.4, this accounted for only 16 per cent of the variance.

It is pertinent next to enquire how durable this intrasubject consistency might be. This question has been studied by Teghtsoonian and Teghtsoonian (1971) using estimations of length and of the area of irregular polygons. They demonstrated a significant intrasubject correlation (c. +0.6) between the exponent estimated for these two attributes, except in the first of five daily sessions which revealed a correlation of about +0.2 only. There was also a significant correlation (c. +0.8) between the exponents estimated for the same attribute on successive days; but this correlation did not persist when subjects were retested one year later. Finally, in a second experiment using the attribute of area only, Teghtsoonian and Teghtsoonian obtained correlations of about +0.4 (not significant, but similar to Ekman *et al.* 1968) between two estimates of the exponent, the second on retesting after an interval of 1 to 56 days; but a correlation of +0.8 on immediate retesting. This suggests a contribution of temporary idiosyncratic differences in the use of number to the variability of individual exponents much greater than the 16 per cent estimated by Ekman *et al.*; within any one experimental session, 64 per cent would seem a more realistic figure.

Since subjects are never given any instruction how differences between successive stimuli are to be categorized, or what numerical ratios are to be used for the different categories in Fig. 11.8, striking individual differences are to be expected.

11.5 THE 'REGRESSION' EFFECT

The point was made in Chapter 5 (pp. 63–5) that subjects could not only assign numbers to stimuli, but also adjust stimuli to match given numbers. Figure 5.4 is one example. When log number is regressed onto log stimulus magnitude, the gradients of the two regression lines differ somewhat, with the estimation gradient systematically the lesser. This was called the 'regression effect' by Stevens and Greenbaum (1966).

The term 'regression effect' is misleading. It invokes an analogy with regression analysis when there are errors in both variables, an analogy which is not appropriate here, as Cross (1973) pointed out. In magnitude estimation the magnitude of the stimulus is known without error and regression of log number onto log magnitude gives an unbiased estimate whatever linear relation might obtain in nature. Likewise, in the production experiment the numbers given to the subject to match are also known without error and regression of log adjusted magnitude onto log number is unbiased in that case. Yet the two regression lines differ systematically. Some other explanation is required.

Typically (e.g. Reynolds and Stevens 1960), the estimation experiment is conducted first, to discover an appropriate set of numbers to give to the same cohort of subjects to match. That set will naturally reflect the ratios between successive numerical estimates uttered in the estimation experiment. Those preferred ratios are indicated by horizontal lines in Fig. 11.8 and reproduced as ticks on the ordinate in Fig. 11.9. But, because the numbers in the production experiment are presented in random order, unrelated to the sequence of stimulus values in the estimation task, the ratio between successive numbers to be matched will sometimes exceed, or fall short if it is less than 1, the range of ratios commonly found between successive numerical estimates. The range of ticks on the ordinate in Fig. 11.9 is therefore extended.

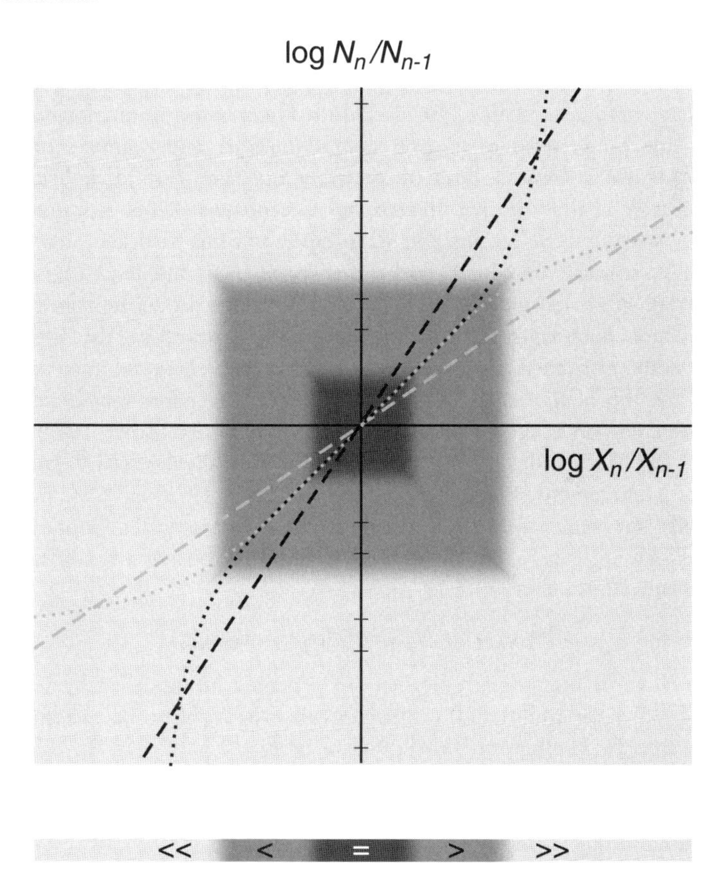

Fig. 11.9 The interaction of ordinal judgment with magnitude production. This is the complementary diagram to Fig. 11.8, showing the classification of numbers into five analogous categories, each with a different distribution of matching stimulus magnitudes. The dotted S-shaped curve from Fig. 11.8 is reproduced here in grey; and the same consideration of a limited range of stimulus magnitudes produces a complementary inverse-S-shaped curve for magnitude production. Even though these expected characteristics align for small stimulus differences, linear regression of log N onto log X (estimation) and of log X onto log N (production data) produces two diverging regression lines (shown as broken lines in grey and in black).

The selection of a stimulus magnitude to match a given number in the production experiment is the converse of the process of estimation. Each number is presumed to be categorized as 'very much less than', 'less than', 'about the same as', 'greater than', or 'very much greater than' its predecessor and a stimulus value chosen, in relation to the value selected on the preceding trial, according to the ordinal scheme set out in Fig. 11.9. In comparison with Fig. 11.8, the numbers to be matched are perceived without error (if differences between subjects in the assignment of numbers to categories are ignored), but the selection of a stimulus magnitude is everywhere subject to variability. Because (for the reason explained above) the range of ratios between successive numbers exceeds that which subjects would naturally use in the estimation experiment, so the argument which leads to the S-shaped relation between the average value of ($\log N_n - \log N_{n-1}$) and the log stimulus ratio ($\log X_n/X_{n-1}$) in estimation (reproduced as the faint dotted line in Fig. 11.9), leads to a complementary curvilinear relation (the black dotted line) in the production experiment. If, now, magnitude productions are regressed onto number and estimates onto stimulus magnitude, the two regression lines (respectively the faint and black broken lines in Fig. 11.9) separate in the way that Stevens and Greenbaum (1966) reported.

Figure 11.9 actually shows assignments with respect to some particular preceding trial. In practice, $\log N_n$ is regressed onto $\log X_n$ (rather than $\log N_n/N_{n-1}$ onto $\log X_n/X_{n-1}$); and in that calculation judgments made with respect to different preceding stimuli are aggregated together without distinction. Such aggregation of technically distinct categories of data tends to obscure whatever curvature of relationship there might be in nature. However, 'Inserting additional stimuli near the top of the range is now a well-known procedure for obtaining a nearly straight-line function on a loglog plot with unpractised observers (Eisler, 1962; J.C. Stevens and Tulving, 1957)' (Poulton 1979, p. 788). Poulton cites the data of J.C. Stevens (1958, fig. 3) and of Montgomery (1975, as replotted by Poulton 1979, fig. 6) as examples.

Substantially the same idea can be formulated mathematically. Suppose that in a magnitude estimation experiment the subject begins by choosing a candidate number ν according to eqn 10.3; i.e.

$$\log \nu_n - \log N_{n-1} = B_n(\log x_n - \log x_{n-1}). \qquad (11.10)$$

The limited range of numerical responses can plausibly be modelled by weighting the candidate $\log \nu$ towards a numerical centre of gravity $\log N_\pi$ after the pattern of response compression seen in Hollingworth's 1909 data in Fig. 2.3 (p. 22). In that figure the amplitudes of reproduced movements are attracted geometrically towards a centre of gravity derived from previous stimuli. The subject then utters a numerical estimate that is a weighted average of $\log \nu_n$ and $\log N_\pi$, i.e.

$$\log N_n = \theta \log \nu_n + (1 - \theta)\log N_\pi, \qquad (11.11)$$

where θ lies between 0 and 1. Combining eqns 11.10 and 11.11 gives

$$\log N_n - \log N_{n-1} = \theta B_n(\log x_n - \log x_{n-1}) + (1 - \theta)[\log N_\pi - \log N_{n-1}]. \qquad (11.12)$$

Taking expectations with respect to $X_n B_n$ and trial $n - 1$ now gives

$$\log N_n = \theta\beta \log X_n + \log c, \qquad (11.13)$$

which is eqn 11.4 with $\theta\beta$ for β.

In the magnitude production experiment the roles of x_n and N_n are reversed. Eqns 11.10, 11.11, and 11.12 are therefore replaced, respectively, by

$$\log \xi_n - \log x_{n-1} = B_n^{-1}(\log N_n - \log N_{n-1}). \tag{11.14}$$

where ξ_n is a candidate match to N_n;

$$\log x_n = \theta \log \xi_n + (1 - \theta)\log X_\pi, \tag{11.15}$$

where X_π is the subject's prior expectation of what the stimulus match might be; and

$$\log X_n = \theta\beta^{-1}\log N_n + \log c' \tag{11.16}$$

where c' is another constant. The (inverse) exponent from eqn 11.16, matching numbers to stimulus magnitudes, is $\theta^{-1}\beta$ which is always greater than the exponent from 11.13, $\theta\beta$, because θ is less than 1. This is the relationship between exponents estimated from magnitude estimation and production discovered by Stevens and Greenbaum (1966) and set out in Fig. 11.9.

11.6 SUMMARY

This summary will set the scene for a counterargument to the explanations proposed in this chapter, a counterargument based on intramodal range effects, which follows in the next chapter. I have so far argued these propositions:

1. Power law data are generated by inducing subjects to assign an approximately geometric distribution of numbers to a geometric series of stimuli. Any method of assignment will do so long as it is not entirely random. Provided the stimulus and response sets are both reasonably uniform with respect to a logarithmic metric, Stevens' Power Law drops out of the regression equation 11.4.
2. The absolute scale of the numbers uttered as magnitude estimates (i.e. the constant c in eqn 11.4) is widely agreed to be arbitrary.
3. The regression coefficient β in eqn 11.4 (the Power Law exponent) is determined (at least within the body of experimental data from Stevens and his colleagues summarized in Tables 11.1, 11.2 and 11.3) chiefly by the geometric range of stimulus magnitudes employed (eqn 11.6). The geometric range of mean response values (within the same body of data) is roughly constant, and nearly independent of the stimulus range. This results from the use of finely tuned instructions to the subjects and from transfer effects which accompany the use of the same subjects in different investigations.
4. Proposition 3 is specific to the body of data summarized in Tables 11.1, 11.2 and 11.3. It is not necessary that the range of numbers used by subjects in magnitude estimation experiments be the same everywhere. In fact, the range of numbers used depends on prior experience and may be manipulated by means of numerical examples included in the instructions to the subjects. The range of numbers used varies widely, as also do the exponents obtained (Marks 1974; Eisler 1976).

12 The stimulus range

The experimental results published by S.S. Stevens and his colleagues were summarized at the end of the preceding chapter in these terms:

1. the Power Law results from inducing subjects to assign an approximately geometric distribution of numbers to a geometric ladder of stimulus values; and
2. the geometric range of numbers is approximately constant from one experiment to another so that the exponent of the Power Law varies as the inverse of the log stimulus range.

These two statements summarize Stevens' results approximately (though not exactly) for comparisons between different stimulus continua, and owe much to Poulton (1979) and Teghtsoonian (1971) respectively. This chapter is concerned with a body of experimental data assembled by Teghtsoonian (1973) which shows that the second generalization does not extend to experiments with different stimulus ranges, but on the *same* continuum. Teghtsoonian's body of data presents a further problem which I examine here.

12.1 INTRAMODAL RANGE EFFECTS

Teghtsoonian (1973, Table 1) tabulated three sets of data which speak to the effect of varying the stimulus range within a specific sensory modality. If the response range were independent of the stimulus range, then the estimated exponent should vary, intramodally, as eqn 11.7. If, on the other hand, the exponent is fixed, a characteristic property of the stimulus attribute being judged, the (log) response range should vary, intramodally, in proportion to the (log) stimulus range. In practice, neither result obtains.

Teghtsoonian's three experimental comparisons comprised:

1. Magnitude estimation of the loudness of a 3 kHz tone by four groups of 16 subjects (reported in greater detail by Teghtsoonian and Teghtsoonian, 1978). Six different amplitudes of tone were presented for judgment centred around 84 dB SPL and separated by equal intervals of 0.5, 1, 2, 4, and 8 dB (stimulus ranges 2.5, 5, 10, 20, and 40 dB) for the different groups.
2. Magnitude estimation of apparent distance from the observer in a natural outdoor setting (Teghtsoonian and Teghtsoonian 1970). Four different groups of subjects judged distances ranging respectively from 5 to 37, 5 to 110, 5 to 480, and 10 to 450 ft.
3. Five otherwise independent studies of the estimation of apparent length (listed by Teghtsoonian 1973, footnote 6).

The summary data (stimulus range and median exponent) from these various experiments are tabulated by Teghtsoonian (1973, p. 12, table 1) and log response range is plotted against log stimulus range in Fig. 12.1. If response range were independent of stimulus range, then the straight lines added to the data points would be level. It is clear that within each stimulus modality response range increases with stimulus range. If, on the other hand, the exponent were independent of the stimulus range, there would be an exact proportionality between the two log ranges and the straight lines would pass through the origin. Instead, the data are fit by a relation of the form

$$\log \mathcal{R} = \beta \log \mathcal{S} + \log c, \tag{12.1}$$

where $\mathcal{S}$ is the geometric stimulus range and $\mathcal{R}$ the corresponding response range. Although this relation is of the same form as the regression in Fig. 11.7 (eqn 11.8), the coefficient β is here much larger, comparable to the typical value of the Power Law exponent.

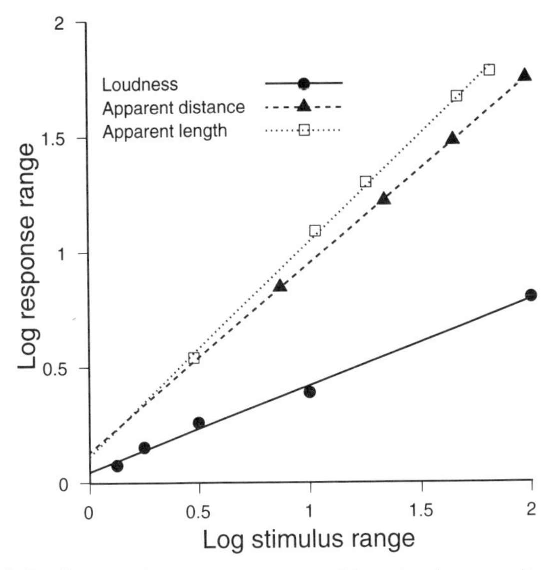

Fig. 12.1 The relation between log response range and log stimulus range for three sets of intramodal comparisons. Data for loudness, apparent distance, and apparent length from Teghtsoonian (1973, p. 12, table 1) and from Teghtsoonian and Teghtsoonian (1978).

An occasional criticism of eqn 12.1 is that geometric stimulus range ($\mathcal{S}$) is a parameter of the experimental design, not a stimulus presented to the subject, and therefore cannot logically be the determinant of the response range. Teghtsoonian rebuts that criticism by citing further data from experiments by Stevens and Poulton (1956), Poulton (1969), and Warren (1970), all of them concerned with the estimation of loudness, but in which the ratio of the estimate of the very first stimulus to the modulus assigned to the standard is compared to the stimulus ratio between the two. The data from those three experiments are plotted in Fig. 12.2 where the standards and their assigned moduli are represented by the filled symbols and the judgments by open symbols. Since the data now relate to specific single judgments (N_1), the previous relation (eqn 12.1) has to be recast as

$$E\{\log N_1 - \log N_0\} = \beta(\log X_1 - \log X_0) + \log c_0, \tag{12.2}$$

where X_0 is the standard and N_0 its modulus, and X_1 the very first stimulus magnitude.

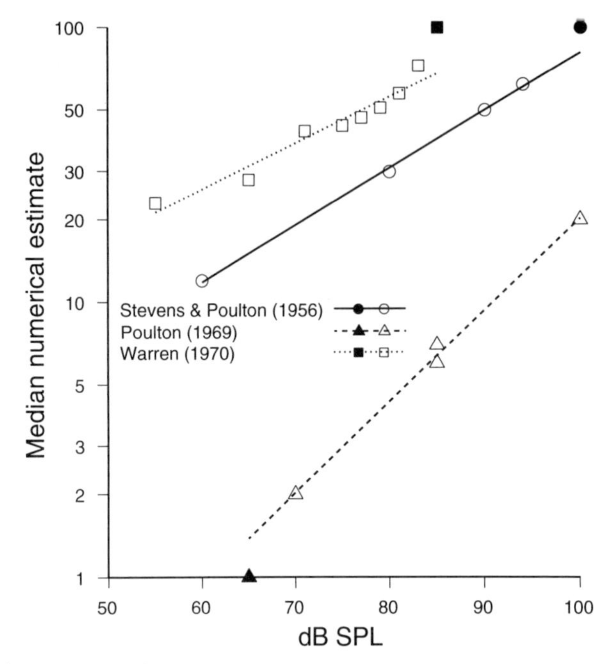

Fig. 12.2 Very first estimates of loudness in relation to distance from the standard in three experiments by Stevens and Poulton (1956), Poulton (1969), and Warren (1970). The standards and their moduli are shown by filled symbols, the judgments by open symbols. The regression lines (eqn 12.2) are fitted to the judgments (open symbols) only. (After Teghtsoonian 1973, p. 16.)

This relation is fitted to the numerical judgments (open symbols only) in Fig. 12.2. Those judgments exhibit the same pattern as the intramodal range data of Fig. 12.1 inasmuch as the linear regression of log response ratio on log stimulus ratio fails to pass through the filled data points (the standards and their moduli), as an exact power law would. The regression lines pass those filled data points on the same side as the regression lines in Fig. 12.1 pass the origin (the gradient of the regression line being in every case too shallow). But in this present case the stimulus ratio is realized explicitly in the relation, to the standard, of the very first stimulus presented to the subject.

In Fig. 12.2 log c_0 is the vertical offset of the regression line from the modulus assigned to the standard. It measures the response one would expect from an extrapolation of the regression line (assuming that extrapolation to be valid) if the standard itself were to be presented as the first stimulus to be judged. It signifies that zero (log) stimulus range does not generate a zero (log) response range. Teghtsoonian's intuition is that the displacement of the extrapolated regression from the standard (passage through the filled data point corresponding to an exact power law) is related to the regression effect described by Stevens and Greenbaum (1966; see pp. 63–5 here).

12.2 VERY FIRST JUDGMENTS

The argument which follows amounts to saying that the regression lines in Fig. 12.2 fail to pass through the moduli assigned to the standards because of subjects' prior expectations what kind of numerical estimate might be appropriate. Subjects sense that an excessively large estimate, relative to the modulus of the standard, would not be acceptable and might even look ridiculous. At the same time they do not expect their very first stimulus to be equal to the standard, especially if that is the only stimulus they are going to be asked to judge, so that an estimate equal to the modulus is also contraindicated. This means that subjects expect, on their first trial at least, to utter an estimate that either exceeds the modulus by a certain ratio or falls short by a similar (inverse) ratio. This idea comes from Teghtsoonian (1973; see also Teghtsoonian and Teghtsoonian 1978) and is merely spelt out here in more explicit detail. With this kind of prior expectation the model below works for both increases and decreases in the stimulus level to be judged.

Suppose the first stimulus to be judged exceeds the standard sufficiently much that the subject perceives it to be greater. Represent the subject's prior idea, how much larger an estimate might reasonably be than the modulus assigned to the standard, by the number N_π, where $N_\pi/N_0 = r_\pi$ ($r_\pi > 1$), a ratio which the subject deems particularly likely. The number N_π is less than the maximum number which the subject is prepared to utter as an estimate, reflecting a certain caution on the part of the subject in choosing his response. Teghtsoonian (1973) comments of the subjects in his own experiment:

Several subjects reported explicitly that since they did not know at the outset how wide a range of intensities they would encounter, they were reluctant to 'use up' extreme numbers for their early judgments. A similar inclination was voiced in even stronger terms for the production procedure. (Teghtsoonian 1973, p. 23).

I adapt the model previously proposed (pp. 190–1) for Stevens and Greenbaum's (1966) 'regression effect'. Suppose that a subject, faced with a very first magnitude estimate, begins by choosing a candidate judgment ν according to eqn 10.3, i.e.

$$\log \nu_1 - \log N_0 = B_1(\log x_1 - \log x_0), \tag{12.3}$$

and then utters a numerical estimate that is a weighted average of $\log \nu_1$ and $\log N_\pi$, i.e.

$$\log N_1 = \theta \log \nu_1 + (1 - \theta)\log N_\pi, \tag{12.4}$$

where θ lies between 0 and 1. Combining eqns 12.3 and 12.4 now gives

$$\begin{aligned}\log N_1 - \log N_0 &= \theta B_1(\log x_1 - \log x_0) + (1 - \theta)(\log N_\pi - \log N_0) \\ &= \theta B_1(\log x_1 - \log x_0) + (1 - \theta)\log r_\pi,\end{aligned} \tag{12.5}$$

which is an equation of the same form as (12.2), fitted to the data in Fig. 12.2.

Equation 12.5 describes what happens when the first stimulus X_1 is greater than the standard X_0. If X_1 is perceived to be less than X_0 ($x_1 < x_0$), the subject's prior expectation is appropriately represented by a number N_π^* where $N_0/N_\pi^* = r_\pi$, the same ratio as before. Then eqn 12.5 has to be replaced by

$$\log N_1 - \log N_0 = \theta B_1(\log x_1 - \log x_0) - (1 - \theta)\log r_\pi, \tag{12.6}$$

reflecting the different prior expectation which applies to estimates of stimuli less than the standard. In eqn 12.6, however, $x_1 < x_0$ and $N_1 < N_0$, so that both equations (12.5 and 12.6) may be written as one in the form

$$|\log N_1 - \log N_0| = \theta B_1 |\log x_1 - \log x_0| + (1 - \theta)\log r_\pi. \qquad (12.7)$$

Equation 12.7 accommodates all of the data in Fig. 12.2, decreases in stimulus value as well as increases.

12.2.1 **Magnitude productions**

In magnitude production the roles of X_1 and N_1 are reversed. Equations 12.3, 12.4, and 12.7 should therefore be replaced respectively by

$$\log \xi_1 - \log x_0 = B_1^{-1}(\log N_1 - \log N_0), \qquad (12.8)$$

where ξ_1 is a candidate match to N_1;

$$\log x_1 = \theta \log \xi_1 + (1 - \theta)\log X_\pi, \qquad (12.9)$$

where X_π ($= r_\pi X_0$) is the subject's prior expectation of what the stimulus match might be; and

$$|\log x_1 - \log x_0| = \theta B_1^{-1} |\log N_1 - \log N_0| + (1 - \theta)\log r_\pi. \qquad (12.10)$$

The (inverse) exponent from eqn 12.10, matching numbers to stimulus magnitudes is $\theta^{-1}B_1$ which is always greater than the exponent from 12.5, θB_1, because θ is less than 1. This is, of course, the relationship between exponents estimated from magnitude estimation and production discovered by Stevens and Greenbaum (1966).

But if a power law exponent were estimated from very first productions only, it would be (substituting stimulus values log X_1, and log X_0 for the perceived values (logx_1 and logx_0).

$$\hat{\beta} = |\log N_1 - \log N_0| / |\log X_1 - \log X_0|$$

$$= \theta^{-1} B_1 |\log N_1 - \log N_0| / \{|\log N_1 - \log N_0| + \theta^{-1} B_1 (1 - \theta)\log r_\pi\}, \qquad (12.11)$$

obtained by substitution from eqn 12.10. A first number N_1, sufficiently close to N_0, the modulus to be matched, would then deliver an estimated exponent (calculated from eqn 12.11) *less than* the value,

$$\theta B_1 |\log N_1 - \log N_0| / \{|\log N_1 - \log N_0| - (1 - \theta)\log r_\pi\}, \qquad (12.12)$$

which is obtained by substitution from eqn 12.7 for magnitude estimation of the corresponding stimulus. This is contrary to the usual relationship between exponents estimated from estimation and from production data. That usual relationship is inverted in this case because, when $|\log N_1 - \log N_0|$ is not much greater than $(1 - \theta)\log r_\pi$, the denominator in eqn 12.12 is not much greater than zero and the relative values of 12.11 and 12.12 are dominated by their respective denominators instead of the factors $\theta^{-1}B_1$ and θB_1 ($\theta^{-1}B_1 > \theta B_1$) which dominate when $\log N_1$ is large.

Figure 12.3 presents one example of an inversion of this relationship from Stevens and Poulton (1956). The estimation data are the same as those shown, by symbols of the same shape, in Fig. 12.2. The production data come from two other experiments within the same study, and have been shifted 10 dB to the right so that the two standards and their moduli superimpose. The exponent estimated from a very first estimate is equal to the gradient of a line drawn from the standard to the judgment data point and that gradient is generally steeper for the production data points (triangles) than for the estimations (circles). This is the relationship described as Stevens and Greenbaum's (1966) 'regression effect'. But if the subjects had been asked to estimate the magnitude of a stimulus greater than 94 dB (to the right of the point of intersection of the two regression lines in Fig. 12.3) and comparison had been made with a comparable magnitude production, that relationship would have inverted. This inversion comes about because the production regression line passes *its* standard and assigned modulus on the opposite side to the estimation regression line. This, in turn, is in accord with the difference between eqn 12.7 for very first estimations and 12.10 for very first productions. Interchange of stimulus values (X_i) and numbers (N_i) effects a change in the sign of the offset $(1-\theta)\log r_\pi$. Teghtsoonian (1973, p. 22, fig. 11) has published another example of this inversion derived from the very first judgments of the subjects in the experiment (Experiment 1 above on p. 192) judging the loudness of a 3 kHz tone and in a comparable production experiment (Teghtsoonian and Teghtsoonian, 1978).

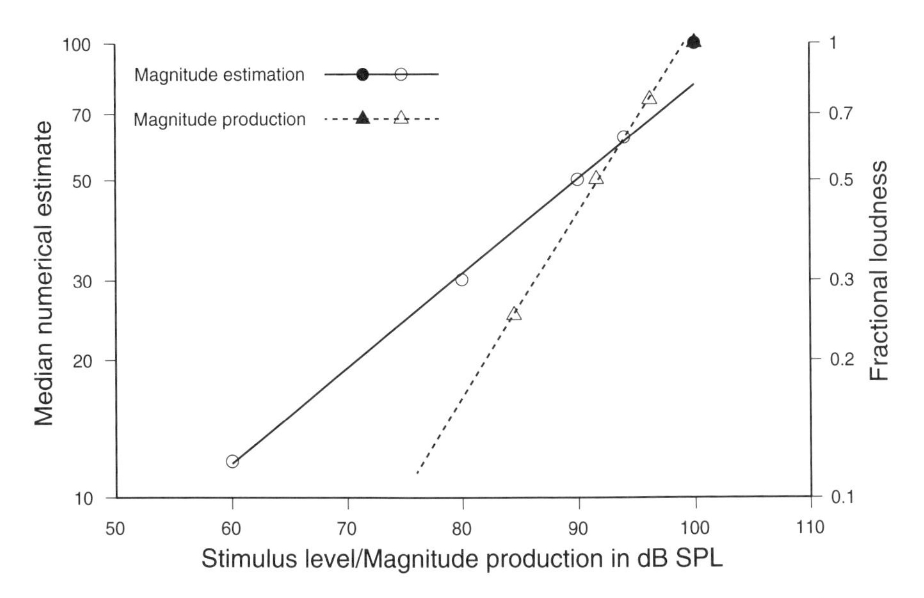

Fig. 12.3 Very first estimates of loudness and very first matches of loudness to numbers in the experiment by Stevens and Poulton (1956). (After Teghtsoonian 1973, p. 22.)

12.2.2 **Range effects**

If an experiment involves estimates of stimuli both above and below the standard, then, for the maximum stimulus presented on some trial *n*, eqn 12.5 gives[1]

$$\log N_{max} - \log N_0 = \theta B_n(\log X_{max} - \log X_0) + (1-\theta)\log r_\pi, \tag{12.13}$$

and for the minimum stimulus on some other trial *m* 12.6 gives

$$\log N_{min} - \log N_0 = \theta B_m(\log X_{min} - \log X_0) - (1-\theta)\log r_\pi. \tag{12.14}$$

To calculate the log response range, N_{max} and N_{min} must be replaced by their means $\overline{N}_{max}$ and $\overline{N}_{min}$ and the random coefficients B_n and B_m by their expectation β. Then

$$\log \overline{N}_{max} - \log \overline{N}_{min} = \theta\beta(\log X_{max} - \log X_{min}) + 2(1-\theta)\log r_\pi, \tag{12.15}$$

or

$$\log \mathcal{R} = \theta\beta \log \mathcal{S} + 2(1-\theta)\log r_\pi, \tag{12.16}$$

which is an equation of the same form as 12.1, describing the variation of exponent with intramodal range in Fig. 12.1.

Figure 12.4 shows the response ranges in the judgment of loudness of a 3 kHz tone for both magnitude estimation (this is Experiment 1 above on p. 192) and production. Four of the estimation ranges have been taken from Teghtsoonian (1973, table 1) and four of the production ranges from Teghtsoonian and Teghtsoonian (1978, fig. 3). But the smallest range in each set of data comes from a replication of these two experiments with a yet smaller range of stimulus values (Teghtsoonian and Teghtsoonian 1978, note 6) carried out some years after the principal series of observations at the suggestion of an editorial referee. It was an inference from Teghtsoonian and Teghtsoonian's argument that, if the ranges of stimulus and numerical values supplied by the experimenter were sufficiently narrow, the usual relation between their estimated exponents would invert, that is, the magnitude production data would show the *shallower* gradient in a plot like Fig. 5.4. In Figs 12.3 and 12.4 each data point affords a separate estimate of the power law exponent and that estimate is equal to the gradient of a line joining the point to the origin (or to the standard and its modulus). While the data in Fig. 12.3 are consistent with this prediction, the regression line fitted to the estimation data has to be extrapolated beyond the actual range of that data. The additional experiment suggested by the referee directly validates the prediction inasmuch as the two sets of data points in Fig. 12.4 physically intersect. For these smallest 0.125 log unit ranges the exponents estimated from the production data were significantly smaller than those from the magnitude estimates, significant at 0.05. This will prove a critical result in relation to the argument which follows below.

[1] The argument has been simplified. Given that each stimulus is compared with its predecessor, one should add an extra bias $(1-\theta)\log r_\pi$ on each trial on which the stimulus exceeds its predecessor and subtract the same bias on each trial on which the stimulus magnitude is less. This makes the actual bias effective on those trials on which X_{min} and X_{max} are presented dependent on the particular sequence of stimuli preceding. But a simple consideration of symmetry applied to a random sequence of stimuli presented for judgment nevertheless dictates an equation of the *form* 12.15, ultimately because the stimulus value X_{max} is always greater than its predecessor and X_{min} always less. Since the quantity $(1-\theta)\log r_\pi$ is a free parameter, not otherwise determined, this simplification is of no consequence.

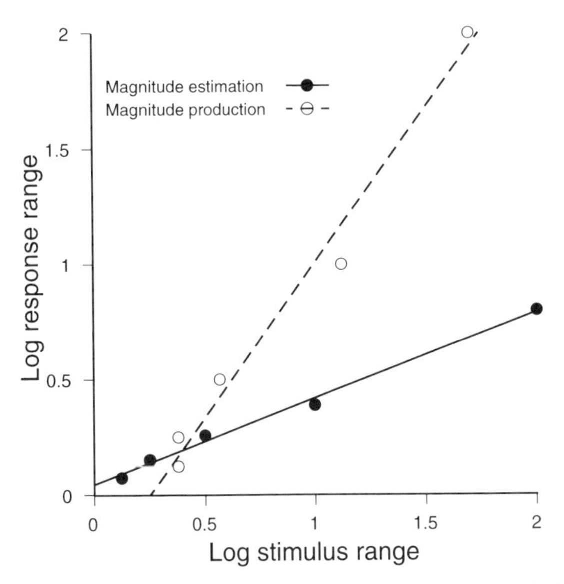

Fig. 12.4 The relation between stimulus range and response range in judging the loudness of a 3 kHz tone. The filled circles are the magnitude production data from Fig. 12.1 (Teghtsoonian 1973). The open circles are comparable magnitude production data from Teghtsoonian and Teghtsoonian (1978).

12.3 COMMENTARY

1. Teghtsoonian's (1973) data possibly understate the effect of varying the stimulus range on a common continuum. Poulton (1989, p. 217, fig. 8.4; pp. 220–221, table 8.2; and p. 225, fig. 8.6) has listed and plotted the results of eight further intramodal comparisons, extant at his time of writing. All of those eight comparisons show a more substantial effect of varying the stimulus range, though in no case does that effect amount to complete reciprocity (numerical range independent of stimulus range). Teghtsoonian has, however, combined estimation experiments with comparable production experiments and his data thereby pose a more acute problem of explanation. The discussion which follows looks at Teghtsoonian's data.

2. Teghtsoonian (1973) has provided an elegant synthesis of his results. The essence of that synthesis is that a subject's prior expectation does not subsist in a preference for a certain set of numbers absolutely, but for a certain *ratio of numerical response* relative to the preceding judgment. Moreover—and this point is critical—that preferred ratio is different according as the stimulus presented for judgment is increased in magnitude over its predecessor or decreased. In the latter case prior expectation settles around the reciprocal $1/r_\pi$ of the ratio in the former case. Teghtsoonian's synthesis works well for experiments in which each subject is asked to make one judgment only (the subjects know in advance that the one stimulus to be judged will be greater/less than the standard), but there are some problems with longer series of trials in which some stimuli are greater, some less than their predecessors.

3. The ratio around which prior expectation settles is different according as the physical

stimulus magnitude is increased over the preceding trial (ratio r_π) or decreased ($1/r_\pi$). So the relative magnitude of the stimulus needs to be known to the subject before the numerical judgment is assigned. That is not impossible; but it implies that the selection of a candidate response in eqn 12.3 is an internal mental event ('This stimulus is weaker than the last one. Do I give it "50" or "25"?'), rather than just a convenient mathematical fiction, and it ought for that reason to be possible somehow to obtain a judgment uncontaminated by prior expectation.

4. What happens when a stimulus value is repeated? Teghtsoonian himself ducked this question:

> Before speculating about what the significance of the additive constant [in eqn 12.2] *is*, it may be useful to suggest first what it is not. It should not be construed as implying that a stimulus ratio of unity (successive presentations of identical stimulus intensities) will yield a judgmental ratio greater than unity. Although such a result, suggesting a time-order error, is conceivable, it is conceptually simpler to consider only those cases in which a subject can readily distinguish between successive intensities. When the latter define differences that fall into the region of uncertainty, it seems likely that the character of a subject's judgments will change (probably falling into a bimodal distribution). It is not at all clear what results are to be expected in this case, but it is unlikely that extrapolation of the function obtained from clearly discriminable pairs would provide a satisfactory prediction. (Teghtsoonian 1973, pp. 18–19)

If such a repeated value is sometimes judged 'greater' and sometimes 'less', with a different prior expectation applying according to that judgment, then the variability of the numerical response ought to be increased thereby and the correlation with the preceding response lessened. There is no indication of a reduced correlation in Figs 9.1 or 10.4 for stimuli repeated exactly.

5. The nub of the problem is that the generalization which worked in Chapter 11 for comparisons between different continua and between magnitude estimation and production (that is, contraction of the absolute response range about some centre of gravity) does not extrapolate to intramodal comparisons. The alternative idea which Teghtsoonian has introduced (contraction about one or the other of two response ratios, according to the perceived relation between successive stimulus values) does not obviously work for intermodal comparisons. There is no problem with experiments in which subjects make one judgment only. The subjects know (or can easily guess from the manner in which the task is explained to them) whether the stimulus to be judged will lie above or below the standard, in which case a prior expectation centred about a specific ratio is not distinct from one centred about a specific number. The problem is specifically concerned with the experiments reproduced in Figs 12.1 and 12.4.

The ideas of (a) contraction of the numerical response about an absolute centre of gravity (pp. 190–1) and (b) contraction of the ratio of successive responses about one of two preferred ratios, the ratio dependent on the perceived relation between successive stimulus values, might both be regarded as attempted descriptions of some common internal process, at present imperfectly understood, descriptions oriented towards different sets of experimental findings. I complete this chapter with yet a third way of looking at experiments with different stimulus ranges on the same continuum.

12.4 ORDINAL JUDGMENT OF DIFFERENT RANGES OF STIMULI

Figure 12.5 presents a graphical model oriented towards the analysis of very first judgments such as the data from Stevens and Poulton in Fig. 12.3. The stimulus values in that kind of experiment all lie on the same side of the standard (so that Fig. 12.5 reproduces only the bottom left-hand corner of Fig. 11.9) where the conjectured relationship between stimulus magnitude and assigned number (grey dotted curve) is curvilinear. The corresponding relation for very first magnitude productions (black dotted line) curves in the opposite direction. So, when a linear regression line is fitted to data from these two kinds of experiment (the values of the independent variables—the stimuli to be judged or the numbers to be matched—being all offset to the same side of the standard and its modulus), the gradients of the two regression lines are slewed in opposite directions, as shown. That pattern provides a qualitative account of the disposition of data points in Fig. 12.3. One

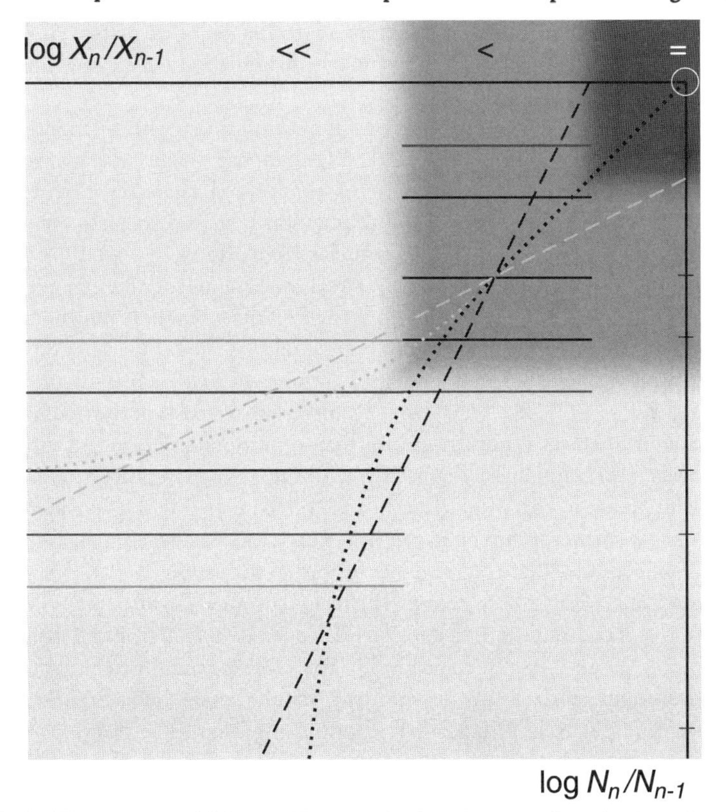

Fig. 12.5 Ordinal judgment model for very first magnitude estimates and productions. It is assumed that subjects know that the stimulus to be judged will be less than the standard, or the number to be matched less than its modulus (cf. Fig. 12.3). The previous categorization of stimulus/numerical ratios applies and the present diagram is a reproduction of the bottom left-hand corner of Fig. 11.9. If, however, the range of stimuli presented for estimation, or numbers for adjustment, is offset from the standard and its modulus, linear regression onto that one-sided set of experimental values gives slewed regression lines which by-pass the origin in the same qualitative pattern that is seen in Fig. 12.3.

could alternatively model the slew of each regression line as a contraction of the selected response about a centre of gravity which is itself the response ordinarily assigned to some stimulus lying in the centre of the range of values presented for judgment (eqns 12.3–12.10). That is the way in which Teghtsoonian formulated his account of very first judgments. At this stage of the argument the distinction between the two is not an empirical matter—the experiments are insufficiently precise—but merely one of style.

Now envisage a full-scale experiment (Fig. 12.4) in which subjects judge a series of stimuli and successive values may increase as well as decrease. To model that kind of experiment we must return to Fig. 11.9. Ratios between successive stimulus values exceed unity as often as they fall short, and randomization of the order of presentation ensures that the values of log ratios between successive stimuli are evenly distributed about zero. Linear regressions of both magnitude estimates and productions are slewed, and in opposite directions, as before (in the explanation of the 'regression effect', pp. 188–90). But if that slew be alternatively modelled as the contraction of the selected response about some centre of gravity, considerations of symmetry force that centre of gravity to be zero (log 1). At this point there is a specific divergence from Teghtsoonian's formulation which will shortly lead to a difference in experimental prediction.

Looking again at Fig. 11.9, it appears that if the stimulus range be much increased (or the numerical range in the production task), the response range will increase less than proportionately because of the curvature of the dotted characteristics. In short, the exponents estimated from estimation and production tasks will increasingly diverge. This is consistent with the data from the intramodal comparisons in Fig. 12.4 in which the exponent estimated from each data point is equal to the gradient of a line joining it to the origin. If, on the other hand, the stimulus range or the numerical range is reduced, the estimated exponents from the two experiments should be similar (because only the central parts of the curvilinear characteristics in Fig. 11.9 are now involved). This also is consistent with the data in Fig. 12.4. But what cannot happen on the basis of the graphical model in Fig. 11.9 is an estimation exponent greater than a production exponent, any production exponent, because the curvilinear characteristic for the estimation task (grey dotted curve) is nowhere steeper than that for production (black dotted curve). This is *incompatible* with the data point for the smallest production range in Fig. 12.4. The experiment from which that data point was obtained therefore requires further examination.

The experiment with 3 kHz tones (Teghtsoonian and Teghtsoonian 1978) initially compared sets of six stimuli centred about 84 dB, spaced at 1, 2, 4, and 8 dB and covering ranges of 5, 10, 20 and 40 dB, respectively. The corresponding production experiments asked for matches to similar sets of six numbers, equally spaced on a logarithmic scale, and covering ranges respectively of 0.25, 0.5, 1, and 2 log units. The additional experiments (Teghtsoonian and Teghtsoonian 1978, Note 6) replicated this design over stimulus/numerical ranges of 2.5 dB and 0.125 log units. The authors refer to 'special difficulties associated with the use of such short ranges' which presumably relate to the difficulty of discriminating between the different stimulus values. Jesteadt *et al.* (1977b, table B-I) report the Weber fraction for discrimination of the amplitude of 2 and 4 kHz tones at 80 dB SL to be about 0.12 in energy units, which is about 0.5 dB, the spacing of the stimuli in the estimation task. This Weber fraction of 0.12 (0.06 in units of amplitude) relates to a 2AFC threshold criterion of 71 per cent correct, resulting from the use of a staircase procedure—

barely discriminable. To judge from Fig. 12.5 this does not cause any problems in the estimation task; there are simply a relatively large number of trials on which the stimulus is judged to be the same as on the preceding trial. But in the production task a new constraint intrudes.

The number to be matched is perceived without error, so that a proportionate increase of 6 per cent is perceived as a definite increase, requiring, according to the inverse of the ordinal scheme 10.2, a definite increase in the stimulus level. That increase cannot be so small as 0.5 dB because, purely from considerations of the discriminability of the stimuli, so small a change would not be perceived as a 'definite increase'. In fact, it appears from Fig. 12.4 that subjects in this repeated production experiment with the very narrow 2.5 dB range spaced their stimulus matches as widely as did the previous subjects with the 5 dB range (1 dB spacing), plausibly because that spacing is the closest at which the different matches can be discriminated with the clarity that the numbers provided to the subject for matching seemed to require. In short, the observed stimulus range matched to the narrowest numerical range does not mean what it appears to mean and does not actually controvert the graphical explanation set out here.

12.5 CONCLUSION

The various results on intramodal range effects assembled by Teghtsoonian (1973) impose an exquisite constraint on what one might otherwise conclude about the origin of the power law exponent. To a first approximation the *inter*modal range effects in Fig. 11.5 are compatible with the idea that the range of numerical responses is an independent variable, effectively fixed by the experimenter. The *intra*modal effects in Fig. 12.1 are clearly not. While both sets of results can be accommodated by assumptions (but different assumptions) about the subjects' prior expectations, the two explanations are not obviously compatible. The intermodal results require some prior limit on the *range of numbers* which subjects might use; the intramodal effects seem to require some assumption about the *acceptable ratio* of one number to its predecessor.

But consider how such prior expectations on the part of the subject might exercise their effects. Subjects do not know the range of stimuli to be judged until they have completed the experiment; stimulus range is not itself presented to the subjects. They can proceed only by judging each stimulus in relation to its predecessor, and human judgment of that relationship appears to be no better than ordinal. Successive choices on that basis, occurring in a full-scale magnitude estimation experiment, cause the numbers uttered by different subjects to diverge. That process has been exhibited in the experiment by J.C. Stevens and Tulving (1957; see pp. 153–5), and it is a reasonable presumption that the asymptotic limit to the trial-to-trial increase in the variability of log numerical estimates is imposed, ultimately, by subjective considerations about what numbers it might be reasonable to utter. The experimental expression of range effects, both intermodal and intramodal, is therefore dynamic and more complex than either of the simple ideas explored so far.

In an attempt to resolve the apparent conflict between the two explanations for range effects, one for intermodal effects, the other for intramodal, I have endeavoured to subsume both categories of phenomena within the scheme of ordinal judgment set out at the beginning of Chapter 10. The gist of that explanation runs as follows. A wide stimulus range, such as is naturally used when the prime objective is a precise estimate of the power law exponent, will generate many pairs of successive stimuli of which the second is 'very much greater than' or 'very much less than' the first. This will tend to spread the range of numerical responses to its limits. But in experiments with a much smaller stimulus range there will be fewer large differences between successive stimuli and a narrower spread of numerical estimates. But the attempt has been no more than qualitative, and it cannot yet be said that it affords any improvement in understanding. Further research is needed, particularly into the detailed use of numbers by individual subjects in magnitude estimation experiments. Until that is accomplished, the findings on intramodal range effects should be put on hold. They do not, to my mind, yet provide an adequate basis for objection to the explanation of Stevens' Power Law proposed in the previous chapter.

13 How, then, can sensation be measured?

It is now 135 years since Fechner published his *Elemente der Psychophysik*, but psychologists are still very far from agreement on how to measure sensation. For one hundred years or so this matter languished, uncontested, in default of any viable alternative proposal to Fechner's Law. But for the past 40 years, since S.S. Stevens' (1957b) 'On the psychophysical law', controversy has been continuous. But not even with the resources and sophisticated instrumentation of modern laboratories is there any sight of agreement. Why?

I suggest—and this has been the undercurrent of this book—that there is no empirical substrate around which agreement might crystallize. Of course, there are real experiments which have been performed, thousands of them, and therefore real behaviour of subjects to study. But the particular question to which those experiments have ultimately been addressed is artificial—a question without empirical reference. The traditional idea of sensation is succinctly expressed by Luce (1981, p. 197): '. . . a physical stimulus is transduced into some sort of distinctive neural activity which, under processing by the central nervous system, is ultimately perceived as a sensation.' That is the idea I wish to abandon. I emphasize, instead, that it is the stimulus that is perceived, not the neural activity; and the stimulus is perceived as an object 'out there', not as an internal sensation (internal stimuli such as pain and tickle excepted). A theory for the experiments surveyed in this book, and many other experiments besides, must therefore take the following schematic form.

A stimulus is perceived as an external event set in the context of all the other contemporaneous stimuli available to perception. The fact that the stimulus for magnitude estimation is presented nearly devoid of context does not induce a different mode of perception; it merely leads to an impoverished percept. The subject's judgment of the stimulus relates to the external event it is perceived to be and for that reason is influenced by the context. The manner in which that judgment—indeed, the entire percept—is related to the stimulus and the context in which it is presented is a problem for experimental psychology. When that problem has been solved at the psychological level of description, another problem awaits, because the entire perceptual process must somehow be realized in neural activity within the brain. The point I make is that the evidence so far to hand does not support any intermediate continuum at the psychological level of description which might reasonably be labelled 'sensation'. While the underlying pattern of sensory neural activity is obviously germane to the perceptual process, not even that can be identified as 'sensation', essentially because there is no corresponding psychological entity. Although this rejoinder might seem no more than a philosophical quibble, it does matter in practice. Experiments by different investigators, seeking to measure the perception of that neural activity as sensation by different methods, have found no basis for agreement.

13.1 A SUMMARY OF THE ARGUMENT

More than any other single idea, it was Fechner's conception of a 'physics of the mind' which prompted the emergence of experimental psychology as a separate science in the middle of the last century. Fechner's psychophysics envisaged internal sensations increasing somehow in parallel with physical stimuli and subject to internal laws analogous to the laws of the classical physics of his day. The first step in the study of this internal domain must be to identify the relation between the physical and the psychophysical. Hence Fechner's Law.

There have been many philosophical, and more recently mathematical, arguments produced to constrain what form this internal domain might take, and it is important not to be seduced by such arguments. What philosophy and mathematics *can* accomplish is to identify those conceptions which are internally inconsistent, and therefore do not need investigation. What philosophy and mathematics *cannot* do is to tell us what that internal domain is like independently of empirical evidence. The need for experimental investigation cannot be circumvented. And what philosophy and mathematics might have done, but failed to do, was to inform experimental psychologists that the questions they were ultimately asking of the subjective domain were not empirical questions, answerable by experimental investigation. Most of the conclusions that can now be drawn from the repeated failure of experiments to answer such questions were anticipated in the nineteenth century, but were not taken to heart.

In this regime Fechner's Law reigned supreme in default of any viable alternative—until Stevens rose to the challenge. The ensuing controversy between Fechner's logarithmic law and Stevens' power law as candidate relations between the intensity of the sensory experience and the magnitude of the physical stimulus can now be seen to be extra-empirical. But, as it happened, repeated replication of basic experimental results in Stevens' laboratory—magnitude estimation, the estimation of inverse attributes, magnitude production, and cross-modality matching—gradually won the day in this artificial controversy. Fechner's Law can be defined operationally as a metric within which the properties of difference discriminations may conveniently be formulated. But that was not the sense in which Stevens conceived of internal sensation.

Stevens envisaged magnitude estimation and similar procedures as a direct method of studying the workings of sensory processing, and even suggested that the power law to which his mean magnitude estimates invariably conformed was realized at an early stage in the sensory pathway. Although a number of apparent physiological parallels were discovered, such evidence is no more than coincidental. If, for example, such a study had failed to exhibit the desired parallel, that would have been because the physiological recording had been taken from the wrong location in the sensory pathway, or from a different (non-human) species. Such excuses, available for the disposal of contrary results, dispose of the confirmatory evidence too. More to the point, while it is manifest that subjective experience is underwritten by neural processes in the brain, the nature of that relation appears much more complicated than Stevens' Power Law.

One problem for Stevens' Law was that the judgment of differences of sensation dictated a different scale with a different exponent to the judgment of ratios. An extensive ratio scale should support addition and subtraction as well as multiplication; Stevens' scales did not. One device to accommodate these otherwise incompatible results was the idea that the numbers uttered as magnitude estimates were not direct measures of the sensation experienced, but had their own subjective values to which they were also related by a power law. But further complication of the stimulus ensembles to be judged, in particular the judgement of total loudness of pairs of tones presented simultaneously, showed that that kind of amendment of Stevens' original idea led only to an escalation of hypothetical power law stages incorporating the additional free parameters that were needed to accommodate the data.

A more subtle development was the suggestion that the judgment of single stimuli, in isolation, was meaningless, only relations between stimuli providing a basis for judgment. If this is so, the judgment of single stimuli, as in Stevens' ultimate development of magnitude estimation with no explicit standard, is always relative to some other stimulus, implicit in the experimental procedure. Analysis of the correlations between successive magnitude estimates by Baird *et al.* (1980), among others, showed this to be so; the stimulus presented on the preceding trial provides an implicit point of reference for the present judgment. Now, if only the relation between a pair of stimuli provides a basis for judgment, then there need be no particular relationship between the judgment of differences between pairs of stimuli, explicitly presented as such, and the judgment of 'single' stimuli relative to some other unspecified reference. Within such a relational theory a single stimulus has no independent significance, and between any two stimuli there can be only one relation to be judged. An individual stimulus may have a highly regular, though statistical, effect on the pattern of activity in the sensory pathway. But, for that pattern to issue in a judgment, there must be some actual standard of comparison. Measuring instruments—rulers, photometers, sound level meters, weighing machines—each embody a set of implicit standards. The reason why a relational theory is required for the experiments surveyed here is that a human subject does not. So the ostensible judgment of differences in sensation and of ratios of sensation must be related, at least monotonically. Rule *et al.* (1981) showed this to be, seemingly, false.

One particular instance of a relation theory, the idea of matching some number of consecutive just-noticeable differences on one dimension with an equal number on another, presented a model of, initially, great intellectual appeal. It promised, *prima facie*, to answer many problems, including the problem of a rapprochement between Stevens' 'direct' experimental methods on the one hand and traditional experiments on sensory discrimination on the other. But such a matching of just-noticeable differences between stimulus dimensions dictates a specific relation between the Power Law exponent and the Weber fraction which is not observed in nature. Indeed, comparison of magnitude estimation with threshold discriminations between the same stimuli shows the former to be much the more variable by, typically, two orders of magnitude. So great is the difference that the two kinds of experiment must be viewed as studying distinct psychological processes; no rapprochement of the kind proposed is possible.

There remained the possibility that the power law results obtained repeatedly by Stevens and his colleagues derived from a careful balancing of the sequential constraints operative on different trials of the experiment, chiefly through careful randomization. The set of stimulus values used in Stevens' experiments was most often chosen to be geometrically spaced. If the subjects could be induced to utter a similar geometric array of numerical responses, the Power Law was assured. This same idea also explains a curious and very precise relation that obtains between the Power Law exponent (as estimated in Stevens' laboratory) and the geometric range of stimuli used in the experiment. It would be necessary, as part of this explanation, for magnitude estimates to be very variable; and, indeed, they are. That great variability of individual estimates and of responses in other similar procedures is compatible with the suggestion that the underlying judgments are no better than ordinal, 'greater than', 'about the same', or 'less'.

But while the idea of a fixed range of numerical responses makes accurate sense of comparisons between different sensory modalities, similar comparisons of experiments employing different ranges of stimulus values within the same modality do not agree. Magnitude estimates are demonstrably subject to a variety of extraneous influences, and a more detailed characterization is required of those prior ideas and expectations which each subject brings with him to the experimental task.

13.2 THE INTERPRETATION OF INTROSPECTIVE REPORTS

The argument of the preceding chapters has been inconclusive; it has almost been a running around in circles. In retrospect it is easy to see where experimental psychology went wrong. Stevens (1956b) introduced his method of magnitude estimation in which he took the numbers uttered by his subjects at face value, as direct measures of their experiences. That is a practice which experimental psychologists, most experimental psychologists, learned to eschew long ago.

In the first two decades of this century psychologists at the University of Würzburg especially, and at other universities as well, turned their attention to the study of thinking using the method of introspective report. Subjects would be asked to solve some suitable mental problem; the time taken to produce an answer would be measured; and the subject then asked for an introspective report of all that had passed through his mind during that period of time. Some laboratories claimed to record thoughts (or elements of thinking) unaccompanied by sensory images. Such 'imageless' thoughts went against philosophical tradition, a tradition going back to Aristotle, but were at the same time supported by contemporary investigations in many different laboratories, not only at Würzburg. The one laboratory to oppose the idea of imageless thought was Cornell where research was directed by Titchener. Titchener objected that the subjects at Würzburg were committing the 'stimulus error', that is, they were frequently reporting the object of their thoughts (which might indeed be imageless) rather than the thought itself. Subjects in Titchener's laboratory invariably reported images with all their thoughts (Humphrey 1951, pp. 119–22).

It will seem to present-day psychologists that this is a splitting of hairs, moreover of imaginary hairs. Those experiments on thinking used only a small number of subjects who were mostly professional colleagues of the investigators. As subjects they would have been well acquainted with the purpose of each investigation and believers in the local point of view concerning imageless thought. The only reliable result was a near perfect correlation between the report (or failure to make report) of the occurrence of imageless thoughts and the laboratory in which the investigation was carried out. And the lesson for experimental psychologists is that, without independent corroboration, introspective evidence should *not* be taken at its face value. Psychologists who disregard this dictum are liable to involve themselves in artificial arguments.

This is the mistake that Stevens made. The entire programme of research in his laboratory proceeded without any independent corroboration of the validity of people's magnitude estimates. Indeed, how could there be such corroboration? But the seeming impossibility of such corroboration does not mean that scientists should proceed without it; it means, instead, that the question addressed lacks the empirical basis needed for an answer to be agreed and that scientists should not proceed at all. That is the nub of the matter.

In my stricture against the taking of introspective reports at face value, I do not mean to imply that such reports are worthless, of no interest at all. On the contrary! What one's subjects say, especially spontaneously, is often a rich source of interpretative ideas, and the wise experimenter listens carefully to what his subjects want to tell him. For example,

> Another problem we encounter is due to the fact that some *O*s seem to make their estimates on an interval-scale, or even on an ordinal scale, instead of on the ratio-scale we are trying to get them to use. One *O* says that all he can do with the set of variables is to try to keep them in a consistent order. He gives one of the variables a number and then if the next is fainter he gives it some smaller number; if it is louder he gives it a larger number. He is pretty good at ordering the variables and seldom makes a reversal, but he is clearly using only an ordinal scale. (Stevens 1956b, p. 23)

Stevens persisted in his view of sensation, even in the face of contrary introspections from certain of his subjects.

13.3 WHAT EXPERIMENTAL FINDINGS CAN BE RELIED UPON?

The great volume of experimental work and argument surrounding attempts to measure sensation involves many assumptions which have ultimately proven unfounded and, in consequence, many experiments which cannot now mean what they have long been thought to mean. What results of tested reliability can be saved from this? I suggest the following which I set in an order of importance.

13.3.1 The respective variabilities of sensory discrimination and of psychophysical judgment

Six examples in Chapter 8 (pp. 120–2) show that the typical variability of magnitude estimates, especially from Stevens' laboratory, is about two orders of magnitude greater than the variability attaching to threshold discriminations with the same stimuli (the two variabilities being expressed with respect to the square of the log stimulus metric). Figure 10.2 presents essentially the same finding from absolute identification with the added detail that the variability of category judgment increases as the square of the log stimulus range. This finding has a surprising number of different implications:

1. Magnitude estimation and similar judgments involve some additional psychological process over and above that studied in threshold measurements. That additional process contributes perhaps 99 per cent of the variability of magnitude estimates and similar judgments and therefore dominates those kinds of experiment. It follows that Fechner's Law

and Stevens' Power Law relate to two different psychological processes. I call the second of these processes 'sensory judgment'. Although the intrinsic variability of the stimuli which limits sensory discrimination also contributes to sensory judgment, it contributes an insignificant proportion of the whole and can be ignored. The idea of a rapprochement between discriminability scales and magnitude estimates (e.g. Krueger 1989) is therefore misconceived. So also is the idea of a systematic relation between the Power Law exponent and the Weber fraction examined in Chapter 8.

2. The great difference in variability between threshold discriminations and magnitude estimates arises because the latter are excessively variable. A magnitude estimate is but weakly determined by the stimulus presented and, to that extent, is influenced by all sorts of other factors—instructions to the subject, prior experience, and the sequence of preceding stimuli, among others. My preferred example to illustrate this point is the study of the autokinetic effect by Sherif (1937). The subject is seated in complete darkness, nothing visible except a tiny pin-point of light. The subject is told that the light will move and he is to estimate, in inches, the distance through which it moves. In fact, the light is stationary throughout; but, because there is no way in which the subject can relate the location of the light to himself—the light is much too weak to reveal anything but itself—it appears unstable. In this way naive subjects were induced to make judgments, seemingly real judgments, which actually lacked any physical basis. In Sherif's (1937) experiment each real subject participated in company with a confederate of the experimenter posing as a second subject. Both subjects, naive and confederate, announced their judgments orally for the experimenter to write down. In this way the real subject was exposed to the confederate's 'judgments'. The same confederate, paired with different (real) subjects, uttered 'judgments' around 2, 3, 4, . . . up to 8 inches. The judgments of the real subjects are set out in Table 13.1.

Table 13.1 Median judgments and ranges (inches) in Sherif's (1937) autokinetic experiment

'Judgments' by confederate								
	Norm	2	3	4	5	6	7	8
	Range	1–3	2–4	3–5	4–6	5–7	6–8	7–9
Judgments by real subjects								
1st group session	Median	3.36	4.25	4.61	5.20	5.50	5.94	7.40
	Range	1–5	1–10	2–8	3–6	3–7	3–8	4–12
2nd session alone	Median	2.62	3.77	4.57	5.21	5.42	6.18	7.83
	Range	1–4	1–5	3–6	3–6	3–7	4–8	6–9

The effect of the confederate's pre-programmed responses on the real subjects' judgments is plain to see. Some of the real subjects were aware of their partner's influence; some were not. Some of them thought they were resisting the influence from their fellow subject; but that was not so. The real subjects were asked to come back another day to repeat the experiment alone. On that repetition, in the absence of the confederate, the influence of that confederate's judgments in the first session showed up even more strongly, if that were at all possible. What this experiment demonstrates is that if there is no sensory basis for judgment, there is no way in which uninformed subjects can resist even the subtlest of suggestions. Relative lack of sensory basis and the intrusion of extraneous influences go together. Although magnitude estimation and other 'direct' procedures do not leave the subjects entirely devoid of sensory basis for their responses, Sherif's autokinetic experiment nevertheless provides a salutary model to guide the interpretation of such data.

3. If a measure of internal sensation is to be obtained from magnitude estimation, or from any other recommended procedure, it must be based on a full understanding of the experiment in question. Acceptance of such a measure merely on the basis of someone's say-so, even the say-so of so influential a psychologist as S.S. Stevens, leads nowhere. It is necessary to understand at a quantitative level the part played by all those kinds of extraneous factors which influence the subjects' judgments in order to be sure that the measure of sensation is not arbitrary. Nothing less will serve to distinguish a true measure of internal sensation from extraneous biases. It should be noted that a scale of internal sensation will not necessarily be a part of that quantitative understanding because we do not know *a priori* that there is a quantitative sensation to be measured. Stevens was aware of this potential arbitrariness: '*Os* can give back Fechner's law in their magnitude-judgments provided they are taught to do so—but it takes a lot of teaching' (Stevens 1956b, p. 16). It may well be that it is easier to design an experiment with naive subjects to yield direct judgments in accord with the Power Law than with Fechner's Law, but that does not make the Power Law an intrinsic property of the state of nature. It is more significant that Rowley and Studebaker (1969; see p. 75 here) experienced the contrary with their audiology students. The kind of quantitative understanding I have in mind will include an account of the way in which some at least of the extraneous factors bear on subjects' numerical responses. Many studies have already been published to identify what some of those extraneous factors are; but we also need to know how they combine together. What is needed is, approximately, an analysis of variance of magnitude estimates that will apportion different elements of the very great variability of the judgments to their respective sources. Although Stevens paid due attention to the variability of his data (whence the examples to prove the point in relation to sensory discrimination), he was unable to see it as an integral product of the intervening process. For Stevens, successive judgments were independent observations and their variability just so much experimental error: 'If the data can be appropriately averaged, it does not matter how widely the variability may range, provided the number of independent measurements can be increased' (Stevens 1971, p. 440).

13.3.2 **The correlation of successive log magnitude estimates**

The typical pattern of correlation between successive log magnitude estimates, varying with the difference in log stimulus magnitude, has been illustrated in Figs 9.1, 10.6, and 10.7. Those figures have been reproduced from one of a number of studies under the authorship of D.M. Green and R.D. Luce, among others, and the overall pattern of findings is succinctly summarized by Green *et al.* (1980). To my mind, this is the most indicative single finding of all, to date.

1. It implies, first, that magnitude estimates are relative judgments, relative to the

stimulus presented on the preceding trial and the number assigned to it. When a stimulus value is repeated, to within ± 5 dB, the correlation between the successive log numerical assignments is frequently +0.8 or thereabouts. This means that about two-thirds ($0.8^2 = 0.64$) of the variance of the second assignment is inherited from its predecessor which must therefore have been used as a point of reference. This same conclusion is supported by a variety of other perceptual phenomena surveyed in Chapter 6. For these reasons a theory of magnitude estimation has to be a relation theory; mapping theories, which include the idea promoted by S.S. Stevens, have to be discarded.

2. The manner in which the correlation between successive log magnitude estimates varies with the stimuli further implies that the variability of judgment increases sharply with the difference between successive log stimulus magnitudes. The use of the previous stimulus and its numerical assignment as a point of reference is obvious only for small differences between one stimulus and its successor. But since the subject cannot know whether the log stimulus difference is to be large or small until he has judged the stimulus, the manner of that judgment must be independent of the difference. The sharply decreased correlation between the log numbers assigned to successive stimuli when the difference between their log magnitudes is large must therefore mean that the variability of the second assignment increases sharply with that difference. The curves fitted to the correlations in Figs 9.1, 10.6, and 10.7 are calculated on the basis of that variability increasing as the square of the difference in log magnitude from one stimulus to the next, and that relation is confirmed by the absolute identification data from Braida and Durlach (1972) in Fig. 10.2. The final step in this argument is the remark that variability increasing as the square of the stimulus difference is the natural result of a purely ordinal scheme of judgment which achieves no more than identifying one stimulus as 'greater than', 'about the same as', or 'less than' its predecessor.

3. If the judgment of one stimulus in relation to another is no better than ordinal, then it may be satisfactorily formulated with respect to physical stimulus magnitude itself. We can know about the internal psychophysical machinery of the subject only through the medium of that subject's judgments, and those judgments do not, as yet, support any internal scale distinct from the physical. Judgments, allegedly of internal sensation, may be equally well interpreted as judgments of the magnitude of the stimulus as it is perceived. There is no experimental basis for introducing any distinct intermediary under the label 'sensation'. The size of the retinal image cannot be judged except by means of a biased mental calculation based on its perceived size. The spectrum of sound reaching the two ears cannot be distinguished from its interpretation in terms of the location of the source. The heaviness of a weight cannot be abstracted from its size, except by closing the eyes.

4. All this would appear to be a thoroughgoing espousal of Titchener's 'stimulus error'. But the 'stimulus error' is no error. The real error, the 'sensation error', subsists in supposing there to be some separate continuous measure of sensation which might be revealed through experiments such as magnitude estimation.

13.3.3 The complex of phenomena distinguishing difference discrimination from increment detection

This is the collection of generalizations set out in Table 4.1 and exemplified in Chapters 3 and 4 (and also, in more detail, in Laming 1985, 1986, 1987, 1988a,b). These phenomena collectively may be succinctly accommodated by a χ^2 model formulated in terms of a natural physical measure of the stimulus. They have the following implication.

In view of the criticism I have made of the interpretation of all the work stemming, directly or indirectly, from Stevens' Power Law, one might now be tempted to return to Fechner's Law as a measure of internal sensation. The logarithm of stimulus magnitude plays a central role in the normal model (eqn 3.2) which provides a precise and accurate account of the principal properties of discriminations between two separate stimuli. It therefore has an operational significance; though to label it 'sensation' on that account is to use the term in quite a different manner to Stevens. But the normal model is not unique. Equally accurate numerical predictions can be obtained from the χ^2 model and, what is especially to the point, the χ^2 model can accommodate the phenomena of increment detection as well. If one decides to use the label 'subjective sensation' in a purely operational manner, then the χ^2 model has to be preferred because it accommodates much the greater range of phenomena; and the operational measure identified by that model turns out to be the natural physical measure of the stimulus.

It thus happens that, whichever route the experimental psychologist follows, Stevens' 'direct' methods of scaling or the operational interpretation of experiments on sensory discrimination, leads back to the natural physical measure of the stimulus as the underlying metric. Existing experimental methods do not identify any distinct measure of internal sensation.

13.4 HOW, THEN, CAN SENSATION BE MEASURED?

It may seem curious to ask this question at the end of 13 chapters arguing that there is no sensation to be measured, not, at least, in a manner distinct from the physical magnitude of the stimulus. But it is none the less true, as was illustrated on the very first page of this book, that our judgments of luminance, of sound level, of weight, sometimes diverge greatly from physical reality. While that divergence cannot be successfully interpreted in terms of an internal sensation which grows as some non-linear transform of the physical stimulus, the divergence does not thereby cease to exist. There is still a practical problem remaining, and two examples indicate how it might be addressed.

13.4.1 **Simultaneous contrast**

Figure 13.1 is a reproduction of Fig. 6.6 with two differences. The middle two small grey squares have been removed and the grey square on the black background has been made a little darker so as to match the appearance of the grey on the white. If the reflectance of a grey on a black background be taken as standard, the reflectance of this particular grey measures the subjective appearance of the grey on the white and, moreover, measures it in physical stimulus units. That is to say, subjective sensation might be measured as the physical intensity of the matching stimulus. The study by Heinemenn (1955; see pp. 83–5 and 104–5) is nothing more than an elaborate realization of this idea.

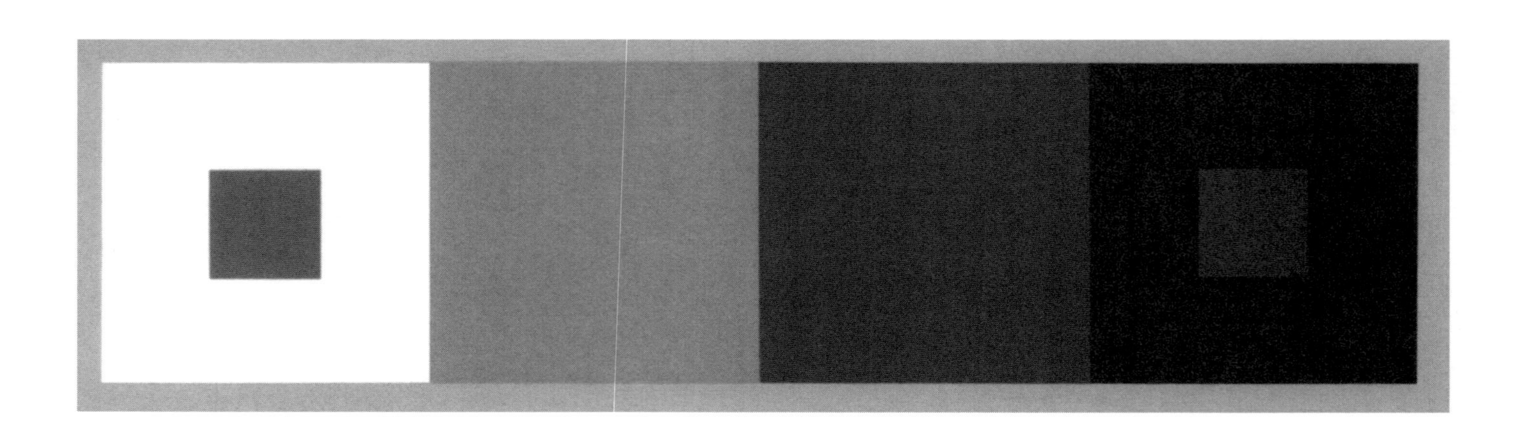

Fig. 13.1 A copy of Fig. 6.7, but with the middle two of the small grey squares removed. In addition, the grey square on the black background has been made a little darker to match, subjectively, the appearance of the grey on the white.

But the value of such a measurement depends on the context, on the background, of the match. One could say that the grey square on the white ground matches itself; and one could also take the reflectance of that grey square (on the white ground) as the measure of the subjective appearance of the grey on the black. There can be no absolute measure of sensation; all one can say is that these levels of reflectance seen against these particular backgrounds appear to match. That degree of ambiguity is the natural consequence of there being no direct measure of internal sensation.

13.4.2 **Tactile roughness**

As a second example, Fig. 13.2 shows the stimulus surfaces used by Connor *et al.* (1990) in a study to identify the neural correlate of tactile roughness. Each surface consists of an array of conical pimples on a plastic sheet, with three different sizes of pimple. The spacing of the pimples is uniform across each strip, but steadily increasing from left to right along the length. The investigation by Connor *et al.* was prompted by the observation that these stimulus strips, already in use for neurophysiological investigations, felt fairly smooth at each end and roughest in the middle, at an intermediate spacing of the pimples.

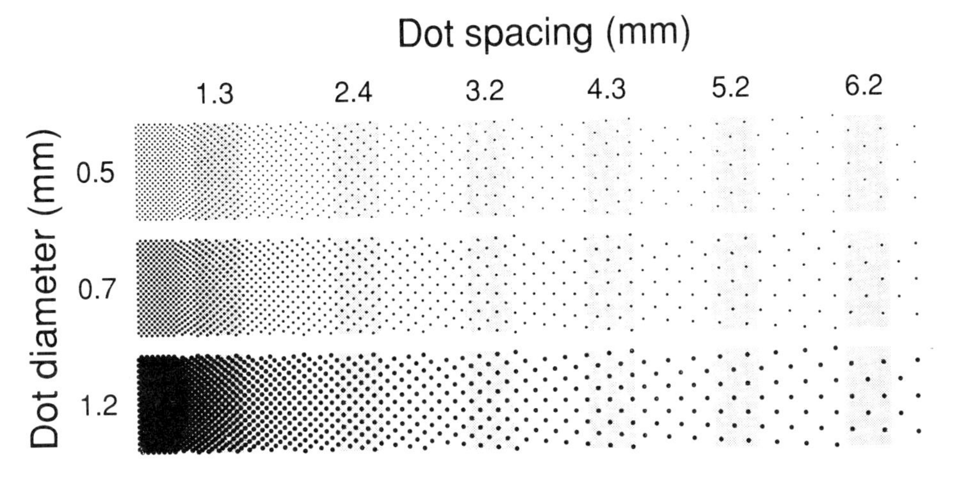

Fig. 13.2 The stimulus surfaces used in the study of tactile roughness by Connor *et al.* (1990). The surfaces consist of pimples (truncated cones) embossed on a plastic sheet. The shaded areas are the regions used as stimuli in the experiments. (From 'Tactile roughness: neural codes that account for psychophysical magnitude estimates' by C.E. Connor, S.S. Hsiao, J.R. Phillips, and K.O. Johnson, *Journal of Neuroscience*, 1990, vol. 10, p. 3824. © 1990, Society for Neuroscience. Reproduced by permission.)

The difficulty in investigating tactile roughness is that while the sensation, subjectively, is quite clear, its physical correlate is uncertain. Abrasive papers are classified in terms of a 'grit' number which is the number of meshes per linear inch in the grading sieve. Stevens and Harris (1962) had a panel of 10 observers estimate both the roughness and smoothness of each of a set of 10 abrasive papers (grit nos 24 to 320) twice each and obtained power law exponents of about 1.5. But abrasive papers present a stimulus surface of random structure which makes neurophysiological data more difficult to interpret.

Six areas of each strip, as indicated in Fig. 13.2, were selected for experimental use, making a total of 18 stimuli. Since the perceived roughness of the pimples depended on their spacing, but not in a monotonic manner, Connor *et al.* asked human subjects to estimate the roughness of these 18 stimuli and established a pragmatic numerical scale thereby. They then showed that perceived roughness correlated well with the variability of neural discharge—not the mean firing rate, but its variability—of slowly adapting fibres innervating Merkel discs in the finger pad of macaque monkeys. A subsequent investigation (Connor and Johnson 1992) showed that the specific neural correlate appeared to be spatial variation of the rate of discharge from one receptive field to another. Maximal roughness was reported for a pimple spacing of 3.2–4.3 mm and this correlated with spatial variation in neural response on a scale of about 2 mm which, in turn, represents about two afferent spacings in the finger pad.

According to all preceding argument, however, there is no quantitative internal sensation of roughness to be measured. Yet, at a practical level, this application of magnitude estimation worked—worked well. Critical to that success was the use of the selfsame stimuli in both human magnitude estimation and in the simian neurophysiological experiments, establishing thereby a direct correlation between samples of human magnitude estimates and patterns of neural discharge. The experimental data could have been analysed purely on the basis of rank order; there was no need of any intervening theory about subjective sensation.

As things turned out, the relationship between mean magnitude estimate and the variance of neural discharge was linear (Connor *et al.* 1990, Fig. 10), and this perhaps requires some further explanation. Given a sufficient number of different stimuli, the difficulty of distinguishing pairwise between some of them, a difficulty which is represented in the scheme of judgment 10.1, makes the assignment of numerical estimates a little better than ordinal, but not so regular as an interval scale. Roughly speaking, the difficulties of discriminating one stimulus from another impose a constraint on the magnitude estimates assigned to adjacent stimuli, adjacent in terms of perceived roughness, sorting the scale out locally. But that difficulty of discrimination is directly related to the information carried by the primary neural fibres and thereby to the discriminative cue which the investigation sought to discover. All that encouraged a linear relationship between estimates and neural cue.

What these two examples show is that we have cultural expressions for entities which do not admit objective measurement, not at least in the present state of scientific knowledge. The entities are not thereby illusory, because independent judges can agree about which grey levels in Fig. 13.1 appear to match or about the relative roughness of segments of the stimulus patterns in Fig. 13.2. This is the context in which Fechner (1860) proposed an intermediate internal continuum called 'sensation'. We are accustomed to say of a light that it is 'bright' or 'dim', of a sound that it is 'loud' or 'soft', and of a weight that it is 'heavy' or 'light'. On that basis Fechner and generations of experimental psychologists after him have supposed that there are quantities such as brightness, loudness, and heaviness to be measured. The thrust of the argument running throughout this book has been that there is no empirical way to identify such continua. It is all an illusion of grammar.

But the problems of why certain grey levels in Fig. 13.1 seem to many different people to match and why people agree about the roughness of different textures do not thereby go away. It is just that those problems and others like them—specifically how people perceive entities which cannot be objectively measured—have to be solved without recourse to an internal scale of sensation.

Appendix A—Notes on the experiments summarized in Tables 8.2 and 8.3

This appendix sets out brief descriptions of the experiments from which the Weber fractions and Power Law exponents plotted in Fig. 8.2 and listed in Tables 8.2 and 8.3 have been estimated. Those estimates have, of necessity, had to be based on whatever published data happened to be available and the choice has been further constrained by the requirement that the stimuli used in corresponding discrimination and magnitude estimation experiments be similar. In the view of this requirement, I have frequently chosen to disregard the magnitude estimation exponent said to be typical of some particular dimension in favour of a value estimated from some particular experiment which provided a reasonable match to some other experiment from which a corresponding estimate of the Weber fraction could be drawn.

While experiments with some attributes show a precise conformity to Weber's Law (eqn 1.1) down to about the absolute threshold, other attributes seem to require the generalized form of the law (eqn 3.3). One possible reason for the difference has been suggested on pp. 36–7. I have taken the value of Θ in the generalized equation as the appropriate estimate of the Weber fraction. It is, at least asymptotically, correct for large stimulus magnitudes. In addition, some of the Weber fractions have been determined by the method of constant stimuli (or similar 2AFC method), others by the method of average error and, in one case (Taves 1941), by the quantal method devised by Stevens *et al.* (1941). The method of average error is commonly supposed, after Kellogg (1929; see also Laming 1986, pp. 23–4), to give a smaller Weber fraction than the method of constant stimuli. The quantal method is known to be unreliable (Laming 1974). But there are, no doubt, many other deficiencies in the comparisons listed in the tables which receive no mention.

Finally, a few studies provide estimates of both the Weber fraction and the Power Law exponent within the one investigation, often using the same apparatus and the same subjects. Since such studies eliminate a potentially large source of variability which might otherwise obscure a relation between the two quantities of interest, I have included a number of such studies which do not otherwise satisfy present-day standards of precision and reliability. The extreme example is Merkel's (1889b) pre-electronic study of the intensity of sounds created by dropping steel balls onto pieces of wood, with the Power Law exponent estimated from experiments on the doubling or halving of stimulus intensities.

A.1 **Weber fractions and Power Law exponents from different sources listed in Table 8.2**

A.1.1 *Amplitude of Gaussian noise*

Harris (1950, Expt I) presented his subjects with two 1 s bursts of Gaussian noise with a spectrum extending from 100 to 7000 Hz. The method of constant stimuli was used at levels from 5 to 40 dB SL. The mean thresholds from four subjects (see Laming 1986, p. 11, fig. 1.9) give an average Weber fraction ($\Delta A_{rms}/A_{rms}$) of 0.064.

Stevens and Guirao (1962) reported a magnitude estimation experiment with Gaussian noise of bandwidth 500 to 5000 Hz at levels from 35 to 95 dB SPL. The exponent of the power function fitted to their aggregate data was 0.25 with respect to energy or 0.50 with respect to r.m.s. amplitude.

A.1.2 *Amplitude of pure tones*

Jesteadt *et al.* (1977b) used a 2AFC staircase procedure to measure the threshold for 1 kHz tones presented for 500 ms each. They report an average 71 per cent threshold of 0.43 dB at 80 dB SPL; this is equivalent to a Weber fraction of 0.063 in terms of amplitude, adjusted to 75 per cent correct.

Stevens (1956b) obtained an exponent of 0.6 re amplitude from a variety of experiments using various ranges of 1 kHz tones of arbitrary duration.

A.1.3 *Amplitude of vibration applied to the fingertip*

Craig (1974) measured thresholds for discriminating between two 200 ms bursts of 160 Hz vibration presented through a 6 mm contactor projecting through a rigid surround. The Weber fraction was 0.245 (see Laming 1986, p. 141, fig. 8.3).

Stevens (1968), matching the sensations produced by different frequencies of vibration, obtained exponents of 0.77 for the matching of 125 to 60 Hz and 0.66 for matching 250 to 60 Hz. The vibrating stimuli were presented to the fingertip through a 6 mm contactor. Interpolation suggests an exponent of 0.74 at 160 Hz. Earlier Stevens (1959c) had obtained an exponent of 0.94 in a magnitude estimation experiment with 1 s bursts of 60 Hz vibration, again presented to the fingertip through a 6 mm contactor. Multiplying 0.94 by 0.74 suggests an exponent of 0.70 at 160 Hz.

A.1.4 *Contrast of sinusoidal grating*

Legge (1981) studied the discrimination of contrast with a 2 c/deg grating 10° high × 13° wide presented for 200 ms at a mean luminance of 10 cd/m^2. Different experiments used various stimulus configurations and psychophysical methods, but the results overall gave a difference threshold increasing as the 0.59 power of stimulus contrast. At the mid-range contrast of 0.06 the Weber fraction was about 0.15.

Gottesman *et al.* (1981) reported a magnitude estimation experiment with 2 c/deg gratings, 6.8° high × 8.1° wide, presented for 5 s at a mean luminance of 10 cd/m^2. Twelve different stimulus values were used, spaced geometrically from 0.006 to 0.6 contrast. The average exponent from three groups of subjects was 0.64.

A.1.5 *Fingerspan*

Gaydos (1958) measured the discrimination of different widths of fingerspan using widths ranging from 17.7 to 100 mm in three different experiments. The average Weber fraction was 0.021.

Stevens and Stone (1959) reported a magnitude estimation experiment using widths of fingerspan from 2.3 to 63.7 mm. Their estimated exponent was 1.33.

A.1.6 *Lifted weight*

Fechner (1860) measured the difference threshold for weights from 300 to 3000 g using himself as subject. The data are plotted in Laming (1986, p. 6, fig. 1.4) and give a Weber fraction of 0.059.

Rule and Curtis (1976) report a magnitude estimation experiment with weights from 25 to 6400 g. The weights themselves were hidden from the subjects who lifted them by means of fishing lines passing through holes in a horizontal surface. The exponent was 0.92.

A.1.7 *Lifted weight (smaller stimulus range)*

Oberlin (1936, Expt I) measured thresholds for weights from 50 to 550 g using the method of constant stimuli. The data (see Laming 1986, p. 6, fig. 1.4) give a Weber fraction of 0.043.

Stevens and Galanter (1957) reported a magnitude estimation experiment using weights from 17 to 196 g and another using weights from 17 to 645 g with no standard weight supplied. The exponent estimated from these two experiments was 1.17.

A.1.8 *Luminance*

Leshowitz *et al.* (1968) presented a stimulus 1° in diameter in Maxwellian view for 320 ms to the dark-adapted eye. For a temporal 2AFC discrimination between two successive flashes they obtained Weber fractions of 0.22 and 0.18 from their two subjects. The average is 0.20. This is very similar to the value obtained by Cornsweet and Pinsker (1965) with a spatial 2AFC discrimination between two stimuli of 50' arc diameter presented for 4.5 ms only to the dark-adapted eye. Their Weber fraction for a 71 per cent threshold determined by a staircase technique was 0.17 (see Laming, 1986, p. 271, fig. B.2). Adjusted to 75 per cent correct, this Weber fraction becomes 0.21.

Onley (1960) conducted a comparable magnitude estimation experiment using a stimulus 1° in diameter presented for 275 ms in central fixation to the dark-adapted eye. The luminances ranged from about –1.6 to +3.8 log mL; the estimated exponent was 0.29.

A.1.9 *Pressure on the skin*

Gatti and Dodge (1929) applied a single hair mounted on the arm of a chemical balance to a single touch point on the volar surface of the forearm. Thresholds were measured by the method of limits at standard forces of 0.1 to 0.8 g wt. The data are plotted by Laming (1986, p. 1, fig. 1.1) and give a Weber fraction of 0.171.

J.C. Stevens and Mack (1959) estimated the magnitude of the pressure of a disc on the palm of the hand. The total forces used ranged from 0.5 to 6 lbs wt and were applied through discs of diameters 0.19, 0.50, and 1.25 inches. The Power Law exponent was independent of the diameter of the disc and averaged 1.1.

A.1.10 *Smell*

Stone and his colleagues (Stone 1963; Stone and Bosley 1965; Stone *et al.* 1962) have measured difference thresholds for six different odorous substances which all smell rather like vinegar. The odour was mixed with purified air in a specific concentration and supplied to a naturally breathing subject for 10 s. The two concentrations to be compared in the method of constant stimuli were both presented in this way separated by a further 10 s period of purified air. Thresholds were calculated from the aggregate judgments of a panel of subjects, and the difference thresholds measured from the six substances are reasonably consistent with a Weber fraction of 0.17 (see Laming 1986, p. 3, fig. 1.2; 1987, p. 13, fig. 1).

Berglund *et al.* (1971) report magnitude estimation experiments with 28 different odorous substances, but not including any of the six studied by Stone and his colleagues. The substances were dissolved, mostly in diethyl phthalate, and kept in glass tubes, from whence they were presented to the subjects on wads of cotton wool. Seven different concentrations of each odorant were prepared in geometric series of concentrations, each concentration being twice its predecessor. The Power Law exponents estimated from these experiments varied somewhat from one odorant to another; the median value was 0.15.

A.1.11 *Taste—'sip and spit' method*

Schutz and Pilgrim (1957) report difference thresholds for caffeine, citric acid, sodium chloride, and sucrose using the method of single stimuli. The subjects were given 6 ml of solution in a 1 oz glass; this solution was squirted round the mouth, spat out, and the mouth rinsed. Thresholds were estimated from the aggregate judgments of a panel of 10 subjects and yielded these estimates of the Weber fraction: caffeine, 0.25; sodium chloride, 0.11; sucrose, 0.14 (see Laming 1987, p. 14).

Stevens (1969) presented 4 cc of solution in a small 'shot' glass for magnitude estimation, the mouth being thereafter rinsed with tap water. He reported these values of the Power Law exponent: quinine sulphate (bitter, concentrations 0.001–0.023 per cent), 1.0; sodium chloride (concentrations 0.5–26 per cent), 1.35; sucrose (concentrations 3.1–50 per cent), 1.3.

A.1.12 *Temperature—cold*

Johnson *et al.* (1973) reported a study of the discrimination of cooling pulses applied to the ball of the thumb through a silver thermode, 12 mm in diameter. Difference thresholds were measured for the discrimination between cooling pulses of different magnitudes from 0 to −10 °C with respect to skin temperatures (physiological zeros) of 29, 34, 39, and 41 °C using the method of constant stimuli. All the four base temperatures gave the same Weber fraction of 0.017 (see Laming 1986, p. 142).

J.C. Stevens and Stevens (1960) used aluminium cylinders heated in a water bath to the desired temperature. These were applied to the ventromedial surface of the forearm at temperatures from 0.5 to 27.7 °C. Physiological zero was taken to be 31 °C, but was not precisely controlled. The exponent estimated from these authors' magnitude estimation experiment was 1.0.

A.1.13 *Visual extent*

Volkmann (1863) suspended three quartz threads from a beam with weights. The vertical points of support of the threads could be adjusted by micrometer screws, and the subject's task was to set the outer two threads to be equidistant from the central one. This experiment was carried out for visual separations between the threads of up to 20° of visual angle. Taking the probable error of adjustment as the measure of the difference threshold gave a Weber fraction of 0.008 (see Laming 1986, p. 8, fig. 1.6).

Teghtsoonian and Teghtsoonian (1971) used markers on an aluminium bar to indicate the visual extents in a magnitude estimation experiment. Using a range of distances from 0.50 to 60 inches (the latter distance being equivalent to a visual angle of 45°), they obtained an exponent of 0.93.

A.2 **Weber fractions and Power Law exponents from the same source listed in Table 8.3**

A.2.1 *Cain (1977a,b)—Smell*

Cain (1977a) presented n-amyl alcohol and n-butyl alcohol in glass vessels, with the subject sniffing the odorant from a wad of cotton wool soaked in the solution. The Weber fractions were estimated to be: n-amyl alcohol, 0.163; n-butyl alcohol, 0.068. In both cases the Power Law exponent was 0.48.

In the second study (Cain 1977b) the odorants were presented in an air olfactometer. A cotton wad soaked in a solution of a specific concentration was placed on a perforated glass platform which divided the olfactometer into two compartments. Air flowed in through a port in the lower part of the vessel, below the perforated platform, and the subject sniffed the odorant from a port in the upper part of the vessel, from above the platform. For n-amyl butyrate the Weber fraction was 0.091 and the Power Law exponent 0.26; for n-amyl alcohol the Weber fraction was 0.042 (note that this is only one-quarter of the value in the previous investigation) and the exponent 0.48 (which is unchanged).

A.2.2 *Graf et al.* (1974)—Luminance

The stimuli were two 1° luminous discs separated by 3° vertically and presented for 4 s. One group of 24 subjects saw them simultaneously, another group successively, separated by a 10 s delay. Difference thresholds were measured using the method of constant stimuli at two different luminance levels (0.035 and 111 ft-L). The mean of the four Weber fractions (two groups × two luminances) was 0.146. Magnitude estimation used nine stimulus luminances from 0.035 to 350 ft-L and either 0.035 or 111 as standard. The geometric mean exponent was 0.31.

A.2.3 *Indow (1967)—Saturation of red*

Red and white light were mixed in a rotating square prism. The colours were produced by passing white light through adjacent red and white filters and viewed through an aperture

$1° \times 0.8°$. By adjusting the location of the filters relative to the prism, the relative proportion of each filter scanned by the prism could be set to produce any desired saturation of red. Difference thresholds were measured by the method of average error and gave a Weber fraction of 0.004. Magnitude estimation of redness over the range 20–100 per cent redness gave an exponent of 1.8.

A.2.4 *Indow and Stevens (1966)—Hue*

Indow and Stevens produced variable colour mixtures by means of the same system as Indow (1967), mixing red and green light in a rotating square prism. By adjusting the location of two adjacent colour filters relative to the prism, the relative proportion of each filter scanned by the prism could be set to produce any desired mixture of the primary colours. Indow and Stevens selected two ranges of hue for study, one bounded by red (R) and a reddish yellow (Y') and the other by yellow (Y) and a yellowish green (G').

Difference thresholds were measured by the method of average error and gave these Weber fractions: $R–Y'$, 0.004; $G'–Y$, 0.020. Magnitude estimation of redness in the $R–Y'$ range (26–100 per cent redness) gave an exponent of 2.0, and yellowness 1.9; the average is 1.95. Magnitude estimation of greenness in the $G'–Y$ range (again with 26–100 per cent greenness) gave an exponent 1.8 and yellowness 1.6, average 1.7.

A.2.5 *Krueger (1984)—Numerousness*

Krueger used a random distribution of Xs over a 25×35 matrix on a computer printout to study numerousness. Difference thresholds were measured using the method of constant stimuli with respect to standard numbers of 25, 100, and 400 Xs (the maximum possible in the matrix being 875). The Weber fractions were 0.126, 0.117, and 0.081 at these three standard values, average 0.108. Magnitude estimation employed 12 arrays of Xs varying in number from 10 to 400 presented twice in different random orders. The estimated exponent was 0.81.

A.2.6 *McBurney (1966) and McBurney et al.* (1967)—*Taste, using the 'flow' method*

In the second of these two studies McBurney *et al.* measured the difference threshold for sodium chloride at the single concentration of 0.1 M. The surface of the extended tongue was divided into two halves by a plastic dam. The two concentrations to be compared were allowed to flow onto opposite sides of the tongue, which was irrigated with distilled water for at least 20 s between successive trials. The difference threshold was 18 mM, giving a estimate of the Weber fraction from this one datum only of 0.18.

In the first of the two studies McBurney reported magnitude estimates of the concentration of sodium chloride solutions allowed to flow onto the tongue as above. Eight different concentrations were presented (0.001 to 1.0 M and distilled water) combined with four different adapting concentrations irrigating the tongue in between stimulations. Log magnitude estimate turned out to be highly non-linear as a function of stimulus concentration in the region of the adapting level. But, when the adaptation was provided by a concentration of 0.001 M, the magnitude estimates conformed satisfactorily to a power law over the entire suprathreshold range with exponent 0.41.

A.2.7 *Merkel (1888)—Luminance*

In this very early study of the discrimination of luminance, the stimuli were frosted glass apertures, 3 cm in diameter, viewed with the right eye only through reduction tubes. The source of light was a paraffin lamp, and the luminance of the frosted glass was manipulated according to the inverse square law by movement of the light source. The just-noticeable difference was determined by the method of adjustment, and the geometric average of several individual determinations of the Weber fraction was 0.132. A Power Law exponent can be estimated from a second experiment on the doubling of a given luminance. The geometric average of the ratio of doubled luminance to the original was 1.945, which is equivalent to an exponent of 1.042.

A.2.8 *Merkel (1889a)—Pressure*

A beam, balanced on a knife edge, bore on the index finger via a plate, either 1 or 7 mm thick. The Weber fraction for the discrimination of different pressures was about 0.1, ignoring a steep rise in this fraction at low pressures. Doubling the apparent pressure actually required an increase of 2.408 times (geometric average), which is equivalent to a Power Law exponent of 0.79.

A.2.9 *Merkel (1889b)—Noise*

In this paper Merkel reported experiments on the intensity of the noise produced by Wundt's 'Fall Apparat'. With this equipment the stimulus was produced by dropping a steel ball from a certain height onto a piece of wood. The energy of the sound produced was taken to be equal to the loss of potential energy calculated as the product of the weight of the ball times the height from which it was dropped less the height of its rebound. The Weber fraction was about 0.3 (ignoring the increased values at low stimulus levels). Doubling the apparent level of the noise required a physical stimulus ratio of 2.028 (geometric average), which is equivalent to an exponent of 0.98.

A.2.10 *Merkel (1894)—Length of line*

In this study the stimuli were two lines 0.4 mm thick situated end to end. Each could be adjusted by a screw thread. Four experiments are reported in which one of the lines is set to be (a) just not noticeably different, (b) just noticeably different, (c) double the length, and (d) half the length in relation to a given standard. Using the probable errors of adjustment in these four experiments and expressing those probable errors as fractions of their respective mean adjustments gives a Weber fraction for all four experiments taken together of 0.005. The mean adjustments from the doubling and halving experiments in relation to the standard lengths are equivalent to a Power Law exponent of 1.15.

A.2.11 *Panek and Stevens (1966)—Saturation of red*

Panek and Stevens created a red of variable saturation by covering a cylinder with red and grey papers, the red of unspecified colorimetric purity, the grey of 0.2 reflectance. The cylinder was entirely red at one end and entirely grey at the other, the proportion of red decreasing linearly along the length of the cylinder. The cylinder was rotated at 2000 r.p.m. and viewed through a reduction tube which afforded a stimulus of 2.8° diameter with the appearance of a luminous field rather than a surface colour. The degree of saturation of the stimulus thus produced could be varied by changing the point at which the rotating cylinder was viewed.

Difference thresholds for the saturation of red in stimuli of 0.5 s duration were determined both by the method of constant stimuli and by the method of single stimuli with the standard presented once only at the beginning of a series of stimuli to be judged. These two procedures gave very similar thresholds and a Weber fraction estimated at 0.025. An experiment on the magnitude estimation of the same stimuli, with the degree of saturation ranging from 20 to 100 per cent, gave an exponent of 1.7.

A.2.12 *Taves (1941)—Numerousness*

Taves studied the discrimination of numerosity with stimuli consisting of a field of bright circular dots on a dark ground presented tachistoscopically for 0.2 s. Thresholds were measured by rapidly following one stimulus by another and, in an experiment using the quantal design of Stevens *et al.* (1941), a Weber fraction of 0.205 was obtained. Other experiments on fractionation and bisection gave results indicative of a Power Law exponent of 1.59.

A.2.13 *Treisman (1963)—Temporal duration*

Intervals of time were defined by the duration of a tone. Treisman's Experiment 5, using the method of constant stimuli with two temporal intervals presented in succession for discrimination, gave thresholds equivalent to a Weber fraction of 0.061 (adjusted to 75 per cent correct). Experiment 7, presenting a similar range of stimulus durations (0.9–5.5 s) for magnitude estimation, gave a Power Law exponent of 0.89.

References

Aczél, J. (1966). *Lectures on functional equations and their applications.* Academic Press, New York.

Adler, H.E. (trans.) (1966). Translation of *Elements of psychophysics,* Vol. 1. by G.T. Fechner. Holt, Rinehart and Winston, New York.

Adrian, E.D. and Matthews, R. (1927). The action of light on the eye. Part I. The discharge of impulses in the optic nerve and its relation to the electric changes in the retina. *Journal of Physiology,* **63**, 378–414.

Alpern, M., Rushton, W.A.H., and Torii, S. (1970). Signals from cones. *Journal of Physiology,* **207**, 463–75.

Anderson, N.H. (1970). Averaging model applied to the size–weight illusion. *Perception & Psychophysics,* **8**, 1–4.

Anderson, N.H. (1972). Cross-task validation of functional measurement. *Perception & Psychophysics,* **12**, 389–95.

Anderson, N.H. (1974). Algebraic models in perception. In *Handbook of perception,* Vol. 2 (ed. E.C. Carterette and M.P. Friedman), pp. 215–98. Academic Press, New York.

Arend, L.E., Buehler, J.N., and Lockhead, G.R. (1971). Difference information in brightness perception. *Perception & Psychophysics,* **9**, 367–70.

Attneave, F. (1962). Perception and related areas. In *Psychology: a study of a science,* Vol. 4 (ed. S. Koch), pp. 619–59. McGraw-Hill, New York.

Auerbach, C. (1971). Interdependence of Stevens' exponents and discriminability measures. *Psychological Review,* **78**, 556.

Baird, J.C., Lewis, C., and Romer, D. (1970). Relative frequencies of numerical responses in ratio estimation. *Perception & Psychophysics,* **8**, 358–62.

Baird, J.C., Kreindler, M., and Jones, K. (1971). Generation of multiple ratio scales with a fixed stimulus attribute. *Perception & Psychophysics,* **9**, 399–403.

Baird, J.C., Green, D.M., and Luce, R.D. (1980). Variability and sequential effects in cross-modality matching of area and loudness. *Journal of Experimental Psychology: Human Perception and Performance,* **6**, 277–89.

Banks, W.P. and Hill, D.K. (1974). The apparent magnitude of number scaled by random production. *Journal of Experimental Psychology,* **102**, 353–76.

Bartoshuk, L.M. (1968). Water taste in man. *Perception & Psychophysics,* **3**, 69–72.

Bartoshuk, L.M., McBurney, D.H., and Pfaffmann, C. (1964). Taste of sodium chloride solutions after adaptation to sodium chloride: implications for the 'water taste'. *Science,* **143**, 967–8.

Beck, J. and Shaw, W.A. (1967). Ratio-estimations of loudness-intervals. *American Journal of Psychology,* **80**, 59–65.

Berglund, B., Berglund, U., Ekman, G., and Engen, T. (1971). Individual psychophysical functions for 28 odorants. *Perception & Psychophysics,* **9**(3B), 379–84.

Birnbaum, M.H. (1978). Differences and ratios in psychological measurement. In *Cognitive theory,* Vol. 3 (ed. N.J. Castellan, Jr and F. Restle), pp. 33–74. Erlbaum, Hillsdale, NJ.

Birnbaum, M.H. (1980). Comparison of two theories of 'ratio' and 'difference' judgments. *Journal of Experimental Psychology: General,* **109**, 304–19.

Birnbaum, M.H. (1982a). Controversies in psychological measurement. In *Social attitudes and psychophysical measurement* (ed. B. Wegener), pp. 401–85. Erlbaum, Hillsdale, NJ.

Birnbaum, M.H. (1982b). Problems with so-called 'direct' scaling. In *Selected sensory methods: problems and approaches to hedonics* (ed. J.T. Kuznicki, R.A. Johnson, and A.F. Ritkiewic), pp. 34–48. ASTM Special Technical Publication 773, American Society for Testing Materials, Philadelphia.

Birnbaum, M.H. and Elmasian, R. (1977). Loudness 'ratios' and 'differences' involve the same psychophysical operation. *Perception & Psychophysics*, **22**, 383–91.

Birnbaum, M.H. and Mellers, B.A. (1978). Measurement and the mental map. *Perception & Psychophysics*, **23**, 403–8.

Birnbaum, M.H. and Veit, C.T. (1974). Scale convergence as a criterion for rescaling: information integration with difference, ratio, and averaging tasks. *Perception & Psychophysics*, **15**, 7–15.

Borg, G., Diamant, H., Ström, L., and Zotterman, Y. (1967). The relation between neural and perceptual intensity: a comparative study on the neural and psychophysical response to taste stimuli. *Journal of Physiology*, **192**, 13–20.

Boring, E.G. (1921). The stimulus-error. *American Journal of Psychology*, **32**, 449–71.

Boring, E.G. (1942). *Sensation and perception in the history of experimental psychology.* Appleton-Century-Crofts, New York.

Boring, E.G. (1950). *A history of experimental psychology* (2nd edn). Appleton-Century-Crofts, New York.

Boudreau, J.C. (1965). Stimulus correlates of wave activity in the superior–olivary complex of the cat. *Journal of the Acoustical Society of America*, **37**, 779–85.

Boynton, R.M. (1989). About assumptions and exponents. *Behavioral and Brain Sciences*, **12**, 271.

Braida, L.D. and Durlach, N.I. (1972). Intensity perception. II. Resolution in one-interval paradigms. *Journal of the Acoustical Society of America*, **51**, 483–502.

Brentano, F. (1874). *Psychologie vom empirischen Standpunkt.* Dunker & Humblot, Leipzig. [*Psychology from an empirical standpoint* (trans. A.C. Rancurello, D.B. Terrell, and L.L. McAlister, 1973). Routledge & Kegan Paul, London.]

Bridgman, P.W. (1922, revised 1931). *Dimensional analysis.* Yale, New Haven.

Brown, W. (1910). The judgment of difference. *University of California Publications in Psychology*, **1**, 1–71.

Brysbaert, M. and d'Ydewalle, G. (1989). Unifying psychophysics: and what if things are not so simple? *Behavioral and Brain Sciences*, **12**, 271–3.

Brysbaert, M. and d'Ydewalle, G. (1990). The difference between stimulus and background: an explanation of the psychophysical function based on partition scales? In *Psychophysical explorations of mental structures* (ed. H-G. Geissler, M.H. Müller, and W. Prinz), pp. 58–70. Hogrefe & Huber, Toronto.

Burgess, A. and Barlow, H.B. (1983). The precision of numerosity discrimination in arrays of random dots. *Vision Research*, **23**, 811–20.

Cain, W.S. (1977a). Differential sensitivity for smell: 'noise' at the nose. *Science*, **195**, 796–8.

Cain, W.S. (1977b). Odor magnitude: coarse vs. fine grain. *Perception & Psychophysics*, **22**, 545–9.

Campbell, F.W. and Kulikowski, J.J. (1966). Orientational selectivity of the human visual system. *Journal of Physiology*, **187**, 437–45.

Campbell, F.W., Nachmias, J. and Jukes, J. (1970). Spatial-frequency discrimination in human vision. *Journal of the Optical Society of America*, **60**, 555–9.

Churcher, B.G. (1935). A loudness scale for industrial noise measurements. *Journal of the Acoustical Society of America*, **6**, 216–26.
Cohen, M. and Narens, L. (1979). Fundamental unit structures: a theory of ratio scalability. *Journal of Mathematical Psychology*, **20**, 193–232.
Connor, C.E. and Johnson, K.O. (1992). Neural coding of tactile texture: comparison of spatial and temporal mechanisms for roughness perception. *Journal of Neuroscience*, **12**, 3414–26.
Connor, C.E., Hsiao, S.S., Phillips, J.R., and Johnson, K.O. (1990). Tactile roughness: neural codes that account for psychophysical magnitude estimates. *Journal of Neuroscience*, **10**, 3823–36.
Cornsweet, T.N. (1970). *Visual perception*. Academic Press, New York.
Cornsweet, T.N. and Pinsker, H.M. (1965). Luminance discrimination of brief flashes under various conditions of adaptation. *Journal of Physiology*, **176**, 294–310.
Cox, D.R. (1962). *Renewal theory*. Methuen, London.
Craig, J.C. (1974). Vibrotactile difference thresholds for intensity and the effect of a masking stimulus. *Perception & Psychophysics*, **15**, 123–7.
Craik, K.J.W. (1938). The effect of adaptation of differential brightness discrimination. *Journal of Physiology*, **92**, 406–21.
Craik, K.J.W. (1966). *The nature of psychology* (ed. S.L. Sherwood). Cambridge University Press, Cambridge.
Cross, D.V. (1973). Sequential dependencies and regression in psychophysical judgments. *Perception & Psychophysics*, **14**, 547–52.
Crovitz, H.F. (1976). Perceived length and the Craik–O'Brien illusion. *Vision Research*, **16**, 435.
Curtis, D.W. (1970). Magnitude estimations and category judgments of brightness and brightness intervals: a two-stage interpretation. *Journal of Experimental Psychology*, **83**, 201–8.
Curtis, D.W. and Mullin, L.C. (1975). Judgments of average magnitude: analyses in terms of the functional measurement and two-stage models. *Perception & Psychophysics*, **18**, 299–308.
Curtis, D.W. and Rule, S.J. (1972). Magnitude judgments of brightness and brightness difference as a function of background reflectance. *Journal of Experimental Psychology*, **95**, 215–22.
Curtis, D.W. and Rule, S.J. (1977). Judgment of duration relations: simultaneous and sequential presentation. *Perception & Psychophysics*, **22**, 578–84.
Curtis, D.W. and Rule, S.J. (1980). Fechner's paradox reflects a nonmonotone relation between binocular brightness and luminance. *Perception & Psychophysics*, **27**, 263–6.
Curtis, D.W., Attneave, F., and Harrington, T.L. (1968). A test of a two-stage model of magnitude judgment. *Perception & Psychophysics*, **3**, 25–31.
Dawson, W.E. (1971). Magnitude estimation of apparent sums and differences. *Perception & Psychophysics*, **9**, 368–74.
De Valois, R.L., Jacobs, G.H., and Jones, A.E. (1962). Effects of increments and decrements of light on neural discharge rate. *Science*, **136**, 986–8.
de Vries, H. (1943). The quantum character of light and its bearing upon threshold of vision, the differential sensitivity and visual acuity of the eye. *Physica*, **10**, 553–64.
Delboeuf, J. (1873). Étude psychophysique. Recherches théoriques et expérimentales sur la mesure des sensations et spécialement des sensations de lumière et la fatigue. *Mémoires couronnés et autres mémoires publiés par l'Academie Royale des Sciences, des Lettres et des Beaux-Arts de Belgique*, 23.

Dodge, F.A. Jr, Knight, B.W., and Toyoda, J. (1968). Voltage noise in *Limulus* visual cells. *Science*, **160**, 88–90.

Dorfman, D.D. (1981). Warren's physical correlate theory: correlation does not imply causation. *Behavioral and Brain Sciences*, **4**, 192–3.

Egan, J.P. (1948). The effect of noise in one ear upon the loudness of speech in the other ear. *Journal of the Acoustical Society of America*, **20**, 58–62.

Ehrenberger, K., Finkenzeller, P., Keidel, W.D., and Plattig, K.H. (1966). Elektrophysiologische Korrelation der Stevensschen Potenzfunktion und objektive Schwellenmessung am Vibrationssinn des Menschen. *Pflüger's Archiv für die Gesamte Physiologie des Menschen und der Tiere*, **290**, 114–23.

Eisler, H. (1962). Empirical test of a model relating magnitude and category scales. *Scandinavian Journal of Psychology*, **3**, 88–96.

Eisler, H. (1963a). How prothetic is the continuum of smell? *Scandinavian Journal of Psychology*, **4**, 29–32.

Eisler, H. (1963b). Magnitude scales, category scales, and Fechnerian integration. *Psychological Review*, **70**, 243–53.

Eisler, H. (1976). Experiments on subjective duration 1865—1975: a collection of power function exponents. *Psychological Bulletin*, **83**, 1154–71.

Ekman, G. (1956). Discriminal sensitivity on the subjective continuum. *Acta Psychologica*, **12**, 233–43.

Ekman, G. (1958). Two generalized ratio scaling methods. *Journal of Psychology*, **45**, 287–95.

Ekman, G. (1959). Weber's Law and related functions. *Journal of Psychology*, **47**, 343–52.

Ekman, G. (1962). Measurement of moral judgment: a comparison of scaling methods. *Perceptual and Motor Skills*, **15**, 3–9.

Ekman, G. and Åkesson, C. (1965). Saltness, sweetness, and preference: a study of quantitative relations in individual subjects. *Scandinavian Journal of Psychology*, **6**, 241–53.

Ekman, G. and Künnapas, T. (1962). Scales of aesthetic value. *Perceptual and Motor Skills*, **14**, 19–26.

Ekman, G. and Künnapas, T. (1963a). A further study of direct and indirect scaling methods. *Scandinavian Journal of Psychology*, **4**, 77–80.

Ekman, G. and Künnapas, T. (1963b). *Scales of masculinity and femininity: a further study of direct and indirect scaling methods.* Report, Psychological Laboratory, University of Stockholm, No. 162.

Ekman, G., Hosman, B., Lindman, R., Ljungberg, L., and Åkesson, C. (1968). Interindividual differences in scaling performance. Perceptual and Motor Skills, **26**, 815–23.

Elmasian, R. and Birnbaum, M.H. (1984). A harmonious note on pitch: scales of pitch derived from subtractive model of comparison agree with the musical scale. *Perception & Psychophysics*, **36**, 531–7.

Engen, T. and McBurney, D.H. (1964). Magnitude and category scales of the pleasantness of odors. *Journal of Experimental Psychology*, **68**, 435–40.

Falmagne, J-C. (1985). *Elements of psychophysical theory.* Oxford University Press, Oxford.

Fechner, G.T. (1851). *Zend-Avesta oder Über die Dinge des Himmels und das Jenseits. Vom Standpunkt der Naturbetrachtung.* Voss, Leipzig.

Fechner, G.T. (1860). *Elemente der Psychophysik.* Breitkopf and Härtel, Leipzig. [*Elements of Psychophysics*, Vol. 1 (trans. H.E. Adler, 1966). Holt, Rinehart and Winston, New York.]

Fechner, G.T. (1877). *In Sachen der Psychophysik.* Breitkopf and Hártel, Leipzig.

Ferguson, A., Meyers, C.S., Bartlett, R.J., Banister, H., Bartlett, F.C., *et al.* (1940). Quantitative estimates of sensory events. *Advancement of Science*, **1**, 331–349.

Fitzmaurice, C. (1992). Compensation for personal injury: a psychophysical study of monetary awards in and out of court. Unpublished Ph.D. thesis, University of Manchester.

Fitzmaurice, C. and Moreland, J.D. (1995). Weberian characteristics in number preferences. Paper delivered to European Mathematical Psychology Group, Regensburg, 6 September.

Fletcher, H. (1929). *Speech and hearing.* Van Nostrand, New York.

Fuortes, M.G.F. (1959). Initiation of impulses in visual cells of *Limulus. Journal of Physiology*, **148**, 14–28.

Fuortes, M.G.F. and Hodgkin, A.L. (1964). Changes in time scale and sensitivity in the ommatidia of *Limulus. Journal of Physiology*, **172**, 239–63.

Galanter, E. and Messick, S. (1961). The relation between category and magnitude scales of loudness. *Psychological Review*, **68**, 363–72.

Garner, W.R. (1954a). A technique and a scale for loudness measurement. *Journal of the Acoustical Society of America*, **26**, 73–88.

Garner, W.R. (1954b). Context effects and the validity of loudness scales. *Journal of Experimental Psychology*, **48**, 218–24.

Garner, W.R. (1958). Half-loudness judgments without prior stimulus context. *Journal of Experimental Psychology*, **55**, 482–5.

Garner, W.R. (1959). The development of context effects in half-loudness judgments. *Journal of Experimental Psychology*, **58**, 212–19.

Garner, W.R. (1962). *Uncertainty and structure as psychological concepts.* Wiley, New York.

Garner, W.R. and Hake, H.W. (1951). The amount of information in absolute judgments. *Psychological Review*, **58**, 446–59.

Gatti, A. and Dodge, R. (1929). Über die Unterschiedsempfindlichkeit bei Reizung eines einzelnen, isolierten Tastorgans. *Archiv für die Gesamte Psychologie*, **69**, 405–26.

Gaydos, H.F. (1958). Sensitivity in the judgment of size by finger-span. *American Journal of Psychology*, **71**, 557–62.

Geiger, P.H. and Firestone, F.A. (1933). The estimation of fractional loudness. *Journal of the Acoustical Society of America*, **5**, 25–30.

Gescheider, G.A. (1981). In defense of a sensory process theory of psychophysical scaling. *Behavioral and Brain Sciemces*, **4**, 194.

Gescheider, G.A., Wright, J.H., and Polak, J.W. (1971). Detection of vibrotactile signals differing in probability of occurrence. *Journal of Psychology*, **78**, 253–60.

Gibson, J.J. (1950). *The perception of the visual world.* Houghton Mifflin, Boston, MA.

Gottesman, J., Rubin, G.S., and Legge, G.E. (1981). A power law for perceived contrast in human vision. *Vision Research*, **21**, 791–9.

Graf, V., Baird, J.C., and Glesman, G. (1974). An empirical test of two psychophysical models. *Acta Psychologica*, **38**, 59–72.

Green, D.M. and Luce, R.D. (1974). Variability of magnitude estimates: a timing theory analysis. *Perception & Psychophysics*, **15**, 291–300.

Green, D.M. and Swets, J.A. (1966). *Signal detection theory and psychophysics.* Wiley, New York.

Green, D.M., Luce, R.D., and Duncan, J.E. (1977). Variability and sequential effects in magnitude production and estimation of auditory intensity. *Perception & Psychophysics*, **22**, 450–6.

Green, D.M., Luce, R.D., and Smith, A.F. (1980). Individual magnitude estimates for various distributions of signal intensity. *Perception & Psychophysics*, **27**, 483–8.

Gregory, R.L. and Ross, H.E. (1967). Arm weight, adaptation, and weight discrimination. *Perceptual and Motor Skills*, **24**, 1127–30.

Gregson, R.A.M. and Russell, P.N. (1965). Psychophysical power law exponent value for sucrose intensity. *Perceptual and Motor Skills*, **20**, 294.

Guilford, J.P. (1931). Some empirical tests of the method of paired comparisons. *Journal of General Psychology*, **5**, 64–77.

Guilford, J.P. (1954). *Psychometric methods* (2nd edn). McGraw-Hill, New York.

Hagerty, M. and Birnbaum, M.H. (1978). Nonmetric tests of ratio vs. subtractive theories of stimulus comparison. *Perception & Psychophysics*, **24**, 121–9.

Hake, H.W. and Garner, W.R. (1951). The effect of presenting various numbers of discrete steps on scale reading accuracy. *Journal of Experimental Psychology*, **42**, 358–66.

Ham, L.B. and Parkinson, J.S. (1932). Loudness and intensity relations. *Journal of the Acoustical Society of America*, **3**, 511–34.

Hamblin, R.L., Bridger, D.A., Day, R.C., and Yancey, W.L. (1963). The interference-aggression law? *Sociometry*, **26**, 190–216.

Hamer, R.D., Verrillo, R.T., and Zwislocki, J.J. (1983). Vibrotactile masking of Pacinian and non-Pacinian channels. *Journal of the Acoustical Society of America*, **73**, 1293–303.

Hanna, T.E., von Gierke, S.M., and Green, D.M. (1986). Detection and intensity discrimination of a sinusoid. *Journal of the Acoustical Society of America*, **80**, 1335–40.

Hardin, C. and Birnbaum, M.H. (1990). Malleability of 'ratio' judgments of occupational prestige. American *Journal of Psychology*, **103**, 1–20.

Harper, R.S. and Stevens, S.S. (1948). A psychological scale of weight and a formula for its derivation. American *Journal of Psychology*, **61**, 343–51.

Harper, R. and Stevens, S.S. (1964). Subjective hardness of compliant materials. Quarterly *Journal of Experimental Psychology*, **16**, 204–15.

Harris, J.D. (1950). The effect of sensation-levels on intensive discrimination of noise. *American Journal of Psychology*, **63**, 409–21.

Harris, J.D. (1963). Loudness discrimination. *Journal of Speech and Hearing Disorders* (Monograph Supplement No. 11).

Hartline, H.K. and Graham, C.H. (1932). Nerve impulses from single receptors in the eye. *Journal of Cellular and Comparative Physiology*, **1**, 277–95.

Heidelberger, M. (1987). Fechner's indeterminism: from freedom to laws of chance. In *The probabilisitic revolution*, Vol. 1, *Ideas in history* (ed. L. Krueger, L.J. Daston, and M. Hiedelberger), pp. 117–56. MIT Press, Cambridge, MA.

Heidelberger, M. (1988). Fechner's Leib-Seele-Theorie. In *G.T. Fechner and psychology* (ed. J. Brozek and H. Gundlach), pp. 61–77. Passavia Universitätsverlag, Passau.

Heidelberger, M. (1993). Fechner's impact for measurement theory. *Behavioral and Brain Sciences*, **16**, 146–8.

Heidelberger, M. (1994). The unity of nature and mind: Gustav Theodor Fechner's non-reductive materialism. In *Romanticism in science: science in Europe, 1790–1840* (ed. S. Poggi and M. Bossi), pp. 215–36. Kluwer, Dordrecht.

Heinemann, E.G. (1955). Simultaneous brightness induction as a function of inducing- and test-field luminances. *Journal of Experimental Psychology*, **50**, 89–96.

Hellman, R., Scharf, B., Teghtsoonian, M., and Teghtsoonian, R. (1987). On the relation between the growth of loudness and the discrimination of intensity for pure tones. *Journal of the Acoustical Society of America*, **82**, 448–53.

Hering, E. (1925). Grundzüge der Lehre vom Lichtsinn. In *Handbuch der Gesamten Augenheilkunde*, Vol. 3, *Physiologische Optik* (ed. T. Axenfeld and A. Elschnig), Ch. XII. Springer, Berlin.

Hess, R.F. and Nordby, K. (1986). Spatial and temporal limits of vision in the achromat. *Journal of Physiology*, **371**, 365–85.

Hollingworth, H.L. (1909). The inaccuracy of movement. *Archives of Psychology*, No. 13.

Holway, A.H. and Pratt, C.C. (1936). The Weber-ratio for intensitive discrimination. *Psychological Review*, **43**, 322–40.

Hood, D.C. and Finkelstein, M.A. (1979). Comparison of changes in sensitivity and sensation: implications for the response-intensity function of the human photopic system. *Journal of Experimental Psychology: Human Perception and Performance*, **5**, 391–405.

Hood, D.C. and Finkelstein, M.A. (1981). On relating physiology to sensation. *Behavioral and Brain Sciences*, **4**, 195.

Humphrey, G. (1951). *Thinking: an introduction to its experimental psychology*. Methuen, London.

Hunt, R.W.G. (1953). Characteristic curves of the human eye. *Journal of Photographic Science*, **1**, 149–58.

Hurvich, L.M. (1981). *Color vision*. Sinauer, Sunderland, MA.

Indow, T. (1961). [An example of motivation research applied to product design.] *Chosa To Gijutsu*, **102**, 45–60 (in Japanese).

Indow, T. (1967). Saturation scales for red. *Vision Research*, **7**, 481–95.

Indow, T. and Stevens, S.S. (1966). Scaling of saturation and hue. *Perception & Psychophysics*, **1**, 253–71.

Ittelson, W.H. (1952). *The Ames demonstrations in perception*. Princeton University Press, Princeton, NJ.

James, W. (1890). *The principles of psychology*. Henry Holt, New York.

Jeffress, L.A. (1964). Stimulus-oriented approach to detection. *Journal of the Acoustical Society of America*, **36**, 766–74.

Jeffreys, H. and Jeffreys, B.S. (1966). *Methods of mathematical physics* (3rd edn). Cambridge University Press, Cambridge.

Jesteadt, W., Luce, R.D., and Green, D.M. (1977a). Sequential effects in judgments of loudness. *Journal of Experimental Psychology: Human Perception and Performance*, **3**, 92–104.

Jesteadt, W., Wier, C.C. and Green, D.M. (1977b). Intensity discrimination as a function of frequency and sensation level. *Journal of the Acoustical Society of America*, **61**, 169–77.

Johnson, K.O., Darian-Smith, I. and LaMotte, C. (1973). Peripheral neural determinants of temperature discrimination in man: a correlative study of responses to cooling skin. *Journal of Neurophysiology*, **36**, 347–70.

Johnson, N.L. (1949). Systems of frequency curves generated by methods of translation. *Biometrika*, **36**, 149–76.

Kanizsa, G. (1955). Margini quasi-percettivi in campi con stimolazione omogenea. *Rivista di Psicologia*, **49**, 7–30.

Keidel, W.D. and Spreng, M. (1965). Neurophysiological evidence for the Stevens power function in man. *Journal of the Acoustical Society of America*, **38**, 191–5.

Kellogg, W.N. (1929). An experimental comparison of psychophysical methods. *Archives of Psychology*, No. 106.

Kern, E. (1952). Der Bereich der Unterschiedsempfindlichkeit des Auges bei festgehaltenem Adaptationszustand. *Zeitschrift für Biologie*, **105**, 237–45.

Khintchine, A.Y. (1960). *Mathematical methods in the theory of queueing* (trans. D.M. Andrews and M.H. Quenouille). Griffin, London.

Kiang, N.Y-S., Watanabe, T., Thomas, E.C., and Clarke, L.F. (1965). *Discharge patterns of single fibers in the cat's auditory nerve*. MIT Press, Cambridge, MA.

Kiesow, F. (1925/26). Über die Vergleichung linearer Strecken und ihre Beziehung zum Weberschen Gesetze. *Archiv für die Gesamte Psychologie*, **52**, 61–90; **53**, 433–46; **56**, 421–51.

Knibestöl, M. and Vallbo, Å.B. (1980). Intensity of sensation related to activity of slowly adapting mechanoreceptive units in the human hand. *Journal of Physiology*, **300**, 251–67.

Knudsen, V.O. (1928). 'Hearing' with the sense of touch. *Journal of General Psychology*, **1**, 320–52.

Koh, S.D. (1965). Scaling musical preferences. *Journal of Experimental Psychology*, **70**, 79–82.

Kornbrot, D.E. (1984). Mechanisms for categorization: decision criteria and the form of the psychophysical function. *British Journal of Mathematical and Statistical Psychology*, **37**, 184–98.

Krantz, D.H. (1971). Integration of just-noticeable differences. *Journal of Mathematical Psychology*, **8**, 591–9.

Krantz, D.H. (1972). A theory of magnitude estimation and cross-modality matching. *Journal of Mathematical Psychology*, **9**, 168–99.

Krantz, D.H., Luce, R.D., Suppes, P., and Tversky, A. (1971). *Foundations of measurement*, Vol. 1, *Additive and polynomial representations*. Academic Press, New York.

Krauskopf, J. (1967). Heterochromatic stabilized images: a classroom demonstration. *American Journal of Psychology*, **80**, 634–7.

Krueger, L.E. (1984). Perceived numerosity: a comparison of magnitude production, magnitude estimation, and discrimination judgments. *Perception & Psychophysics*, **35**, 536–42.

Krueger, L. (1989). Reconciling Fechner and Stevens: toward a unified psychophysical law. *Behavioral and Brain Sciences*, **12**, 251–320.

Kruskal, J.B. (1964). Nonmetric multidimensional scaling: a numerical method. *Psychometrika*, **29**, 115–29.

Kuffler, S.W. (1953). Discharge patterns and functional organization of mammalian retina. *Journal of Neurophysiology*, **16**, 37–68.

Kulikowski, J.J. (1976). Effective contrast constancy and linearity of contrast sensation. *Vision Research*, **16**, 1419–31.

Künnapas, T. and Sillén, M. (1964). *Measurement of 'political' preferences: a comparison of scaling methods*. Report No. 172, Psychological Laboratory, University of Stockholm.

Künnapas, T. and Wikstroem, I. (1963). Measurement of occupational preferences: a comparison of scaling methods. *Perceptual and Motor Skills*, **17**, 611–94.

Laird, D.A., Taylor, E., and Wille, H.H. Jr (1932). The apparent reduction of loudness. *Journal of the Acoustical Society of America*, **3**, 393–401.

Laming, D. (1968). *Information theory of choice-reaction times*. Academic Press, London.

Laming, D. (1973). *Mathematical psychology*. Academic Press, London.

Laming, D. (1974). The sequential structure of the quantal experiment. *Journal of Mathematical Psychology*, **11**, 453–72.

Laming, D. (1984). The relativity of 'absolute' judgements. *British Journal of Mathematical and Statistical Psychology*, **37**, 152–83.

Laming, D. (1985). Some principles of sensory analysis. *Psychological Review*, **92**, 462–85.

Laming, D. (1986). *Sensory analysis*. Academic Press, London.

Laming, D. (1987). The discrimination of smell and taste compared with other senses. *Chemistry and Industry*, 5 Jan, 12–18.

Laming, D. (1988a). Précis of *Sensory analysis*. *Behavioral and Brain Sciences*, **11**, 275–96.

Laming, D. (1988b) A reexamination of *Sensory analysis*. *Behavioral and Brain Sciences*, **11**, 316–39.

Laming, D. (1989a). Experimental evidence for Fechner's and Stevens's laws. *Behavioral and Brain Sciences*, **12**, 277–81.

Laming, D. (1989b). On relating visual phenomena to physiological observation. In *Seeing contour and colour* (ed. J.J. Kulikowski, C.M. Dickinson, and I.J. Murray), pp. 659–70. Pergamon Press, Oxford.

Laming, D. (1991a). Contrast sensitivity. In *Vision and visual dysfunction*, Vol. 5, *Limits of vision* (ed. J.J. Kulikowski, V. Walsh, and I.J. Murray), pp. 35–43. Macmillan, London.

Laming, D. (1991b). Reconciling Fechner and Stevens? *Behavioral and Brain Sciences*, **14**, 188–91.

Laming, D. (1991*c*). Spatial frequency channels. In *Vision and visual dysfunction*, Vol 5, *Limits of vision* (ed. J.J. Kulikowski, V. Walsh, and I.J. Murray), pp. 97–105. Macmillan, London.

Laming, D. (1992). Springer's lines and Hermann's grid. *Ophthalmic and Physiological Optics*, **12**, 178–82.

Laming, D. (1994). Psychophysics. In *Companion encyclopedia of psychology*, Vol. 1 (ed. A.M. Colman), pp. 251–77. Routledge, London.

Laming, D. (1997). A critique of a measurement-theoretic critique. *British Journal of Psychology*, in press.

Laming, D. and Marsh, D. (1988). Some performance tests of QUEST on measurements of vibrotactile thresholds. *Perception & Psychophysics*, **44**, 99–107.

Laming, J. and Laming, D. (1996). J. Plateau: On the measurement of physical sensations and on the law which links the intensity of these sensations to the intensity of the source. J. Plateau: Report on 'Psychophysical study. Theoretical and experimental research on the measurement of sensations, particularly sensations of light and of fatigue' by Mr Delboeuf. *Psychological Research*, **59**, 134–44.

Land, E.H. (1959). Experiments in color vision. *Scientific American*, May, 84–99.

Land, E.H. (1974). Smitty Stevens' test of retinex theory. In *Sensation and measurement* (ed. H.R. Moskowitz, B. Scharf, and J.C. Stevens), pp. 363–8. Reidel, Dordrecht.

Lane, H.L., Catania, A.C., and Stevens, S.S. (1961). Voice level: autophonic scale, perceived loudness, and effects of sidetone. *Journal of the Acoustical Society of America*, **33**, 160–7.

Legge, G.E. (1979). Spatial frequency masking in human vision: binocular interactions. *Journal of the Optical Society of America*, **69**, 838–47.

Legge, G.E. (1981). A power law for contrast discrimination. *Vision Research*, **21**, 457–67.

Leshowitz, B., Taub, H.B. and Raab, D.H. (1968). Visual detection of signals in the presence of continuous and pulsed backgrounds. *Perception & Psychophysics*, **4**, 207–13.

Lindsay, P.H. and Norman, D.A. (1977). *Human information processing: an introduction to psychology* (2nd edn). Academic Press, New York.

Link, S.W. (1992). *The wave theory of difference and similarity*. Erlbaum, Hillsdale, NJ.

Linker, E., Moore, M.E. and Galanter, E. (1964). Taste thresholds, detection models, and disparate results. *Journal of Experimental Psychology*, **67**, 59–66.

Lockhead, G.R. (1992). Psychophysical scaling: judgments of attributes or objects? *Behavioral and Brain Sciences*, **15**, 543–601.

Luce, R.D. (1959). On the possible psychophysical laws. *Psychological Review*, **66**, 81–95.

Luce, R.D. (1962). Comments on Rozeboom's criticisms of 'On the possible psychophysical laws'. *Psychological Review*, **69**, 548–51.

Luce, R.D. (1964). A generalization of a theorem of dimensional analysis. *Journal of Mathematical Psychology*, **1**, 278–84.
Luce, R.D. (1981). Physical correlate theory: a question and a prediction. *Behavioral and Brain Sciences*, **4**, 197–8.
Luce, R.D. (1990). 'On the possible psychophysical laws' revisited: remarks on cross-modal matching. *Psychological Review*, **97**, 66–77.
Luce, R.D. (1993). Let's not promulgate either Fechner's erroneous algorithm or his unidimensional approach. *Behavioral and Brain Sciences*, **16**, 155–6.
Luce, R.D. and Edwards, W. (1958). The derivation of subjective scales from just noticeable differences. *Psychological Review*, **65**, 222–37.
Luce, R.D. and Galanter, E. (1963). Discrimination. In *Handbook of mathematical psychology*, Vol. I (ed. R.D. Luce, R.R. Bush, and E. Galanter), pp. 191–243. Wiley, New York.
Luce, R.D. and Green, D.M. (1974). The response ratio hypothesis for magnitude estimation. *Journal of Mathematical Psychology*, **11**, 1–14.
Luce, R.D. and Green. D.M. (1978). Two tests of a neural attention hypothesis for auditory psychophysics. *Perception & Psychophysics*, **23**, 363–71.
Luce, R.D. and Mo, S.S. (1965). Magnitude estimation of heaviness and loudness by individual subjects: a test of a probabilistic response theory. *British Journal of Mathematical and Statistical Psychology*, **18**, 159–74.
Luce, R.D. and Narens, L. (1983). Symmetry, scale types, and generalizations of classical physical measurement. *Journal of Mathematical Psychology*, **27**, 44–85.
Luce, R.D. and Narens, L. (1985). Classification of concatenation measurement structures according to scale type. *Journal of Mathematical Psychology*, **29**, 1–72.
Luce, R.D. and Tukey, J.W. (1964). Simultaneous conjoint measurement: a new type of fundamental measurement. *Journal of Mathematical Psychology*, **1**, 1–27.
Luce, R.D., Green, D.M., and Weber, D.L. (1976). Attention bands in absolute identification. *Perception & Psychophysics*, **20**, 49–54.
Luce, R.D., Nosofsky, R.M., Green, D.M., and Smith, A.F. (1982). The bow and sequential effects in absolute identification. *Perception & Psychophysics*, **32**, 397–408.
MacKay, D.M. (1963). Psychophysics of perceived intensity: a theoretical basis for Fechner's and Stevens' laws. *Science*, **139**, 1213–16.
MacKay, D.M. (1973). Lateral interaction between neural channels sensitive to texture density? *Nature*, **245**, 159–61.
Macmillan, N.A. and Creelman, C.D. (1991). *Detection theory: a user's guide*. Cambridge University Press, Cambridge.
Mansfield, R.J.W. (1973). Brightness function: effect of area and duration. *Journal of the Optical Society of America*, **63**, 913–20.
Mansfield, R.J.W. (1975). Neuronal mechanisms subserving brightness coding in monkey visual cortex. *Society for Neuroscience Abstracts*, **1**, 56.
Mansfield, R.J.W. (1981). Sensory coding: the search for invariants. *Behavioral and Brain Sciences*, **4**, 198–9.
Marcel, A.J. (1983). Conscious and unconscious perception: experiments on visual masking and word recognition. *Cognitive Psychology*, **15**, 197–237.
Markowitz, J. and Swets, J.A. (1967). Factors affecting the slope of empirical ROC curves: comparison of binary and rating responses. *Perception & Psychophysics*, **2**, 91–100.
Marks, L.E. (1974). On scales of sensation: prolegomena to any future psychophysics that will be able to come forth as science. *Perception & Psychophysics*, **16**, 358–76.
Marks, L.E. (1978a). Binaural summation of the loudness of pure tones. *Journal of the Acoustical Society of America*, **64**, 107–13.

Marks, L.E. (1978*b*). PHONION: translation and annotations concerning loudness scales and the processing of auditory intensity. In *Cognitive theory*, Vol. 3 (ed. N.J. Castellan and F. Restle), pp. 7–31. Erlbaum, Hillsdale, NJ.

Marks, L.E. (1979a). A theory of loudness and loudness judgments. *Psychological Review*, **86**, 256–85.

Marks, L.E. (1979b). Sensory and cognitive factors in judgments of loudness. *Journal of Experimental Psychology: Human Perception and Performance* **5**, 426–43.

Marks, L.E. and Bartoshuk, L.M. (1979). Ratio scaling of taste intensity by a matching procedure. *Perception & Psychophysics*, **26**, 335–9.

Marks, L.E. and Cain, W.S. (1972). Perception of intervals and magnitudes for three prothetic continua. *Journal of Experimental Psychology*, **94**, 6–17.

Marrocco, R.T. (1972). Maintained activity of monkey optic tract fibers and lateral geniculate nucleus cells. *Vision Research*, **12**, 1175–81.

Mashhour, M. (1965). Note on the validity of the power law. *Scandinavian Journal of Psychology*, **6**, 220–4.

Masson, A. (1845). Etudes de photometrie électrique. *Annales de Chimie et de Physique, 3rd series*, **14**, 129–95.

Matthews, B.H.C. (1931). The response of a muscle spindle during active contraction of a muscle. *Journal of Physiology*, **72**, 153–74.

McBurney, D.H. (1966). Magnitude estimation of the taste of sodium chloride after adaptation to sodium chloride. *Journal of Experimental Psychology*, **72**, 869–73.

McBurney, D.H. and Pfaffmann, C. (1963). Gustatory adaptation to saliva and sodium chloride. *Journal of Experimental Psychology*, **65**, 523–9.

McBurney, D.H., Kasschau, R.A. and Bogart, L.M. (1967). The effect of adaptation on taste jnds. *Perception & Psychophysics*, **2**, 175–8.

McGill, W.J. (1967). Neural counting mechanisms and energy detection in audition. *Journal of Mathematical Psychology*, **4**, 351–76.

Mellers, B.A. and Birnbaum, M.H. (1982). Loci of contextual effects in judgment. *Journal of Experimental Psychology: Human Perception and Performance*, **8**, 582–601.

Mellers, B.A., Davis, D.M., and Birnbaum, M.H. (1984). Weight of evidence supports one operation for 'ratios' and 'differences' of heaviness. *Journal of Experimental Psychology: Human Perception and Performance*, **10**, 216–30.

Merkel, J. (1888). Die Abhängigkeit zwischen Reiz und Empfindung. I. *Philosophische Studien*, **4**, 541–94.

Merkel, J. (1889a). Die Abhängigkeit zwischen Reiz und Empfindung. II. *Philosophische Studien*, **5**, 245–91.

Merkel, J. (1889b). Die Abhängigkeit zwischen Reiz und Empfindung. III. *Philosophische Studien*, **5**, 499–557.

Merkel, J. (1894). Die Methode der mittleren Fehler, experimentell begründet durch Versuche aus dem Gebiete des Raummasses. *Philosophische Studien*, **9**, 53–65, 176–208, 400–28.

Mittenecker, E. (1974). Der Einfluß der Erfahrung auf die psychophysische Skalierung. *Psychologische Beiträge*, **16**, 288–99.

Montgomery, H. (1975). Direct estimation: effect of methodological factors on scale type. *Scandinavian Journal of Psychology*, **16**, 19–29.

Mountcastle, V.B. and Powell, T.P.S. (1959). Neural mechanisms subserving cutaneous sensibility, with special reference to the role of afferent inhibition in sensory perception and discrimination. *Bulletin of the Johns Hopkins Hospital*, **105**, 201–32.

Mountcastle, V.B., Talbot, W.H., Sakata, H., and Hyvärinen, J. (1969). Cortical neuronal mechanisms in flutter-vibration studied in unanesthetized monkeys. Neuronal periodicity and frequency discrimination. *Journal of Neurophysiology*, **32**, 452–84.

Murray, D.J. (1993). A perspective for viewing the history of psychophysics. *Behavioral and Brain Sciences*, **16**, 115–86.

Nachmias, J. and Steinman, R.M. (1965). Brightness and discriminability of light flashes. *Vision Research*, **5**, 545–57.

Narens, L. and Luce, R.D. (1976). The algebra of measurement. *Journal of Pure and Applied Algebra*, **8**, 197–233.

Narens, L. and Luce, R.D. (1986). Measurement: the theory of numerical assignments. *Psychological Bulletin*, **99**, 166–80.

Narens, L. and Mausfeld, R. (1992). On the relationship of the psychological and the physical in psychophysics. *Psychological Review*, **99**, 467–79.

Newman, E.B. (1933). The validity of the just noticeable difference as a unit of psychological magnitude. *Transactions of the Kansas Academy of Science*, **36**, 172–5.

Oberlin, K.W. (1936). Variation in intensitive sensitivity to lifted weights. *Journal of Experimental Psychology*, **19**, 438–55.

O'Brien, V. (1958). Contour perception, illusion and reality. *Journal of the Optical Society of America*, **48**, 112–9.

Onley, J.W. (1960). Brightness scaling of white and colored stimuli. *Science*, **132**, 1668–70.

Panek, D.W. and Stevens, S.S. (1966). Saturation of red: a prothetic continuum. *Perception & Psychophysics*, **1**, 59–66.

Plateau, J. (1872a). Étude psychophysique—recherches théoriques et expérimentales sur la mesure des sensations et spécialement des sensations de lumière et la fatigue; par M. Delboeuf. Rapport de M.J. Plateau. *Bulletins de L'Academie Royale des Sciences, des Lettres et des Beaux-Arts de Belgique, 2me Sér.*, **34**, 250–62.

Plateau, J. (1872b). Sur la mesure des sensations physiques, et sur la loi qui lie l'intensité de ces sensations à l'intensité de la cause excitante. *Bulletins de L'Academie Royale des Sciences, des Lettres et des Beaux-Arts de Belgique, 2me Sér.*, **33**, 376–88.

Pollack, I. (1949). The effect of white noise on the loudness of speech of assigned average level. *Journal of the Acoustical Society of America*, **21**, 255–8.

Pollack, I. (1952). The information of elementary auditory displays. I. *Journal of the Acoustical Society of America*, **24**, 745–9.

Pollack, I. (1953). The information of elementary auditory displays. II. *Journal of the Acoustical Society of America*, **25**, 765–9.

Popper, R., Parker, S., and Galanter, E. (1986). Dual loudness scales in individual subjects. *Journal of Experimental Psychology: Human Perception and Performance*, **12**, 61–9.

Poulton, E.C. (1967). Population norms of top sensory magnitudes and S.S. Stevens' exponents. *Perception & Psychophysics*, **2**, 312–6.

Poulton, E.C. (1968). The new psychophysics: six models for magnitude estimation. *Psychological Bulletin*, **69**, 1–19.

Poulton, E.C. (1969). Choice of first variables for single and repeated multiple estimates of loudness. *Journal of Experimental Psychology*, **80**, 249–53.

Poulton, E.C. (1979). Models for biases in judging sensory magnitude. *Psychological Bulletin*, **86**, 777–803.

Poulton, E.C. (1989). *Bias in quantifying judgments*. Erlbaum, Hove, UK.

Poulton, E.C., Simmonds, D.C.V., Warren, R.M., and Webster, J.C. (1965). Prior context and fractional versus multiple estimates of the reflectance of grays against a fixed standard. *Journal of Experimental Psychology*, **69**, 496–502.

Poulton, E.C., Simmonds, D.C.V., and Warren, R.M. (1968). Response bias in very first judgments of the reflectance of grays: numerical versus linear estimates. *Perception & Psychophysics*, **3**, 112–4.

Pradhan, P.L. and Hoffman, P.J. (1963). Effect of spacing and range of stimuli on magnitude estimation judgments. *Journal of Experimental Psychology*, **66**, 533–41.

Prandtl, A. (1927). Über gleichsinnige Induktion und die Lichtverteilung in gitterartigen Mustern. *Zeitschrift für Sinnesphysiologie*, **58**, 263–307.

Ratliff, F. (1965). *Mach bands: quantitative studies on neural networks in the retina.* Holden-Day, San Francisco.

Rawdon-Smith, A.F. and Grindley, G.C. (1935). An illusion in the perception of loudness. *British Journal of Psychology*, **26**, 191–5.

Reese, T.S. and Stevens, S.S. (1960). Subjective intensity of coffee odor. *American Journal of Psychology*, **73**, 424–8.

Reynolds, G.S. and Stevens, S.S. (1960). Binaural summation of loudness. *Journal of the Acoustical Society of America*, **32**, 1337 –44.

Richardson, L.F. and Ross, J.S. (1930). Loudness and telephone current. *Journal of General Psychology*, **3**, 288–306.

Riesz, R.R. (1928). Differential intensity sensitivity of the ear for pure tones. *Physical Review*, **31**, 867–75.

Risset, J.C. (1969). Pitch control and pitch paradoxes demonstrated with computer-synthesized sounds. *Journal of the Acoustical Society of America*, **46**, 88(A).

Robinson, G.H. (1976). Biasing power law exponents by magnitude estimation instructions. *Perception & Psychophysics*, **19**, 80–4.

Rose, A. (1948). The sensitivity performance of the human eye on an absolute scale. *Journal of the Optical Society of America*, **38**, 196–208.

Rose, J.E., Brugge, J.F., Anderson, D.J., and Hind, J.E. (1967). Phase-locked response to low-frequency tones in single auditory nerve fibers of the squirrel monkey. *Journal of Neurophysiology*, **30**, 769–93.

Rosner, B.S. (1965). The power law and subjective scales of number. *Perceptual and Motor Skills*, **21**, 42.

Rowley, R.R. and Studebaker, G.A. (1969). Monaural loudness–intensity relationships for a 1000-Hz tone. *Journal of the Acoustical Society of America*, **45**, 1186–92.

Rozeboom, W.W. (1962a). Comment. *Psychological Review*, **69**, 552.

Rozeboom, W.W. (1962b). The untenability of Luce's principle. *Psychological Review*, **69**, 542–7.

Rule, S.J. (1969). Equal discriminability scale of number. *Journal of Experimental Psychology*, **79**, 35–8.

Rule, S.J. (1971). Discriminability scales of number for multiple and fractional estimates. *Acta Psychologica*, **35**, 328–33.

Rule, S.J. (1972). Comparisons of intervals between subjective numbers. *Perception & Psychophysics*, **11**, 97–8.

Rule, S.J. and Curtis, D.W. (1973*a*). Conjoint scaling of subjective number and weight. *Journal of Experimental Psychology*, **97**, 305–9.

Rule, S.J. and Curtis, D.W. (1973*b*). Reevaluation of two models for judgments of perceptual intervals. *Perception & Psychophysics*, **14**, 433–6.

Rule, S.J. and Curtis, D.W. (1976). Converging power functions as a description of the size–weight illusion: a control experiment. *Bulletin of the Psychonomic Society*, **8**, 16–8.

Rule, S.J. and Curtis, D.W. (1977). Subject differences in input and output transformations from magnitude estimation of differences. *Acta Psychologica*, **41**, 61–5.

Rule, S.J. and Curtis, D.W. (1982). Levels of sensory and judgmental processing: strategies for the evaluation of a model. In *Social attitudes and psychophysical measurement* (ed. B. Wegener), pp. 107–22. Erlbaum, Hillsdale, NJ.

Rule, S.J. and Curtis, D.W. (1985). Ordinal properties of perceived average duration: simultaneous and sequential presentations. *Journal of Experimental Psychology: Human Perception and Performance*, **11**, 509–16.

Rule, S.J. and Markley, R.P. (1971). Subject differences in cross-modality matching. *Perception & Psychophysics*, **9**, 115–17.

Rule, S.J., Curtis, D.W., and Markley, R.P. (1970). Input and output transformations from magnitude estimation. *Journal of Experimental Psychology*, **86**, 343–9.

Rule, S.J., Laye, R.C., and Curtis, D.W. (1974). Magnitude judgments and difference judgments of lightness and darkness: a two-stage analysis. *Journal of Experimental Psychology*, **103**, 1108–14.

Rule, S.J., Curtis, D.W., and Mullin, L.C. (1981). Subjective ratios and differences in perceived heaviness. *Journal of Experimental Psychology: Human Perception and Performance*, 7, 459–66.

Rule, S.J., Mahon, M.L., and Curtis, D.W. (1983). Composition rule for perceived duration of simultaneous events. *Perception & Psychophysics*, **34**, 569–72.

Rushton, W.A.H. (1959). A theoretical treatment of Fuortes's observations upon eccentric cell activity in *Limulus*. *Journal of Physiology*, **148**, 29–38.

Rushton, W.H.A. (1969). Colour perception in man. In *Processing of optical data by organisms and by machines* (ed. W. Reichardt), pp. 565–79. Academic Press, New York.

Savage, C.W. (1970). *The measurement of sensation.* University of California Press, Berkeley.

Scharf, B. (1961). Complex sounds and critical bands. *Psychological Bulletin*, **58**, 205–17.

Scheerer, E. (1987). The unknown Fechner. *Psychological Research*, **49**, 197–202.

Scheerer, E. (1989). Conjuring Fechner's spirit. *Behavioral and Brain Sciences*, **12**, 288–90.

Scheerer, E. (1992). Fechner's inner psychophysics. Its historical fate and present status. In *Cognition, information processing and psychophysics: basic issues* (ed. H-G. Geissler, S.W. Link, and J.T. Townsend), pp. 3–21. Erlbaum, Hillsdale, NJ.

Schneider, B. and Parker, S. (1990). Does stimulus context affect loudness or only loudness judgments? *Perception & Psychophysics*, **48**, 409–18.

Schutz, H.G. and Pilgrim, F.J. (1957). Differential sensitivity in gustation. *Journal of Experimental Psychology*, **54**, 41–8.

Sellick, P.M. and Russell, I.J. (1980). The responses of inner hair cells to basilar membrane velocity during low frequency auditory stimulation in the guinea pig cochlea. *Hearing Research*, **2**, 439–45.

Sellin, T. and Wolfgang, M.E. (1964). *The measurement of delinquency.* Wiley, New York.

Semb, G. (1968). The detectability of the odor of butanol. *Perception & Psychophysics*, **4**, 335–40.

Shepard, R.N. (1964). Circularity in judgments of relative pitch. *Journal of the Acoustical Society of America*, **36**, 2346–53.

Shepard, R.N. (1978). On the status of 'direct' psychophysical measurement. In *Minnesota studies in the philosophy of science*, Vol. 9, *Perception and cognition. Issues in the foundations of psychology* (ed. C.W. Savage), pp. 441–90. University of Minnesota Press, Minneapolis.

Shepard, R.N. (1981). Psychological relations and psychophysical scales: on the status of 'direct' psychophysical measurement. *Journal of Mathematical Psychology*, **24**, 21–57.

Sherif, M. (1937). An experimental approach to the study of attitudes. *Sociometry*, **1**, 90–8.

Stevens, J.C. (1958). Stimulus spacing and the judgment of loudness. *Journal of Experimental Psychology*, **56**, 246–50.

Stevens, J.C. and Guirao, M. (1964). Individual loudness functions. *Journal of the Acoustical Society of America*, **36**, 2210–13.
Stevens, J.C. and Mack, J.D. (1959). Scales of apparent force. *Journal of Experimental Psychology*, **58**, 405–13.
Stevens, J.C. and Marks, L.E. (1965). Cross-modality matching of brightness and loudness. *Proceedings of the National Academy of Sciences of the United States of America*, **54**, 407–11.
Stevens, J.C. and Shickman, G.M. (1959). The perception of repetition rate. *Journal of Experimental Psychology*, **58**, 433–40.
Stevens, J.C. and Stevens, S.S. (1960). Warmth and cold: dynamics of sensory intensity. *Journal of Experimental Psychology*, **60**, 183–92.
Stevens, J.C. and Stevens, S.S. (1963). Brightness function: effects of adaptation. *Journal of the Optical Society of America*, **53**, 375–85.
Stevens, J.C. and Tulving, E. (1957). Estimations of loudness by a group of untrained observers. *American Journal of Psychology*, **70**, 600–5.
Stevens, J.C., Mack, J.D., and Stevens, S.S. (1960). Growth of sensation on seven continua as measured by force of handgrip. *Journal of Experimental Psychology*, **59**, 60–7.
Stevens, S.S. (1936). A scale for the measurement of a psychological magnitude: loudness. *Psychological Review*, **43**, 405–16.
Stevens, S.S. (1951). Mathematics, measurement, and psychophysics. In *Handbook of experimental psychology* (ed. S.S. Stevens), pp. 1–49. Wiley, New York.
Stevens, S.S. (1956a). Calculation of the loudness of complex noise. *Journal of the Acoustical Society of America*, **28**, 807–32.
Stevens, S.S. (1956b). The direct estimation of sensory magnitudes—loudness. *American Journal of Psychology*, **69**, 1–25.
Stevens, S.S. (1957a). Calculating loudness. *NOISE Control*, September, 11–22.
Stevens, S.S. (1957b). On the psychophysical law. *Psychological Review*, **64**, 153–81.
Stevens, S.S. (1959a). Cross-modality validation of subjective scales for loudness, vibration, and electric shock. *Journal of Experimental Psychology*, **57**, 201–9.
Stevens, S.S. (1959b). Measurement, psychophysics, and utility. In *Measurement: definitions and theories* (ed. C.W. Churchman and P Ratoosh), pp. 18–63. Wiley, New York.
Stevens, S.S. (1959c). Tactile vibration: dynamics of sensory intensity. *Journal of Experimental Psychology*, **57**, 210–18.
Stevens, S.S. (1961a). On the psychophysics of sensory function. In *Sensory communication* (ed. W.A. Rosenblith), pp. 1–33. MIT Press, Cambridge, MA.
Stevens, S.S. (1961b). To honor Fechner and repeal his law. *Science*, **133**, 80–6.
Stevens, S.S. (1962). In pursuit of the sensory law (2nd Klopsteg Lecture). Northwestern University Technological Institute, Evanston, IL.
Stevens, S.S. (1966a). A metric for the social consensus. *Science*, **151**, 530–41.
Stevens, S.S. (1966b). Matching functions between loudness and ten other continua. *Perception & Psychophysics*, **1**, 5–8.
Stevens, S.S. (1966c). Power-group transformations under glare, masking, and recruitment. *Journal of the Acoustical Society of America*, **39**, 725–35.
Stevens, S.S. (1968). Tactile vibration: change of exponent with frequency. *Perception & Psychophysics*, **3**, 223–8.
Stevens, S.S. (1969). Sensory scales of taste intensity. *Perception & Psychophysics*, **6**, 302–8.
Stevens, S.S. (1970). Neural events and the psychophysical law. *Science*, **170**, 1043–50.
Stevens, S.S. (1971). Issues in psychophysical measurement. *Psychological Review*, **78**, 426–50.

Stevens, S.S. (1975). *Psychophysics: introduction to its perceptual, neural, and social prospects* (ed. G. Stevens). Wiley, New York.

Stevens, S.S. and Galanter, E.H. (1957). Ratio scales and category scales for a dozen perceptual continua. *Journal of Experimental Psychology*, **54**, 377–411.

Stevens, S.S. and Greenbaum, H.B. (1966). Regression effect in psychophysical judgment. *Perception & Psychophysics*, **1**, 439–46.

Stevens, S.S. and Guirao, M. (1962). Loudness, reciprocality, and partition scales. *Journal of the Acoustical Society of America*, **34**, 1466–71.

Stevens, S.S. and Guirao, M. (1963). Subjective scaling of length and area and the matching of length to loudness and brightness. *Journal of Experimental Psychology*, **66**, 177–86.

Stevens, S.S. and Guirao, M. (1964). Scaling of apparent viscosity. *Science*, **144**, 1157–8.

Stevens, S.S. and Harris, J.R. (1962). The scaling of subjective roughness and smoothness. *Journal of Experimental Psychology*, **64**, 489–94.

Stevens, S.S. and Poulton, E.C. (1956). The estimation of loudness by unpracticed observers. *Journal of Experimental Psychology*, **51**, 71–8.

Stevens, S.S. and Stone, G. (1959). Finger span: ratio scale, category scale, and jnd scale. *Journal of Experimental Psychology*, **57**, 91–5.

Stevens, S.S. and Volkmann, J. (1940). The relation of pitch to frequency: a revised scale. *American Journal of Psychology*, **53**, 329–53.

Stevens, S.S., Morgan, C.T., and Volkmann, J. (1941). Theory of the neural quantum in the discrimination of loudness and pitch. *American Journal of Psychology*, **54**, 315–35.

Stevens, S.S., Carton, A.S., and Shickman, G.M. (1958). A scale of apparent intensity of electric shock. *Journal of Experimental Psychology*, **56**, 328–34.

Stone, H. (1963). Determination of odor difference limens for three compounds. *Journal of Experimental Psychology*, **66**, 466–73.

Stone, H. and Bosley, J.J. (1965). Olfactory discrimination and Weber's Law. *Perceptual and Motor Skills*, **20**, 657–65.

Stone, H., Ough, C.S., and Pangborn, R.M. (1962). Determination of odor difference thresholds. *Journal of Food Science*, **27**, 197–202.

Stone, J. and Fabian, M. (1968). Summing properties of the cat's retinal ganglion cell. *Vision Research*, **8**, 1023–40.

Swets, J.A. (1961). Is there a sensory threshold? *Science*, **134**, 168–77.

Swets, J.A., Tanner, W.P. Jr, and Birdsall, T.G. (1961). Decision processes in perception. *Psychological Review*, **68**, 301–40.

Talbot, W.H., Darian-Smith, I., Kornhuber, H.H. and Mountcastle, V.B. (1968). The sense of flutter-vibration: comparison of the human capacity with response patterns of mechanoreceptive afferents from the monkey hand. *Journal of Neurophysiology*, **31**, 301–34.

Tanner, W.P. Jr and Swets, J.A. (1954). A decision-making theory of visual detection. *Psychological Review*, **61**, 401–9.

Tasaki, I. (1954). Nerve impulses in individual auditory nerve fibers of guinea pig. *Journal of Neurophysiology*, **17**, 97–122.

Taves, E.H. (1941). Two mechanisms for the perception of visual numerousness. *Archives of Psychology*, No. 265.

Teas, D.C., Eldredge, D.H., and Davis, H. (1962). Cochlear responses to acoustic transients: an interpretation of whole-nerve action potentials. *Journal of the Acoustical Society of America*, **34**, 1438–59.

Teghtsoonian, M. and Teghtsoonian, R. (1971). How repeatable are Stevens's power law exponents for individual subjects? *Perception & Psychophysics*, **10**, 147–9.

Teghtsoonian, R. (1971). On the exponents in Stevens' Law and the constant in Ekman's Law. *Psychological Review*, **78**, 71–80.
Teghtsoonian, R. (1973). Range effects in psychophysical scaling and a revision of Stevens' law. *American Journal of Psychology*, **86**, 3–27.
Teghtsoonian, R. (1974). On facts and theories in psychophysics: does Ekman's law exist? In *Sensation and measurement* (ed. H.R. Moskowitz, B. Scharf, and J.C. Stevens), pp. 167–76. Reidel, Dordrecht.
Teghtsoonian, R. and Teghtsoonian, M. (1970). Scaling apparent distance in a natural outdoor setting. *Psychonomic Science*, **21**, 215–16.
Teghtsoonian, R. and Teghtsoonian, M. (1978). Range and regression effects in magnitude scaling. *Perception & Psychophysics*, **24**, 305–14.
Teghtsoonian, R., Teghtsoonian, M., and Baird, J.C. (1995). On the nature and meaning of sinuosity in magnitude-estimation functions. *Psychological Research*, **57**, 63–9.
Thouless, R.H. (1931a). Phenomenal regression to the 'real' object. I. *British Journal of Psychology*, **21**, 339–59.
Thouless, R.H. (1931b). Phenomenal regression to the 'real' object. II. *British Journal of Psychology*, **22**, 1–30.
Thouless, R.H. (1932). Individual differences in phenomenal regression. *British Journal of Psychology*, **22**, 216–41.
Thurstone, L.L. (1927). A law of comparative judgment. *Psychological Review*, **34**, 273–86.
Thurstone, L.L. and Chave, E.J. (1929). *The measurement of attitude.* University of Chicago Press.
Titchener, E.B. (1905). *Experimental psychology*, Vol. II, *Quantitative experiments*, Part I, *Student's manual.* Macmillan. New York.
Torgerson, W.S. (1958). *Theory and methods of scaling.* Wiley, New York.
Torgerson, W.S. (1961). Distances and ratios in psychophysical scaling. *Acta Psychologica*, **19**, 201–5.
Treisman, M. (1963). Temporal discrimination and the indifference interval: implications for a model of the 'internal clock'. *Psychological Monographs*, **77**, No. 576.
Tumarkin, A. (1981). A biologist looks at psycho-acoustics. *Behavioral and Brain Sciences*, **4**, 207.
Vallbo, Å.B. (1995). Single-afferent neurons and somatic sensation in humans. In *The cognitive neurosciences* (ed. M.S. Gazzaniga), pp. 237–252. MIT Press, Cambridge, MA.
van Brakel, J. (1993). The analysis of sensations as the foundation of all sciences. *Behavioral and Brain Sciences*, **16**, 163–4.
van Nes, F.L. (1968). Experimental studies in spatiotemporal contrast transfer by the human eye. Unpublished doctoral thesis, University of Utrecht.
van Nes, F.L. and Bouman, M.A. (1967). Spatial modulation transfer in the human eye. *Journal of the Optical Society of America*, **57**, 401–6.
Veit, C.T. (1978). Ratio and subtractive processes in psychophysical judgment. *Journal of Experimental Psychology: General*, **107**, 81–107.
Verrillo, R.T. (1962). Investigation of some parameters of the cutaneous threshold for vibration. *Journal of the Acoustical Society of America*, **34**, 1768–73.
Viemeister, N.F. (1970). Intensity discrimination: performance in three paradigms. *Perception & Psychophysics*, **8**, 417–19.
Volkmann, A.W. (1863). *Physiologische Untersuchungen im Gebiete der Optik.* Breitkopf and Härtel, Leipzig.
von Helmholtz, H.L.F. (1909–11). *Handbuch der physiologischen Optik* (3rd edn). Voss, Hamburg. [*Treatise on physiological optics* (trans. ed. J.P.C. Southall, 1924–5). Optical Society of America.]

von Kries, J. (1882). Ueber die Messung intensiver Grössen und über das sogenannte psychophysische Gesetz. *Vierteljahrsschrift für Wissenschaftliche Philosophie*, **6**, 257–94.

von Loewenich, V. and Finkenzeller, P. (1967). Reizstärkenabhängigkeit und Stevenssche Potenzfunktion beim optisch evozierten Potential des Menschen. *Pflügers Archiv für die Gesamte Physiologie des Menschen und der Tiere*, **293**, 256–71.

Ward, L.M. (1973). Repeated magnitude estimations with a variable standard: sequential effects and other properties. *Perception & Psychophysics*, **13**, 193–200.

Ward, L.M. (1979). Stimulus information and sequential dependencies in magnitude estimation and cross-modality matching. *Journal of Experimental Psychology: Human Perception and Performance*, **5**, 444–59.

Ward, L.M. and Lockhead, G.R. (1971). Response system processes in absolute judgment. *Perception & Psychophysics*, **9**, 73–8.

Ware, C. and Cowan, W.B. (1983). The chromatic Cornsweet effect. *Vision Research*, **23**, 1075–7.

Warren, R.M. (1958). A basis for judgments of sensory intensity. *American Journal of Psychology*, **71**, 675–87.

Warrren, R.M. (1965). Lightness of gray in the presence of white. *Perceptual and Motor Skills*, **21**, 925–6.

Warren, R.M. (1969). Visual intensity judgments: an empirical rule and a theory. *Psychological Review*, **76**, 16–30.

Warren, R.M. (1970). Elimination of biases in loudness judgments for tones. *Journal of the Acoustical Society of America*, **48**, 1397–1403.

Warren, R.M. (1977). Subjective loudness and its physical correlate. *Acustica*, **37**, 334–46.

Warren, R.M. (1981). Measurement of sensory intensity. *Behavioral and Brain Sciences*, **4**, 175–223.

Warren, R.M. (1989). Sensory magnitudes and their physical correlates. *Behavioral and Brain Sciences*, **12**, 296–7.

Warren, R.M. and Poulton, E.C. (1960). Basis for lightness-judgments of grays. *American Journal of Psychology*, **73**, 380–87.

Warren, R.M. and Poulton, E.C. (1962). Ratio- and partition-judgments. *American Journal of Psychology*, **75**, 109–14.

Warren, R.M. and Poulton, E.C. (1966). Lightness of grays: effects of background reflectance. *Perception & Psychophysics*, **1**, 145–8.

Warren, R.M. and Warren, R.P. (1956). Effect of the relative volume of standard and comparison-object on half-heaviness judgments. *American Journal of Psychology*, **69**, 640–43.

Warren, R.M. and Warren, R.P. (1958). Basis for judgments of relative brightness. *Journal of the Optical Society of America*, **48**, 445–50.

Warren, R.M. and Warren, R.P. (1968). *Helmholtz on perception: its physiology and development.* Wiley, New York.

Wasserman, G.S. (1991). Neural and behavioral assessments of sensory quality. *Behavioral and Brain Sciences*, **14**, 192–3.

Watson, C.S., Rilling, M.E., and Bourbon, W.T. (1964). Receiver-operating characteristics determined by a mechanical analog to the rating scale. *Journal of the Acoustical Society of America*, **36**, 283–8.

Weber, E.H. (1834). *De pulsu, resorptione, auditu et tactu.* Köhler, Leipzig. [*De tactu*, (trans. H.E. Ross, 1978), Academic Press, London.]

Weber, E.H. (1846). *Der Tastsinn und das Gemeingefühl.* In Handwörterbuch der Physiologie (ed. R. Wagner), Vol. III, pp. 481–588. Vieweg, Brunswick. [*Der Tastsinn*, (trans. D.J. Murray, 1978). Academic Press, London.]

Westheimer, G. (1972). Visual acuity and spatial modulation thresholds. In *Handbook of sensory physiology*, Vol. VII/4, *Visual psychophysics* (ed. D. Jameson and L.M. Hurvich), pp. 170–87. Springer-Verlag, Berlin.

Whittle, P. (1986). Increments and decrements: luminance discrimination. *Vision Research*, **26**, 1677–91.

Whittle, P. (1994). Contrast brightness and ordinary seeing. In *Lightness, brightness, and transparency* (ed. A.L. Gilchrist), pp. 111–57. Erlbaum, Hillsdale, NJ.

Woodworth, R.S. (1938). *Experimental psychology*. Henry Holt, New York.

Zotterman, Y. and Diamant, H. (1959). Has water a specific taste? *Nature*, **183**, 191–2.

Zuriff, G.E. (1972). A behavioral interpretation of psychophysical scaling. *Behaviorism*, **1**, 118–33.

Zwislocki, J.J. and Jordan, H.N. (1986). On the relations of intensity jnd's to loudness and neural noise. *Journal of the Acoustical Society of America*, **79**, 772–80.

Author index

Italic numbers denote references to figures

Subject index

Italic numbers denote references to figures

VERMONT STATE COLLEGES
0 0003 0627549 4